Communications
in Computer and Information Science

2787

Series Editors

Gang Li, *School of Information Technology, Deakin University, Burwood, VIC, Australia*
Joaquim Filipe, *Polytechnic Institute of Setúbal, Setúbal, Portugal*
Zhiwei Xu, *Chinese Academy of Sciences, Beijing, China*

Rationale

The CCIS series is devoted to the publication of proceedings of computer science conferences. Its aim is to efficiently disseminate original research results in informatics in printed and electronic form. While the focus is on publication of peer-reviewed full papers presenting mature work, inclusion of reviewed short papers reporting on work in progress is welcome, too. Besides globally relevant meetings with internationally representative program committees guaranteeing a strict peer-reviewing and paper selection process, conferences run by societies or of high regional or national relevance are also considered for publication.

Topics

The topical scope of CCIS spans the entire spectrum of informatics ranging from foundational topics in the theory of computing to information and communications science and technology and a broad variety of interdisciplinary application fields.

Information for Volume Editors and Authors

Publication in CCIS is free of charge. No royalties are paid, however, we offer registered conference participants temporary free access to the online version of the conference proceedings on SpringerLink (http://link.springer.com) by means of an http referrer from the conference website and/or a number of complimentary printed copies, as specified in the official acceptance email of the event.

CCIS proceedings can be published in time for distribution at conferences or as post-proceedings, and delivered in the form of printed books and/or electronically as USBs and/or e-content licenses for accessing proceedings at SpringerLink. Furthermore, CCIS proceedings are included in the CCIS electronic book series hosted in the SpringerLink digital library at http://link.springer.com/bookseries/7899. Conferences publishing in CCIS are allowed to use Online Conference Service (OCS) for managing the whole proceedings lifecycle (from submission and reviewing to preparing for publication) free of charge.

Publication process

The language of publication is exclusively English. Authors publishing in CCIS have to sign the Springer CCIS copyright transfer form, however, they are free to use their material published in CCIS for substantially changed, more elaborate subsequent publications elsewhere. For the preparation of the camera-ready papers/files, authors have to strictly adhere to the Springer CCIS Authors' Instructions and are strongly encouraged to use the CCIS LaTeX style files or templates.

Abstracting/Indexing

CCIS is abstracted/indexed in DBLP, Google Scholar, EI-Compendex, Mathematical Reviews, SCImago, Scopus. CCIS volumes are also submitted for the inclusion in ISI Proceedings.

How to start

To start the evaluation of your proposal for inclusion in the CCIS series, please send an e-mail to ccis@springer.com.

Flavio Corradini · Knut Hinkelmann ·
Hanlie Smuts · Barbara Re
Editors

Society 5.0

5th International Conference Society 5.0 2025
San Benedetto Del Tronto, Italy, June 25–27, 2025
Revised Selected Papers

 Springer

Editors
Flavio Corradini [iD]
University of Camerino
Camerino, Italy

Hanlie Smuts [iD]
University of Pretoria
Pretoria, South Africa

Knut Hinkelmann [iD]
FHNW University of Applied Sciences
and Arts Northwestern Switzerland
Olten, Switzerland

Barbara Re [iD]
University of Camerino
Camerino, Italy

ISSN 1865-0929   ISSN 1865-0937 (electronic)
Communications in Computer and Information Science
ISBN 978-3-032-15462-0   ISBN 978-3-032-15463-7 (eBook)
https://doi.org/10.1007/978-3-032-15463-7

This Springer imprint is published by the registered company Springer Nature Switzerland AG
The registered company address is: Gewerbestrasse 11, 6330 Cham, Switzerland

If disposing of this product, please recycle the paper.

Preface

It is with great pleasure that we write this preface to the Proceedings of the 5th International Conference on Society 5.0 held from 25–27 June 2025 in San Benedetto del Tronto, Italy. The Society 5.0 Conference 2025 was hosted by the University of Camerino, Italy. This multi- and interdisciplinary conference is continuing to grow into a premier international conference series with steering committee members from FHNW University of Applied Sciences and Arts Northwestern Switzerland, the University of Pretoria (South Africa), the University of Camerino (Italy), the Universidad EAFIT (Colombia), the Technical University of Mauritius, the Business School of the Shenzhen Technology University (China), the Universiti Malaysia Kelantan (Malaysia), and Putra Business School (Malaysia).

The theme of the 2025 Conference on Society 5.0 was *"Co-Existence Between Human Being and Machine Being"*. In a rapidly evolving digital society, the growing interaction between humans and machines is redefining the boundaries of all aspects and stages of our life cycle. This emerging "collaboration" has the potential to drive forward social good, foster a more equitable, sustainable and responsible future, while properly addressing (complex) global challenges. However, this significant and pervasive interaction also requires a careful engagement with the ethical and social issues that arise alongside these innovations.

The conference provided an important and timely opportunity to contribute to the vision of Society 5.0--a human-centered society that increasingly relies on a "fair pact" between human being and machine being with the aim of shaping a future where everyone benefits, while ensuring justice, inclusivity, and sustainability for the generations to come.

For the 2025 Society 5.0 conference we encouraged contributions from experienced and young researchers and practitioners from industry. We sincerely thank all organizers, partners, authors, and reviewers without whom this conference would not have been realised.

Technical Information

We received 64 research papers which were sent out for review to our Society 5.0 program committee. 24 full research papers were selected for the proceedings of the Society 5.0 Conference 2025, which are published in this Springer CCIS volume (which translates to an acceptance rate of 38%) after a rigorous, single-blind review process. Further 15 submissions were invited for presentation at the conference; the papers are published as a separate report.

The program committee comprised 44 members from 15 different countries across the world. Each paper was reviewed by three members of the program committee in a rigorous review process. The review was organized using Easychair, avoiding potential conflicts of interest when assigning the reviewers. Criteria such as the following were taken into consideration: Relevance to Society 5.0, Significance, Technical Quality, Scholarship, and Presentation, which included quality and clarity of writing.

Thank you to all the authors and program committee members, and congratulations to the authors whose research was accepted for publication in these proceedings.

June 2025

Knut Hinkelmann
Hanlie Smuts
Flavio Corradini
Barbara Re

Organization

General Chairs

Flavio Corradini   University of Camerino, Italy
Barbara Re   University of Camerino, Italy

Program Committee Chairs

Knut Hinkelmann   FHNW University of Applied Sciences and Arts Northwestern Switzerland, Switzerland
Hanlie Smuts   University of Pretoria, South Africa

Workshop and Doctoral Symposium Chair

Massimo Callisto De Donato   University of Camerino, Italy

Organization Committee

Fabrizio Fornari (Chair)   University of Camerino, Italy
Massimo Callisto De Donato   University of Camerino, Italy
Devid Montecchiari   FHNW University of Applied Sciences and Arts Northwestern Switzerland, Switzerland
Roberta Cocci Grifoni (Chair)   University of Camerino, Italy
Jessica Piccioni (Chair)   University of Camerino, Italy
Matteo Leonesi (Chair)   University of Camerino, Italy
Luca Mozzoni (Chair)   University of Camerino, Italy
Alessio Galassi (Chair)   University of Camerino, Italy
Niccolò Francioni (Chair)   University of Camerino, Italy
Filippo Lampa (Chair)   University of Camerino, Italy
Massimiliano Sampaolo (Chair)   University of Camerino, Italy

Program Committee

Ahmad Shaharudin Abdul Latiff	Putra Business School, Malaysia
Marc Aeschbacher	FHNW University of Applied Sciences and Arts Northwestern Switzerland, Switzerland
Sara Aguilar-Barrientos	Universidad EAFIT, Colombia
Luis Alvarez Sabucedo	Universidade de Vigo, Spain
Luis Anido Rifón	Universidade de Vigo, Spain
Dimitris Apostolou	University of Piraeus, Greece
Carolina Ardila-López	Universidad EAFIT, Colombia
Aleesha Boolaky	University of Technology Mauritius, Mauritius
Massimo Callisto De Donato	University of Camerino, Italy
Hemant Chittoo	University of Technology, Mauritius, Mauritius
Roberta Cocci Grifoni	University of Camerino, Italy
Flavio Corradini	University of Camerino, Italy
Barbara Eisenbart	FHNW University of Applied Sciences and Arts Northwestern SwitzSwitzerland, Switzerland
Sunet Eybers	University of South Africa, South Africa
Hans-Georg Fill	University of Fribourg, Switzerland
Fabrizio Fornari	University of Camerino, Italy
Rouxan Fouche	University of the Free State, South Africa
Aurona Gerber	University of the Western Cape, South Africa
Marie Hattingh	University of Pretoria, South Africa
Dikky Indrawan	IPB University, Indonesia
Stephan Jüngling	FHNW University of Applied Sciences and Arts Northwestern Switzerland, Switzerland
Gordana Kierans	MGT OPEN j.d.o.o., Croatia
Emanuele Laurenzi	FHNW University of Applied Sciences and Arts Northwestern, Switzerland, Switzerland
Andreas Martin	FHNW University of Applied Sciences and Arts Northwestern Switzerland, Switzerland
Machdel Matthee	University of Pretoria, South Africa
Heiko Maus	German Research Center for Artificial Intelligence DFKI, Germany
Tendani Mawela	University of Pretoria, South Africa
Mohd Zulkifli Muhammad	Universiti Malaysia Kelantan, Malaysia
Wynand Nel	University of the Free State, South Africa
Kesseven Padachi	University of Technology, Mauritius
Needesh Ramphul	University of Technology, Mauritius
Barbara Re	University of Camerino, Italy
Sandra Schlick	FHNW University of Applied Sciences and Arts Northwestern Switzerland, Switzerland

Riana Steyn	University of Pretoria, South Africa
Agnis Stibe	Riga Technical University, Latvia
Rainer Telesko	FHNW University of Applied Sciences and Arts Northwestern Switzerland, Switzerland
Ronald Tombe	Kisii University, Kenya
Alta Van der Merwe	University of Pretoria, South Africa
Ludger Van Elst	German Research Center for Aritificial Intelligence DFKI, Germany
Silke Waterstraat	FHNW University of Applied Sciences and Arts Northwestern Switzerland, Switzerland
Lizette Weilbach	University of Pretoria, South Africa
Hans Friedrich Witschel	FHNW University of Applied Sciences and Arts Northwestern Switzerland, Switzerland
Endrit Xhina	University of Tirana, Albania

Additional Reviewers

Daniel Borcard	University of Fribourg, Switzerland
Marcel Bühlmann	University of Fribourg, Switzerland
Simon Curty	University of Fribourg, Switzerland
Felix Härer	FHNW University of Applied Sciences and Arts Northwestern Switzerland, Switzerland
Tim Kröncke	FHNW University of Applied Sciences and Arts Northwestern Switzerland, Switzerland
Devid Montecchiari	FHNW University of Applied Sciences and Arts Northwestern Switzerland, Switzerland
Mirnal Mungra	University of Technology, Mauritius
Minh Khoi Nguyen	RMIT University Vietnam, Vietnam
Varouna Ramgoolam	University of Technology, Mauritius
Manuel Renold	FHNW University of Applied Sciences and Arts Northwestern Switzerland, Switzerland
Maja Spahic Bogdanovic	FHNW University of Applied Sciences and Arts Northwestern Switzerland, Switzerland

Steering Committee Chairs

Hanlie Smuts	University of Pretoria, South Africa
Knut Hinkelmann	FHNW University of Applied Sciences and Arts Northwestern Switzerland, Switzerland

Steering Committee

Ahmad Shaharudin Abdul Latiff	Putra Business School, Malaysia
Marc Aeschbacher	FHNW University of Applied Sciences and Arts Northwestern Switzerland, Switzerland
Sara Aguilar-Barrientos	Universidad EAFIT, Colombia
Roselina Ahmad Saufi	Universiti Malaysia Kelantan, Malaysia
Flavio Corradini	University of Camerino, Italy
Noorshella Che Nawi	Universiti Malaysia Kelantan, Malaysia
Zhuoqi Ding	Shenzhen Technology University, China
Natalia Escobar Pemberthy	Universidad EAFIT, Colombia
Aurona Gerber	University of Western Cape, South Africa
Stephan Jüngling	FHNW University of Applied Sciences and Arts Northwestern Switzerland, Switzerland
Gordana Kierans	Shenzhen Technology University, China
Kesseven Padachi	University of Technology, Mauritius
Arie Hans Verkuil	FHNW University of Applied Sciences and Arts Northwestern Switzerland, Switzerland
Wan Fadzilah Wan Yusoff	Putra Business School, Malaysia

Contents

Current Educational Approaches for Cyber-Safety Awareness in South African Schools: A Systematic Literature Review

Nolufefe Ali[✉] and Elmarie Kritzinger

College of Science, Engineering and Technology, School of Computing, University of South Africa (Unisa), PO Box 392, Pretoria 0003, South Africa
`33784205@mylife.unisa.ac.za, kritze@unisa.ac.za`

Abstract. In an era of rapid technological advancement, traditional thinking and living patterns are being disrupted, underscoring the need for improved cyber-safety awareness. This is especially critical for vulnerable groups such as school learners, who face heightened risks due to limited knowledge of online threats. This study examines current educational approaches to cyber safety in South African schools, aiming to identify existing gaps and strengths. Employing the PRISMA framework, a systematic literature review was conducted, analysing 92 out of 286 articles on cyber safety published between 2012 and 2024. The research reveals the current state of cyber-safety education. The results contribute to the academic discourse and offer guidance for policymakers to advance cyber-safety regulations in South African schools.

Keywords: Cyber safety · learner awareness · educational approaches · South Africa · school environment · online threats · cyber risk management

1 Introduction

School learners face significant cyber risks such as cyberbullying, harassment and self-harm necessitating early educational interventions to boost awareness, yet despite understanding these threats, students often fail to apply safe practices, endangering themselves and others [1–5]. Existing approaches undermined by poor curriculum integration, insufficient teacher training, reactive measures and fragmented policies underscore the urgent need for innovative strategies that effectively embed cyber-safety into learners' online behaviour [6–10]. Developing country schools face persistent cyber-safety challenges most notably a lack of integrated policies and support mechanisms [11] while evolving threats and technological advances demand updated strategies and resources [12, 13]; yet research has scarcely examined how educational approaches can be tailored to enhance cyber-safety awareness in school environments [14]. This paper reviews cyber-safety awareness approaches in South African schools, outlines its methodology, and presents results and discussion.

F. Corradini et al. (Eds.): Society 5.0 2025, CCIS 2787, pp. 1–12, 2026.
https://doi.org/10.1007/978-3-032-15463-7_1

2   Systematic Literature Review

Cyber-safety refers to the protection of individuals, especially young people, from online risks such as cyberbullying, exposure to harmful content, and online exploitation. As internet access expands, learners are increasingly vulnerable to these threats, which can negatively affect their well-being, academic performance, and digital development. Educational institutions are thus under pressure to implement effective cyber safety education, yet in contexts like South Africa, such efforts are often hampered by resource limitations and inconsistent policy implementation. This review situates itself within this landscape to explore current educational approaches to cyber safety awareness in South African schools.

3   Methodology

Guided by the research question *"How can educational approaches be adapted to enhance cyber-safety awareness through a holistic and integrated approach?"* (Table 1), this article systematically reviews pedagogical methods, curriculum design, delivery modes, teacher training and student engagement in South African schools. Employing a systematic literature review, studies published between 2012 and 2024 were identified, evaluated and synthesised to reflect current challenges and best practices amid evolving cyber threats, digital education technologies and policies providing a rigorous foundation for enhancing school-based cyber-safety awareness.

3.1   Scoping Keywords

The database search strategy included the keywords as displayed:

Table 1. Search keywords

Cyber approaches: *Silo approaches* OR *Short-term approaches* Reactive* *Peer to peer* *Curriculum* *Web-based* *Game-based*
AND: *Policies and standards* *Parental involvement* *Once-off initiatives* *Cyber education*
AND: *School* *Government* *Leadership* OR *Governance* *Policies* OR *Procedures*
AND: *Cyber safety* OR *Cyber awareness*
NOT: *Technical cyber security*

Based on the keyword search results, the keywords were occasionally rephrased to enhance search accuracy. The screening process involved several stages: initially, articles were assessed by their titles. Subsequently, abstracts were analysed to further determine relevance. Finally, entire articles were reviewed to ensure that their content was pertinent to the study's focus.

3.2 Preferred Reporting Items for Systematic Reviews and Meta-analyses (PRISMA)

To ensure the accurate reporting of this study, the researchers adhered to the Preferred Reporting Items for Systematic Reviews and Meta-Analyses (PRISMA) guidelines [15]. The literature search was conducted across multiple databases, including the Unisa research database repository, Google Scholar, ACM Digital Library, ScienceDirect, IEEE Xplore, Springer, ResearchGate, Sabinet African Journals, and Theses and Dissertations. To assess the credibility of the sources, the citation counts for each article were reviewed. This section below introduces the categorisation of articles based on thematic relevance and methodological rigor, along with the inclusion and exclusion criteria used to ensure the selection of studies aligns with the research objectives.

3.3 Inclusion and Exclusion Criteria

In this study, inclusion/exclusion criteria (Table 2) ensured selection of English, peer-reviewed journal articles published between 2012 and 2024 that report empirical, hypothesis-driven research on educational approaches to cyber-safety awareness in South African schools, while excluding reviews, opinion pieces, duplicates and any studies involving unauthorized or illicit media content. A consolidated literature matrix was then created to synthesise these high-quality contributions, categorise the diverse strategies employed and inform future cyber-safety initiatives.

Table 2 is a literature matrix that provides a summary of 92 authors who identified multiple approaches for cyber-safety awareness in South African schools. The literature matrix intends to present all pieces of evidence into a single logical argument. In analysing the approaches, the researchers designed the literature matrix to identify more patterns in the research to make insightful inferences and convey the research findings in a refined manner.

3.4 Article Categorisation

The selected articles were retrieved from a total of 92 books and journal articles encompassing the fields of information systems, education, and computer science. The study conducted a detailed analysis of these articles to elucidate the various approaches that have an impact on cyber-safety awareness in schools. During the analysis, the studies were categorised based on thematic similarities. Efforts were made to identify and emphasise both commonalities and differences in the findings across the studies.

4 ATLAS.ti Analysis

To systematically analyze the selected literature, the researcher employed a literature matrix to organize key themes and concepts. This structured approach facilitated the coding process within ATLAS.ti, enabling the identification of patterns and recurring terms. To further enhance the analysis, a word cloud was generated to visually represent the frequency of word occurrences, providing insights into the most prominent topics within the dataset.

Table 2. Consolidated literature matrix consolidating authors and existing educational approaches for cyber-safety awareness in South African schools:

Article	Authors	Approaches
1, 6, 7, 8, 10, 12, 19, 29, 30	Kritzinger, 2016; Spiering, 2018; Cilliers and Chinyamurindi, 2020; Jabbar, Al-Shboul, Tannous, Banat, and Aldreabi, 2019	Curriculum, incident management, policies and standards, school and government, silo approaches, parental involvement, collaboration, integration, leadership and governance
2, 16, 22, 28, 34, 41, 45, 50	Farhangpour, Maluleke, and Mutshaeni, 2019; Kritzinger and Lautenbach, 2022; Paluckaite and Zardeckaite-Matulaitiene, 2026; Artz, Burton, Ward, Leoschut, Phyfer, Lloyd, Kassanjee, and Mottee, 2016	Policies and standards, compliance, cyber-safety awareness, policy and compliance, behavioural aspects
3, 4, 11, 18, 25, 39	Jabbar, Al-Shboul, Tannous, Banat, and Aldreabi, 2019; de Lange and von Solms, 2012; Pencheva, Hallett, and Rashid, 2020; Burne and Burton, 2017; Saxena, Kotiyal, and Goudar, 2012	Parental involvement, collaboration, integration, monitoring and evaluation
5, 9, 22, 27, 32, 37	Kritzinger, 2017; Smit, 2015; Kortjan, 2013; von Solms and von Solms, 2019	Silo approaches, leadership and governance, policy and compliance
33, 60, 61	Dhawan, 2020; El Asam, and Katz, 2018; Moyo, Tsokota, Ruvinga, and Kangara, 2022	Cyber risks, learner awareness, user awareness and education
36, 38, 44, 46, 48, 49, 51	Tshabalala, Mduduzi, and Ndeye-Ndereya, 2013; Butnaru, Niță, Anichiti, and Brînză, 2021; Ivy, Kelley, Cook, and Thomas, 2020; Mezzalira and Guzzo, 2015; Walsh, Wallace, Ayling, and Sondergeld, 2020	Incident management, cyber-safety awareness, policy and compliance, risk management
55, 56, 57	Van Boekel, Peek, and Luijkx, 2017	Positive effects of cyberspace, internet use
70, 71, 72, 81	Byrne and Burton, 2017; Gamhewage, Mahmoud, Tokar, Attias, Mylonas, Canna, and Utunen, 2022; Atlam, Alenezi, Alassafi, and Wills, 2018	Cyberbullying and peer-to-peer violence, online interaction
87, 88, 89	Fraser and O'Brien, 2020; Meyer, 2024	Social networks and online interaction, online threats
64, 76, 80	Kritzinger, 2014; Yin, and Chen, 2022; Islam, 2019	Learner awareness of online dangers, online time and exposure
90, 91	Chizanda, Agola, and Rodrigues, 2022; Raju, Rahman, & Ahmad, 2022	Cyber-safety education, behavioural factors, policy and compliance

4.1 Word Cloud

Word clouds in ATLAS.ti visually map word frequency—with size indicating occurrence—across documents, codes and quotations to highlight prevalent terms and themes, assess coding consistency and flag areas for deeper investigation. Currently, one cloud depicts pre-coding interactions and another uses coded quotations, underscoring the alignment between dominant interview topics and the established coding framework.

4.1.1 Word Cloud of Responses

A word cloud is a visual representation of text data, where word size reflects frequency or importance in a dataset. In this research, Fig. 2 presents a word cloud generated from literature on cyber-safety awareness in South African schools, with larger words indicating more frequently mentioned concepts. This visualization effectively highlights key terms and themes, illustrating dominant topics and common trends in the research.

Fig. 1. Word cloud of responses (all documents)

Figure 1 illustrates the initial phase of thematic analysis using a word cloud generated from responses across all 92 documents in ATLAS.ti, highlighting key terms and themes relevant to the study—such as teachers, schools, learners, cyber risks, cyber safety, awareness, education, parents, and curriculum.

4.1.2 Word Cloud of Coded Responses

The word cloud visually represents the most common themes and keywords emerging from the coded responses, highlighting the key patterns and insights from the data.

Fig. 2. Word cloud of coded responses

Figure 2 illustrates the initial phase of thematical analysis through a word cloud derived from responses of coded responses only on ATLAS.ti. This visualisation emphasises key terms relevant to the study, highlighting themes identified in the research, such as parents, teachers, schools, learners, government, cyber safety, awareness, education, parents, curriculum, and others.

4.1.3 The Value of the Word Cloud in This Study

Figures 1 and 2 illustrate the value of word clouds in capturing shared nuances within the data, where bold and enlarged words indicate frequently cited themes, reflecting the depth of interpretation by the researcher [16]. Word clouds, as visual representations of word frequency from interviews, documents, and other sources, rely on both the visibility of tokens in the analysis software and the researcher's interpretive insight [17]. Figures 2 and 3 offer a visual summary of the systematic literature review on educational approaches to cyber-safety awareness in schools, supporting further content analysis and enhancing the "verbose interpretation of the full rich [collected] data" [18], thereby reinforcing the study's validity.

4.2 Code List with Frequency

In analysing cyber-safety awareness initiatives in South African schools, a detailed code list was developed to categorise and quantify key themes and categories identified in the literature, supporting a structured understanding of the factors influencing cyber-safety education and highlighting prevalent challenges and opportunities. Table 3 presents this code list, showing themes, categories, and associated codes with their frequencies, thereby offering insights into the complexity of cyber-safety initiatives. The "Grounded" column in Table 3 indicates the number of instances or pieces of evidence supporting each theme—for example, the value "19" reflects 19 instances where the theme "Once-off, short-term initiatives: Curricular integration" is supported by data, underscoring the validity and relevance of the findings.

In this study, interview data were coded in ATLAS.ti v24 using an inductive thematic-analysis approach per [19], allowing themes to emerge directly from the data. Open coding generated initial, flexible codes, which were then grouped into broader themes during a second coding cycle; redundant and irrelevant codes were merged or discarded and differentiated by colour. Upon reaching code saturation, a refined thematic framework was constructed and visualised through network maps illustrating relationships among themes and codes.

4.2.1 Agreement Between Grouped Documents and Themes

Using code-occurrence analysis in ATLAS.ti, the data is organized around themes, categories, and codes. In Table 4, "themes" represent key concepts, while "approaches" are specific strategies addressing those themes. The "Non-SA" and "South Africa" columns show where data originates, and "totals" reflect the overall frequency of each theme and approach. This type of analysis helps identify patterns and trends in qualitative research by showing how often particular codes appear across data sources.

Table 3. Code list

Themes	Category	Code	Frequency
Cyber-safety initiatives and education	Once-off, short-term initiatives	• Curricular integration	19
		• Curriculum renewal	43
		• Game-based	5
		• Peer to peer	14
		• Response protocols	5
		• Short-term effects	6
		• Silo approaches	16
	Partnerships and collaboration	• Collaboration	24
		• Collaborative outcomes	1
		•Cyber-safety education strategies	22
		• Industry	3
		• Management boards	2
		• Parental involvement	26
		• School and government	27
		• Stakeholder roles	49
		• Learner reception	4
	Pedagogical challenge of cyber safety	•Challenges in implementation	8
		•Curricular content (education)	82
		•Innovative educational tools for cyber safety awareness	13
		• Integration to curriculum	20
		• Interactivity	6
		• Pedagogical approaches	13
		•Teacher preparedness/perception/attitude	14
		• Evaluation mechanisms	12
		• Monitoring and evaluation	7
		•Policies and procedures, incident management (committee)	3
		• Proactive	2
		•Reporting, consequence management, and penalties	22
		• Skilled attackers	2
		•Learner reception/understanding ICT	9
		• Teacher preparedness	4
Regulatory and compliance frameworks	Government regulations and compliance	• Code of good practice	2
		• Compliance issues	6
		• Cybersecurity culture	7
		• Government oversight	5
		•Incident response/strategy	36
		•Leadership and governance	13
		• Policies and procedures	52
		• Policy enforcement	4
		• Regulatory compliance	4
		• Regulatory gaps	7
		•Enforcement of legislation, policies and procedures	3
		• Leadership support	2
		• Policy development	6
		• Proactive and preventive attitude	40
		•Teacher training	44
	School and government	•Cultural factor effect on security awareness	13
		•Government support/challenges	13
		• Infusion of cyber safety in every school subject	2
		• Inter-institutional collaboration	4
		• Policy alignment	4
		• Recommendations for cyberbullying	23
		• Schools policy on ICT (use of electronic devices)	16
		• Learner gadget /internet use and risk of ICT/awareness	126
		• Learner ICT bullying others/misuse of ICT	65

Table 4. Code-occurrence analysis table

Themes	Approaches	Non-SA	South Africa	Totals
Cyber-safety educational approaches	139	46	60	245
Monitoring and evaluation	28	7	13	48
Regulatory and compliance frameworks	159	79	177	415
Totals	326	132	250	708

5 Findings

This study provides critical insights into cyber-safety education, categorised into four areas: short-term initiatives, the importance of partnerships, pedagogical challenges, and regulatory frameworks. Each category highlights key aspects and challenges, offering a comprehensive understanding of the current landscape. Based on the themes and categories outlined in Tables 3 and 4, developing a holistic approach to cyber-safety awareness in South Africa schools can significantly benefit from the theoretical building blocks and checklists. Through comprehensive curriculum integration and regularly updated curricula, the cyber-safety initiatives can ensure that learners are learning about current threats and best practices, making the education timely and *relevant*. Interactive learning tools foster *engagement*, making complex concepts easier to understand and retain. Through *cross-disciplinary learning* cyber safety can be integrated into various subjects to reinforce the importance of these skills across different contexts, helping learners understand its relevance in everyday life. Through robust partnerships and collaboration, a holistic cyber-safety approach can also benefit from the building blocks and checklists. Through *community involvement* parents, industry experts, and community members can create a support network that reinforces learning at home and in the community, as well as *support from authorities* by collaboration with the government. The theoretical building blocks or checklists that could guide the development and implementation of effective cyber-safety strategies:

5.1 Theoretical Building Blocks for Cyber-Safety Initiatives

The theoretical building blocks for cyber-safety initiatives outline essential components for creating effective cyber-safety programmes in educational settings. Each section focuses on key areas such as curriculum integration, robust partnerships, effective implementation strategies, clear response protocols, regulatory frameworks, and pedagogical approaches. The accompanying checklist provides actionable steps to ensure these building blocks are effectively applied, fostering a comprehensive and proactive approach to cyber safety in schools. The occurrences next to each component indicate the frequency with which that particular element has been highlighted or emphasised in the context of the study or framework. For example, a higher number of occurrences suggest that the component is particularly important or commonly referenced in discussions about cyber-safety initiatives. This quantitative measure helps prioritise areas for focus and implementation, guiding educators and policymakers in developing effective strategies. The building blocks and their components are:

5.1.1 Building Block 1: Comprehensive Curriculum Integration

- **Curricular renewal**: Regularly update the curriculum to include current cyber-safety topics (43 occurrences).
- **Interactivity**: Incorporate interactive learning tools to enhance engagement (6 occurrences).
- **Integration across subjects**: Infuse cyber-safety concepts into various subjects (2 occurrences).

5.1.2 Building Block 2: Robust Partnerships and Collaboration

- **Stakeholder engagement**: Involve parents, industry, and community stakeholders in developing strategies (49 occurrences).
- **School-government collaboration**: Establish strong ties between schools and government entities to support initiatives (27 occurrences).
- **Parental involvement**: Encourage active participation from parents in cyber-safety education (26 occurrences).

5.1.3 Building Block 3: Effective Implementation Strategies

- **Teacher preparedness**: Ensure teachers are well-trained and confident in delivering cyber-safety content (44 occurrences).
- **Peer-to-peer learning**: Promote peer-to-peer initiatives to enhance understanding (14 occurrences).
- **Innovative educational tools**: Utilise innovative tools for raising cyber-safety awareness (13 occurrences).

5.1.4 Building Block 4: Clear Response Protocols

- **Incident response strategy**: Develop clear protocols for responding to cyber incidents (36 occurrences).
- **Monitoring and evaluation**: Establish mechanisms to assess the effectiveness of cyber-safety initiatives (7 occurrences).
- **Reporting procedures**: Create straightforward reporting processes for cyberbullying and misuse of ICT (22 occurrences).

5.1.5 Building Block 5: Regulatory and Compliance Frameworks

- **Policies and procedures**: Implement clear policies on ICT usage and cyber safety (52 occurrences).
- **Government oversight**: Ensure compliance with national regulations and best practices (5 occurrences).
- **Cultural considerations**: Address cultural factors that have an impact on security awareness (13 occurrences).

5.1.6 Building Block 6: Pedagogical Approaches

- **Addressing challenges**: Identify and tackle implementation challenges (8 occurrences).
- **Evaluation mechanisms**: Develop tools for evaluating student understanding and programme effectiveness (12 occurrences).
- **Proactive measures**: Adopt a proactive attitude toward preventing cyberthreats (40 occurrences).

5.1.7 Building Block 7: Focus on Learner Understanding and Engagement

- **Learner reception**: Assess how well learners understand ICT risks and cyber safety (9 occurrences).
- **Skilled attacker awareness**: Educate learners about potential threats and how to respond (2 occurrences).
- **Consequence management**: Establish clear consequences for ICT misuse (22 occurrences).

5.2 Checklist for Implementation

- **Curriculum Development:** Integrate cyber-safety as a core, year-round strand across all grade levels and subjects, updating content annually to address emerging threats (e.g. deepfakes, novel social-media risks) and drawing on established competency frameworks—such as Franqueira et al.'s six-category model—to balance threat recognition, safe behaviours and digital resilience.
- **Stakeholder Engagement:** Forge continual partnerships with parents, caregivers and community organisations via workshops, newsletters and co-design sessions, since evidence shows that community-based programmes involving schools, families and policymakers substantially increase students' adoption of safe online practices.
- **Teacher Training:** Embed cyber-safety into both pre-service curricula and at least six hours of in-service professional development per year, combining theoretical grounding, hands-on simulations and peer coaching to boost teachers' confidence and effectiveness in delivering cyber-safety lessons.
- **Clear Policies:** Establish and widely circulate an ICT-use policy grounded in the "identify–protect–detect–respond–recover" cycle, with explicit sections on acceptable online behaviour, data privacy and reporting procedures, ensuring visibility in student handbooks, staff memos and the school intranet.
- **Incident Management:** Create a tailored Cyber Incident Response Plan (CIRP) that designates a response team, defines roles and maps communication flows (including legal and insurance contacts), and rehearse it annually through tabletop exercises and post-incident reviews.
- **Cultural Sensitivity:** Customize content, examples and delivery methods to reflect local languages, belief systems and community norms, as culturally attuned programmes yield higher engagement and more enduring behaviour change.
- **Monitoring Tools:** Employ a mixed-methods evaluation—quantitative surveys and incident logs, qualitative focus groups with teachers and parents, and LMS-based analytics within a Plan–Do–Study–Act cycle, using "lessons learned" reviews after each incident to iteratively refine curriculum and policies.

This framework offers schools an integrative blueprint for cyber-safety initiatives—spanning curriculum design, policy enforcement and community engagement—that addresses educational, regulatory and social dimensions while cultivating cybersecurity awareness and proactive prevention among learners, educators and parents. By detailing stakeholder collaboration mechanisms, it fosters a resilient culture and supportive environment that prioritises collective defence against evolving cyberthreats.

6 Contribution of the Research

This research advances both theory and practice by pinpointing critical needs—shifting from ad hoc efforts to an integrated curriculum, forging stakeholder partnerships, enhancing teacher development, tightening regulatory enforcement and embedding rigorous monitoring—to guide educators and policymakers in creating adaptive, sustainable school-based cyber-safety programmes. It further articulates a long-term vision for protective policies that foster a proactive culture of cyber awareness among learners.

7 Conclusion

This study categorises cyber-safety education into short-term initiatives, partnerships, pedagogical challenges and regulatory frameworks, revealing critical gaps and underscoring the need for a multifaceted approach that combines robust strategies, stakeholder collaboration, ongoing monitoring and firm regulation to secure learners' digital environments. It furnishes policymakers and educational institutions with data-driven insights into current threat landscapes, evidence-based best practices, and frameworks for vulnerability assessment and tailored risk management. Finally, it delivers actionable recommendations for crafting supportive policies, designing targeted training programmes and establishing collaboration mechanisms among schools, government agencies and cybersecurity experts to fortify collective defences.

Acknowledgements. This article was developed from the PhD thesis under the supervision of Professor Elmarie Kritzinger. The researchers declare no conflict of interest. Both authors contributed towards all sections of the paper and have approved its final version.

References

1. Siddiqi, S., Khan, M., Ahmed, R.: The risks and opportunities of cyberspaces for school learners. Educ. Res. Rev. **18**(2), 180–194 (2020)
2. Scholtz, B., Kritzinger, E., Botha, J.: Enhancing cyber safety awareness through school-based initiatives. J. Cyber Saf. Stud. **15**(4), 234–249 (2019)
3. Vilander, J.: Bridging the knowing-doing gap: the role of attitude in information security awareness. Master's Thesis. University of Jyväskylä, Jyväskylä (2021)
4. Gillam, L.: The disconnect between cyber safety awareness and behavior: a study of student practices. Comput. Educ. **92**, 25–38 (2019)
5. Mezzalira, S., Guzzo, A.: Evaluating student response to cyber safety training programs. Int. J. Cyber Educ. **17**(2), 211–225 (2024)

6. Shyshkanova, I., Zaytseva, I., Frydman, H.: Motivating students to apply cyber safety knowledge: innovative approaches. J. Dig. Saf. Educ. **12**(3), 88–102 (2027)
7. Ivy, J., Roberts, M., and Clarke, T. Challenges in implementing effective cyber safety education: a review of educational technology research & development **68**(2), 215–230 (2020)
8. Gcaza, N., von Solms, S.: Evaluating the effectiveness of cyber safety policies in South African schools. J. Inf. Secur. **28**(1), 55–70 (2017)
9. Walsh, K., et al.: Best Practice framework for online safety education: results from a rapid review of the international literature, expert review, and stakeholder consultation. Int. J. Child-Comput. Inter. **33** (2022)
10. Witsenboer, J.W.A., Sijtsma, K., Scheele, F.: Measuring cyber secure behavior of elementary and high school students in the Netherlands. Comput. Educ. **186**, 104536 (2022)
11. Meyer, M.: Recent developments in cyber safety policies for South African schools. S. Afr. J. Educ. **44**(1), 15–30 (2024)
12. Pospisil, R.: Long-term effects of cyber safety training in educational settings. Int. J. Cyber Educ. **22**(3), 303–315 (2018)
13. Byrne, C., Burton, D.: Addressing cyber safety challenges in South African schools: a review of current approaches. J. Educ. Technol. **32**(2), 145–160 (2017)
14. Page, M.J. et al.: The PRISMA 2020 statement: an updated guideline for reporting systematic reviews Syst. Rev. Meta-Anal. (2021)
15. Jansen, R.: Utilising Word Clouds (ATLAS.ti TM 22) in a Qualitative Research project focusing on Music Education in South Africa. University of Free State (2023)
16. Friese, S., Soratto, J., Pires, D.: Carrying out a computer-aided thematic content analysis with ATLAS.ti. IWMI Working Pap. **18** (2018)
17. Turner, D.: Word Clouds and word frequency analysis in qualitative data from Quirkos Qualitative Research. Blog (2022). https://www.quirkos.com/blog/post/word-clouds-and-word-frequency-analysis-in-qualitative-data/
18. Braun, V., and Clarke, V.: Reflecting on reflexive thematic analysis. Qualit. Res. Sport. Exerc. Health **13**(2), 1–21 (2021)

Data Security Compliance – An Application-Oriented Solution for Small Businesses

Petra Maria Asprion[✉][iD], Tanja Tschan, and Sherdel Käppler[iD]

University of Applied Sciences and Arts Northwestern Switzerland FHNW, Windisch, Switzerland
{petra.asprion,sherdel.kaeppler}@fhnw.ch,
tanja.tschan@students.fhnw.ch

Abstract. In the last decade, compliance management and data security have become increasingly critical for businesses, driven by evolving regulations. Small companies, in particular, face challenges in navigating complex regulatory landscapes and implementing effective data security compliance processes or even better sufficient management systems. To address this problem, this research developed an application-oriented solution, the "Action Plan for Data Security Compliance" (Act4DSC), a structured, evidence-based and easy-to-use tool designed to guide small businesses through the initial steps of data security compliance. Utilizing design science methodology, Act4DSC integrates the NIST Cybersecurity Framework 2.0 as its foundational structure with practitioner insights from several qualitative expert interviews. The Act4DSC offers a step-by-step approach, including regulatory alignment, stakeholder considerations, prioritization, data criticality classification, and gap analysis. Expert evaluations confirm its usability, adaptability, and structured guidance, making data security compliance more accessible for smaller businesses. Act4DSC fills a critical gap by tailoring compliance solutions for smaller businesses, bridging the divide between theoretical frameworks and practical implementations.

Keywords: Cybersecurity · Data Security Compliance (DSC) · Framework · Tool

1 Introduction

With evolving standards and rising expectations, Data Security Compliance (DSC) is increasingly essential to modern business operations. Data security involves policies to protect sensitive information from misuse and loss, while DSC ensures adherence to regulatory laws and industry standards. Amid rapid technological change, the unchecked use of Artificial Intelligence (AI), and growing cyber threats, DSC helps mitigate risks and safeguard sensitive data (Marotta and Madnick, 2021; Stevens et al., 2020). However, small businesses often face significant challenges in understanding regulations and navigating in complex standards or frameworks, particularly their periodic revisions, such as

F. Corradini et al. (Eds.): Society 5.0 2025, CCIS 2787, pp. 13–24, 2026.
https://doi.org/10.1007/978-3-032-15463-7_2

updates to the EU's General Data Protection Regulation (GDPR) in 2018 (Tikkinen-Piri et al., 2018), the International Organization for Standardization (ISO) standards in 2021, or the Swiss Federal Act on Data Protection (FADP) in 2023 (Romanou, 2018, p. 109; Guirguis et al., 2021, p. 16).

These difficulties are compounded by limited resources and expertise, leaving smaller businesses disproportionately vulnerable to compliance failures (Ebert & Widmer, 2018, pp. 1, 3).

A review of existing literature (Sect. 2) reveals a lack of frameworks or tools that address the intersection of data security and compliance management, particularly those tailored to the needs of small businesses. This absence of structured and applicable supporting material for smaller businesses leaves these companies without clear guidance on bridging the gap between compliance requirements and practical implementation. As a result, small businesses struggle to identify and implement the necessary measures for effective compliance with data security regulations (Mikkelsen et al., 2017, p. 1). To address this problem, this research introduces the "Action Plan for Data Security Compliance" (Act4DSC), a tool designed to integrate compliance management and data security. The necessity of developing Act4DSC exists because current frameworks primarily focus on general compliance or are tailored to larger organizations. In contrast, Act4DSC uniquely integrates DSC principles with actionable implementation guidance, specifically addressing the resource constraints and operational needs of small businesses. Drawing on insights from a comprehensive literature review, Act4DSC prioritizes practical implementation through step-by-step instructions, clearly defined responsibility assignments, and structured review cycles. By focusing on the unique challenges faced by small businesses, Act4DSC simplifies compliance processes and promotes sustainable and scalable digital security practices.

This research aims to answer the central research question: What elements and processes are of relevance to support small businesses to manage DSC? To address this question comprehensively, the research is guided by the following sub-questions:

- SQ1: What process should be followed to build a DSC management system?
- SQ2: What elements differentiate DSC from general compliance?
- SQ3: How can these elements be included in the process to reach DSC?

The scope of this research includes compliance with data security regulations, laws, and standards, focusing on regulations most relevant – as case study - to Swiss companies. Global standards such as GDPR, ISO, and FADP form the foundation of compliance requirements for Swiss businesses. In this context, standards refer to non-legally binding publications from institutions such as ISO, which often offer industry-specific certifications. Regulations, on the other hand, are enforceable rules defined by authoritative bodies. As methodology, we employed Design Science Research (DSR), which emphasizes the development and evaluation of practical artifacts that enhance organizational information systems. DSR is particularly suited to this research as it emphasizes iterative development and refinement, focusing on functionality and practical utility rather than rigid design processes or theoretical foundations (Peffers et al., 2018, p. 131). This approach allows for the flexible development of Act4DSC, accommodating diverse strategies and evaluation methods throughout its creation.

This paper is structured to reflect its dual aims: artifact development and practical application. Section 2 presents the literature review methodology, including key terms, criteria, categorization, and a summary of findings. Section 3 overviews the supporting research, covering methods and the tool's core elements—action planning, stakeholder alignment, and compliance. Section 4 presents the results, followed by conclusions addressing the research questions and future directions.

2   Literature Review

The objective of the literature review was to analyze existing research on DSC Management (DSCM) and related tools, leveraging insights to inform and guide the development of the Act4DSC tool. The review followed Kitchenham's systematic approach, encompassing three main phases: planning, conducting, and reporting (Kitchenham, 2004, p. 8). Primary resources included Elicit, Google, and Google Scholar, platforms known for their extensive repositories of high-quality, peer-reviewed scientific literature.

Key terms for searching loops were selected strategically to ensure a focused analysis of relevant contributions in the field. The used key terms included "security compliance management," "regulations," "standards," and "personal data." Synonyms and related phrases, such as "digital protection regulations" and "compliance tools," were incorporated to broaden the search scope. The key terms were chosen to align directly with the research objectives and questions; for example, "action planning" highlighted the practical aspects of DSC implementations, while "regulatory alignment" emphasized adherence to laws and standards. This approach ensured that the search captured both theoretical foundations and applicable solutions.

In addition, strict inclusion and exclusion criteria were applied to maintain the quality and relevance of the reviewed literature. Included sources comprised peer-reviewed articles and credible organizational publications focusing on DSC, compliance management, or tools for small businesses. Only literature published between 2000 and 2024, and written in English or German, was considered to ensure accuracy and relevance. The reviewed literature was systematically organized into six categories based on relevance and thematic focus, as seen in Table 1.

Scientific contributions were selected based on an evaluation of their introductions, abstracts, conclusions, and, when available, recommendations for further research. Peer-reviewed literature was presumed to meet quality standards, while articles lacking peer review, published before 2000, or unrelated to DSC were excluded. Exceptions were made for high-quality, non-peer-reviewed reports from reputable organizations. Notable examples include the draft of the NIST Cybersecurity Framework 2.0 (2023), Statista data on office software usage in Switzerland, and Mikkelsen et al.'s (2017) McKinsey & Company article discussing GDPR implementation challenges.

3   Research Design and Application

This research utilized DSR adhering to design-oriented research principles that focus on creating artifacts to solve specific problems and deliver measurable benefits (Österle et al., 2011, pp. 8–9). The process was guided by Hevner et al.'s (2004, p. 83) "Design

Table 1. Important contributions used as foundation for Act4DSC

Group	Description	Authors
Frameworks and Standards for Data Security Compliance	Structured frameworks, methodologies, and standards that guide organizations in implementing DSC	Cofino et al., 2023; Ebert & Widmer, 2018; Federal Act on Data Protection, 2023; Fischermanns, 2013; Marotta & Madnick, 2021; NIST, 2023; NIST, 2024; Rüegg-Stürm & Grand, 2020; Tikkinen-Piri et al., 2018; Voigt & Von dem Bussch, 2017
Legislative Analysis and Regional Contexts	Implications of data security laws and regional regulatory environments	Guirguis et al., 2021; Krystlik, 2017; Romanou, 2018
Practical Implementation Strategies	Actionable steps for achieving compliance	Garber, 2018; Mikkelsen et al., 2017; Voigt & Von dem Bussch, 2017
Sector-Specific Insights	Impact of DSC regulations on various industries	Stevens et al., 2020
Small and Medium-Sized Enterprises (SME) Focus	SMEs' unique challenges, such as resource and expertise limitations	Ebert & Widmer, 2018
Compliance Principles and Management Systems	Foundational principles for building compliance systems	Bay & Hastenrath, 2021; Beglinger & Michel, 2014; TÜV Nord Group, n.d.;

as a Search Process" and organized into five-phases (1) awareness of problem, (2) suggestion, (3) development, (4) evaluation, and (5) conclusion, whereby phases 3 and 4 were repeated in iterative loops (Hevner & Chatterjee, 2010, p. 27).

3.1 Phase 1 – Awareness

The awareness phase establishes the foundation for the development of ActDSC. It began with identifying the knowledge gap, the absence of frameworks that integrate data security and compliance management. Through a literature review, the gap's impact was analyzed to provide an understanding of its significance. Building on these findings, an initial draft of Act4DSC was developed and subjected to iterative evaluation. This process led to an assessment that validated the tool's relevance and effectiveness in subsequent research phases.

3.2 Phase 2 – Suggestion

This phase drew inspiration from the NIST Cybersecurity Framework 2.0 (NIST, 2023, 2024) and Bay and Hastenrath's compliance implementation case study (2021, pp. 121–122). Act4DSC was conceptualized as a tool to generate actionable compliance plans, helping organizations prioritize and sequence regulatory requirements (Garber, 2018, p. 15). Microsoft Excel was chosen as the tool's platform, due to Excel's widespread use in Switzerland (Statista, n.d.), and the tool's design was structured around NIST's "CSF Organizational Profile" (NIST, 2024, p. 6). Additional design elements came from Bay and Hastenrath's (2021) practical compliance guidelines and Voigt and Von dem Bussche's (2017) data protection processes. This methodology follows the plan-do-check-act (PDCA) model, allowing for continuous improvement through iterative cycles (Cofino et al., 2023, pp. 85–86).

3.3 Phase 3a – Initial Development

The initial development process for Act4DSC involved six distinct steps:

Step 1 -- Use Case Definition: this step involves scoping the organizational profile and gathering regulatory information. Key sub-processes include defining the scope, identifying relevant regulations, specifying regulatory details, and clarifying stakeholder expectations. Inspired by NIST (2024, p. 6) and Voigt and Von dem Bussche (2017, p. 248), this phase provided alignment with organizational and stakeholder requirements.

Steps 2 & 3 -- Target Profile and Current Situation Analysis: the target profile establishes future compliance goals, while the current situation analysis evaluates existing practices. These steps involve mapping, categorizing, and prioritizing requirements, laying the groundwork for gap analysis (NIST, 2023, p. 10). The resulting scores for fulfillment and prioritization guided the development of the action plans.

Steps 4 & 5 -- Gap Analysis and Action Plan Development: the gap analysis quantifies discrepancies between current and target profiles through metrics like the fulfillment and gap rates. The fulfilment rate measures how well each requirement is currently met based on the user's input regarding their existing context (scope, regulations, specific requirements, stakeholders, and expectations). It is then compared against the desired context to determine compliance progress. The gap rate is the inverse of the fulfilment rate, indicating the extent of non-compliance or the remaining effort needed to achieve full alignment with the target requirements. The Act4DSC prioritizes and sequences tasks by outlining required actions, timelines, and responsibilities to address identified gaps (NIST, 2024, p. 6; Voigt & Von dem Bussche, 2017, p. 245).

Step 6 -- Continuous Improvement: the final step focused on continuously refining the compliance processes and action plan. Adjustments were made based on evaluation feedback to increase both efficacy and functionality. Frameworks by NIST (2024), Bay and Hastenrath (2021), and Voigt and Von dem Bussche (2017) guided this phase.

3.4 Phase 4a -- Initial Evaluation

An informal expert interview with the Head of Master Data Management and Processes at a Swiss retail company provided feedback on the first draft of Act4DSC. Suggestions included:

- Simplifying navigation and layout by removing redundant worksheets and repositioning interactive elements.
- Optimizing forms and processes to reduce user fatigue and clarifying stakeholder responsibilities.
- Refining the action plan by integrating effort estimation and improving categorization.

3.5   Phase 3b – Iterative Development

Further development involved iterative refinements based on expert feedback. Adjustments to Act4DSC included usability improvements, such as optimized navigation, simplified step numbering, and clearer process views. Additional changes to the Act4DSC handbook, the accompanying technical documentation and users' manual of the Act4DSC tool, inclusive content revisions such as addressing interpretive challenges, offering detailed guidance, updated definitions, and the creation of actionable insights. Process categories were aligned with models like the ´St. Gallen Management Model´ (Rüegg-Stürm & Grand, 2020) and the ´FAU Process Model´ (Fischermanns, 2013). The subsequent iterations involved:

- **Loop 1:** feedback informed navigation redesigns, adjustments to stakeholder related steps, and the inclusion of an optional effort estimation feature. Mapping and prioritization steps were reorganized for logical flow.
- **Loop 2:** expanded guidance for scoping processes, including data location and regional regulations (Ebert & Widmer, 2018; Krystlik, 2017). Fixed requirements were temporarily added but later removed for flexibility.
- **Loop 3:** recommendations from an ICT-Safety Officer emphasized flexible scoping, example measures, and automating regulatory analysis for future consideration.
- **Loop 4:** added features included review responsibilities, data criticality classification, and archiving capabilities. Terminology was refined, and handbook updates emphasized interdisciplinary collaboration and knowledge sharing.

3.6   Phase 4b – Iterative Evaluation

Act4DSC was evaluated using a semi-structured interview format with practitioners from a large Swiss retail company, following the criteria outlined in Prat et al. 's (2014) framework. Stakeholders included four evaluators from various departments to utilize their diverse perspectives. In total, five qualitative informal to semi-formal interviews were conducted with the following complementary expert roles: the Head of Master Data Management and Processes, the Head of Compliance, the ICT-Safety Officer, and an Internal Revision Officer.

Metrics for evaluation included usability, adaptability, and clarity, assessed through descriptive feedback, and quantitative scoring to compare the degree to which each criterion was fulfilled. Points were assigned using a three-point scale: "1" indicated the criterion was poorly or not fulfilled, requiring immediate adjustment; "2" represented partial fulfillment, suggesting adjustments in future iterations; and "3" signified the criterion was well fulfilled, with no immediate adjustments necessary.

The developed tool scored 2 out of 3 points overall, with specific strengths identified in its structured guidance and adaptability for smaller businesses. Recommendations focused on usability enhancements, stakeholder visibility, and improved navigation, all of which informed subsequent iterations. Post-evaluation updates addressed identified gaps, including terminology refinements, corrected formulas, and streamlined steps. Handbook updates emphasized tool customization and addressed common pitfalls.

4 Result – The Act4DSC

Through iterative development and evaluation with experts from the field as described in Sect. 3, Act4DSC was incrementally developed according to the experts' suggestions and wishes. Act4DSC has demonstrated its practicality in supporting smaller Swiss companies in achieving DSC. By combining flexibility, adaptability, and structured guidance with the accompanied handbook, the tool fulfills the need for a tailored, research-based approach to compliance management for the target group of smaller businesses.

4.1 Landing Page

Figure 1 shows the landing page, depicting a chalkboard figure climbing steps labeled "Step by Step". The climbing figure symbolizes progress by illustrating that businesses can follow the step-by-step methodology embedded in the Act4DSC tool to navigate compliance challenges. To the right of the image is a description of the goal of the tool, while the tabs at the bottom label the steps that are used to create a compliance plan.

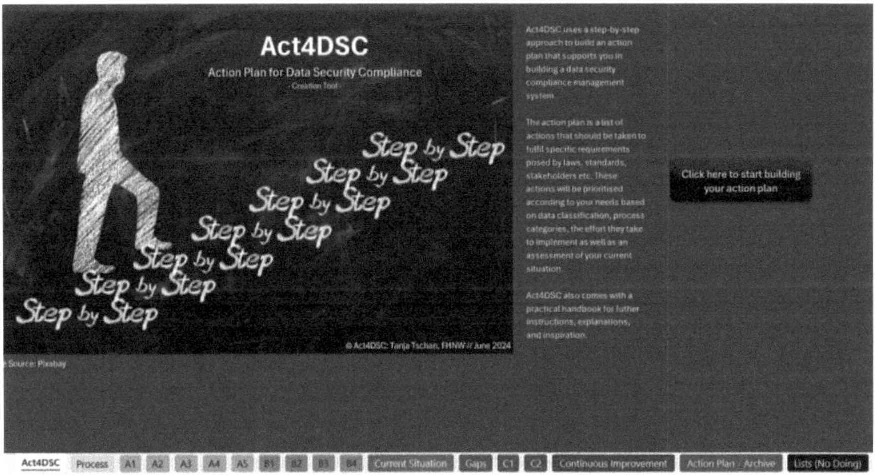

Fig. 1. Act4DSC Landing Screen (Excel-based tool)

4.2 Process Overview

Figure 2, a screenshot, shows an overview of the necessary steps to build an action plan in the Act4DSC tool, presented as an Excel spreadsheet. This (first) sheet, "Process", provides a structured, step-by-step approach to building a data security compliance

(DSC) management system. The processes outlined in Fig. 2 are: Context, Target Profile, Current Situation, Gaps, Action Plan, and Continuous Improvement.

Context begins with A1 Scope, where organizations determine which regional regulations apply based on data types, processes, and storage locations. A2 Regulations identifies the legal requirements governing data practices and specifies which will be addressed in the Act4DSC run. A3 Regulation Specifications clarifies the exact demands of these regulations. In A4 Stakeholders, organizations identify those affected by data processes. The final step, A5 Stakeholders Expectations, captures and prioritizes stakeholder concerns and requirements for compliance.

The Target Profile step starts with B1 Requirements, translating stakeholder expectations and regulations into specific compliance needs. In B2 Mapping, these are categorized by data criticality, regulatory scope, and process segmentation. B3 Category Prioritization then ranks categories and subcategories by importance. Finally, B4 Target Profile compiles this into a structured priority list.

Process	
Context	Define the context and gather the needed information for this run of Act4DSC.
A1 Scope	
A2 Regulations	
A3 Regulation Specifications	
A4 Stakeholders	
A5 Stakeholder Expectations	
Target Profile	
B1 Requirements	Dissect the previously listed regulation specifications and stakeholder expectations into specific requirements.
B2 Mapping	Map these requirements with different levels of process catagories for your companies processes.
B3 Category Prioritisation	Prioritise which categories and their sub-levels are most important for your company.
B4 Target Profile	Summary of the targeted requirements and their segment categorization. Calculation of a prioritzation value in the background.
Current Situation	Create the current profile by analysing and assessing the situation based on the requirements and mapping done in step B1 and B2.
Gaps	Analyse the gaps between the current profile and the target profile by calculating a fulfilment score, a fulfilment rate and a gap rate accordingly.
Action Plan	
C1 Action Order	The order in which the requirements should be tackled through actions is calculated based the corresponding requirement's previously calculated priority value and gap rate.
C2 Action Plan	Define and plan the actions that will be taken to fulfil each requirements.
Continuous Improvement	Continuously review the process, action plan, and the results. This step facilities the continuous improvement process by summarizing the date gathered in the previous steps.
Click here to start. ➡	

Fig. 2. Act4DSC: Process Overview

In the Current Situation step, organizations assess their current compliance status by reviewing the prioritized requirements and inputting their fulfillment status. Next, Gap calculates the fulfillment rate, indicating how well each requirement is met, and the gap rate, representing the remaining compliance effort needed.

The Action Plan addresses the compliance gaps. C1 Action Order determines the sequence in which actions should be taken based on priority value and gap rate. C2 Action Plan outlines specific tasks required to meet legal, regulatory, and stakeholder requirements. These actions are prioritized based on data classification, process categories, implementation effort, and an assessment of the organization's current security standing.

In the final step, Continuous Improvement, allows ongoing refinement of the DSC process by summarizing data from the previous steps. Organizations can then update the status of each requirement, action, and compliance measures to track progress and identify necessary adjustments.

4.3 Accompanied Handbook

To make the tool easily accessible for new users and practitioners, a handbook was created alongside the actual tool and evaluated using appropriate criteria. The handbook, provided as a Word document, offers additional instructions, explanations, and examples to support the application of Act4DSC. Together, the Act4DSC tool and the handbook equip small businesses with the knowledge and strategies they need to enhance DSC. The handbook named can be downloaded for application or further research (https://drive.switch.ch/index.php/s/C2wVNtbTsrKM4Tq).

5 Discussion

A notable limitation of this research is that Act4DSC's evaluation was conducted within a rather large Swiss retail company rather than the small businesses it aims to support. This choice was driven by the access it provided to a diverse range of departments and subject matter experts, ensuring comprehensive feedback from recognized experts with the same background. However, this may limit the direct applicability of some findings to smaller organizations, underscoring the need for future testing in environments more representative of the target demographic. This discrepancy is acknowledged, and broader real-world testing within actual SME environments is a key area for future research. In terms of practical implementation, the success of Act4DSC also depends on user support and dissemination strategies. Future development could include:

- Support materials and workshops to guide onboarding and adoption by SMEs.
- Partnerships with SME associations and chambers of commerce for broader dissemination and trust-building.

5.1 Research Questions Response

This research aims to fill a research gap that exists in many areas, namely focusing on the needs of small businesses in the compliance environment and their ability to cope with DSC. In this context three research questions were derived (Sect. 1) and will be discussed in the following.

SQ1: Building a DSC management system requires a structured approach that integrates foundational principles and iterative steps. Sufficient procedures were identified in the literature (Sect. 2) that were used for the development of the Act4DC: TÜV's compliance-securing structures, processes, and measures (TÜV Nord Group, n.d.), the five key elements, including management commitment, risk analysis, training, and audits from SwissHoldings/Economiesuisse (Beglinger & Michel, 2014, pp. 6–7). IN addition, the approach from Bay and Hastenrath's (2021, p. 121) and the NIST Cybersecurity Framework 2.0's model (NIST, 2024, p. 7) with its practical methodologies. Voigt and

Von dem Bussche (2017, p. 245) recommended a view on adaptability, and a systematic review, underscoring that robust compliance systems require processes tailored to organizational needs while remaining dynamic to regulatory changes. The methods, models and recommendations listed were used to develop the process structure of the Act4DSC (Fig. 2).

SQ2: Since the focus of this research was on data security compliance and a tool was to be designed and evaluated precisely for this perspective, it was necessary to work out the special features of DSC, particularly regarding general compliance. DSC differs from general compliance primarily in its level of detail and focus. As a specialized field, it ensures adherence to regulations protecting confidentiality, integrity, and the availability of data, as well as the fundamental rights of individuals regarding personal data (FADP, 2023). Public scrutiny was identified as an important key differentiator; concerns over privacy and data misuse drive the need for transparency in data handling (Guirguis et al., 2021). Companies must disclose data usage to build trust. Additionally, data classification plays a crucial role in risk prioritization. Organizations must determine (a) where personal and sensitive data is processed, (b) where data is stored (on-premises or via third parties), and (c) which regional regulations apply. Unlike general compliance, data security compliance requires continuous risk assessment and adaptation to evolving privacy concerns and regulatory landscapes.

SQ3: Incorporating DSC elements requires heightened specificity compared to general compliance processes. Act4DSC achieves this by tailoring processes to the unique demands of data security, such as classifying data based on criticality, identifying processes involving personal data, and addressing storage and regional regulatory considerations. Additionally, the related handbook provides detailed guidance on targeted data security measures, ensuring comprehensive coverage of data security requirements. These features enable organizations to build robust compliance systems tailored to their operational contexts while addressing the specific challenges of data security.

5.2   Conclusion and Further Directions

Hevner et al.'s fourth guideline for DSR emphasizes the importance of clear and verifiable contributions in design artifacts, foundations, and methodologies (2004, p. 83). This research effectively followed this principle, with the literature review identifying the research gap and the original design enabling a structured, iterative process for an artifact, a tool development to support smaller businesses with its DSC problem. Act4DSC addresses the identified gaps in DSC by providing a tailored solution for smaller businesses, which are often underserved by existing frameworks. It bridges the divide between theoretical compliance models and practical application by integrating the NIST Cybersecurity Frameworks (2023, 2024) with actionable steps and detailed guidance.

This research not only contributes to academia by extending design science principles but also offers a tangible tool for practitioners, enabling smaller organizations to navigate complex regulatory landscapes effectively. The iterative development process, driven by stakeholder feedback, ensures that Act4DSC remains practical, adaptable, and responsive to real-world challenges.

Feedback from semi-formal interviews with experts from the field indicated that Act4DSC is effective for smaller companies without existing data security frameworks. The tool received positive evaluations for its structured approach, actionable guidance, and adaptability to varying organizational needs. Practitioners noted its ability to streamline compliance efforts, with suggestions for further enhancing usability and stakeholder engagement.

Future directions for Act4DSC include:

- Broader Testing and Validation: conducting pilot implementations in small businesses settings to validate its effectiveness and adaptability across diverse organizational contexts.
- Localisation: expanding accessibility by translating the tool and handbook into other languages to make it easier for the users of smaller businesses.
- Integration of automation and AI: Enhancing functionality through automated regulatory analysis and AI-driven recommendations; this could help to identify relevant (new) regulations and streamline compliance processes.
- Adaptation for larger organizations: Investigating modifications to accommodate the needs of medium-sized and large businesses, broadening the tool's applicability.

Act4DSC's structured and iterative design positions it as a promising solution for smaller companies navigating the complexities of DSC. With further refinement and testing, it has the potential to become a widely adopted resource, contributing to stronger data security practices and regulatory adherence across various sectors.

References

Bay, K.C., Hastenrath, K.: Compliance Management Systeme: Praxiserprobte Elemente, Prozesse und Tools. Helbing & Lichtenhahn (2021)

Beglinger, J., Michel, A.: Fundamentals of effective compliance management. Swissholdings/Economiesuisse (2014)

Cofino, C., et al.: New management standard for digital data protection using a PDCA model anchored to ISO/IEC 27001 and R.A. 10173. Int. J Emerg. Technol. Adv. Eng. **13**(5), 84–89 (2023)

Ebert, N., Widmer, M.: Datenschutz in Schweizer Unternehmen 2018 - Eine Studie des Instituts für Wirtschaftsinformatik und des Zentrums für Sozialrecht. ZHAW School of Management and Law (2018)

FADP, Federal Act on Data Protection: https://www.fedlex.admin.ch/eli/cc/2022/491/en. Accessed 11 Feb 2025

Fischermanns, G.: Praxishandbuch Prozessmanagement. Das Standardwerk auf Basis des BPM Framework ibo-Prozessfenster. 11th edn. vol.9. Dr. Götz Schmidt, Gießen (2013)

Garber, J.: GDPR – compliance nightmare or business opportunity? Comput. Fraud Secur. **2018**(6), 14–15 (2018)

Guirguis, K., Pleger, L., Dietrich, S., Mertes, A., Brüesch, C.: Datenschutz in der Schweiz – eine quantitative analyse der gesellschaftlichen Bedenken und Erwartungen an den Staat. Yearb. Swiss Adm. Sci. **12**(1), 16–30 (2021)

Hevner, A., Chatterjee, S.: Design science research in information systems. In: Design Research in Information Systems, Integrated Series in Information Systems, vol. 22. Springer, Boston, MA (2010)

Hevner, A., March, S., Park, J., Ram, S.: Design science in information systems research. MIS Q. **28**(1), 75 (2004)

ISO, International Organization for Standardization. https://www.iso.org/obp/ui/en/#iso:std:iso:22300:ed-3:v1:en. Accessed 11 Feb 2025

Kitchenham, B.: Procedures for Performing Systematic Reviews (Joint Technical Report TR/SE-0401; Keele University Technical Report). Keele University (2004)

Krystlik, J.: With GDPR, preparation is everything. Comput. Fraud Secur. **2017**(6), 5–8 (2017)

Mikkelsen, D., Soller, H., Strandell-Jansson, M.: The EU data-protection regulation—compliance burden or foundation for digitization? McKinsey & Company (2017)

NIST, National Institute of Standards and Technology: The NIST cybersecurity framework 2.0—draft (NIST CSWP 29 ipd; p. NIST CSWP 29 ipd). National Institute of Standards and Technology (2023)

NIST, National Institute of Standards and Technology: The NIST cybersecurity framework 2.0 (NIST CSWP 29; p. NIST CSWP 29). National Institute of Standards and Technology (2024)

Marotta, A., Madnick, S.: Convergence and divergence of regulatory compliance and cybersecurity. Issues Inf. Syst. **22**(1) (2021)

Österle, H., et al.: Memorandum on design-oriented information systems research. Eur. J. Inf. Syst. **20**(1), 7–10 (2011)

Peffers, K., Tuunanen, T., Niehaves, B.: Design science research genres: introduction to the special issue on exemplars and criteria for applicable design science research. Eur. J. Inf. Syst. **27**(2), 129–139 (2018)

Prat, N., Comyn-Wattiau, I., Akoka, J.: Artifact evaluation in information systems design science research – a holistic view. In: PACIS 2014 Proceedings, 23. AIS Electronic Library (AISeL) (2014)

Romanou, A.: The necessity of the implementation of privacy by design in sectors where data protection concerns arise. Comput. Law Secur. Rev. **34**(1), 99–110 (2018)

Rüegg-Stürm, J., Grand, S.: Das St. Galler Management-Modell. Management in einer komplexen Welt. (2nd ed.). Haupt, UTB (2020)

Statista. https://www.statista.com/outlook/tmo/software/productivity-software/office-software/switzerland?currency=CHF. Accessed 11 Feb 2025

Stevens, R., et al.: Compliance cautions: investigating security issues associated with U.S. digital-security standards. In: Proceedings 2020 Network and Distributed System Security Symposium. Network and Distributed System Security Symposium, San Diego, CA (2020)

Tikkinen-Piri, C., Rohunen, A., Markkula, J.: EU general data protection regulation: changes and implications for personal data collecting companies. Comput. Law Secur. Rev. **34**(1), 134–153 (2018)

TÜV NORD: Compliance Management Systeme – warum sie so wichtig sind und was Unternehmen bei der Umsetzung beachten müssen. https://www.tuev-nord.de/de/unternehmen/bildung/wissen-kompakt/moderne-arbeitswelt/compliance-management-im-unternehmen/. Accessed 11 Feb 2025

Voigt, P., von dem Bussche, A.: Practical implementation of the requirements under the GDPR. In: The EU General Data Protection Regulation (GDPR), pp. 245–249 Springer, Cham (2017)

DAOMod: A Modeling Method for Token Economy and Voting Protocol Specification

Sowelu Avanzo[1]([⊠])[iD], Daniele Pautasso[1][iD], Irene Domenicale[1][iD], Alex Norta[2,3,4][iD], Claudio Schifanella[1][iD], and Marie Hattingh[4][iD]

[1] University of Torino, Turin, Italy
`{soweluelios.avanzo,daniele.pautasso,irene.domenicale,`
`claudio.schifanella}@unito.it`
[2] Tallinn University, Tallinn, Estonia
`alex.norta.phd@ieee.org`
[3] Dymaxion OÜ, Tallinn, Estonia
[4] University of Pretoria, Pretoria, South Africa
`marie.hattingh@up.ac.za`

Abstract. Decentralized Autonomous Organizations (DAOs) are a type of Decentralized Applications (DApps) that utilize smart contracts to support governance processes. DAO development is especially challenging due to the complexity of designing and validating their token economies and voting protocols. In addition, DAOs suffer from the scalability, usability, and complexity limitations faced by all DApps. Although different approaches address some of the issues mentioned in isolation, a holistic model-driven method for DAO design is lacking. To address this gap, we propose a modeling method that supports crucial DAO design and development phases. The approach is evaluated in an in vivo case study. This involves modeling a novel application of DAOs that facilitates the production and distribution of peer-to-peer media content. Although previous DAO development approaches provide modeling languages, ontologies, and platform-dependent decision models, our solution advances the field by proposing a stepwise, platform-independent DAO specification guidance. This ensures early-stage involvement of both technical and non-technical stakeholders by means of visual notation.

Keywords: Decentralized Autonomous Organization · blockchain

1 Introduction

Decentralized Autonomous Organizations (DAOs) represent a special class of decentralized applications that use smart contracts–computer programs running in a blockchain-based environment–to enable decentralized governance processes [8].

In recent years, a wide variety of novel real-world applications have been proposed and increasing scientific research has been conducted on the topic [8].

F. Corradini et al. (Eds.): Society 5.0 2025, CCIS 2787, pp. 25–37, 2026.
https://doi.org/10.1007/978-3-032-15463-7_3

Several of these applications are crucial for empowering citizens and solving societal challenges, hence making DAOs a key pillar of Society 5.0. However, the researchers also highlighted that the development of DAOs still involves a significant degree of complexity and discussed the main issues that limit the utility of DAOs [4]. In particular, since the governance of DAOs is strongly dependent on incentive mechanisms and tokenization of resources, these systems face challenges in the design and validation of suitable token economies–systems where digital tokens are used for coordination, allocation of resources, and rewarding contributions within decentralized networks [4]. Moreover, the selection of an appropriate voting protocol further adds to this complexity, as various mechanisms have been developed [16], each with distinct implications on governance and suitability for different project requirements. In addition to the above, DAOs face structural limitations in terms of complexity, usability, and scalability, as all DApps [19].

Recently, various approaches to support the development of DAOs have been proposed. In particular, the decision model in [5] reduces the complexity of selecting a suitable DAO deployment platform, based on the project requirements. However, the constraining factors for this decision model are the dependency on platform availability and the lack of interoperability of existing solutions [4,5].

On the other hand, platform-independent design approaches focus on specific DAO design issues while lacking a holistic method, or they lack concrete stepwise guidance. Trusted DApp Modeling (T-DM) [19] and IContractML 2.0 [12] are examples that address the complexity of DApp and smart contract development. However, they lack suitability for specifying voting protocols and token economies of DAOs. In contrast, the decision model in [16] facilitates the selection of a suitable voting protocol, but does not address token economy design. Recent methods and theoretical frameworks facilitate token economy design [6,18], but lack suitability for the specification of other aspects of DAOs.

T-DM was recently extended (ET-DM) to achieve suitability for the specification of token economies and voting systems of DAOs [3]. While this recent contribution proposes a standard language for the specification and communication of DAO requirements, it fails to provide stepwise guidance for developers and non-technical users to select suitable design options for their project. This limits the usability and pragmatic usefulness of the modeling language.

Since a comprehensive methodology for specifying DAO token economies and voting protocols, also considering DApp structural challenges, is still lacking, we shall address this gap by responding to the following Research Question (RQ): *How to develop a method that enables the specification of platform-independent models of DAOs with suitable token economies and voting protocols?* Responding to this main RQ involves defining a set of measures for the utility of DAOs (nonfunctional requirements), and derive a set of suitable steps that guide modeling and facilitate the selection of suitable design features based on the prioritized NFRs of the project. To create a separation of concerns, we deduce the following sub-research questions: *What are the reference non-functional requirements of the token economies and voting protocols of DAOs?* (**RQ1**) and *What are the* *method steps that enable the specification of DAOs using ET-DM diagrams?* (**RQ2**).

By applying the Design-Science Research (DSR) methodology [13], a structured framework to address unsolved organizational problems by iterative development and evaluation of IS artifacts, including constructs, models and methods, we design the DAOMod method, which guides users in the process of modeling Extended T-DM diagrams to respond to the main RQ. This involves making two main contributions. Firstly, we generate reference NFRs of DAO voting protocols and token economies based on extant literature (RQ1) (detailed in Sect. 3). Secondly, we define a set of suitable method steps that guide modeling and facilitate the selection of suitable design features based on the prioritized NFRs of the project, detailed in Sect. 4 (RQ2).

The utility of the approach is evaluated through an *in vivo* case study of a DAO, which aims to automate and disintermediate the production and distribution of independent media content, with empirical analysis discussed in Sect. 5, and outcomes in Sect. 6, along with future research outlook. The subsequent section presents related work, along with the background information necessary for the reader to understand the contributions of the article, and the running-case problem addressed by the DSR artifacts generated.

2   Preliminaries

Section 2.1 introduces the running case problem addressed by DAOMod, followed by related work and the ET-DM modeling notation in Sect. 2.2.

2.1   Running Case

The White Rabbit DApp addresses challenges in minority-language media distribution, where mainstream platforms often overlook niche content due to perceived low profitability. It enables users to share and purchase films in a decentralized manner, ensuring fair compensation for all involved in content creation, marketing, and distribution. A Chrome extension[1] identifies user-searched films and redirects them to legal viewing options, including cinemas, licensed platforms, or peer-to-peer streaming with traceable payments to rights holders. The integration of the White Rabbit system with the DAOs could make its governance more decentralized and community-driven. DAOs in this context would enable filmmakers and other stakeholders to collectively and transparently make decisions regarding crucial platforms policies. These decisions may include the selection of suitable viewing fees, or of adequate distribution channels for a given content. This participatory governance could improve the loyalty of users to the platform, as it would align the platform's operations with the needs and interests of the community. However, the implementation of DAOs in this context requires that governance features be carefully designed, in order to avoid reproducing the centralization dynamics that currently affect the mainstream media industry.

---

[1] https://chromewebstore.google.com/detail/white-rabbit/nmapoiplonbfadgdnnnkjo akgjdifikn.

2.2   Background and Related Work

This section provides a brief discussion of the state-of-the-art of DAO development methods. The study in [17] proposes a method focused on the design of the governance of blockchain systems. While DAOs may be adopted to manage the governance of a blockchain network, they are applicable to a wider range of use cases, as shown in [8]. This limits the suitability of the method for DAO design and development. The model-based, process-driven engineering approach proposed in [21] effectively guides the selection of suitable on-chain and off-chain functions in blockchain-augmented organizations. However, it primarily focuses on organizational structure and process coordination, without addressing token economy mechanisms or voting protocol design. Modeling languages and ontologies facilitate DAO development. In particular, the DECENT ontology, presented in [14] models decentralized governance constructs. Although DECENT provides a conceptualization of the rules and policies on which the governance of a DAO is based, it does not model how rules and policies are concretely executed by smart contracts. The DAO-ML modeling language facilitates the specification of organizational structures of DAOs [2], but it lacks suitability for token economy design. By contrast, ET-DM provides a suitable notation for the specification of token economies and voting protocols of DAOs. However, none of the mentioned modeling languages guides developers in the process of specifying DAO models and in selecting suitable features for the modeled DAO.

Table 1 defines the elements of the T-DM extension (ET-DM) to specify decision-making protocols and token economies. The complete syntax definition is presented in [3]. Both in the original T-DM Requirement Diagram syntax [19], based on goal models, and its extension, a system's primary *goal* is *decomposed* into subordinate goal elements and finally assigned to agents (human or autonomous) to facilitate the specification of complex large-scale systems. These models include *quality goals* for non-functional requirements elicitation and *emotional goals* for expected agent sentiment in executing system functions. These are *associated to* relevant *goals*. T-DM also introduces the *on-chain execution type*, enabling early-stage decisions on which functions require blockchain execution based on *quality goals*. In the T-DM extension, a further *execution type* is included: *Snapshot* execution records data off-chain while ensuring on-chain integrity, enhancing scalability, and security [20]. The ET-DM specifies elements that detail the main functional areas of the DAOs. The Organisation Goal represents the DAO's mission. It decomposes into *Treasury* elements, that manage financial tokenized resources, *Decision-Making Methods*, specifying voting protocols and *Token Manager* elements enabling issuance of tokens. *Token Managers decompose into Token* types issued by the DAO itself, while *Treasuries decompose into Tokens* that are managed but non-issued by the DAO. Mechanisms enforce governance rules via *pre-* and *post-conditions*. *Resource* elements specify the entitlement to (material or immaterial) resources a *Token* they are *associated to* provides. The concrete execution of DAO functions is detailed by *decomposing* elements whose *execution type* is *on-chain* into Assets (state variables), Transactions (functions), and Data Stores (DAO data management functions).

Table 1. Extended T-DM Elements and Properties [3,19].

Element	Notation	Description	Properties
Goal		Target state of a system function.	ID; name; execution_type;
Quality Goal		Success criterion for a goal.	ID; description;
Emotional Goal		Desired user sentiment.	ID; description;
Organization Goal		DAO system's organizational mission.	ID; DAO_name; mission_statement;
Treasury		Manages DAO's tokenized reserve.	ID; name; fiscal_policy_Goal;
Decision-Making		Voting protocol of the DAO.	ID; name; DM_method; DM_scope; voting_requirement; proposal_requirement;
Mechanism		Implementation of a governance rule.	ID; precondition; postcondition; trigger; executive_action; mechanism_type;
Token		Token type in the DAO economy.	ID; token_name; utility; transferable; fungibility;
Proposal		Specifies the characteristics of proposal objects.	ID; name; allowed_state; parameter;
Resource		Tokenized resource (material or immaterial).	ID; name; resource_type;
Token Manager		Component that handles token issuance.	ID; name; tokenomic_goal;
Snapshot		System function implementing the snapshot technique.[20]	ID; name; execution_type;
Asset		Smart contract state variables.	ID; name; parameter;
Transaction		State transition in a smart contract.	ID; function_name; operation;
Data Store		DAO data storage or indexing function.	ID; name; data_stored; public;
Agent		Actor interacting with the system.	ID; name; autonomous;
Decomposition		Splits high-level goals into sub-goals.	parent_ID; child_ID;
Association		Links between related elements.	source_ID; target_ID;
On-Chain		Function executed on the blockchain.	ID; name; execution_type;

3 Reference Requirements of DAOs

Recent research has classified key DAO system requirements but lacks a comprehensive discussion of NFRs from the perspective of token economy and voting protocol design. For example, [9] discusses NFRs for voting protocols but not token economy design, while [3] models Reference Functional Requirements for both but lacks NFR classification. Figure 1 provides an overview of the NFRs for DAO systems based on the three relevant perspectives of *decision-making, token economy design* and *Execution.*

Under the leftmost column of the table, we identify NFRs of voting protocols of DAOs based on extant literature. In particular, *Security* is needed, as these often implement mechanisms to protect against malicious attacks and unauthorized tampering [9,15]. *Efficiency* in decision-making consists in requiring minimal time to reach a decision. Moreover, decision-making protocols should ensure scalability as participation grows [9]. *Effectiveness* is achieved by provid-

PERSPECTIVES		
Decision-Making	**Token Economy**	**Execution**
Secure	Diversified - TE/TA	Secure
Effcient	Dependable - TE/TA	Upgradable
Effective	Profitable - TE/TA	Extensible
Accountable	Incentive-Aligning - TE/TA	Scalable
Expressive	Sustainable - TE/TA	Trustable
Inclusive	Liquid - TA	Verifiable
	Stable -TA	Interoperable
	Abundant/Rare - TE/TA	Performant

Fig. 1. Reference Requirements of DAO systems. NFRs of token economies can apply to Tokenized Assets (TA) if they refer to a specific token type, to the overall token economy of the DAO (TE), or can be used in both contexts (TE/TA).

ing comprehensive information to voters, enabling well-informed decisions [9]. *Simplicity* involves developing usable and straightforward protocols and interaction mechanisms to lower participation barriers [15]. *Accountability* is maintained through mechanisms that increase voters' responsibility by requiring a commitment in terms of tokenized resources, time, or reputation, as discussed in [15]. Decision-making protocols are sufficiently *expressive* if they allow voters to indicate the intensity of their preferences, using methods such as weighted or range voting [15]. Finally, *inclusivity* ensures an equitable participation, preventing power concentration, and promoting broad user engagement [10].

In the central column of the table, we introduce reference NFRs for DAO token economies and tokenized assets. As shown in the third column of the table, some of the listed NFRs apply to the entire token economy, while others apply to individual tokenized assets only. Other NFRs can refer to both contexts. Firstly, *diversification* is required for token economies to mitigate risk by reducing the impact of adverse events on any single asset [22]. This implies for individual DAOs that they store several types of token in their treasury, whose price fluctuations are uncorrelated. *Dependability* refers to the need to minimize the risk of counterparty credit for the stakeholders of the DAO and the organization through suitable mechanisms, such as those described in [1] and [11]. *Profitability* ensures regular returns to stakeholders, improving ecosystem viability [1,22]. *Incentive aligning* token economies fosters behavior that supports system goals through rewards and penalties.

Sustainability relates to the long-term value appreciation [15]. For tokenized assets, liquidity is maintained through suitable issuance mechanisms and automated market makers [1,7,15]. Price *Stability* is achieved by avoiding volatility with price management and collateralization [15].

Diverse studies, such as [19], discuss NFRs of DApps, to which we refer for the Execution Layer of DAOs. NFRs of the Execution layer ensure reliable operation of DAOs by addressing key aspects such as *security, verifiability, trustability*. These requirements are met by the presence of suitable on-chain functionalities. *Off-chain* functions ensure *usability, scalability* and *extensibility*. Furthermore, *upgradability* and *interoperability* are desirable requirements for this class of systems. The rightmost column of the table reports the list of such NFRs, highlighting their importance and applicability within the DAO execution layer.

4   DAO Requirement Modeling

Given the complexity of the DAO domain, a method guiding developers and non-technical stakeholders in the process of modeling DAO systems along with their token economies is needed, as highlighted in [4]. Therefore, we propose steps to guide users in modeling DAOs using the ET-DM language [3], as this provides a standardised visual notation for this domain. Table 2 outlines the proposed method steps for specifying DAOs. Users should first define the root goal as either an *Organization Goal* for an individual DAO or a *Goal* In the former case, the model concerns an individual DAO, whereas in the latter, a

Table 2. DAO Requirement Modeling Steps

Task	Description
1. Root Goal Definition	Define the root as an *Organization Goal* (if the system modeled is an individual DAO) or a *Goal*.
2. Organization Goal Definition	Decompose root goal into subgoals specifying *execution type* (*on/off-chain, snapshot*). Define DAO mission and metadata per each DAO modeled.
3.Organization Goal Refinement	Refine Organization Goal into *Goal* elements for governance. Define *Data Store* if needed.
4. Decision-Making Definition	Specify *Decision-Making* elements, governance areas, execution type, and proposal/voting requirements.
5. Decision-Making Refinement	Decompose *Decision-Making* element into *mechanisms* that cover the four crucial phases of decision-making [16]: • **Initiation:** Specify *voting/proposal rights* and *decision-making support mechanisms*. • **Ratification:** Specify *vote polling* and *vote tallying mechanisms*. • **Implementation:** Decompose *proposal execution mechanisms*. • **Monitoring:** Set *dispute resolution mechanisms*.
6. Fiscal Policy Definition	Decompose *Organization Goal* into *Treasury*, define fiscal policies, token types, and capital gain strategies.
7. Tokenomics Definition	Decompose the *Token Manager* into token types, define issuance (*airdrop, sale, cap*), and apply *abundant/rare* attributes.
8. Smart Contract Refinement	Refine on-chain elements into *assets*, decompose into *transactions* to specify smart contract state variables and functions (if this level of detail is needed).
9. Agent Specification	Define *autonomous/human* agents, associate them with functions, and optionally assign *emotional goals*.

more complex system which includes a DAO sub-system is modeled, such as a platform enabling DAO deployment (**Step 1**).

Subsequently (**Step 2**), the root goal is associated with relevant *Quality Goal* elements (if any), defining the NFRs of the entire system. If a *Goal* element is used, decompose it into sub-goals until *Organization Goals* are defined. Per each of those elements, metadata including and execution type (*on-chain, off-chain, snapshot*). Include *Data Store* elements when necessary. Subsequently, each refining *Organization Goal* is refined into *Goal* elements indicating the sub-functions of each DAO (**Step 3**).

Among the children elements of each DAO modeled, one or more *Decision-Making* element is specified (**Step 4**), indicating the voting protocol(s) used in that DAO. The *DM_scope* property specifies the separate governance areas of interest for each of them. The selection of *Decision Making (DM) methods* depends on the quality attributes chosen among the reference NFRs in the left column of Fig. 1. Based on the quality attributes chosen, users textually specify the decision-making method (*DM_method*) that best suits their needs. Quality attributes of the Execution layer (rightmost column in Fig. 1) can also be associated to *Decision-Making Method* elements to guide the selection of the appropriate *execution type*. The *proposal_requirement* and *voting_requirement* attributes are specified at this stage, which affect the degree of *inclusivity, security* and *accountability* realized by the protocol. Solutions involving *allowlists* are used to enhance the security of the protocol by increasing control over the system, but may limit its degree of *inclusivity*.

Requiring users to own a certain amount of a given token type can be used as a way to make the protocol more *accountable* and *secure*. Each *Decision-Making Method* decomposes into *Mechanism* elements to support the four crucial decision-making phases of voting (Table 2). Governance tokens may be *airdropped* for higher *inclusivity*, while mechanisms entailing *elections* or *invitations* prioritize security and efficiency. Requiring *token purchase* may be a suitable criterion to make participants *accountable* for their decisions, although it may limit *inclusivity*. Support mechanisms may also be specified to meet the quality goals associated to the element. In particular, *Proof-of-Personhood* increases *security, proposal screening efficiency*, and vote delegation enhances *simplicity* of the voting system. In addition, *incentive mechanisms* may be provided to encourage participation and improve *accountability*. In the **Initiation phase**, *Mechanism* elements for the *voting* and *proposal right* allocation are selected. (*airdrop, election, proof-of-personhood, proposal screening, vote delegation*). Subsequently, *mechanisms* supporting the **Ratification phase** are selected. These specify how *vote polling* and *vote tallying* are conducted. A more *expressive* ballot allows voters to rank options or provide detailed input, making the process more *effective*, but also more complex. Conversely, a *simpler* ballot streamlines participation but may limit nuanced preferences. In vote tallying, quorum affects *inclusivity*, as requiring a minimum number of participants ensures a greater representation but may slow decision making. *Vote weighting* can further impact *inclusivity* and *simplicity*: favoring users with more governance tokens can reduce equal participation and add complexity to the process. The **Implementation** phase establishes *proposal execution* mechanisms, supporting autonomous execution if *security* is prioritized. Finally, the *Monitoring* phase may be supported by specifying suitable *dispute resolution* Mechanisms to enhance *security* and *accountability*. Finally, each *mechanism* is associated with relevant *quality goals* from the third column of Fig. 1, and their *execution type* is selected based on such requirements. Subsequently, developers decompose Organization Goals into the Treasury elements (**Step 6**), indicating the collectively managed wallets of the DAO and specifying the respective goals of the *fiscal policy* associated to them.

Each of those is associated with quality attributes in the central column of the Fig. 1 that can be applied to the token economy of DAO. These facilitate the selection of the foreseen capital gain sources (*profitability*) for the DAO and the expected degree of *diversification* for the tokens managed by that specific treasury. Based on these requirements, Treasury elements are refined into token types that the DAO shall manage as part of its operations. Once token types are specified, the relevant quality goals from the central column of Fig. 1 can be assigned to individual token elements. Quality goals assigned to the Treasury elements and token types guide their decomposition into *Mechanism* types. If *Dependability* is prioritized, as in the case where users deposit or stake funds, it should be *associated* to the *Treasury* element. In this case, *Resource Allocation* mechanisms to mitigate counterparty credit risk and ensure predictable financial commitments. Similarly, *Profitability* and *Sustainability* requirements are addressed by decomposing *Treasury* or *Token* elements into *Price Control* mechanisms, which regulate price fluctuations reducing market risk. *Exchange* mechanisms facilitate automated token conversion, ensuring *liquidity* when required. If *incentive alignment* is a priority, *Incentive* mechanisms distribute rewards and penalties to encourage desired behavior. Subsequently, the Token Manager of the DAO is decomposed from the Organization Goal.

The token types implemented and issued by the DAO itself (**Step 7**) are therefore decomposed from this element. Similar decomposition rules as those applied to Tokens in Step 6, with the added specification of *Issuance Mechanisms*, as tokens are minted by the DAO. The Token Issuance Mechanism defines key attributes such as preconditions, postconditions, and triggers, determining distribution methods (sale or airdrop) and supply constraints (capped or uncapped). The choice of issuance strategy depends on the token's *abundance* or *rarity*. Deflationary policies enhance scarcity for a store of value, while inflationary policies promote adoption as a medium of payment [15]. Subsequently, if greater specification detail is needed, On-chain functions are decomposed into *assets*. These represent the state variables of the smart contracts of the DAO. Each of these decomposes into *transactions*, representing the functions of each smart contract. **Step 9** concludes the specification process by defining Agents that execute functions of the DAO. These can be *human* (organizational roles) or *autonomous* (software entities).

The selection of a suitable execution type (on-chain, snapshot-based, or off-chain) depends on the non-functional requirements (NFRs) associated with the DAO's functionalities. When a system function must be verifiable, secure, or trustable, but performance and scalability are not primary concerns, on-chain execution is preferred [19]. For functionalities that require both verifiability and security while also maintaining performance and scalability, a snapshot-based execution is more appropriate, as it relies on off-chain computation, while maintaining an acceptable degree of *security*, *trustability* and *verifiability* of data, which are stored *on-chain* [20]. In other cases, off-chain execution is preferred [19]. These Execution Type selection heuristics apply to Goal, Mechanism, Decision Making Method elements at each step described.

5 Evaluation

This case study models, using the steps described in the method, the DAO subsystem of the White Rabbit platform, managing the ownership of intellectual property (IP), resolving conflicts related to its attribution, and distributing revenues as reported in the *mission statement* of the Organization Goal in Fig. 2. The DAO decision-making process includes both off-chain and on-chain *mechanisms*, and is associated to *privacy*, *effectiveness*, and *security* NFRs. The *vote polling* and *vote tallying* mechanisms are executed *off-chain*, prioritizing *performance*, while an *on-chain proposal execution mechanism* updates IP contracts when consensus on attribution is reached, ensuring *verifiability*. The token economy is then specified (Steps 6–7). The **Film Industry Token (FIT)** is a fungible token (FT) with financial and usage utility, enabling payments for access to the content. The **Access Token (AT)**, represented as an NFT, grants film viewing rights, while the **Intellectual Property Token (IP)**, also an

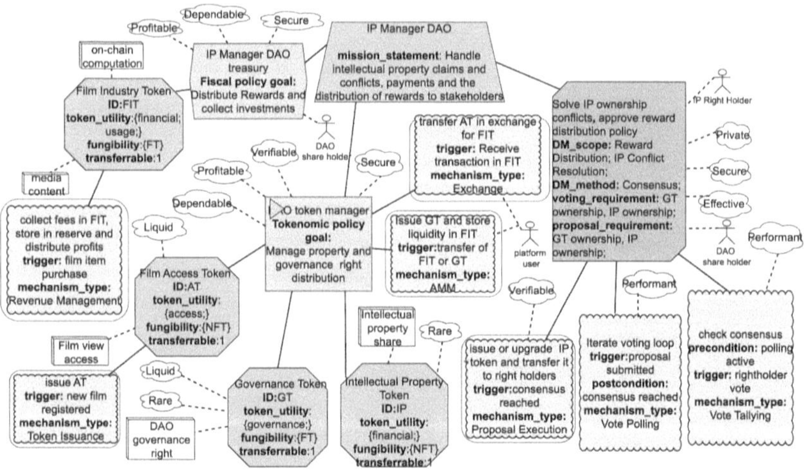

Fig. 2. Extended Requirement Diagram of IP Manager DAOs.

NFT, embodies ownership claims and related financial returns. The **Governance Token (GT)** provides voting rights over profit-sharing policies and the fees charged by the DAO for IP registration. *Liquidity* for governance tokens is maintained through an Automated Market Maker (AMM), while an on-chain *Revenue Management mechanism* ensures financial *sustainability* of the DAO. This collects fees from content sales, redistributes revenues to IP rights holders, and stores reserves to support DAO operations. The XML files encoding the diagram reported are included in[2] and validated by means of the Python script provided, ensuring the syntactic correctness of the ET-DM models.

6   Discussion and Conclusion

This article presents the development and evaluation of DAOMod, a holistic modeling method for DAOs. This is developed by first investigating reference non-functional requirements of DAOs discussed in the literature. Subsequently, we propose step-by-step guidelines for modeling DAOs using the modeling language developed in [3]. The method proposed guides developers in selecting suitable design features based on the non-functional requirements elicited. The approach is evaluated through an *in vivo* case study. This demonstrates the real-world applicability of the method. The method steps enabled the modeling of a DAO addressing the challenges of decentralized IP management, ensuring that rights holders receive fair compensation. Unlike other model-driven methods [19,21], the DAOMod guidelines facilitate the visual specification of the token economy and voting protocol design of the system. Due to the high degree of complexity of the DAO domain, the syntax used includes a large number of constructs. This complexity is addressed by the modeling method, which supports developers in the adoption of the modeling language. To further increase the usability of the approach, we plan to implement dedicated tool support for the modeling language. Moreover, since the modeling method is focused on static modeling of DAOs, we foresee its extension to incorporate dynamic aspects needed to capture the evolving nature of DAOs. This will provide support for the simulation and formal verification of token economies of DAOs. Finally, a more comprehensive evaluation of the approach is needed, which may include quantitative evaluation by means of surveys with industry experts.

Acknowledgments. This project is funded by the Estonian "Personal research funding: Team Grant (PRG)" project PRG1641 and PON REACT-EU (A. IV.5).

References

1. Alao, O., Cuffe, P.: Structuring special purpose vehicles for financing renewable generators on a blockchain marketplace. IEEE Trans. Ind. Appl. **58**(2), 1478–1489 (2021)

---

[2] https://github.com/SoweluAvanzo/DAOMod/tree/master/DAOMod%20Schemas%20and%20Models.

2. Avanzo, S., Norta, A., Linares, J., Schifanella, C., Hattingh, M.: Dao-ml: A modelling language for the specification of decentralized autonomous organization governance. Methods **13**, 16 (2024)
3. Avanzo, S., Norta, A., Linares, J., Schifanella, C., Hattingh, M.: Extending trusted DAPP modeling for decentralized autonomous organization development. In: Prieto, J., Vargas, R.P., Lage, O., Machado, J.M., Bálint, M. (eds.) Blockchain and Applications, 6th International Congress, pp. 140–149. Springer Nature Switzerland, Cham (2025)
4. Avanzo, S., Norta, A., Schifanella, C.: A modelling approach for a high utility decentralized autonomous organization development. In: 5th International Congress on Blockchain and Applications (BLOCKCHAIN'23). Guimarães, Portugal (2023)
5. Baninemeh, E., Farshidi, S., Jansen, S.: A decision model for decentralized autonomous organization platform selection: Three industry case studies. Blockchain: Res. Appl. **4**(2), 100127 (2023)
6. Barrera, C., Hurder, S.: Cryptoeconomics: Designing Effective Incentives and Governance Models for Blockchain Networks Using Insights From Economics. Tech. rep, Blockchain Research Institute (2020)
7. Bartoletti, M., Chiang, J.H.Y., Lluch-Lafuente, A.: A theory of automated market makers in DeFi (2022)
8. Bonnet, S., Teuteberg, F.: Decentralized autonomous organizations: a systematic literature review and research agenda. Int. J. Innov. Technol. Manage. 2450026 (2024)
9. Fan, Y., Zhang, L., Wang, R., Imran, M.A.: Insight into voting in DAOS: conceptual analysis and a proposal for evaluation framework. IEEE Network (2023)
10. Faqir-Rhazoui, Y., Arroyo, J., Hassan, S.: A scalable voting system: validation of holographic consensus in daostack. Technical Report (2021)
11. Fries, C.P., Kohl-Landgraf, P.: Smart derivative contracts (detaching transactions from counterparty credit risk: Specification, parametrisation, valuation). Available at SSRN 3163074 (2018)
12. Hamdaqa, M., Met, L.A.P., Qasse, I.: icontractml 2.0: A domain-specific language for modeling and deploying smart contracts onto multiple blockchain platforms. Inf. Softw. Technol. **144**, 106762 (2022)
13. Hevner, A.R., March, S.T., Park, J., Ram, S.: Design science in information systems research. Manag. Inf. Syst. Q. **28**(1), 6 (2008)
14. Kaya, F., Gordijn, J.: Decent: An ontology for decentralized governance in the renewable energy sector. In: 2021 IEEE 23rd Conference on Business Informatics (CBI), vol. 1, pp. 11–20. IEEE (2021)
15. Kivilo, S.: Designing a Token Economy: Incentives, Governance, and Tokenomics. Master's thesis, Tallinn University of Technology, MSc in Business Information Technology (2023). https://doi.org/10.13140/RG.2.2.13326.13124
16. Kurniawan, W., Jansen, S., van der Werf, J.M.: Voting mechanism selection for decentralized autonomous organizations. Technical Report
17. Pelt, R.v., Jansen, S., Baars, D., Overbeek, S.: Defining blockchain governance: a framework for analysis and comparison. Inf. Syst. Manage. **38**(1), 21–41 (2021)
18. Schubert, N., Obermeier, D., Kohlbrenner, F., Sandner, P.: Development of a token design framework. In: 2021 IEEE International Conference on Decentralized Applications and Infrastructures (DAPPS), pp. 30–38. IEEE (2021)
19. Udokwu, C.J.: A modelling approach for building blockchain applications that enables trustable inter-organizational collaborations (2022)

20. Wang, Q., et al.: An empirical study on snapshot DAOS. arXiv preprint arXiv:2211.15993 (2022)
21. Yue, K.B.: Blockchain-augmented organizations (2020)
22. Ziegler, C., Welpe, I.M.: A taxonomy of decentralized autonomous organizations (2022)

From Consumer Sovereignty to Algorithm-Dependency? The Case of Shopping Agents

Mathias Binswanger[(✉)]

University of Applied Sciences and Arts, Northwestern Switzerland, 4600 Olten, Switzerland
`mathias.binswanger@fhnw.ch`

Abstract. Most consumption and investment decisions are still made by humans today. But we already witness that such decisions are increasingly transferred to algorithms. The newest example, which caught a lot of attention, is the shopping agent "Operator", which was launched by Open AI in the beginning of 2025. Advanced algorithms not only automatically identify needs but also search for optimal products and purchasing options and possess the potential to carry out the corresponding transactions themselves. They become "autonomous consumer buying agents", or, in short, shopping agents, which are supposed to enable better consumption decisions in an environment of an ever-increasing and constantly changing variety of products. Consumers may save a lot of time, as shopping agents can screen a much larger number of products much faster than humans. Moreover, shopping agents can evaluate all offers based on criteria, which are supposed to be relevant to individual users. But at the same time, consumers gradually become dependent on shopping agents and lose their sovereignty. They have to "trust" decisions made by AI-based algorithms, which, however, do not necessarily make decisions in favor of consumers but rather in favor of their operators.

Keywords: Shopping Agents · Artificial Intelligence · Information Asymmetry Market Power

1 Introduction

Self-learning algorithms based on AI have the potential to make economic processes increasingly independent of human intervention. Today, we still assume that consumption and investment decisions or the choice of a particular candidate in an application process are made by humans. But we can already see that such decisions are increasingly transferred to algorithms. The newest example, which caught a lot of attention, is the shopping agent "Operator", which was launched by Open AI in the beginning of 2025. AI-driven algorithms are superior to humans in several ways. They can analyze much larger amounts of data in much less time, without getting tired. They are in operation 24 h a day as continuously optimizing agents and are therefore able to make purchasing or investment decisions faster and 'better' than their human counterparts.

F. Corradini et al. (Eds.): Society 5.0 2025, CCIS 2787, pp. 38–49, 2026.
https://doi.org/10.1007/978-3-032-15463-7_4

The more humans are replaced by algorithms, the more efficiently many economic processes will work. But on the other hand, we become increasingly dependent on AI-driven agents. The more sophisticated they get, the more they represent black boxes to their users. And users can never be sure whether these agents really choose the options, which are the best for them. Market power and information asymmetry allow Big-Tech companies to pursue their own interests, when offering AI-based devices (Binswanger, 2024a).

The paper is organized as follows. Section 2 explains how shopping agents are likely to shape consumption in the future and how they will gradually make decisions on behalf of their users. Section 3 emphasizes the information asymmetry between providers of shopping agents and users, which allows providers to influence and manipulate consumption. In Sect. 4 the focus is on market power associated with Big-Tech companies, which also facilitates the use of shopping agents to increase their own profits. Section 5 summarizes the results and draws some conclusions.

2 How Shopping Agents Will Make Decisions on Behalf of Consumers

The focus in this paper is on consumers and decisions about consumption. However, the following reasoning also applies to investment goods and thus to markets, where suppliers and buyers are companies. Generally, we talk about AI driven algorithms, which become AI agents. Such AI agents are often defined as "autonomous software systems that can reason, make decisions, and pursue goals with creativity and flexibility for you." (Desai and Riedl, 2025, p. 8). They are different from earlier applications because instead of simply talking about what you should do, AI Agents can do the things it suggests on your behalf without the user actually being involved.

For certain consumer goods, the shift of decision making from humans to algorithms is already apparent, although traditionally not very spectacular. For example, ThinQ washing machines from LQ can automatically reorder detergent when it runs low, and dishwashers from LQ do the same for washing capsules. There are coffee machines, printers or even smoke detectors that can reorder coffee capsules, ink and batteries. And in the US, algorithms are already being used to book campsites or make appointments with authorities (Kowalkiewicz, 2020). But this is just the beginning. Advanced algorithms not only automatically identify needs but also search for optimal products and purchasing options and then carry out the corresponding transactions themselves. In this way, they become 'autonomous consumer buying agents (CBA)' (Weber et al., 2020) or simply autonomous agents, which in the reminder of the paper we will refer to as shopping agents (e.g. Hong, 2024).

Three stages of development can be distinguished in which algorithms based on AI increasingly become independent of humans and independently make economically relevant decisions (see Gal and Elkin-Koren, 2018). Currently, most of the known algorithms, which autonomously purchase goods, are still in the first stage where a predefined product is purchased. For example, the dishwashers mentioned above always buy the same detergent from the same supplier, and no real choice is involved. The aim here is to ensure the supply of certain consumer goods. This can prove to be a very lucrative business for certain suppliers, because it guarantees them demand for certain products such as washing powder.

The interesting development starts in the second stage, when consumer preferences come into play and a genuine selection process is involved. Algorithms controlled by preferences can carry out a comprehensive search for offers of goods or services on the internet. They can find the best offer for the user, because the algorithm knows, for example, which flavors or colors the user prefers, or whether they prefer a sporty or elegant style. However, these preferences are not yet the result of AI-controlled processes but are based on information provided by the customers themselves or they are inferred from previous orders.

In the third stage, AI and self-learning algorithms become the decisive factor. Decisions are no longer based on predetermined preferences, but algorithms are able to predict preferences for decisions regarding the purchase of new products, which the customer has never bought before. Above all, this requires a lot of data about consumer behavior. This data is collected, organized and stored in huge databases, which can be used by algorithms based on AI to create individual user profiles. These profiles are built on revealed preferences concerning decision made in the past. These user profiles allow the algorithms to make predictions about future decisions of individual users.

But self-learning algorithms can develop even more abilities. If these algorithms were to make decisions based solely on data about our past behavior, they would rarely surprise or inspire us with anything new. But AI-based algorithms can also suggest unexpected – or non-obvious – purchases, thereby delighting the user with surprises. For example, an algorithm, which knows my personal preferences also knows that I occasionally make unexpected purchases to break out of my usual consumption routine.

We can also imagine how online comparison sites such as comparis.ch (in Switzerland) or check24.de (in Germany) will work in the future. If we visit these comparison sites today (2025), we quickly realize that AI is not involved yet. But we can easily imagine how they are likely to evolve in the next couple of years. Currently, we use these sites to get an overview of a specific market. For example, in Switzerland, people must choose a health insurance provider on an annual basis, which covers their mandatory health insurance. An online comparison provider such as comparis.ch pretends to help with this choice by showing the current rates of all insurance companies as well as the average customer ratings of these companies. But finally, people still must choose the insurance company by themselves.

Making such a choice can quickly turn into a tedious, time-consuming task. It is relatively easy to find the cheapest insurance offer, but unfortunately customer satisfaction often leaves something to be desired. The service is poor and/or you must wait a long time for your money when you submit claims to the company. Therefore, it might be better to choose a slightly more expensive health insurance provider, where customer satisfaction is at an acceptable level. However, since customer reviews are often contradictory, this is not an easy task. It would be more convenient if an algorithm could find the "best offer" and sign the contract with the health insurance company after having searched all offers and ratings within a short period of time. This would save customers a lot of time, which otherwise they must spend on this time-consuming selection. And they can be "sure" that the optimal offer will be chosen because the algorithm takes care of the individual preferences regarding price and quality (ratings).

This is precisely the development that we are likely to see in the future. Self-learning algorithms will search the internet for "best" offers and purchase the products, without human involvement. Consumers will no longer be bothered by decision making. They feel confident that the shopping agent will choose the "best" and "most affordable" offer based on previously revealed preferences. Thus, shopping agents will gradually replace human beings as consumers. They will make consumption decisions, which causes demand to become increasingly independent of human beings.

But how does the algorithm know which offer is "the best'" for me? The algorithm will only be able to acquire such knowledge with the help of AI. If the algorithm has access to a large data set, which contains information about my previous consumption behavior, it will soon know what is best for me. It can predict what I really care about. It knows my preferences regarding price and quality. For a cheapskate, the algorithm will select the cheapest offer because it knows that quality matters less than price. For a quality-oriented customer, on the other hand, the algorithm will give quality a higher weighting and, therefore, will choose a more expensive offer where customer reviews are more favorable. And the algorithm can also use data, which is not directly connected to the choice of the best health insurance. Price sensitivity and quality awareness can also be inferred from decisions related to other products. The more data on past decisions the algorithm includes, the better informed it is and the "better" decisions it can make. And the data does not even need to be restricted to former buying decisions. The algorithms also know which sites I typically visit on the internet, and it can track my travels or my contacts on social media, which provide information about aspects of my personality that may also be relevant for selecting the optimal health-insurance provider.

Selecting the appropriate health insurance provider is a relatively simple selection process. The question, whether we should choose a health insurance plan or not, does not arise, because health insurance in Switzerland is mandatory. And relatively few criteria (price, quality) are relevant for making an optimal decision. But AI-based algorithms can go much further, and not only decide which health insurance provider, which yoghurt or which car is best for me. They can also decide whether I should buy yoghurt or rather switch to a fruit curd. Or they can make an educated guess whether it makes sense buying a car or whether I would be better off using public transport. Consumers often will be happy to accept decisions made by AI, as we feel overwhelmed by too many options. As Koenig (2019, p. 450, own translation) writes: "If people are willing to enter into the relationship with machines…., it is probably because they are thereby enveloped in a comfortable blanket of intelligent decision support that is able to adapt to the idiosyncrasies and dispositions of individuals."

Shopping agents therefore have the potential to make life easier for consumers in two ways (see also Gokhale, 2025):

- better consumption decisions in an environment of an ever-increasing and constantly changing variety of products (optimization),
- saving time when making consumption decisions (convenience).

Both improvements, better decision making and time savings, are important in a world where the variety of products is constantly increasing. The only thing that is not growing is time itself. As before, there are only 24 h in a day. This means that consumers have to make more choices and decisions in the time available to them. People generally enjoy making choices, but only as long as the various options can be monitored and there are clear criteria for deciding which option is best. If there is not enough time for screening and monitoring all the options and the selection must be made under time pressure, the joy of choice quickly turns into an agony of choice. This phenomenon has been described as a multi-option treadmill (Binswanger, 2006).

This increase in diversity of products is also the result of constant attempts to boost sales (Binswanger, 2019). People buy more yoghurts, if there is a large variety in flavors. Suppliers try to diversify their products to make their supply more attractive. The world of consumption turns into an ever-increasing buffet, where the supply is constantly changing. Suppliers of goods and services constantly try to reinforce the multi-option treadmill. But in the future, they will also claim to mitigate the multi-option treadmill by advertising the use of shopping agents. Since shopping algorithms can search for a much larger range of products within a much shorter time scale than humans, the increase in variety and thus the multi-option treadmill is likely to become even more prevalent. However, many times it is not a real variety, but variety is artificially enhanced by adding more flavors, shapes and other features to the same product (Binswanger, 2006). This pseudo-variety makes it more difficult to compare products between different providers. If comparison is easy, people tend to buy where they get a product at the cheapest price. Therefore, telecommunications companies usually try to make offers for calling packages, which cannot directly be compared to the packages offered by competitors. This is an example of a pseudo-variety, as all they offer are gigabytes, which are the same, no matter whether they come from company A or company B.

3 Information Asymmetry Between Providers and Users of Shopping Agents

In reality, users can never be sure whether AI-based algorithms make decisions exclusively in their favor. Perhaps they are guided by vested interests and try to lurk users into making certain purchases or favor certain providers or products. This problem already exists today, when we analyze traditional comparison sites like comparis.ch (see Sect. 2), which do not make use of AI yet. If, again, we look at the comparison of health-insurance providers, we should be suspicious about the ratings of particular insurance companies. Because, once we switch to alternative comparison sites, they often provide ratings, which are at odds with the ratings on comparis.ch. Moreover, comparis.ch has been criticized several times for presenting a biased selection of insurance providers, leaving out those, who do not pay sufficiently high commissions. But if we cannot fully trust currently existing comparison sites, why should we trust AI-based algorithms making allegedly optimal decisions?

Many consumers try to solve the problem by visiting different comparison sites to get better information about a specific market. Therefore, the problem might be solved by establishing a meta-comparison site that compares the results of different comparison sites. The ratings of all comparison sites would be collected and weighed according to certain criteria. However, such a meta-comparison site would have to be operated by providers that are independent of the providers of comparison sites. In practice, this could hardly be guaranteed, and we would never be sure what interests are behind a meta-comparison site. Therefore, we could never fully trust them, and it is likely that several competing meta-comparison sites would pop up after some time. Do we therefore need to develop meta-meta comparison sites that compare all meta-comparison sites?

Of course, such an attempt would be futile, because the problem is just shifted to a higher level. Therefore, some experts and politicians call for more regulation as it is already done within the EU by the recently decided AI act. Such regulations are supposed to make sure that an algorithm only acts in the interest of its user and does not pursue any other goals. But how can the government ensure the "benevolence" of an algorithm (see Binswanger, 2024b)? The more sophisticated AI-based, self-learning algorithms become, the less transparent the decisions or predictions coming from these algorithms will be. Extensive tests would have to be carried out to investigate how they react to changes in the decision environment. But there would be no guarantee that an algorithm would make the same decisions again under slightly different circumstances. As they learn from previous experience they may decide differently today, as compared to yesterday even if you ask them to perform the same task. In short, even the most sophisticated testing method cannot guarantee "fair" or "unbiased" functioning of an algorithm. To achieve this goal, the government itself would have to develop algorithms under transparent and controllable conditions. But the government does not have the expertise to be an innovator in this field and it is unable to play such a role.

Ultimately, consumers have no choice but to trust the decisions or predictions of self-learning algorithms, because transparency remains wishful thinking. There is also a fundamental information asymmetry that affects all the markets where AI applications are advertised. Economists are familiar with information asymmetries, especially on markets for health services, where healthcare providers are typically better informed than consumers (patients). For example, a doctor is better informed about how successful or unsuccessful a particular treatment is likely to be than a patient. The way the doctor presents the therapy to the patient can strongly influence the patient's demand. If the doctor plays down the side effects and mentions success stories, it is likely that the patient will undergo the treatment. Ultimately, patients have no other choice than trusting doctors to make the right recommendations. The situation is quite similar regarding AI-based shopping agents. Consumers must trust them because there is no way of knowing exactly how and why they make certain choices. But this trust is built on shaky grounds. Providers of algorithms have a constant incentive to manipulate the decisions of users in a way that primarily serves their own interest, as law professors Ariel Ezrachi and Maurice Stucke made clear in their book "Virtual Competition", already published in 2016.

A few examples may serve to illustrate this point. In Australia the Australian Competition and Consumer Commission (ACCC) investigated online hotel booking sites and found that the search results on some hotel booking sites were influenced by the amount of the commission a hotel pays to the comparison site. And the ACCC also found that the comparison site Trivago violated Australian consumer law. Its ranking algorithm was significantly influenced by payments from online hotel booking sites to Trivago. However, Trivago's users were unaware of this, as Trivago presents itself as an impartial, objective and transparent organization (ACCC, 2020). Of course, it might be argued that there are a few black sheep everywhere, but that fraudulent behavior is not the rule but an exception. This may be true, but we can never be sure whether we are also manipulated by AI-driven algorithms or not, because there is no clear evidence to prove it. In the literature, there are discussions of so-called 'dark patterns', which relate to attempts to influence user behavior by designing the interface between user and AI application in such a way that the user decides in the interest of the providers and against his or her own interests (e.g. Mathur et al. 2019).

Another example concerns Amazon's buy-box algorithm. For companies who offer their products on Amazon's platform, the main concern is how their products will get into the buy box. This is an electronic shopping cart that potential buyers can fill with the products they want to buy and then order directly by clicking the buy button. Amazon has emphasized many times that its buy-box algorithm is an AI-based, impartial customer assistant that selects the seller with the offer that best suits the needs of the customer. When testifying before the House Judiciary Committee in 2019, Amazon's Associate General Counsel, Nate Sutton, told members of Congress: "Our algorithm aims to predict what customers are going to want to buy, and we apply the same criteria to that, whether it's a third-party seller or Amazon". (quoted from Mitchell and Sussmann, 2019).

But in fact, there is evidence that Amazon has designed its buy-box algorithm to produce results that serve its own interests at the expense of sellers and consumers (Mitchell and Sussmann, 2019; Raval, 2022). In 2020, the House Antitrust Subcommittee Report (Nadler and Cicilline, 2020, p. 1) stated that Amazon's control and reach across its many business lines allows it to disadvantage competitors. Amazon, therefore, can favor its own offers over those of third parties.

However, few specialists know how the buy-box algorithm works in detail, and which factors it weighs in which way. Even within Amazon, this is a closely guarded secret. For third-party sellers the buy-box algorithm represents a black box (Raval, 2022, p. 3). This uncertainty, in turn, created a new business opportunity for a whole range of consulting firms who try to offer their advice to companies selling their products on the Amazon platform. One of the largest players is called Feedvisor, a company which claims to offer "AI-driven, data-backed, 360 degree E-marketplace optimization performance, which leads to powerful solutions to scale profitability on Amazon". Feedvisor pretends to understand how the buy-box algorithm works and allegedly has identified more than a dozen variables, which are supposed to increase the chance for conquering the buy box. These factors include, for example, the seller's rating by customers, shipping time, stock availability, delivery reliability and sales volume.

Are decisions made by the buy-box algorithm therefore based on objective criteria? There is sufficient evidence which casts doubt on such a conclusion. It has been found that Amazon itself, when it is among the vendors of a certain product, "wins" the buy box with increased frequency – even when competing with highly rated sellers who offer the same product at significantly lower prices. According to Feedvisor (2020) and other consulting firms, the reason for this is that Amazon awards itself high scores in the metrics, which the algorithm uses for its decisions. By favoring itself in customer ratings, Amazon can win the buy box even with an inflated price. Amazon's goal, however, is not to sell everything itself, but to maximize its profits. In some cases, as described above, this means convincing customers to buy its own offers. In other cases, it is more profitable for Amazon to promote a third party and collect a commission of 15 per cent for most items (Mitchell and Sussmann, 2019), along with (in many cases) significant fees for its services. Amazon's insider knowledge about the buy-box algorithm allows the company to use this algorithm to its own advantage.

Feedvisor is an example of how the use of an AI-based algorithm (Amazon's buy-box algorithm) triggers the development of further AI-based algorithms. Certain algorithms react to the decisions of other algorithms without human beings being involved in this process anymore. Just as Amazon's buy-box algorithm is a black box to the user, the algorithms used by Feedvisor are also black boxes. Customers of Feedvisor cannot be sure whether the algorithms used by Feedvisor really act in their interest. Does using the services of Feedvisor really improve their chances of entering the buy box, or are the algorithms mainly driven by Feedvisor's own interests? We should also be aware of the fact that Feedvisor's services are only needed as long as Amazon's buy-box algorithm remains a black box. The more complex and opaquer Amazon's buy-box algorithm appears to the outside world, the more valuable the services of Feedvisor will be.

The interaction between Amazon's and Feedvisor's algorithms described above illustrates what we are likely to see in the future: algorithms will interact with algorithms independently of human beings and thus also influence market developments. Marketing will become very different from what it is today. Traditionally, marketing has been about designing, placing and pricing products in such a way that customers notice them and want to buy them. But when algorithms make purchasing decisions, human customers are no longer the important target group for marketing. Instead, the aim is to "convince" algorithms to buy a particular product. Thus, you must know according to which criteria algorithms will make purchasing decisions. Based on this knowledge you can offer your products in such a way that shopping agents will find them as quickly as possible and identify them as the best offer (Binswanger, 2024a, p. 186–187).

As soon as one side of the market uses algorithms based on AI, the other side of the market will respond with algorithms accordingly. When sellers are confronted with shopping agents on a large scale, they react with their own strategies, which are already being discussed in the literature as "AI engine optimization (AIEO) strategies" (Jonker and Koch, 2023). To ensure that their offers are selected by the shopping agents, companies need to understand how the underlying algorithms make decisions and align their content strategy accordingly. Or they can try to influence the shopping algorithms to favor their own products. Marketing thus becomes a process in which algorithms try to persuade other algorithms about the products of a company, or, to put it in other words, algorithms try to seduce other algorithms to select certain products.

In the ideal case, this works as described already in an article from 2017 on the online portal 'The Innovation Machine' (Krasadakis, 2017). AI-based algorithms search on behalf of consumers to find the best offers. The algorithms attempt to negotiate the best conditions for their users based on parameters that users have classified as important (e.g. quality) and based on market conditions (especially price). Shopping agents then repeatedly "meet" with the sellers' own agents until they receive sufficiently improved offers for a specific product. Both algorithms are supposed to act in the interest of their user (consumer, seller) thus enabling better and cheaper consumption decisions as markets work more efficiently as compared to the situation, where human consumers or sellers were involved.

4 Big-Tech Companies and How They Take Advantage of Market Power

Another important aspect regarding markets for AI-based products is the market power associated with Big-Tech companies (Alphabet, Amazon, Apple, Meta, Microsoft in the USA or Tencent and Alibaba in China). These companies can influence prices and market conditions to their advantage as they often do not face competition. Big-Tech companies not only dominate leading virtual platforms, but they are also far ahead of other companies, when it comes to the development of AI-based algorithms and they have access to enormous amounts of data, which is the basis of AI. But if markets are dominated by a few large players, the outcome is not necessarily to the benefit of consumers (see for example, Shaleen et al., 2024). At first glance, it looks like consumers are the main beneficiaries from shopping agents, as they allow for faster and better consumer decisions. Within a short time, a shopping agent is more familiar with the user's preferences than the user himself. A much larger range of offers can be monitored more rapidly and, ideally, even better prices can be negotiated. And we are not forced to hand over all decisions to shopping agents. For example, we can leave the tedious selection of the best health-insurance deal to a shopping agent but still decide ourselves where to go on holidays next summer.

But such positive evaluations usually ignore the fact that people become increasingly dependent on shopping agents. And the more people become dependent on algorithms, the less they can control the use of these algorithms. Instead, algorithms start to determine what people should do. And there is always a certain doubt whether we are in fact digitally short-changed. Only one thing is for sure: AI-based algorithms and shopping agents are developed with the intention of making money. And making money works best where providers such as Alphabet, Amazon or Meta can also exercise market power. The performance of AI stands and falls with access to big data. AI-based algorithms rely on the permanent collection of data and the monitoring of users. Market power allows the providers of shopping agents to collect an enormous amount of data about the behavior of its users. On the other hand, AI-based algorithms are a black box to their users. Under such conditions, consumers are always at a disadvantage and their behavior can be influenced, manipulated and controlled, which results in higher profits (See Sect. 3).

The more consumers become dependent on shopping agents, the easier it is to manipulate their demand. In the healthcare sector, constant growth has been observed in many countries for decades, and rising healthcare costs are a frequent topic in political debates. The rapid growth in the consumption of healthcare products and services is also related to market failures in the health domain, which favor high growth in health expenditures. First, patients pay only partially out of their own pocket, when consuming healthcare services. Under these circumstances cost-awareness is much less pronounced as compared to a situation where consumers must pay out of their own pockets Second, there is the information asymmetry regarding the functioning of AI-based algorithms. If a doctor, a hospital or a provider of a pharmaceutical product is better informed than the patient about its service or product, providers are able to influence demand to their favor (See Sect. 3). This is very similar in the case of AI applications. A lot of services such as using the Google search engine or Chat GPT are "free" to use. You only pay with your data. And Big-Tech companies also try to take advantage of the information asymmetry by telling potential users how their life will become so much better by using their AI-tools.

Let's return to the example of health insurance companies in Switzerland. And let's assume that a shopping agent selects the ideal health-insurance company for a specific user. The first question that will arise is: who develops and offers these shopping agents? Are they provided by the comparison sites themselves? In this case, there would be a particular incentive to encourage customers to constantly change health insurance companies, since the sites collect a commission every time a new contract is signed. Would it, therefore, be better if the shopping agents came from the health-insurance companies? The answer is likely to be "no" as well. Health insurance companies have a strong interest in selling additional, non-mandatory insurance contracts, because they make more money with these contracts. Therefore, we should expect that insurance-operated agents would mostly be used to promote additional non-mandatory insurance contracts. But an increase in non-mandatory insurance contracts would not really benefit users of the shopping agents but rather benefit health insurance providers.

If market power and information asymmetry are an economic reality, shopping agents are likely to serve not only the interest of their users but also and foremost of their providers. If you control shopping agents, you can ensure an increase in consumption year after year. For example, by influencing shopping agents, Apple would be able to promote new iPhone models through these shopping agents. The algorithms of shopping agents can be designed in a way that they recognize the new models as "best offers" to their users and consequently purchase new iPhone models year after year. Or Netflix could ensure that a new subscription model will be chosen by most users because shopping agents operated by Netflix recognize this model as an "improvement" compared to previous subscription models. Consequently, consumption growth becomes increasingly autonomous, as companies with market power are no longer subject to the whims of human consumers. However, the previously mentioned example of Amazon's buy-box algorithm demonstrates that such biased behavior of shopping agents can never exactly be proven. The lack of transparency in the functioning of AI-based algorithms always protects the providers, because the lack of transparency is an integral part of AI. All AI applications are black boxes as well, because their functioning depends on recognition of spatial and temporal patterns in enormous amounts of data, which is not accessible to the human brain.

5 Conclusion

Ultimately, digital transformation follows the old principle of creative destruction, which is inextricably linked to the capitalist economy. The aim is to gain a competitive advantage over rivals with the help of AI-based algorithms and digital services. This is an often overlooked but central point: the digital transformation is driven by the prospect of making profits. "AI-solutions" tend to be designed in a way that the users of AI systems, algorithms or platforms also serve the economic interests of the providers when they are used. This is not new and was also true when we analyze previous episodes of disruptive innovations. But never has a technological revolution offered such extensive opportunities to influence human behavior. For the first time, it is possible to directly influence and manipulate decisions of consumers and companies. This opens windows of opportunities to promote demand for products and services as especially consumption decisions are transferred from human beings to shopping agents. But consumers often welcome such a development as it makes shopping more convenient. Consumers are likely to adapt to the use of shopping agents.

Of course, there is a huge potential for better consumption decisions in an environment of an ever-increasing and constantly changing variety of products. And consumers can save a lot of time, as shopping agents can screen a much larger number of products in much shorter time as compared to human beings. Moreover, agents can evaluate all offers based on criteria, which are supposed to be relevant to individual users. But at the same time, consumers gradually become dependent on shopping agents and lose their sovereignty. They have to "trust" decisions made by AI-based algorithms, which, however, do not necessarily make decisions in favor of consumers but rather in favor of their operators. But since AI-applications are black boxes to the outside world, it is virtually impossible to present empirical evidence, which "proves" such biases.

Acknowledgments. The author would like to thank two anonymous referees for helpful suggestions and comments.

Disclosure of Interests. The authors have no competing interests to declare that are relevant to the content of this article.

References

ACCC. Trivago misled consumers about hotel room rates (2020)

Binswanger, M.: Die Tretmühlen des Glücks. Herder Verlag, Freiburg (2006)

Binswanger, M.: Der Wachstumszwang – Warum die Volkswirtschaft immer weiterwachsen muss, selbst wenn wir genug haben. Wiley Verlag, Weinheim (2019)

Binswanger, M.: Die Verselbständigung des Kapitalismus. Wie KI Menschen und Wirtschaft steuert und für mehr Bürokratie sorgt. Wiley Verlag, Weinheim (2024a)

Binswanger, M.: More bureaucracy instead of more security or more fairness: the effects of AI regulation. In: Hinkelmann, K., Smuts, H. (eds.) Society 5.0 - 4th International Conference, Society 5.0, Selected Papers, pp. 57–67. Springer (2024b)

Ezrachi, A., Stucke, M.: Virtual Competition: The Promise and Perils of the Algorithm-Driven Economy. Harvard University Press (2016)

Desai, D.R., Riedl, M.: Responsible AI Agents. Georgia Tech Scheller College of Business Research Paper No. 5147666 (2025). Accessed 20 Feb 2025

Feedvisor. The Amazon Buy Box Playbook for Sellers and Retailers. Technical Report (2020)

Gal, M., Elkin-Koren, N.: Algorithmic consumers. Harvard J. Law Technol. **30**(2), 309–353 (2018)

Gokhale, A.: Autonomous AI agents in online retail: the next leap in programmatic media buying. Int. J. Sci. Res. Comput. Sci., Eng. Inf. Technol. **11**, 2713–2722 (2025). https://doi.org/10.32628/CSEIT25112732

Hong, J.W.: Future of shopping: the role of shopping agents (2024). https://yesplz.ai/resource/future-of-shopping-the-role-of-ai-agents-in-transforming-ecommerce-experiences

Jonker, D., Koch. C.: When AI does the shopping, every price is negotiable. SAP-Viewpoints (2023). https://www.sap.com/insights/viewpoints/when-ai-does-the-shopping-every-price-is-negotiable.html

König, P.D.: Die digitale Versuchung. Politische Vierteljahresschrift, vol. 60, no. 3, pp. 441–459 (2019)

Kowalkiewicz, M.: When algorithms go shopping. Published in: Towards Data Science (2020)

Krasadakis, G.: AI Buyer/Seller Negotiation Agents. The Innovation Machine (2017). Accessed 5 Oct 2017

Martens, B.: An economic perspective on data and platform market power. JRC Digital Economy Working Paper 2020–09 (2020)

Mathur, A., et al.: Dark patterns at scale: findings from a crawl of 11K shopping websites. Proc. ACM Hum.-Comput. Inter. **3**(CSCW), 1–32 (2019)

Mitchell, S., Sussmann, S.: How Amazon rigs its shopping algorithm. ProMarket (2019). Accessed 6 Nov 2019

Nadler, J., Cicilline, D.: Investigation of competition in digital markets: majority staff report and recommendations. United States (2020)

Raval, D.: Steering in one click: platform self-preferencing in the Amazon Buy Box. Harvard Law School (2022)

Shaleen K., Hongzhou Z., Araz T.: Why and how is the power of Big Tech increasing in the policy process? The case of generative AI. Policy Soc. **44**(1), 52–69 (2024)

Weber, M., Kowalkiewicz, M., Weking, J., Bohm, M., Krcmar, H.: When algorithms go shopping: Analyzing business models for highly autonomous consumer buying agents. In: Gronau, N., Krasnova, H., Pousttchi, K., Heine, M. (Hrsg.) Entwicklungen, Chancen und Herausforderungen der Digitalisierung: Band 1, Proceedings der 15. Internationalen Tagung Wirtschaftsinformatik 2020. Institut für Wirtschaftsinformatik und Digitale Gesellschaft e.V. Potsdam, Germany, S. 1–16 (2020)

The Role of Digital Twins
in Environmental, Social, and Governance:
A Sustainability Perspective
for Companies

Massimo Callisto De Donato$^{(\boxtimes)}$ ⓘ, Jacopo Mucchietto ⓘ,
and Samuele Mucchietto ⓘ

Computer Science Division, University of Camerino, Via Madonna delle Carceri,
7, 62032 Camerino, Italy
`{massimo.callisto,jacopo.mucchietto,samuele.mucchietto}@unicam.it`
`https://computerscience.unicam.it/`

Abstract. Environmental, Social, and Governance (ESG) is a priority
for companies that are required to adopt innovative strategies for sustainability, compliance, and corporate responsibility. Investors use ESG criteria to evaluate the future financial performance of companies by assessing their level of responsibility and sustainability. National regulations
also require companies to transparently report their ESG performance
in their financial statements. Digital Twin technology is an emerging
innovation that enables companies to create virtual counterparts of real-world entities, including physical assets, processes, and even entire organizations. By integrating real-time data, Digital Twins provide advanced
functionalities such as monitoring, simulation, prediction, and optimization, enhancing operational efficiency and decision-making. In this paper,
we examine the role of Digital Twins in supporting the implementation
of ESG principles within organizations. Our findings are based on experiences with various Italian companies across different sectors undergoing
digital transformation processes. We also discuss key issues that companies must address when integrating ESG principles with Digital Twin
technology.

Keywords: Sustainability · Environmental · Social · Governance ·
Digital Twin · Digital transformation

1 Introduction

Nowadays digital transformation and the green economy are driving the development of a human-centered society, or Society 5.0, where economic growth and the
resolution of social issues coexist, through highly integrated systems and digital technologies [14]. Leveraging technological advancements, humans, machines,
and intelligent systems will work together to foster a sustainable future. The

F. Corradini et al. (Eds.): Society 5.0 2025, CCIS 2787, pp. 50–62, 2026.
https://doi.org/10.1007/978-3-032-15463-7_5

pursuit of a new and sustainable society is also part of the 2030 Agenda, which includes the 17 Sustainable Development Goals (SDGs)[1] proposed by the United Nations (UN) in 2015 to address global challenges and achieve a better and more sustainable future.

In a human-centered society, corporate sustainability and social responsibility have gained increasing importance, driven by the growing expectations of stakeholders. Companies are now asked to redefine their strategies and business models toward a transition to the Industry 5.0 model to achieve sustainable and socially responsible practices [5].

Environmental, Social, and Governance (ESG) framework provides a structured set of principles for assessing company's operations and their impact on the society and the environment, their ethical performance, guiding investors and stakeholders in making informed decisions [10]. The adoption of ESG criteria is no longer a voluntary choice [29]. Companies are now required to report their ESG performance in their financial statements in accordance with national regulations. In Europe, the obligations are regulated by Directive 2022/2464. In Italy, large companies are already required to produce sustainability reports based on ESG criteria, and the same obligation will be extended to listed small and medium-sized enterprises (SMEs) [32].

Digital Twin (DT) is an emerging technology that support organizations in the creation of a comprehensive and dynamic digital representation of physical entities (assets, processes) of the physical space into a digital one using virtual replicas, enabling real-time monitoring, simulation, prediction, optimization and improved decision making [9]. Organizations can be systematically integrated DTs in the production and decision-making processes to assess and drive the implementation of DTs, supporting the understanding and implementation of DTs [22]. Several applications in various domains (e.g. manufacturing, supply chain management, healthcare, smart cities) demonstrate that DTs increase efficiency and optimist operations, improving resource allocation and infrastructure management [36]. Leveraging the integration with other technologies (IoT, computational intelligence, cloud computing) [15], DTs represent an effective tool for the organizations to achieve sustainability objectives thanks to their ability to simulate and monitor organizational operations [18].

In this paper we report on how DTs can be used by companies to become more sustainable, improving their ESG performance across the environmental, social, and governance dimensions. Our considerations are based on the experience we had with various Italian companies which are undergoing digital transformation processes and seeking to implement DTs in their organizations. These companies operate in different sectors such as manufacturing, industry, healthcare and services. The interactions we had with these companies allowed us to identify a set of ESG criteria in which DTs can contribute. We have integrated these findings with the results of the analysis of the scientific literature to highlight relevant resources that companies can consider to initiate sustainable actions based on

---

[1] Sustainable Development Goals: https://sdgs.un.org/goals.

DTs. Finally, we discuss some of the issues that companies need to consider when pursuing ESG principles supported by DT technology.

The paper is organized as follows. Section 2 introduces the ESG principles, regulations and implementation frameworks. Section 3 reports on the contribution of DTs to the ESG principles. Section 4 discusses issues that companies need to consider when pursuing ESG principles and applying DTs. Finally, Sect. 5 summarizes and concludes the paper.

2   Environmental, Social, and Governance

In this section we report on the main concepts related to the ESG principles, regulations and frameworks that companies can adopt for their implementation.

2.1   ESG Principles

ESG principles serve as a guiding framework for integrating sustainability into corporate strategies, and serve as a reference standard used by investors to evaluate the behavior and future financial performance of a company, assessing its level of responsibility and sustainability. The ESG principles take into account financial results as well as the social and environmental impact of company's operations. Figure 1 reports some of the elements in the ESG framework [35].

Fig. 1. Environmental, Social, and Governance dimensions.

The three different dimensions of ESG are defined as follows:

– **Environmental**: Evaluates how a company interacts with the environment. The dimension focuses on various actions such as carbon footprint reduction, energy efficiency, sustainable resource and waste management.

- **Social**: Assesses the impact on and relationships of the company with the employees, stakeholder and the broader society. Examples include ethical business practices, human rights, diversity, and inclusiveness.
- **Governance**: Examines the company's governance policies and management structure. For example, it focuses on how a company is structured, managed and operated to ensure transparency, accountability and ethical leadership.

ESG was introduced as a structured framework by the UN in 2004 with the report "Who Cares Wins", defined in collaboration with a group of leading financial institutions. The report provides guidelines and recommendations on how to better integrate ESG issues into financial decision-making. In 2006, the UN Principles for Responsible Investment (PRI)[2] encouraged financial institutions to integrate ESG principles into their decision-making processes in order to pursue sustainable and responsible investment through the adoption of six key principles. These principles aim to incorporate ESG into investment decisions, active ownership, transparency in ESG disclosures and regular reporting on progress to promote sustainable and responsible financial practices.

Two of the most significant international agreements influencing the development of the ESG principles are the **Paris Agreement**[3] and the **SDGs** of the Agenda 2030. The Paris Agreement has been adopted in 2015 by 195 countries to address climate change by limiting global warming. Each country is required to embody efforts to reduce national emissions and adapt to the impacts of climate change. It also requires countries to report on Nationally Determined Contributions (NDCs), which outline their climate actions and targets. The SDGs were established by the UN in 2015 to strengthen a global partnership for sustainable development through the definition of 17 goals addressing global challenges. These goals cover different aspects (such as poverty, inequality, climate change and environmental degradation) and provide a comprehensive framework for sustainable development, including ESG aspects. Both the Paris Agreement and SDGs serve as global frameworks for sustainability and responsible development, directly influencing the adoption and implementation of the ESG principles in businesses and investments.

2.2   ESG Regulations and Compliance

The adoption of the ESG principles is regulated by different standards and regulations that companies and investors must comply to ensure the transparency and sustainability of their activities [13].

The International Sustainability Standards Board (ISSB) represent a set of reporting standards introduced in 2021 by the International Financial Reporting Standards (IFRS) to promotes a global framework for sustainability-related financial disclosures and provide reliable ESG information for investors and stakeholders. ISSB encompasses several sustainability reporting frameworks,

---

[2] Principles for Responsible Investment: https://www.unpri.org/.
[3] Paris Agreement: https://www.mase.gov.it/pagina/cop-21-laccordo-di-parigi.

such as the Task Force on Climate-related Financial Disclosures (TCFD), Global Reporting Initiative (GRI), and Sustainability Accounting Standards Board (SASB).

At the European level, several regulations and directives have been proposed. The Corporate Sustainability Reporting Directive (CSRD) adopted in 2023 aims to improve transparency and accountability in corporate sustainability reporting and requires companies to disclose information on their ESG practices. The Sustainable Finance Disclosure Regulation (SFDR) introduced in 2021 aims to increase transparency in sustainable finance defining the "do no significant harm" principle (DNSH) as assessment of potential adverse impacts across all environmental objectives. In 2024 the Corporate Sustainability Due Diligence Directive (CSDDD) has been introduced to further strengthen ESG obligations by imposing due diligence requirements on companies regarding human rights and environmental impacts across their value chains.

Italy has aligned its ESG regulations and the CSDDD by introducing Legislative Decree 125/2024 to regulate which types of organizations are obliged to draw up each year the *sustainability report* (*bilancio di sostenibilità*). The Italian regulation establishes a detailed adoption plan leading in the 2029 when large companies and listed Small and Medium-sized Enterprises (SMEs) are required to provide the representation of an organization's sustainability performance in their operations. Additional reports can be issued by companies about the ESG adoption such as: *bilancio ambientale* which describes the environmental strategies and results achieved by the company; *report di sostenibilità* describing the communication process of ESG activities and results; *Dichiarazione non finanziaria* describing how the company's ethical and social impact issues are handled. The National Recovery and Resilience Plan (PNRR) and the adoption of the DNSH reinforce the Italy's commitment to ESG adoption, ensuring that financed investments contribute positively to environmental sustainability.

2.3   ESG Implementation Frameworks

Several standard frameworks for sustainability reporting have been proposed to help organisations to disclose their ESG performance through the application of structured guidelines [13]. For example, a well-known and recognised standard framework has been proposed by the Global Reporting Initiative (GRI), an international organisation that provides standards for sustainability reporting. The GRI framework provides a structured approach to ESG reporting, allowing companies to *assess environmental impacts* (e.g. carbon footprint, waste management, biodiversity conservation), *assess social responsibilities* (e.g. labour practices, human rights, diversity & inclusion), *improve governance transparency* (e.g. anti-corruption policies, executive accountability, supply chain ethics).

Organizations that want to operate in the European Union are required to implement the European Sustainability Reporting Standards (ESRS) defined in the CSDR has a mandatory framework aimed at ensuring alignment with EU climate and sustainability goals while enhancing corporate transparency. Additionally, the Voluntary Reporting Standards for SMEs (VSME) is a voluntary frameworks that enable small and medium companies to report on sustainability aspects without the complexity of larger corporate disclosures, helping them improve their ESG commitment and attract sustainable investments.

3 Digital Twins in ESG Implementation

In this section, we report on the contribution of DT to the ESG principles, highlighting the key areas where DT can be applied and the expected benefits.

3.1 Environmental Dimension

By leveraging real-time data analytics, predictive modeling, and process automation, DTs help organizations optimize resource management, improve energy efficiency, minimize waste, and control emissions.

Energy Efficiency. Optimization of the energy consumption is extremely important for improving environmental sustainability. The objective can relate to different areas and approaches, such as improving operational performance, predicting optimal process execution, as well as education, for example on waste. By applying DTs to real-time energy monitoring, it is possible to help industries to optimize energy consumption across production processes [38]. Using predictive scenarios created through simulation, DTs help to reduce unnecessary energy consumption and minimize environmental impact in various sectors such as industry, buildings, smart cities [4, 25].

Carbon Footprint Reduction. Reduction of carbon footprints involves lowering greenhouse gas emissions through cleaner production methods, renewable energy, and efficient resource utilization in several domains such us industries, buildings management, smart cities. The combination of DT, IoT and Artificial Intelligence (AI), enables in-depth monitoring of processes and operations. By implementing advanced simulation and predictive scenarios, it is possible to support the transition to low-carbon alternatives [40].

Resource Optimization. Efficient resource consumption ensures the sustainability of the usage of materials, minimizing the impact on the environment, promoting circular economy models and responsible production practices. DTs can be used to anticipate the design of virtual models of assets that do not yet exist in the physical world. By using iterative simulation, design inefficiencies can be identified and production processes can be refined. This eliminates the need for physical prototypes and unnecessary materials, reducing environmental impact [37].

Waste Management. Responsible waste management encompasses activities aimed at minimizing waste generation, implementing efficient recycling processes, promoting recycling among citizens, and ensuring compliance with environmental regulations. Companies supporting municipalities in waste management can benefit from the combination of DT and IoT technology to enable the implementation of smarter systems for real-time monitoring of waste tracking, waste production, tracking disposal, and assessing recycling efficiency [6]. For instance, by enhancing simulations and predictions with AI-driven approached, DTs can be used go enhance the efficiency of sewage treatment plants [33].

3.2   Social Dimension

DTs enable the representation of entire environments, processes and equipment through virtual replicas in digital space. This can be extended to the Human Digital Twin (HDT), allowing the modeling of human characteristics, behaviors, and interactions [20]. This opens up the possibility of modeling and analyzing social aspects to improve workplace safety, accessibility, training and inclusion.

Workplace Safety. Providing a safe and healthy working environment involves a number of aspects such as risk prevention measures, safety protocols and compliance with regulations to protect employees from harm. DTs can be used to create virtual replicas of existing workplaces, where safety models can be used for risk assessment and hazard prevention, reducing accidents and improving safety protocols [8,41]. By integrating Virtual Reality, organizations can employ immersive simulations to train employees for emergency response and hazardous work conditions [2].

Training Development. Social advancement also means fostering continuous learning and skills development for employees with relevant competencies, promoting career growth and supporting business innovation. DTs and Virtual Reality enable the creation of digital models that can simulate specific scenarios and allow employees to train and acquire competences by leveraging experience in the virtual environment [26]. Organizations benefit from personalized learning experiences, enhancing employee skill development and long-term retention [23].

Employment Development. Attention to fair labour practices, the promotion of ethical working conditions and the adaptability of the workforce are all aspects that have a direct impact on the social aspects that are relevant to both attracting and engaging employees. DTs facilitate remote working environments, enabling the creation of virtual spaces where employees can collaborate and interact with physical assets remotely [11]. This can break down geographical barriers and enable wider engagement in the organization [16].

Inclusiveness and Diversity. The physical and mental health of employees is important to ensure conditions of well-being. This includes consideration of work-life balance and the overall quality of participation in the organization. By combining digital immersive environments with the simulation capabilities of DTs, the organisation can improve diversity and accessibility in the workplace [39]. This can reduce the physical and logistical barriers that have traditionally limited the participation and accessibility of diverse groups of people [34].

Workforce Well-Being. The integration of DT and wearable IoT devices can be used to monitor operators and enable advanced monitoring services to assess workplace conditions, stress levels and fatigue. Simulation and predictive analytics based on operator DTs can be used by HR departments to optimize work schedules and task allocation based on real-time workforce data [31].

3.3   Governance Dimension

Digital Twin Organization (DTO) can be used to represent different aspect of an organization, including physical assets, processes as well as functional departments [24]. This capability enables organisations to develop DT models that accurately reflect their operational dynamics, improving transparency in operations, governance and regulatory compliance.

Risk Management. Organizations are required to identify risks in their operations and define risk management plans and strategies to deal with them. This allows the organization to increase resilience and minimize unpredictability. DTs and DTOs, used as structural tools in organizations, allow modeling and simulation of virtual replicas of processes, departments, and operations. They support what-if scenario analysis, vulnerability assessment, and real-time decision-making optimization [19, 41].

Transparency and Compliance. Transparency in the implementation of ESG practices is crucial for companies to demonstrate accountability, ethical integrity and compliance. It also helps to prevent greenwashing and misinformation, where companies manipulate sustainability claims to enhance their reputation without making real improvements. DT can be used in combination with Blockchain and IoT technologies, enabling the definition of a trusted digital space where tamper-proof IoT devices provide certified real-time data from the physical space, while Blockchain guarantees transparency, traceability and immutability of transactions over operational data [17].

Financial Efficiency. Organizations should implement strategies to improve their ability to optimist financial resources and reduce expenditure to ensure economic sustainability. This requires organizations to consider useful operational data in order to make effective management decisions. DTs and DTO enable the capture of operational data at multiple levels of the organization (physical assets, business processes, departments and employee interactions). By integrating financial data flows, DTs facilitate a data-driven approach to the simulation and analysis of the financial performance improving financial planning and decision-making [28].

Cooperation. An organization needs to promote a holistic approach based on the closed interaction between departments, teams, and stakeholders, fostering the sharing of the knowledge, operational alignment, ensuring that all parts of the organization work toward common objectives. DT and DTO can be extended to include external operational insights from other organization and citizen [1]. For instance, DT communities promote the idea of knowledge sharing beyond organizational boundaries, fostering a collaborative approach. This facilitates the exchange of information, allowing companies to align around common goals and share sustainability strategies in a profitable way [3].

4   Discussion

In this section, we discuss some of the issues that companies need to consider when implementing ESG principles, as well as integrating DTs.

4.1   ESG Implementation Issues

Implementing ESG principles requires significant effort from companies, ranging from regulatory compliance to financial commitments [21].

Regulation Adoption. From a regulatory perspective, organizations operate in a complex landscape where different countries and regions have different ESG disclosure requirements. For example, at the European level, organizations have to comply with the CSRD and SFDR regulations, while at the national level, such as in Italy, they have to comply with the various sustainability reports mentioned in Sect. 2.2. To this regards, the European Commission recently proposed the Omnibus package[4] in response to concerns about some of these complexities and administrative burdens for companies.

Financial Investment. The adoption of sustainable business practices often requires substantial financial investments since this requires to implement and demonstrate sustainable supply chain practices, invest in ESG reporting infrastructure, access to reliable and standardized data. For small and medium-sized organizations these costs can be particularly burdensome and may lack the financial resources to invest in sustainability initiatives and compliance tools.

Implementation Commitment. ESG reporting requires organizations to have access to reliable data. Many organizations struggle with data gaps, inconsistencies and a lack of consistent reporting frameworks. While several ESG implementation frameworks exist as described in Sect. 2.3, organizations still face difficulties in collecting, processing, and validating ESG data, especially when external suppliers do not also provide transparent ESG information.

4.2   DT Adoption Issues

DTs represent an opportunity for companies to achieve their sustainability goals. At the same time, there are a number of challenges in integrating DTs into internal processes [12,27]. Below we highlight some of the operational steps that need to be considered to enable DTs in the organization.

Infrastructure Deployment. DTs implementation require substantial investment in infrastructure to integrate the physical and the digital spaces in order to synchronize entities and their virtual counterparts which is a requirement for enabling real-time monitoring, simulation, prediction and optimization capabilities. Consequently, companies are required to invest in IoT infrastructures

---

[4] https://ec.europa.eu/commission/presscorner/detail/en/qanda_25_615.

and edge computational layers for real-time data collection, cloud and AI infrastructure for data analysis, simulation and prediction. However, these investments also introduce new challenges that require careful attention, such as rising energy demand linked to digital technologies and advanced AI [7].

Integration Issue. DTs require seamless integration with the IT systems of the organization that may vary from industrial machinery to enterprise software (Enterprise Resource Planning, Product Lifecycle Management, and Supply Chain and Customer Relationship Management). Traditional organizations may have compatibility issues, legacy systems, and a lack of technical expertise, which may lead to difficulties in implementing complete DTs capabilities.

Data Consistency. Since DTs rely on large volumes of data, ensuring data accuracy, consistency, and interoperability across different platforms is a major challenge. Many industries lack standardized data models, making it difficult to synchronize physical and virtual systems efficiently.

Data Privacy Risks. DTs rely on the exchange of data between physical and virtual environments. This can introduce risks in terms of infrastructure vulnerabilities and data security. Cyber-attacks and data breaches are examples of risks that can compromise the integrity of the data held by the organization, which in turn can affect ESG implementation.

5   Conclusion

In this paper we reported on the contribution of DT technology as a valuable tool to support companies in achieving sustainability goals and facilitate the implementation of the ESG principles. We described the capabilities of DTs, based on real-time monitoring, simulation, and predictive optimization, and how they contribute to enable the implementation of energy efficiency, reduce carbon footprints, improve resource consumption and support waste reduction. By enhancing workplace safety, accessibility, and workforce training, DTs foster a more inclusive, equitable, and efficient working environment. DTs can contribute to regulatory compliance, ESG reporting transparency, and corporate risk management, ensuring greater accountability and data-driven decision-making. We have also reported on some of the issues that companies need to consider when implementing ESG practices supported by the integration of DTs.

While there are concerns about the adoption of ESG principles [30], our analysis must encourage companies to continue to invest in sustainability, where DTs can play an important role in green transition processes.

Acknowledgments. This work has been partially supported by the European Union NextGenerationEU - National Recovery and Resilience Plan, Mission 4 Education and Research - Component 2 From research to business - Investment 1.5, ECS_00000041-VITALITY - Innovation, digitalisation and sustainability for the diffused economy in Central Italy - CUP J13C22000430001.

Disclosure of Interests. The author declares no conflict of interest.

References

1. Abdeen, F.N., Sepasgozar, S.M.: City digital twin concepts: a vision for community participation. Environ. Sci. Proc. **12**(1), 19 (2022)
2. Agnusdei, G.P., Elia, V., Gnoni, M.G.: A classification proposal of digital twin applications in the safety domain. Comput. Industr. Eng. **154**, 107137 (2021)
3. Alcaraz, C., Meskini, I.H., Lopez, J.: Digital twin communities: an approach for secure dt data sharing. Int. J. Inf. Secur. **24**(1), 1–19 (2025)
4. Attaran, M., Celik, B.G.: Digital twin: benefits, use cases, challenges, and opportunities. Decis. Anal. J. **6**, 100165 (2023)
5. Barata, J., Kayser, I.: Industry 5.0-past, present, and near future. Procedia Comput. Sci. **219**, 778–788 (2023)
6. Barth, L., Schweiger, L., Benedech, R., Ehrat, M.: From data to value in smart waste management: optimizing solid waste collection with a digital twin-based decision support system. Decision Anal. J. **9**, 100347 (2023)
7. Bashir, N., et al.: The climate and sustainability implications of generative ai (2024)
8. Callisto De Donato, M., Corradini, F., Fornari, F., Re, B., Romagnoli, M.: Design and development of a digital twin prototype for the SAFE Project. In: International Conference on Enterprise Design, Operations, and Computing, pp. 107–122. Springer, Cham (2023). https://doi.org/10.1007/978-3-031-54712-6_7
9. Casadei, R., Fornari, F., Mariani, S., Savaglio, C.: Fluidware Meets Digital Twins, pp. 137–154. Springer, Cham (2024)
10. Chen, S., Song, Y., Gao, P.: Environmental, social, and governance (ESG) performance and financial outcomes: analyzing the impact of ESG on financial performance. J. Environ. Manage. **345**, 118829 (2023)
11. Coupry, C., Noblecourt, S., Richard, P., Baudry, D., Bigaud, D.: BIM-based digital twin and xr devices to improve maintenance procedures in smart buildings: a literature review. Appl. Sci. **11**(15), 6810 (2021)
12. Fornari, F., et al.: Digital twins of business processes: a research manifesto. Internet Things, 101477 (2024)
13. Frecautan, I., Nita, A.: Who is going to win: the EU ESG regulation or the rest of the world?-a critical review. Ann. Univ. Oradea, Econ. Sci. Ser. **31**(2), 109–120 (2022)
14. Fukuyama, M.: Society 5.0: aiming for a new human-centered society. Japan Spotlight **27**(Society 5.0), 47–50 (2018)
15. Grieves, M.: Intelligent digital twins and the development and management of complex systems. Digital Twin **2**, 8 (2022)
16. Havard, V., Jeanne, B., Lacomblez, M., Baudry, D.: Digital twin and virtual reality: a co-simulation environment for design and assessment of industrial workstations. Prod. Manuf. Res. **7**(1), 472–489 (2019)
17. Hemdan, E.E.D., El-Shafai, W., Sayed, A.: Integrating digital twins with IoT-based blockchain: concept, architecture, challenges, and future scope. Wireless Pers. Commun. **131**(3), 2193–2216 (2023)
18. Kamble, S.S., Gunasekaran, A., Parekh, H., Mani, V., Belhadi, A., Sharma, R.: Digital twin for sustainable manufacturing supply chains: current trends, future perspectives, and an implementation framework. Technol. Forecast. Soc. Chang. **176**, 121448 (2022)
19. Liezina, A., Andriushchenko, K., Rozhko, O., Datsii, O., Mishchenko, L., Cherniaieva, O.: Resource planning for risk diversification in the formation of a digital twin enterprise. Accounting (2020)

20. Lin, Y., et al.: Human digital twin: a survey. J. Cloud Comput. **13**(1), 131 (2024)
21. Liou, J.J., Liu, P.Y., Huang, S.W.: Exploring the key barriers to ESG adoption in enterprises. Syst. Soft Comput. **5**, 200066 (2023)
22. Lo, C., Chen, C.H., Zhong, R.Y.: A review of digital twin in product design and development. Adv. Eng. Inform. **48**, 101297 (2021)
23. Longo, F., Padovano, A., De Felice, F., Petrillo, A., Elbasheer, M.: From prepare for the unknown" to "train for what's coming": a digital twin-driven and cognitive training approach for the workforce of the future in smart factories. J. Ind. Inf. Integr. **32**, 100437 (2023)
24. Lyytinen, K., Weber, B., Becker, M.C., Pentland, B.T.: Digital twins of organization: implications for organization design. J. Organ. Des. 1–17 (2023)
25. Ma, S., Ding, W., Liu, Y., Ren, S., Yang, H.: Digital twin and big data-driven sustainable smart manufacturing based on information management systems for energy-intensive industries. Appl. Energy **326**, 119986 (2022)
26. Martínez-Gutiérrez, A., Díez-González, J., Verde, P., Perez, H.: Convergence of virtual reality and digital twin technologies to enhance digital operators' training in industry 4.0. Int. J. Hum. Comput. Stud. **180**, 103136 (2023)
27. Mihai, S., et al.: Digital twins: a survey on enabling technologies, challenges, trends and future prospects. IEEE Commun. Surv. Tutorials **24**(4), 2255–2291 (2022)
28. Murphy, A., et al.: Representing financial data streams in digital simulations to support data flow design for a future digital twin. Robot. Comput. Integr. Manuf. **61**, 101853 (2020)
29. Oliver Yébenes, M.: Climate change, ESG criteria and recent regulation: challenges and opportunities. Eurasian Econ. Rev. **14**(1), 87–120 (2024)
30. Pérez, L., Hunt, V., Samandari, H., Nuttall, R., Biniek, K.: Does ESG really matter—and why. McKinsey Q. **60**(1) (2022)
31. Pivnička, M., Hrušecká, D., Hrbáčková, L.: Introduction of a new flexible human resources planning system based on digital twin approach: a case study. Serb. J. Manage. **17**(2), 361–373 (2022)
32. Pizzi, S., Coronella, L.: Are listed SMEs ready for the corporate sustainability reporting directive? Evidence from Italy. Bus. Ethics, Environ. Responsib. (2024)
33. Rodríguez-Alonso, C., Pena-Regueiro, I., García, Ó.: Digital twin platform for water treatment plants using microservices architecture. Sensors **24**(5), 1568 (2024)
34. Ruiu, P., Nitti, M., Pilloni, V., Cadoni, M., Grosso, E., Fadda, M.: Metaverse & human digital twin: digital identity, biometrics, and privacy in the future virtual worlds. Multimodal Technol. Interact. **8**(6), 48 (2024)
35. Sætra, H.S.: A framework for evaluating and disclosing the ESG related impacts of ai with the SDGS. Sustainability **13**(15), 8503 (2021)
36. Semeraro, C., Lezoche, M., Panetto, H., Dassisti, M.: Digital twin paradigm: a systematic literature review. Comput. Ind. **130**, 103469 (2021)
37. Turan, E., et al.: Digital twin modelling for optimizing the material consumption: a case study on sustainability improvement of thermoforming process. Sustain. Comput. Inform. Syst. **35**, 100655 (2022)
38. Yu, W., Patros, P., Young, B., Klinac, E., Walmsley, T.G.: Energy digital twin technology for industrial energy management: classification, challenges and future. Renew. Sustain. Energy Rev. **161**, 112407 (2022)
39. Zallio, M., Clarkson, P.J.: Designing the metaverse: a study on inclusion, diversity, equity, accessibility and safety for digital immersive environments. Telematics Inform. **75**, 101909 (2022)

40. Zhang, A., Wang, F., Li, H., Pang, B., Yang, J.: Carbon emissions accounting and estimation of carbon reduction potential in the operation phase of residential areas based on digital twin. Appl. Energy **376**, 123155 (2024)
41. Zio, E., Miqueles, L.: Digital twins in safety analysis, risk assessment and emergency management. Reliab. Eng. Syst. Saf. 110040 (2024)

EduPKG: an Ontology for STEM Education

Paolo Campanelli and Alessandro Marcelletti[(✉)]

University of Camerino, 62032 Camerino, Italy
`{paolo.campanelli,alessandro.marcelletti}@unicam.it`

Abstract. STEM education is essential for preparing students for the digital age, fostering critical thinking, problem-solving, and technological literacy. Despite increasing recognition of its importance, challenges persist in effectively selecting and implementing STEM activities. Educators often lack a structured framework to align STEM lessons with student needs, available resources, and pedagogical objectives. In response, we propose EduPKG, an educational ontology designed to streamline STEM activity planning. EduPKG serves as a decision-making tool, enabling educators to select and customize activities that are engaging, feasible, and aligned with learning outcomes. By structuring STEM education around competencies such as problem-solving, creativity, collaboration, and critical thinking, EduPKG enhances lesson planning while ensuring adaptability to diverse educational settings. EduPKG was validated by conducting surveys with experts and analyzing a what-if scenario.

Keywords: STEM education · Education ontology · Curriculum design

1 Introduction

In the digital age, STEM education plays a crucial role in preparing a technologically literate society and preparing students for future careers. Science, Technology, Engineering, and Mathematics are embedded in everyday life, influencing everything from smart devices to professional fields. Developing critical thinking and practical skills from an early age equips students with the competencies needed for an innovation-driven job market [13]. A key approach to encouraging STEM learning is through coding and educational robotics, which actively engage students in computational thinking, creativity, and hands-on problem-solving. Integrating these elements into early education through structured learning modules enhances digital fluency, promotes collaboration, and nurtures an adaptive mindset essential for future technological advancements [18].

One of the main strengths of STEM education is interdisciplinarity, enabling the integration of different subjects to explore real-world applications [2]. Additionally, STEM activities promote creativity by encouraging innovation and hands-on project development [12]. They also enhance logical reasoning and

F. Corradini et al. (Eds.): Society 5.0 2025, CCIS 2787, pp. 63–74, 2026.
https://doi.org/10.1007/978-3-032-15463-7_6

computational thinking, fostering structured problem-solving skills essential for scientific and technological disciplines [14]. Moreover, STEM learning encourages collaborative learning, as students work together to solve problems, share ideas, and develop projects [19].

Despite these benefits, STEM education remains an evolving field, especially in primary and lower secondary schools [3]. Over the past two decades, Europe has made significant strides in digital and STEM education, integrating these subjects into school curricula [5]. Many countries have recognized the growing importance of STEM skills in the modern economy, launching national policies and initiatives to support their development [11].

However, despite the global recognition of the importance of STEM education, significant challenges in this area persist [10]. Specifically, there is a lack of a uniform strategy for selecting and implementing STEM activities. Educators frequently struggle to identify appropriate methodologies, resources, and objectives for STEM projects [9]. For instance, while many schools introduce after-school STEM programs to take advantage of funding opportunities, these initiatives are often designed without a thorough understanding of the pedagogical or technological needs of their target audience. As a result, students miss opportunities to fully engage with and benefit from these activities [4].

For this reason, we propose EduPKG, an educational ontology designed to enhance STEM activity planning by aligning lessons with student needs, available resources, and time constraints. Serving as a decision-making tool, it helps educators and administrators select and customize activities that are both engaging and feasible. EduPKG aims at simplifying lesson planning, fosters key competencies like problem-solving and data literacy, and promotes the 4Cs: Creativity, Collaboration, Communication, and Critical Thinking. The development of EduPKG was based on the Methontology [8] approach, ensuring a systematic process from ontology definition to validation. EduPKG was implemented and validated through a survey with experts and a what-if scenario, demonstrating its ability to support the creation of STEM activities.

The rest of the paper is structured as follows. Section 2 describes the adopted Methontology approach. Section 3 introduces the current state of the art about educational ontologies. Section 4 details the ontology structure which implementation is presented is introduced in Sect. 5. Section 6 and Sect. 7 focus on validation aspects by presenting surveyed experts' feedback and a what-if analysis. Finally, Sect. 8 concludes the work touching future directions.

2   Background

In this section we introduced the foundation of the proposed ontology. Methontology [8] is a widely adopted methodology for ontology engineering, offering a structured approach that covers all stages from knowledge acquisition to evaluation. It ensures the systematic development, refinement, and logical consistency of ontologies, making them suitable for real-world applications. The methodology is structured around three key dimensions: the *Ontology Development Pro-*

cess, which includes phases such as specification, conceptualization, formalization, and evaluation; the *Ontology Life Cycle Activities*, which encompass tasks including knowledge acquisition, integration, and maintenance; and the *Supporting Techniques*, which provide methods for structuring relationships and formal representations. The development process consists of several key phases. The specification phase defines the ontology's purpose, scope, and target users. The knowledge acquisition phase collects essential domain knowledge from experts, literature, and existing models. The conceptualization phase structures knowledge into a formal model, defining entities, relationships, and attributes. The formalization phase converts the conceptual model into a machine-readable format using languages like OWL or RDF. The implementation phase deploys the ontology in a development environment such as Protégé. The evaluation and validation phase ensures the ontology's accuracy, consistency, and usability through reasoning tools and expert feedback.

Methontology was followed as the primary framework for developing the EduPKG ontology, with adaptations tailored to the educational domain. Specifically, in the **conceptualization** phase, core entities, relationships, and attributes were defined to represent different types of learning activities, competencies, instructional methods, and resource classifications. This pase is detailed in Sect. 4. The **formalization** phase was applied in a limited manner, ensuring flexibility for educators while maintaining machine reasoning capabilities using OWL, and is also covered in Sect. 4. The **implementation** phase is thoroughly described in Sect. 5 and was fully realized in Protégé, with well-defined object properties, semantic relationships, and SPARQL queries for practical demonstration. The **evaluation** and **validation** phases are covered in Sect. 6 and Sect. 7, incorporating expert surveys for empirical validation, automated reasoning tools like Pellet and HermiT for consistency checks, and query-based validation using SPARQL. These steps confirmed that the ontology was logically structured and effective for STEM educational planning.

3   State of the Art

Ontology-based approaches in education have been widely used to structure learning objectives, organize educational resources, and model competency-based learning. This section presents the main relevant ontologies for providing structured approaches to learning resource modeling and competency tracking.

PasOnto [6] is an ontology designed to structure learning pathways and competency development in programming education, specifically focusing on Pascal programming language concepts. The ontology models fundamental programming skills, providing a hierarchical structure for learning objectives, prerequisite relationships, and progressive knowledge acquisition in Pascal. While PasOnto is valuable for modeling structured programming education, its scope is limited to Pascal and does not extend to STEM education, interdisciplinary learning, or broader computational thinking concepts. It lacks a structured representation of how programming interacts with other STEM disciplines such as robotics, mathematics, and engineering. Additionally, PasOnto does not incorporate teaching methodologies or resource-based activity design, making it less adaptable for educators planning hands-on computational learning experiences.

ChemOnto [7] is an ontology designed to structure and manage chemical experiments within virtual laboratory environments. It models laboratory materials, chemical products, safety guidelines, and procedural steps, enabling a systematic representation of experimental workflows. By providing a structured framework for virtual chemistry labs, ChemOnto facilitates the organization of experimental tasks, ensuring that learners acquire both procedural knowledge and laboratory safety awareness. While ChemOnto offers a well-defined structure for the representation of chemical experiments, its scope remains discipline-specific, focusing exclusively on chemistry education. The ontology primarily serves as a documentation tool for experimental materials and procedural guidelines, rather than an adaptive learning framework. Notably, it does not incorporate pedagogical methodologies, interdisciplinary learning strategies, or personalized feedback mechanisms, which limits its applicability beyond chemical experimentation. Furthermore, ChemOnto does not extend to broader STEM education domains, particularly those involving coding, computational thinking, or interdisciplinary curricula. As a result, its utility is confined to chemistry laboratories, making it less suitable for guiding lesson planning or supporting adaptive and cross-disciplinary learning approaches within STEM education.

OntoMathEdu [1] is an ontology designed to support mathematics education through a structured representation of mathematical concepts, theorems, and didactic relationships. As a Linked Open Data (LOD) hub, it facilitates automatic knowledge assessment, personalized content recommendations, and semantic annotation of educational materials. Its multi-layered structure—comprising a foundational ontology, a domain ontology, and a linguistic layer—ensures interoperability and multilingual support. While OntoMathEdu effectively organizes mathematical knowledge, its scope remains discipline-specific, lacking integration with broader STEM education. The ontology prioritizes concept classification over activity-based modeling, meaning it does not provide structured lesson plans, interdisciplinary connections, or computational thinking frameworks. Consequently, its applicability beyond mathematics is limited, reducing its utility for STEM-focused pedagogy.

Although PasOnto, ChemOnto, and OntoMath provide structured frameworks for learning resource organization, competency modeling, and subject-specific education, they do not address STEM education, computational thinking, or interdisciplinary learning. Each of these ontologies is highly specialized, focusing on Pascal programming, chemistry feedback mechanisms, or mathematical content structuring, without offering a comprehensive educational framework that supports hands-on, interdisciplinary STEM learning. Furthermore, there is a significant gap in ontology-driven educational research for primary education and early childhood. Most educational ontologies are designed for higher education, professional training, or specific subject domains, leaving STEM-focused models for younger learners largely unexplored. Early exposure to STEM and computational thinking is essential, yet no ontologies provide a structured, competency-based approach to lesson planning in early education.

4   The EduPKG Ontology

In this section we describe the EduPKG ontology, detailing its structure in terms of components, classes, properties, and relationships. The EduPKG ontology is designed to provide a structured model for organizing educational resources, learning activities, teaching methods, and competencies. This ontology enables the clear and reusable representation of knowledge, facilitating adaptation and customization of learning experiences across different educational levels. The ontology was defined through an iterative process based on an analysis of educational needs and available technologies following the Methontology approach.

The EduPKG ontology follows a hierarchical design, grouping elements into different categories. Each **class** in EduPKG represents a core concept in the teaching and learning process and is linked through semantic relationships, ensuring that educational content is logically structured. Table 1 presents the classes and their subclasses, along with a brief description of each.

Table 1. EduPKG Ontology Classes with Subclasses

Class	Description	Subclasses
ActivityType	Categorizes learning activities based on pedagogical approaches.	CollaborativeActivity, CreativeActivity, ExplorationActivity, HandsOnActivity, ProblemSolvingActivity
Competency	Defines skills developed through STEM activities, aligned with DigiComp.	Collaboration, Communication, Creativity, CriticalThinking, DigitalContentCreation, InformationAndDataLiteracy, ProblemSolving, Safety
LearningLevel	Categorizes activities based on student class level.	None
Resource	Defines educational materials supporting activities.	AdvancedResource, DigitalResource, EntryLevelResource, PhysicalResource
Subject	Classifies educational content by discipline, promoting interdisciplinary connections.	Humanities, STEM
TargetType	Defines the intended audience for an Educational Package.	FullClass, JointClass, Kindergarten Teacher, MixedAbilityGroup, PrimaryTeacher, SecondaryTeacher, SmallGroup
TeachingMethod	Defines pedagogical strategies, aligned with constructivist learning theories.	CollaborativeMethod, ExperientialMethod, GamifiedMethod, PassiveMethod
TimeAllocation	Defines the expected duration of learning activities for lesson planning.	None

The EduPKG ontology relies on a structured network of semantic relationships that interconnect different classes. Each property follows the Web Ontology Language (OWL), ensuring a consistent and machine-readable structure. The first set is related to **object properties** shown in Table 2.

Table 2. Properties of Learning Activities

Property	Domain	Range
adoptsTeachingMethod	ActivityType	TeachingMethod
isDesignedFor	ActivityType	TargetType
isPartOfSubject	ActivityType	Subject
isSuitableForLearningLevel	ActivityType	LearningLevel
requiresTimeAllocation	ActivityType	TimeAllocation
targetsCompetency	ActivityType	Competency
usesResource	ActivityType	Resource

The EduPKG ontology includes also a structured set of **data properties**, which provide descriptive attributes for various entities within the ontology. Unlike object properties, which define relationships between different classes, data properties associate an entity with literal values, such as strings, numbers, or categorical labels. The ontology uses four primary data properties shown in Table 3, each contributing to the clarity and usability of the ontology. These properties ensure that resources, activities, and packages contain relevant metadata, improving their retrievability, classification, and applicability in educational contexts.

Table 3. Ontology Properties

Property	Domain	Range	Description
hasDescription	owl:Thing	xsd:string	Provides a textual description for any ontology element.
hasDifficultyLevel	Resource	xsd:string (Base, Advanced)	Classifies resources by difficulty (beginner/advanced).
hasMaterialType	Resource	xsd:string (Digital, Physical)	Differentiates resources as digital or physical.
hasDuration	TimeAllocation	xsd:decimal	Specifies the duration of an activity (in minutes/hours).

5   EduPKG Implementation

This section presents the implementation details of the EduPKG ontology. The ontology was developed using Protégé [17], a widely used open-source ontology editor, and validated with reasoning tools. To demonstrate a possible application, an example of its use through a SPARQL query is provided. The implemented ontology is accessible online[1].

Formal Validation Using Reasoning Tools. The EduPKG ontology was validated using the Pellet [16] and HermiT [15] reasoners to ensure logical consistency, correct classification, and proper object property constraints. The reasoning process confirmed the integrity of the class hierarchy, eliminated semantic redundancies, and ensured accurate mappings between learning activities, resources, teaching methods, and competencies. No inconsistencies or errors were detected, verifying that EduPKG is structurally sound and semantically coherent for integration into intelligent education systems.

Usage Example with SPARQL Queries. Here, an example of using the EduPKG ontology is provided as visible in Listing 1.1 through SPARQL queries. SPARQL is a query language used to retrieve and manipulate data stored in the Resource Description Framework (RDF) format. In Protégé, SPARQL can be integrated to test the ontology's structure and functionality, allowing for efficient extraction and analysis of educational data based on defined relationships and constraints. One of the fundamental objectives of the EduPKG ontology is to enable the retrieval of subject-specific educational activities, ensuring that educators can efficiently access structured lesson plans tailored to different academic disciplines. To demonstrate this functionality, a SPARQL query was executed to retrieve all activities associated with the subject "Science" (line 5) that are designed for the "PrimarySchool" level (line 6). The query also includes descriptions (line 7), required time allocation (line 8), and associated resources (line 9), ensuring that all essential components of an educational activity are accessible.

Listing 1.1. Learning Activities for Primary Science Education Query

```
 1 SELECT ?activity (STR(?description) AS ?cleanDescription)
 2         ?timeAllocation ?resource
 3 WHERE {
 4             ?activity a :ActivityType ;
 5             :isPartOfSubject :Science ;
 6             :isSuitableForLearningLevel :PrimarySchool ;
 7             :hasDescription ?description .
 8   OPTIONAL { ?activity :requiresTimeAllocation ?timeAllocation }
 9   OPTIONAL { ?activity :usesResource ?resource }
10 }
```

The execution of this query successfully retrieved all activities categorized under the *Primary School Science* domain, confirming that subject and level classifications were correctly applied. The results demonstrated that all retrieved activities were correctly categorized under the *Science* subject and associated with a defined learning level, ensuring age-appropriate content. Additionally, optional constraints successfully retrieved time allocation and resource usage where available.

---

[1] https://github.com/PaoloCampanelli/EduPKG-Data.

6   Validation of the EduPKG Ontology

To ensure the EduPKG practical applicability, we conducted a validation process involving education experts. Experts, including teachers and professors, reviewed the ontology, offering valuable feedback to improve its alignment with classroom activities and STEM project planning. To assess the practical relevance and usability of EduPKG, a survey was conducted among educators with direct experience in STEM education and educational technology. The survey aimed to evaluate the challenges educators face when planning STEM activities, their expectations in EduPKG and the potential barriers to adopting such a solution for lesson planning. The participants included secondary and primary school and early childhood educators with teaching experience ranging from 5 to over 30 years. All respondents had previously implemented STEM activities and used various educational technologies, including robotics, coding platforms, and unplugged activities. In the following, we provide an overview of the conducted surveys and relevant outcomes while the full results are available online[2]. All respondents have prior experience with STEM activities and practical usage of technologies such as educational robotics, coding platforms and 3D printing. Before conducting the survey, we asked about the main challenges in planning STEM activities. Time constraints (50%), limited access to educational technology (71.4%), and adapting activities to mixed-ability classrooms (35.7%) emerged as key obstacles. These findings highlight the need for a structured system to help teachers efficiently identify and personalize STEM learning activities.

One of the primary aspects analyzed in the survey was educators' interest in a system like EduPKG. The results, illustrated in Fig. 1, confirm that an ontology-driven system could provide significant support in structuring and implementing STEM lessons (Fig. 1a). Notably, a considerable number of respondents expressed a willingness to adopt the system, especially for structuring resources and optimizing lesson planning time (Fig. 1b).

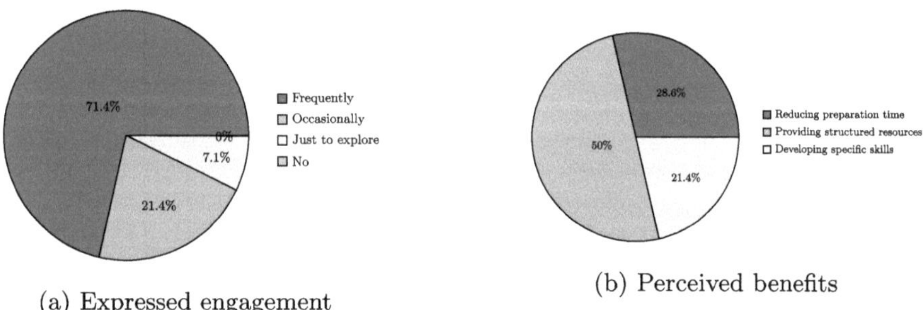

(a) Expressed engagement

(b) Perceived benefits

Fig. 1. Expectations in using EduPKG and planning support.

---

[2] https://github.com/PaoloCampanelli/EduPKG-Data.

Additionally, another key aspect examined was the specific features educators expected from the ontology, as well as the anticipated challenges associated with its implementation (Fig. 2). The survey confirmed the relevance of EduPKG's core features (Fig. 2a), particularly its characterization and adaptability. However, respondents also highlighted concerns related to the complexity of ontology-based systems (Fig. 2b).

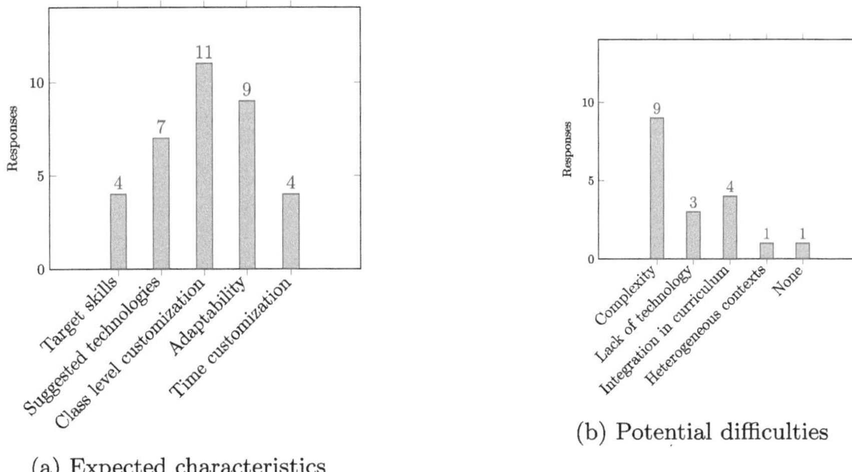

(b) Potential difficulties

(a) Expected characteristics

Fig. 2. Expected characteristics and challenges of EduPKG.

Perceived Utility of EduPKG Among Educators One of the key aspects evaluated in the expert survey was whether educators perceived the EduPKG ontology as a useful tool for their teaching practices. Participants were asked if they believed an ontology-based system for STEM education planning could enhance their instructional activities, and if so, in what ways. The responses collected indicate a strong positive inclination toward EduPKG, with all respondents acknowledging its potential value. However, the specific reasons behind its perceived usefulness varied based on teaching context, subject area, and technological familiarity. The main perspectives expressed by the participants can be categorized as Table 4.

Overall, the survey results highlight EduPKG's potential to enhance STEM education by facilitating lesson planning, aligning with educational frameworks, and supporting personalized learning. While educators recognize its value, key concerns include the need for seamless curriculum integration, user-friendly design, and adaptability across educational levels. Addressing these issues will be crucial for ensuring its practical implementation and widespread adoption. Overall, EduPKG shows promise as an innovative tool for improving STEM education, with further refinement needed to optimize its usability and effectiveness.

Table 4. Main Perspectives on EduPKG Integration

Perspective	Summary
Support for Classroom Integration	EduPKG should seamlessly fit into existing lesson plans and teaching methodologies.
Enhancing STEM Accessibility	It can help more teachers adopt STEM methodologies, even those without specialized training.
Suitability for Early Childhood Education	While not directly applicable, it can support learning in early education settings.
Adaptability to Different Contexts	EduPKG should be flexible to accommodate diverse educational settings and student needs.
Personalization and Student-Centered Learning	It can enhance the customization of teaching resources based on student progress.
Practical and Hands-on Approach	Provides a more interactive and applied learning experience for STEM subjects.
Enhancing Engagement and Motivation	Can make lessons more engaging but requires an analysis of its limitations.
Reinforcing Learning Experiences	Helps consolidate students' STEM learning through structured support.
Providing Structured Didactic Support	Streamlines lesson planning and offers ready-to-use teaching materials.
Facilitating Competency Development	Enables students to develop skills beyond traditional teaching methods.

7   Practical Application of the EduPKG Ontology

To show the potentiality of the EduPKG ontology, this section shows a what-if analysis of a real-world STEM laboratory. In particular, we refer to the *Arduino-based smart greenhouse* project at a Middle School in Urbisaglia city in Italy. The laboratory involved 20 students from 12 to 14 years old and aimed at introducing embedded systems, programming, and home automation using Arduino Starter Kit and mBlock programming platform. Indeed the considered project highlighted significant challenges. Pedagogically, the lesson plan overestimated prior knowledge, leading to cognitive overload and a lack of progressive learning. Technically, mBlock's hardware limitations hindered proper project development. Logistically, the 15-h timeframe proved insufficient forcing a mid-course simplification of objectives. These challenges underscore the need for a structured, competency-based approach, which an ontology-driven system like EduPKG could provide. In the following, we show how EduPKG could have prevented emerged issues by structuring the learning experience more effectively. EduPKG considers parameters such as instructional time, student competencies, resource availability, and pedagogical strategies to suggest the most appropriate learning activity. In this case, EduPKG would have identified the misalignment between the Smart Greenhouse project requirements and the actual learning conditions, recommending a more suitable alternative, namely "PlayArduino".

One of the core advantages of EduPKG is its ability to evaluate instructional feasibility using semantic relationships. The Smart Greenhouse activity required at least 25 h, as indicated by the *requiresTimeAllocation* property, whereas the course schedule only allowed for 15 h. EduPKG would have recognized this mismatch and flagged the activity as unsuitable, ensuring that only activities that fit within the available time frame were considered. Furthermore, the *targetsCompetency* property highlights that the Smart Greenhouse project required advanced programming skills not adequately introduced to the students. The ontology would have determined that a more fundamental Arduino activity was necessary before moving to complex automation tasks, thus avoiding cognitive overload and ensuring a more effective learning pathway. Additionally, EduPKG considers resource compatibility when recommending an activity. The Smart Greenhouse activity relied on mBlock, useful for beginner-level programming but not well-suited for complex real-time sensor automation. Through the *usesResource* property, EduPKG would have assessed that mBlock's limitations made it unsuitable for a project of this scale, reinforcing the decision to recommend an alternative activity better aligned with the available tools.

Teachers could have used EduPKG and adjusted the search parameters to receive support in defining an alternative project, such as PlayArduino. This activity focuses on foundational Arduino skills such as basic circuit assembly, sensor integration, and fundamental programming structures. The ontology's *isSuitableForLearningLevel* property ensures that activities match the educational stage of students, and in this case, it would have prioritized a more structured, guided introduction to Arduino rather than an advanced, self-directed automation project. EduPKG's *adoptsTeachingMethod* property also ensures that pedagogical strategies align with learning objectives. While the Smart Greenhouse project required extensive lecture-based instruction, PlayArduino is designed to encourage hands-on exploration through project-based learning and group collaboration. This alignment with active learning methodologies would have enhanced student engagement, enabling them to experiment with Arduino components in a more intuitive and structured manner.

8   Conclusion and Future Work

STEM education is essential for equipping students with the skills needed in an increasingly technology-driven world. However, selecting and implementing effective STEM activities remains a challenge for educators due to the lack of structured guidance. EduPKG addresses this gap by providing an ontology that aligns STEM activities with specific classroom needs, ensuring accessibility, engagement, and educational impact. By integrating a competency-based approach and fostering the 4Cs—Creativity, Collaboration, Communication, and Critical Thinking—EduPKG enhances the effectiveness of STEM education across various contexts. Future work will focus on the development of a user-friendly application that makes EduPKG accessible to a wider audience, allowing educators to easily plan and customize STEM activities. Additionally, the ontology could be extended to support real-world applications, such as industry-academia collaborations, smart learning environments, and personalized STEM learning pathways. These advancements will further bridge the gap between policy-driven initiatives and classroom realities, ensuring meaningful STEM education for all.

References

1. Avenirovna, N.O., Vitalevich, K.A., Rafikovna, S.L., Konstantinovich, L.E., Viktorovna, F.M., et al.: Ontomathedu: towards an educational mathematical ontology (2015)
2. Bers, M.U.: Coding as a Playground: Programming and Computational Thinking in the Early Childhood Classroom. Routledge (2018)
3. Bocconi, S., Chioccariello, A., Dettori, G., Ferrari, A., Engelhardt, K.: Developing computational thinking in compulsory education-implications for policy and practice. Technical report, Joint Research Centre (Seville site) (2016)
4. Chittum, J.R., Jones, B.D., Akalin, S., Schram, Á.B.: The effects of an afterschool stem program on students' motivation and engagement. Int. J. STEM Educ. **4**, 1–16 (2017)
5. Commission, E.: Resetting education and training for the digital age (2020)
6. Diatta, B., Basse, A., Ouya, S.: Pasonto: ontology for learning pascal programming language. In: EDUCON, pp. 749–754. IEEE (2019)
7. Diatta, B., Basse, A., Ouya, S.: Ontology-based database for chemical experiments: design and implementation. In: Auer, M.E., Tsiatsos, T. (eds.) ICL 2018. AISC, vol. 916, pp. 389–397. Springer, Cham (2020). https://doi.org/10.1007/978-3-030-11932-4_37
8. Fernández-López, M., Gómez-Pérez, A., Juristo Juzgado, N.: Methontology: from ontological art towards ontological engineering. In: AAAI97 Spring Symposium. American Association for Artificial Intelligence (1997). oEG
9. Hossain, M.A., Deehan, J., Gibbs, L.: Unveiling the pedagogical approaches in stem classroom: a scoping review. Int. J. Learn. Teach. Educ. Res. **23**(12), 1–22 (2024)
10. Leung, W.M.V.: Stem education in early years: challenges and opportunities in changing teachers' pedagogical strategies. Educ. Sci. **13**(5) (2023)
11. Ministero dell'Istruzione, d.e.d.R.: Piano nazionale scuola digitale (2015)
12. Papert, S.: Mindstorms: Children, Computers, and Powerful Ideas. Basic Books (1980)
13. Resnick, M.: Lifelong Kindergarten: Cultivating Creativity Through Projects, Passion, Peers, and Play. MIT Press, Cambridge (2017)
14. S. Grover, R.P.: Computational thinking in k–12: a review of the state of the field. Educ. Researcher, **42**(1), 38-43 (2013)
15. Shearer, R.D., Motik, B., Horrocks, I.: Hermit: a highly-efficient owl reasoner. In: Owled, vol. 432, p. 91 (2008)
16. Sirin, E., Parsia, B., Grau, B.C., Kalyanpur, A., Katz, Y.: Pellet: a practical owl-dl reasoner. J. Web Semant. **5**(2), 51–53 (2007)
17. Sivakumar, R., Arivoli, P.: Ontology visualization protégé tools–a review. Int. J. Adv. Inf. Technol. (IJAIT), **1** (2011)
18. Wing, J.M.: Computational thinking. Commun. ACM **49**(3), 33–35 (2006)
19. Y. B. Kafai, Q.B.: Connected Code: Why Children Need to Learn Programming. MIT Press, Cambridge (2014)

Minimum Urban Units (MUUs): A Data-Driven Methodology for Adaptive and Climate-Responsive Urban Planning

Roberta Cocci Grifoni, Rosalba D'Onofrio, Maria Simonetta Bernabei,
Graziano Enzo Marchesani[✉], Mohammadjavad Khodaparast, and Dajla Riera

University of Camerino, School of Architecture and Design "Eduardo Vittoria", Ascoli Piceno,
Italy
`graziano.marchesani@unicam.it`

Abstract. Minimum Urban Units (MUUs) offer a promising approach for adaptive urban planning, facilitating sustainable city development and improving residents' quality of life. Building upon the Local Climate Zone (LCZ) classification, MUUs delineate and characterise a city's physical and environmental attributes, integrating land cover; building morphology; and social, population, mobility, and health data. By using a GIS-based platform and parametric processes, MUUs combine various data types to identify zones that require immediate attention for active intervention. This methodology expands the LCZ classification to introduce risk levels and the projected climate for the next mid-century, serving as a recipe for building climate-resilient cities. Preliminary analyses revealed MUUs' effectiveness of MUUs in categorising urban zones and identifying areas prone to specific environmental stressors or socioeconomic challenges. The flexibility of MUUs allows the incorporation of climate change considerations, sustainable resource use, and community planning. Neural networks will be integrated to identify the complex relationships among environmental factors, socioeconomic indicators, and urban morphology, enabling the prediction of different urban planning scenarios. The MUU project's achievements address data collection and microclimatic analysis challenges, confirming their potential as valuable tools for policymakers and urban planners. Further research and collaboration are needed to refine the open MUU framework, but preliminary findings suggest that MUUs offer a promising pathway towards more adaptive, sustainable, and resilient urban environments.

Keywords: Climate adaptation · Minimum Urban Units (MUU) · Responsive urban planning · Data-Driven Urban Planning · Local Climate Zone (LCZ)

1 Introduction

Global urbanisation and climate change pose significant challenges for urban planning, including housing, mobility, access to services, urban heat islands (UHIs), pollution, and resource management. Effective mitigation and adaptation are crucial for urban sustainability [1, 2], with new methodologies emerging to address issues like UHI [3].

F. Corradini et al. (Eds.): Society 5.0 2025, CCIS 2787, pp. 75–86, 2026.
https://doi.org/10.1007/978-3-032-15463-7_7

However, existing approaches, such as the widely used Local Climate Zone (LCZ) classification, often lack the granularity and multidimensional data integration required to address the localized, interconnected challenges within diverse urban fabrics. Specifically, current methods struggle to simultaneously account for microclimatic variations, socioeconomic disparities, and building-level characteristics at a scale relevant to targeted interventions, such as designing specific street-level heat mitigation measures or assessing localized social vulnerability.

To address these complex urban challenges, this study focused on developing and implementing Minimum Urban Units (MUUs) as an innovative tool for sustainable urban planning. Crucially, the MUU framework is designed to be open source, fostering collaboration and facilitating its adaptation to diverse urban contexts. The primary research objective was to evaluate the effectiveness and transformative potential of MUUs in optimising urban management and enhancing citizens' quality of life.

Specifically, this study addresses the research question: How can a multi-parameter, fine-grained classification system (Minimum Urban Units), building upon the established LCZ framework, effectively integrate diverse data types to provide a more nuanced assessment of micro-scale urban environments suitable for targeted, adaptive, and climate-responsive planning?

Urban planning significantly impacts public health and wellbeing through factors like air quality, healthcare access, and green spaces [4]. MUUs aim to support an integrative approach by incorporating parameters relevant to green spaces, sustainable mobility, and eco-friendly buildings.

MUUs represent a comprehensive approach to urban planning that expands upon the Local Climate Zone (LCZ) concept. This integrated methodology uses various parameters, ranging from energy to socioeconomic and environmental factors, to represent urban systems. These parameter categories were selected to directly address the multifaceted urban challenges, including climate impacts (addressed by Thermal Aspects, Outdoor Quality), public health and liveability (Health, Walkability, Urban Metrics), and resource efficiency (Architecture Quality and Architecture Geometry).

The present study is situated within the framework of the Vitality project, funded by the National Recovery and Resilience Plan (PNRR). Vitality has involved the collaboration of twenty-four organisations – including universities, research centres, and private organisations from Abruzzo, Marche, and Umbria (Italy) – engaged in a multitude of research activities aimed at deepening the understanding of urban environments. Within this extensive and diverse programme, our specific contribution has focused on refining the Local Climate Zones (LCZ) classification within the MUU framework. This objective was pursued through a fine-grained analysis, based on a grid of significantly smaller dimensions than that employed in previous research [5], with the aim of contributing to more resilient and sustainable urban design strategies to address complex challenges.

1.1 Background

The study of urban environment-local climate interaction, vital due to urbanisation and climate change, has seen significant advancements in methods and tools, driven by interdisciplinary convergence and methodological rigor.

Oke's study [6] on urban energy balance established the foundation for a more comprehensive understanding of the crucial role that energy plays in modulating the urban climate. Subsequent research throughout the late 20th and early 21st centuries, including the pivotal work of Masson [7], transitioned towards a mechanistic understanding, increasingly utilising advanced modelling and sophisticated data analysis techniques. This shift represents a significant advancement in the field, allowing for a more detailed and nuanced understanding of the complex urban processes.

Stewart's 2011 critical analysis [8] further propelled the field forward by highlighting the growing awareness of methodological limitations. Stewart's call was for a more rigorous and scientifically defensible approach to collecting and analyzing urban climatic data.

Landmark development was the introduction of the Local Climate Zones (LCZ) concept by Stewart and Oke in 2012 [9], which provided a standardised classification of urban and peri-urban environments, facilitating a more accurate analysis of climatic effects across different geographic areas. Since then, the LCZ framework has been widely applied and expanded, demonstrating its utility in a broad array of urban contexts and planning applications. Lehnert et al. [10] and Zheng et al. [11] effectively demonstrated the efficacy of GIS in analysing complex urban settings using LCZ principles.

The LCZ framework's utility was demonstrated in diverse planning applications [12] including LCZ mapping via remote sensing [13], and UHI analysis [14, 15], with its broad applicability confirmed across numerous cities [16].

The development and application of the LCZ concept paved the way for more refined approaches to urban climate analysis, setting the stage for the introduction of Minimum Urban Units (MUUs) as a more granular and context-aware tool for urban planning.

2 Methodology

2.1 Description of the Theoretical Framework

MUUs expand upon the Local Climate Zone concept, representing urban systems with parameters ranging from energy to socioeconomic and environmental factors.

The MUU technique offers precise urban environment understanding using complex parameters as indicators for developers and municipal managers. These parameters help evaluate ecosystem effects, identify areas for sustainable practices, and link to health and demographic data.

Key parameter categories (detailed in Table 1) include indicators for quality of life and public health like green spaces [17]; urban mobility and infrastructure (e.g., street width, pedestrian/cycling space allocation); environmental factors (e.g., water runoff, solar exposure); and energy/building performance (e.g., WWR, facade orientation, solar factor). These are crucial for sustainability policies, resource management, and energy conservation.

MUUs offer a more precise, detailed analysis than existing tools. This addresses the need, beyond general LCZ classification, to capture finer-grained urban fabric for specific planning applications. In this more focused and specific way, MUUs aim for efficient resource management, improved urban quality of life, and enhanced capacity to address urban growth and environmental problems. Effective strategies require integrating public spaces and heritage, interdisciplinary approaches, and public awareness. Public life is constructed when people engage in various public domains such as streets, squares, parks, and urban spaces between buildings. To emphasise social aspects, MUUs consider factors influencing public life and urban regeneration, where social relationships and community participation shape built environments. This aligns urban regeneration with sustainability principles.

MUUs' fine-grained, context-aware perspectives offer potential solutions to contemporary urban challenges. Effective MUU integration with current planning combines respective strengths. For instance, MUUs' fine-grained, data-rich analysis can complement traditional zoning or master planning, aiming for a more efficient, context-sensitive system. This integration ensures MUU-identified localized vulnerabilities or opportunities inform broader frameworks, leading to more targeted, effective outcomes. This is relevant where other planning models are more precise (e.g., large city centers or regions with significant population density disparities). MUUs are dynamic and responsive to urban conditions. This flexibility is crucial given contemporary technological advancements, population shifts, and climate change challenges. MUUs can be updated for demographic/economic shifts, altered urban density, and other factors, integrating these transformations during city growth or rejuvenation. This beneficial flexibility keeps urban planning dynamic, practical, and responsive to city requirements. Here, big data analysis is critical. It offers new perspectives potentially requiring MUU characteristic changes and helps identify urban structural trends for prompt, precise plan incorporation. However, policies or socioeconomic conditions should drive MUU parameter redesign. These attributes are vital for MUUs' continued relevance as urban planning and development tools.

2.2 MUU Classification Scheme

Minimum Urban Units (MUUs) build upon and enhance the existing local climate zone (LCZ) framework, offering a more nuanced understanding of urban spaces. This innovative approach further enhances and defines the LCZ scheme based on specific parameters, thereby enabling a more refined examination of urban environments, which are not intended to substitute LCZs but to provide a more detailed refinement: Specifically, while LCZs offer a foundational classification based on general morphology and land cover over areas typically 100-500m across, MUUs operate at a finer scale (e.g., 30m grid) allowing the integration of a wider array of parameters (Table 1) within these LCZ-defined areas or even across their boundaries where micro-variations are significant. Therefore, MUUs are best understood as a complementary analytical layer that operates at a higher resolution and integrates a broader set of variables within the foundational spatial typology provided by LCZs, rather than representing a fundamentally distinct paradigm. While LCZs use broad physical and anthropogenic data, MUUs examine smaller urban entities in greater detail and precision.

Integrating MUUs with LCZs involves several key steps. First, it is crucial to determine the LCZs using a highly detailed scale of 30 m, which is suitable for assessing the MUU characteristics. The first step is critical for identifying the different categories of urban landscapes, the features that define them, and the activities that occur within them.

The primary categorisation made by LCZs forms a solid basis for further analysis, as it presents a detailed and multifaceted picture of the investigated urban environment.

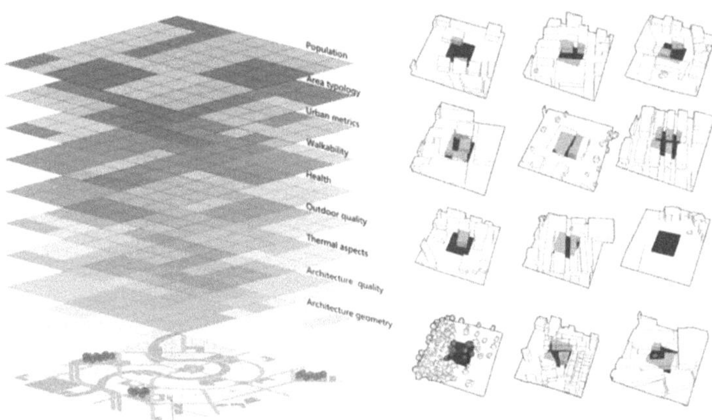

Fig. 1. Urban fabric segmentation was applied to each category, as listed in Table 2. The image represents a thirty-meter grid, where each element has been meticulously selected.

2.3   Criteria for Defining MUUs

Assessing quality of life requires consideration of subjective aspects influenced by social and cultural backgrounds [18]. Indices and scoring systems help to quantify these aspects.

Differentiated data collection includes census data, movement flows (walking, cycling, and public transport), and user demographics. This approach helps understand urban dynamics and identify areas of interest for planning.

Quantitative parameters, such as population density, proportion of green spaces [19], and energy efficiency of buildings, were collected through standardised and easily measurable methods. These data provide clear and tangible indicators that are essential for precisely delineating the MUU characteristics. The methodology presented below is a concrete example of confidently measuring and assessing the residents' perceived well-being.

MUUs are diagnostic frameworks encompassing microclimatic, architectural, and social aspects and can inform reactive urban planning. They identify issues and catalyse actions.

Effective indicators of local public life require identifying stakeholders (age, gender, income, ethnicity), analysing people flows, urban space morphology, and using apps to collect data on vegetation, land use, and building interfaces. A public life database helps identify the best practices.

The development of urban quality can be guided by the existing literature, which provides clear criteria. Gehl initially reported 12 criteria in his studies [20], which later increased to 20. The selection of parameters within categories like 'Urban Metrics', 'Walkability', and 'Outdoor Quality' was partly guided by such people-centered urban quality frameworks. These criteria, ranging from protection against traffic and accidents to opportunities for enjoying the positive aspects of the climate, provide a holistic approach for evaluating urban spaces.

Table 1 provides a comprehensive overview of the key parameters used to define the MUUs grouped into categories. These categories encompass various urban characteristics ranging from population demographics to architectural geometry.

The parameters listed in Table 1 form the foundation for the MUU classification system. Each category contributes to a comprehensive understanding of the urban environment. For instance, the 'Population' category helps us understand the demographic composition of an area, which is crucial for planning social services. The categories of area typology and urban metrics provide insights into the physical structure and functional distribution of the urban fabric. 'Walkability' parameters, informed by research demonstrating the link between streetscape characteristics and pedestrian activity, are essential for assessing the pedestrian-friendliness of an area [21], while 'Health' indicators, drawing upon established methods for correlating urban features with public health outcomes and utilizing recognized metrics like the Liveability Index and the Universal Thermal Climate Index (UTCI), allow us to correlate urban characteristics with public health outcomes [22]. Categories of outdoor quality and thermal aspects are important for understanding the environmental performance of urban areas. Finally, the parameters architecture quality and architecture geometry help assess the quality and energy performance of the built environment.

It is important to note that the data for these parameters come from various sources [23–25], as indicated in the 'Data Sources' column. Some are derived from measures calculated from primary data, whereas others are derived directly from municipal records or monitoring systems. Integrating these diverse data sources is a crucial strength of our MUU approach, which allows a more holistic understanding of the urban environment.

Table 1. Comprehensive Overview of Urban Planning Parameters: This table provides an example of grouping key parameters, such as Architecture Quality, Health, Indoor and Outdoor Usage, Population Dynamics, Walkability, Area Typology, Thermal Aspects, and Geometry.

Category	Parameters	Data Sources
Population	Population age <14, population age >65	Derived measure
Area typology	Zone classification, Vegetation high fraction, Water fraction	Municipality data, derived measure

(continued)

Table 1. (*continued*)

Category	Parameters	Data Sources
Urban metrics	Residence percentage, Amenities percentage, Production percentage, Private percentage, Public percentage, Residence to amenities distance, Residence to production distance, Clinics/Hospital distance, Private outdoor space percentage, Open to public-private Outdoor space percentage, Public space percentage	Municipality data, derived measure
Walkability	Road width, Sidewalk width, Pedestrian Walk score, Cycling walk score, Car walk score, Shady roads	Derived measure
Health	Hospital admissions, Air quality, Water quality, Heat stress index, Death indexes, Liveability index [24]	Hospital data, monitored data
Outdoor quality	Green age, Public green, Private green, RIE index, Runoff, UTCI index [26]	Municipality data, meteorological data, derived measure
Thermal aspects	Solar exposure, Global solar radiation, Roofs incident Solar radiation, Sunlight hours, Average solar absorption	Meteorological data, derived measure
Architecture quality	Building structure, Building insulation, Building age, Energetic class	Municipality data, derived measure
Architecture geometry	Window-to-wall ratio (WWR), Surface building orientation, Building envelope construction	Derived measure

Table 2. Illustrative Data Sample for a Hypothetical MUU in Ascoli Piceno based on Layered Parameters (Fig. 1).

Parameter Category	Parameter Example	Illustrative Value/Category
Population	Population Density	High (>50 inhab/ha)
Area typology	LCZ Classification	Compact Midrise (LCZ 2)
Urban metrics	Residence to amenities dist	Moderate (250–500m)

(*continued*)

Table 2. (continued)

Parameter Category	Parameter Example	Illustrative Value/Category
Walkability	Sidewalk Width	Narrow (<1.5m)
Health	Heat Stress Index (Proxy)	Elevated
Outdoor quality	Vegetation Fraction	Low ($<10\%$)
Thermal aspects	Avg. Summer Surface Temp	High ($>35\,°C$)
Architecture quality	Building Age	Pre-1945
Architecture geometry	Window-to-wall ratio (WWR)	Low ($<15\%$)

As illustrated in Fig. 2, the workflow begins with the input of geometric, administrative, health, and meteorological data into the SQL database. These data undergo transformation and standardisation to meet project requirements. The Grasshopper platform, enhanced with Python scripts, filters data for specific applications. Simultaneously, GIS analysis provides a deeper understanding of urban textures [27].

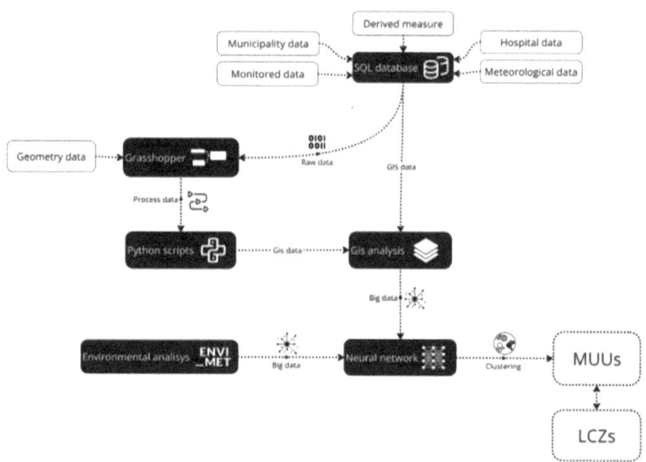

Fig. 2. MUU clustering workflow: GIS analysis and neural network.

3   Preliminary Analysis and Intermediate Results

Preliminary analyses demonstrated the potential of MUUs to address urban challenges. Their fine-grained design enables detailed urban zone categorization, identifying areas susceptible to environmental/socioeconomic issues [28] and allowing targeted interventions. MUUs integrate diverse data layers, offering a nuanced understanding of urban complexity and identifying areas prone to specific stressors (e.g., high UHI effects with vulnerable populations).

Ascoli Piceno (central Italy), with its rich medieval heritage, served as a case study to validate the MUU-centred urban planning approach. This initial MUU delineation integrates LCZ taxonomy (Fig. 3) with population density data (Fig. 4), creating a composite layer identifying urban areas with characteristics conducive to heat island intensification and high population densities. Consequently, this approach highlights areas highly vulnerable to urban overheating. The resultant analysis provides critical information and evidence, informing strategies for wider MUU adoption.

Conceptually, this integration involves overlaying LCZ (Fig. 3) and population density data (Fig. 4) at a common 30x30m grid resolution. Specific criteria identify cells (potential MUUs) with high physical susceptibility to overheating (e.g., LCZ 2 'Compact Midrise', LCZ 3 'Compact Lowrise') and significant populations (e.g., higher density classes in Fig. 4). Preliminary overlay analysis in Ascoli Piceno identified specific zones (e.g., historic center, adjacent residential areas) with this combination of physical and social vulnerability. Although a detailed map of these combined-vulnerability MUUs is part of ongoing research, this 'resultant analysis' is fundamental to prioritize micro-zones for in-depth characterization with all MUU parameters.

Overlaying multiple data layers (Fig. 1) is core to the MUU definition. To illustrate the detailed, multi-parameter data collected for such prioritized MUUs, Table 2 shows a simplified data example for a hypothetical MUU in a critical area of Ascoli Piceno.

This hypothetical MUU's multi-faceted profile indicates high vulnerability: dense population in a heat-retaining urban form (LCZ 2, older buildings with low WWR), low vegetation, narrow sidewalks (affecting walkability), and elevated heat stress indicators. This 30x30m scale characterization pinpoints areas for tailored interventions (e.g., targeted greening, facade improvements, shading), showcasing MUUs' potential utility and feasibility for focused urban planning, even from this initial application.

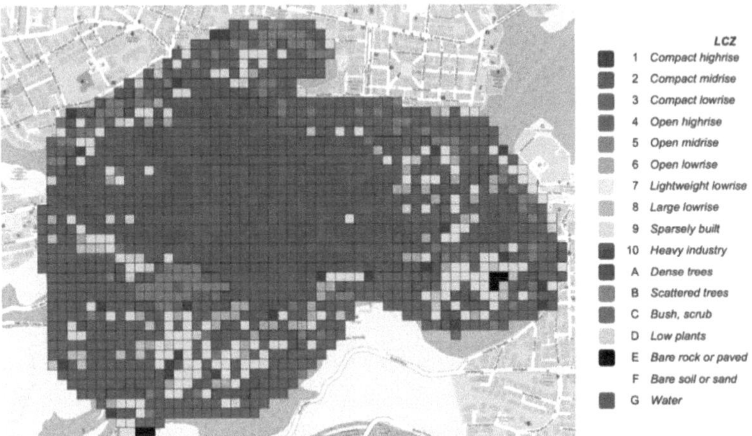

Fig. 3. LCZ map on 30 x 30 grid. This map illustrates the initial findings from the LCZ.

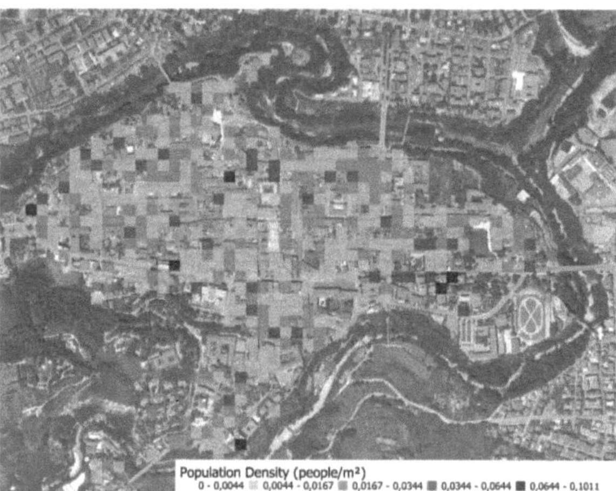

Fig. 4. Population density distribution, crucial for understanding actual population spread.

4 Next Steps and Future Directions

Following data collection and microclimatic analysis, neural network application is planned to define and classify MUUs. These machine learning techniques are suitable for this task due to their ability to model complex, non-linear relationships among the diverse environmental, socioeconomic, and morphological factors in the MUU parameter set (Table 2). Training these networks on collected datasets aims for automatic, nuanced categorization of urban areas into distinct MUU types, potentially uncovering subtle patterns and interactions missed by conventional methods. This data-driven classification should enhance prediction of responses to planning interventions, operationalising the MUU framework and informing proactive strategies.

The MUU project will publicly release its concept and methodology as an open model. This enables global researchers to utilise, test, refine, and expand the MUU framework, fostering wider adoption and contributing to sustainable urban planning.

Future work will involve detailed specification of network architecture, training procedures, and rigorous validation protocols to assess model classification performance and predictive accuracy.

5 Conclusions

The achievements and milestones of the MUU project are promising. The initiative has effectively addressed the challenges related to data collection and microclimatic analysis, which forms the basis of the MUU framework. This data-driven approach has revealed the capabilities of MUUs in identifying the strengths and weaknesses of urban landscapes and in shaping the future of cities. The initial results confirm the potential of MUUs as valuable tools for policymakers and urban planners. In practical terms, MUUs offer decision-makers a framework to move beyond city-wide analyses, enabling data-driven prioritization of micro-zones for targeted climate adaptation investments, localized public health strategies, or infrastructure upgrades based on specific, multi-faceted vulnerability profiles. By integrating MUUs with other modelling tools and urban design practices, cities can proactively manage their environments, improve their quality of life, and contribute to a more sustainable future. It is important to acknowledge the limitations of this study, including the preliminary nature of the case study results and the ongoing development of the automated classification tools. Furthermore, the successful application of the MUU framework is inherently dependent on the availability and quality of fine-grained, multi-source local data, which can pose a significant challenge. Future research should also investigate the methodology's scalability and transferability to diverse urban contexts. Further research and collaboration are needed to refine the MUU framework; however, the preliminary findings are encouraging and suggest that MUUs offer a promising pathway towards more adaptive, sustainable, and resilient urban environments.

Acknowledgments. The authors disclosed receipt of the following financial support for the research, authorship, and publication of this work. This work was supported by the PNRR MUR project ECS_00000041-VITALITY.

References

1. Risk with an innovative indicators-based assessment approach. J. Clean. Prod. **371**, 133496 (2022)
2. Kotharkar, R., Bagade, A., Singh, P.R.: A systematic approach for urban heat island mitigation strategies in critical local climate zones of an Indian city. Urban Climate **34**, 100701 (2020)
3. Cocci Grifoni, R., Tascini, S., Cesario, E., Marchesani, G.E.: Cool façade optimization: a new parametric methodology for the urban heat island phenomenon (UHI). In: Conference Proceedings - 2017 17th IEEE International Conference on Environment and Electrical Engineering and 2017 1st IEEE Industrial and Commercial Power Systems Europe, EEEIC / I and CPS Europe 2017, pp. 1–5. Institute of Electrical and Electronics Engineers Inc., New York (2017)
4. Corburn, J.: Confronting the challenges in reconnecting urban planning and public health. Am. J. Public Health **94**, 541–546 (2004)
5. Moura, A.C.B.D., Nunes, L.V., Paula, D.C.J. de, Souza, N.S., et al.: Characterization of an urban area in the legal amazon using local climate zones (LCZ). Revista Nacional de Gerenciamento de Cidades 11 (2023)
6. Oke, T.: The urban energy balance. Prog. Phys. Geogr. **12**, 471–508 (1988)
7. Masson, V.: A physically-based scheme for the urban energy budget in atmospheric models. Bound.-Layer Meteorol. **94**, 357–397 (2000)
8. Stewart, I.: A systematic review and scientific critique of methodology in modern urban heat island literature. Int. J. Climatol. **31** (2011)
9. Stewart, I., Oke, T.: Local climate zones for urban temperature studies. Bull. Am. Meteor. Soc. **93**, 1879–1900 (2012)
10. Lehnert, M., Geletič, J., Husák, J., Vysoudil, M.: Urban field classification by "local climate zones" in a medium-sized Central European city: the case of Olomouc (Czech Republic). Theoret. Appl. Climatol. **122**, 531–541 (2015)
11. Zheng, Y., et al.: GIS-based mapping of local climate zone in the high-density city of Hong Kong. Urban Clim. (2017)

12. Perera, N., Emmanuel, R.: A "Local Climate Zone" based approach to urban planning in colombo, sri lanka. Urban Clim. **23**, 188–203 (2016)
13. Wang, C., Middel, A., Myint, S., Kaplan, S., Brazel, A., Lukasczyk, J.: Assessing local climate zones in arid cities: the case of Phoenix, Arizona and Las Vegas, Nevada. ISPRS J. Photogrammetry Remote Sens. (2018)
14. Leconte, F., Bouyer, J., Claverie, R., Pétrissans, M.: Using Local Climate Zone scheme for UHI assessment: evaluation of the method using mobile measurements. Build. Environ. **83**, 39–49 (2015)
15. Hammerberg, K., Brousse, O., Martilli, A., Mahdavi, A.: Implications of employing de-tailed urban canopy parameters for mesoscale climate modelling: a comparison between WUDAPT and GIS databases over Vienna, Austria. Int. J. Climatol. **38** (2018)
16. Bechtel, B., Demuzere, M., Mills, G., Zhan, W., Sismanidis, P., Small, C., Voogt, J.: SUHI analysis using local climate zones—a comparison of 50 cities. Urban Clim. (2019)
17. Cicea, C., Pirlogea, C.: Green spaces and public health in urban areas. Theor. Empirical Res. Urban Manag. (2011)
18. Marans, R.W., Stimson, R.J. (eds.): Investigating Quality of Urban Life: Theory, Methods, and Empirical Research. Springer, Netherlands (2011)
19. Addas, A.: Influence of urban green spaces on quality of life and health with smart city design. Land **12**, 960 (2023)
20. Gehl, J.: Città per le persone. Maggioli, Santarcangelo di Romagna (2017)
21. Li, X., Santi, P., Courtney, T.K., Verma, S.K., Ratti, C.: Investigating the association between streetscapes and human walking activities using google street view and human trajectory data. Trans. GIS **22**, 1029–1044 (2018)
22. Dennis, M., Cook, P.A., James, P., Wheater, C.P., Lindley, S.J.: Relationships between health outcomes in older populations and urban green infrastructure size, quality and proximity. BMC Public Health **20**, 626 (2020)
23. Demuzere, M., et al.: A global map of local climate zones to support earth system modelling and urban-scale environmental science. Earth Syst. Sci. Data **14**, 3835–3873 (2022)
24. Higgs, C., Badland, H., Simons, K., Knibbs, L.D., Giles-Corti, B.: The urban liveability index: developing a policy-relevant urban liveability composite measure and evaluating associations with transport mode choice. Int. J. Health Geograph. **18**, 14 (2019)
25. He, S., Zhang, Y., Zhang, J.: Urban local climate zone mapping and apply in urban environment study. IOP Conf. Ser.: Earth Environ. Sci. **113**, 012055 (2018)
26. Fiala, D., Havenith, G., Bröde, P., Kampmann, B., Jendritzky, G.: UTCI-Fiala multi-node model of human heat transfer and temperature regulation. Int. J. Biometeorol. **56**, 429–441 (2012)
27. Quan, S.J., Bansal, P.: A systematic review of GIS-based local climate zone mapping studies. Build. Environ. **196**, 107791 (2021)
28. Ozdemir, S.: Unveiling environmental resilience: a data-driven multi-criteria decision-making approach. Environ. Impact Assess. Rev. **108**, 107607 (2024)

Cultural Influences on Human Cybersecurity Behaviour: A Study of Switzerland and Cameroon

Franka Ebob Enow Ebai[1]([envelope]) [iD], Simon Eyongabane Ako[2] [iD], Bettina Schneider[1] [iD],
George Fonkeng Epah[2], Gaius Ngong Mufua[2], Willibroad Abongwa Acho[2],
Williams Boma[2], Williams Boma[2], Delbert Akom Afumbom[2],
Veronica Ika K. Visemih[2], Samuel Nemkul Lackbuin[2], and Mary Feh[2]

[1] University of Applied Sciences and Arts Northwestern Switzerland, Basel, Switzerland
Franka.ebai@fhnw.ch
[2] Biaka University of Buea, Buea, Cameroon

Abstract. Culture—be it national or organizational culture—shapes the behaviour, mindset and decision-making of individuals. Since human behaviour is considered the most vulnerable link in the security chain, it is worth examining the relationship between culture and human behaviour in the field of cybersecurity. This paper examines culture as a fundamental element of cybersecurity, highlighting its impact on security awareness, decision-making, and risk perception. Specifically, we explore how national and organisational culture shape cybersecurity practices in cross-cultural contexts. Using a qualitative approach, we conduct episodic and focus group interviews with cybersecurity professionals, educators, Chief Security Officers, and students from diverse educational backgrounds in Switzerland and Cameroon. Our findings reveal that cultural dimensions such as power distance, individualism, and uncertainty avoidance significantly influence cybersecurity behaviour. This study expands the body of literature on culture and individual cybersecurity behaviour and provides new, practical implications for integrating culture into cybersecurity training in educational institutions and organisations.

Keywords: Cross-cultural Contexts · Culture · Human Cybersecurity Behaviour

1 Introduction

Security risks transcend borders affecting both developed and developing countries. Evidence of this includes such attacks as the WannaCry Ransomware and the NotPetya attacks that occurred in 2017. These cyber-attacks impacted multiple organisations in countries around the globe [1]. About 88% of data breaches are caused by employees' mistakes, and humans are termed the weakest link in the security chain [2]. Although often ignored, authors such as [3] and [4] have highlighted the importance of human factors in cybersecurity. Risky cybersecurity behaviour has been linked to human traits such as internet addiction and a dismissive attitude to threats [3] as well as time pressure [4].

F. Corradini et al. (Eds.): Society 5.0 2025, CCIS 2787, pp. 87–97, 2026.
https://doi.org/10.1007/978-3-032-15463-7_8

Considering the role of human behaviour in data breaches, it is important to examine how one's cultural background and/or the culture of their work environment influences human action in relation to cybersecurity. This is particularly relevant because cultural background, also referred to as national culture, influences an individual's way of life and decision-making process [5]. Similarly, organisational culture also shapes individuals' behaviour as it comprises a system of shared values that define what is important and shared norms that guide appropriate attitudes and behaviours [6].

While researchers continue to explore the role of human behaviour in cybersecurity, the influence of culture—both national and organisational—on cybersecurity behaviour remains underexamined. Some existing studies [7] and [8] have emphasised the importance of fostering a cybersecurity culture within organisations. However, culture-specific elements, stemming from the organisational environment and national culture, that influence human cybersecurity behaviour remain largely unexplored. Therefore, the gap we aim to address lies in understanding how cultural-specific factors—both at the organisational and national levels—shape human cybersecurity behaviour.

We therefore address two main research objectives: 1) To investigate the role of national culture in human cybersecurity behaviour in Switzerland and in Cameroon. 2) To investigate the role of organisational culture in human cybersecurity behaviour in Switzerland and in Cameroon. Our findings will be valuable for cybersecurity practitioners across government, education, and industry, enabling them to adapt cybersecurity policies and training for students and workers. Our aim is not to compare Switzerland and Cameroon in terms of which country is better regarding cybersecurity. Rather, we seek to identify key cultural contexts from both countries that influence human cybersecurity behaviour. Therefore, we focus specifically on the cultural and organisational contexts of the two countries.

In the next sections, we present our theoretical framework, literature review, methodology, discuss key findings and conclude.

2   Theoretical Framework and Literature Review

2.1   Theoretical Framework

To research cultural factors impacting individual cybersecurity behaviour, we primarily focused on Hofstede's Cultural Dimensions as the basis for our work. Although we also drew slightly on the Iceberg Theory of Culture to identify key elements that define organisational culture, our overall aim was to link the identified national and organisational elements to Hofstede's cultural dimensions.

Referring to the Iceberg theory, the larger portion of an organisation's culture – about 90%, is hidden [9]. This includes core values, customs, beliefs, and assumptions, while the remaining 10% forms the visible part, such as, greetings, music and dress code. The elements were explored through our conducted interviews.

Hofstede Cultural Dimensions: Cameroon and Switzerland. Here, we primarily illustrate how the two countries differ culturally, reinforcing our aim to understand how national culture might influence human cybersecurity behaviour. These differences can be examined through the following dimensions: *Power distance, Individualism, Uncertainty avoidance, long term orientation, and indulgence.* Due to Cameroon not being among the investigated countries in Hofstede's original study, we mainly relied on the study of [10] and [11] to draw some cultural aspects of Cameroon.

Power Distance (PDI). Switzerland is a low-power distance society [12]. There is a belief in minimizing inequality among people. Power within organizations is decentralized, with employees expecting to be consulted and managers relying on the experience of their employees. Cameroon has a score of 54 for PDI [10], which is lower than coutries in West Africa but higher than of Western nations like Germany and USA with lower PDI scores.

Individualism (IDV). Switzerland is classified as an "I" society. Individuals prioritize taking care of themselves and their immediate social circles [12]. Meanwhile, Cameroon is a collective society [10]. In such a society, people are integrated into strong, cohesive in-groups from birth [13].

Uncertainty Avoidance (UAI). In Switzerland, the French-speaking strongly prefers rigid rules and structured environments than the German-speaking region [12]. Similarly, the Cameroonian society prefers avoiding uncertainty [11]. Managers in the country do not like ambiguous conditions. However, this finding is contradicted by [10], who found that Cameroon has low uncertainty avoidance, implying that the society tolerates uncertainty.

Long Term vs. Short-Term Orientation. In Switzerland, there is a preference for traditional cultures and norms that emphasize long-standing values and practices. Cameroon, on the other hand, leans towards short term orientation relative to other African countries. This demonstrates that society is present-oriented with a focus on quick results [10].

Indulgence. In Switzerland, people have a strong willingness to enjoy life, a positive attitude and a high value for leisure activities. Meanwhile, Cameroon values moderate restraint due to social norms [10].

2.2   Literature Review

Guided by the theoretical framework, we conducted a literature review on the impact of culture on cybersecurity, considering both national and organisational contexts.

The Role of National Culture in Cybersecurity.   Hofstede's Cultural Dimensions have mainly been related to a countries' cybersecurity development (for instance, [14]; [15]; [16]), individuals' cybersecurity behaviour and privacy (for instance, [17]; [18]; [19]). Referring to the level of cybersecurity development, countries associated with low power distance, low uncertainty avoidance, high individualism, high long-term orientation and high masculinity show a high level of cybersecurity development based on the analysis of global cybersecurity index of 2015 [14].

Countries linked to short term orientation tend to pay less attention to their long-term security. Hence, they demonstrate low level of cybersecurity maturity [15]. Cybersecurity maturity is also lower in high power distance countries due to heavy reliance on the leaders to ensure security. Meanwhile, people in individualistic society lean towards keeping their online identities private.

Further, surveying over 4'650 people, consisting of Chief Information Security Officers (CISOs), Chief Security Officers, and Chief Technology Officers (CTOs) in various business regions revealed that an individual's intention to comply with security policies positively correlates with masculinity, power distance, and long-term orientation [17]. On the other hand, research investigations in Ghana and USA showed that uncertainty avoidance played a significant role in individuals' security behavioural intention relative to individualism and collectivism. That is, people from cultures with high uncertainty avoidance express high discomfort when faced with unfamiliar risks. They also have high levels of self-efficacy, and they perceive risk-mitigation costs to be lower [18]. While individuals from collectivist societies perceive response cost to avoid risks to be lower.

The Role of Organisational Culture in Cybersecurity.   Robust top management commitment, proficient IT personnel, and regular training ensure an organisation's cybersecurity readiness [20]. Including cybersecurity considerations into business strategies as well as security professionals in decision-making processes enhance cybersecurity behaviour in organisations [8]. Additionally, the involvement of leadership in security topics and processes lures employees to positively react to security measures and enhances their cognitive understanding in cybersecurity management [21]. Contrarily, [22] found no significant link between top management commitment to security and employees' security compliance.

Fostering a pro-security culture within organisations also positively influences cybersecurity behaviour [8]. Organisational culture also positively correlates with security culture and information security awareness. Individuals in organisations with a stronger security culture are likely to demonstrate more security awareness [7]. Community, a component of security, is one of the positive influences on employees' security compliance behaviour [22]. While aspects such as rule-orientation was found to not impact employees' compliance attitude.

Our literature review revealed that there is still room to apply Hofstede's cultural dimensions to the analysis of national and organizational culture in the context of human cybersecurity development. Only a few studies have applied this framework in relation to country-level cybersecurity development, particularly considering a European and an African country. Past studies have also overlooked the role of broader organisational culture—beyond security-specific initiatives—including implicit factors like norms and branding. These gaps justify our aim to explore these cultural influences and connect them to Hofstede's theory.

3   Methodology and Data Collection

To develop a theory in an under-researched area, we adopted a qualitative approach, gathering data through episodic interviews and focus groups. Additionally, we employed a cross-sectional research design, collecting data at a single point in time [23].

The episodic interview is a combination of narrative interviews and semi-structure interviews [24, p. 208]. The method enables research participants to present their experiences in a general, comparative form [25, p. 2]. Following the example of [24, p. 289], we started by asking a generative narrative question aimed at stimulating the interviewee's narrative, then listened attentively and guided the interviewee to certain scenarios where need be.

Focus group interviews refer to *"group discussion that gathers together people from similar backgrounds or experiences to discuss a specific topic of interest to the researcher"* [26]. This interviewing method is suitable for sensitive topics [27], and is therefore well-suited for our study which touches on culture. Following the method of [26], after welcoming the participants, we introduced the interviewing team, explained the purpose of the study, and how the focus group discussion will be done. Then we led with an ice breaker question – for example, *what comes to your mind when they hear of cybersecurity?* Next, we asked the questions in our interview guide without disrupting the flow of the discussion.

We chose our interview participants through purposive sampling strategy. That is, sampled cases of participants ought to be relevant to the research question [28, p. 418]. In this light, we chose participants based on their field of work and field of study in Switzerland and Cameroon.

Nine episodic interviews were conducted in Switzerland via Zoom, while six in-person episodic interviews took place in Cameroon. The participants included cybersecurity teachers, specialists, CTOs and general employees. Two focus group discussions were held in Cameroon: one with five ICT and Engineering students and another with eight students from various backgrounds, including business, nursing, and education. In Switzerland, we primarily conducted one focus group with five Business Information Systems students. A second focus group was planned but was not conducted due to time constraints and difficulty in reaching students from various fields.

To analyse our data, we applied both the In-vivo and descriptive coding methods, as elaborated by [29, p. 74]. First, we captured short phrases or words in the participants' own language to highlight their individual voices. These formed our first-level codes. Next, we summarized the data into a word or short phrase to create second-level codes, applying the descriptive coding method [29]. This approach allowed us to draw connections between these codes and make comparisons.

4   Main Findings

We present key findings from our qualitative study in Switzerland and Cameroon. A summary of the main findings is also displayed in Table 1 below.

4.1   The Role of National Culture in Human Cybersecurity Behaviour

The Perspective of Interviewees in Switzerland. Perspectives of the interviewees in Switzerland unravelled such national cultural elements geographical and personal contexts, regulatory influences, attitude to trust and privacy, and fear of the unknown.

Starting with **geographical and background contexts**, a few interviewees explained that people based in countries with strong cybersecurity development will demonstrate higher cybersecurity awareness than those in countries with a lower level of cybersecurity development. Additionally, people's upbringing, such as their attitude towards work and self-discipline, can influence how they approach cybersecurity.

Secondly, all interviewees pointed to the **influence of rules or power distance** on cybersecurity behaviour. Some stated that in certain countries, cybersecurity policies should be enforced more strictly to influence people's behaviour. The state plays a central role in such cases. In cultures with high respect for authority, people are more likely to strictly follow established guidelines and may hesitate to speak up, even when they notice something suspicious.

Furthermore, **trust** emerged as a cultural element that influences how people from certain cultures approach cybersecurity and can be exploited by hackers. One interview participant pointed out that some Swiss may easily trust others because they live in a generally safe country.

Moreover, another cultural element **concerns people's knowledge and approach to privacy**. Some interviewees mentioned that data privacy awareness positively affects cybersecurity behaviour. However, one argued that privacy concerns and the tendency to avoid sharing, such as information about experiences with cyberattacks, could hinder the development of a solid cybersecurity culture. Similarly, individuals from cultures that prioritize privacy, and restraint may overlook cyber threats originating from a more collectivist perspective.

Finally, people's **attitude towards the unknown** was mentioned by half of the total interviewees. They explained that individuals who tend to enjoy the moment or are open to taking risks may fall prey to scams. On this point regarding the unknown, one participant explained how their Swiss employees would question policies, while employees from other cultures tend to accept the same policies without resistance.

The Perspective of Interviewees in Cameroon. Our analysis showed that cultural elements influencing human cybersecurity behaviour include cultural vulnerability, religious beliefs, attitude toward sharing, resistance to change, policy and governance, and trust. In terms of cultural vulnerability, some interviewees mentioned that the lack of cybersecurity resources in local languages negatively impacts people's cybersecurity behaviour.

Regarding **religious beliefs**, some interviewees stated that some Cameroonians may believe their faith can shield them from digital harm, prompting less caution online. This belief also connects to the **attitude towards sharing**. The act of sharing links, such as Christian messages via WhatsApp, can inadvertently expose people to social engineering attacks. On another note, three interviewees explained that some communities can become more resilient against cyberattacks by sharing collective knowledge and experiences. Meanwhile, negative cybersecurity behaviour can arise when individuals prioritize personal needs over the safety of the community, potentially compromising collective security in favour of individual convenience.

Another argument was linked to Cameroon's **lack of comprehensive frameworks and policies**, which results in people not taking cybersecurity seriously in the country. This leads to cybersecurity vulnerabilities, particularly in rural areas. Finally, **trust** was also identified as a cultural element by many Cameroonian interviewees. A few interviewees mentioned that Cameroonians have a mindset of blind trust in authorities, making them more susceptible to cyberattacks.

4.2 The Role of Organisational Culture in Human Cybersecurity Behaviour

The Perspective of Interviewees in Switzerland. Some identified organisational cultural elements include communication style & transparency, authority and Hierarchy, work-related factors and training or skill development. First, some interviewees argued that open **communication and transparency** would enable employees to understand what is happening in other sectors of the company, including the organisation's stance on security. Concerning **hierarchy,** most interviewees in Switzerland highlighted that lower-level employees in highly hierarchical organisations may become overly dependent on leaders for cybersecurity-related decisions. The perspectives of such employees may also be overlooked, or they may act against their own judgement to please their superiors.

Moreover, having **clear objectives** beyond just a vision can positively influence people's cybersecurity behaviour. Clear cybersecurity objectives help establish the organisation's stance and set expectations for both employees and customers.

Lastly, in terms of **work pressure**, some interviewees noted that employees may pay less attention to security measures when under high pressure or dealing with excessive workloads. Additionally, employees in certain departments may be more likely to click on phishing links than those in other departments due to the nature of their work.

The Perspective of Interviewees in Cameroon. From this side, we saw factors like the organisational environment, policy and governance, training and awareness, company structure and vision, and work pressure. Referring to the **organisational environment**, some of our interviewed cybersecurity experts revealed that many Cameroonian companies lack a cybersecurity culture, with security-related policies either absent or not effectively implemented. Additionally, envy and jealousy among employees in the workplace can lead them to deliberately violate some of the organisation's security procedures.

Regarding **training and awareness**, most organisations do not prioritise cybersecurity education. Furthermore, proactive practices such as frequent password changes are often neglected. **Company structure and vision** were also identified as cultural factors by some interviewees. The use of a top-down approach can discourage lower-level employees from actively participating in cybersecurity matters, as they may feel that their opinions are not valued.

Lastly, some interviewees highlighted employees' **poor digital mindset** and lack of interest in cybersecurity. For instance, some staff do not fully understand the significance of web cookies and occasionally grant strangers access to their machines, increasing the risk of cybersecurity intrusions.

Table 1. Summary of Main Findings

Cultural Factors Influencing Individual Cybersecurity Behaviour from **Empirical Study**		
	National	**Organisational**
Switzerland	• Influence of geographical contexts • Influence of rules • Attitude towards trust • Attitude towards privacy • Attitude towards uncertainty	• Influence of communication • Influence of hierarchy • Influence of clear objective • Influence of work pressure
Cameroon	• People's religious beliefs • Attitude towards sharing • Lack of cybersecurity frameworks	• Influence of work environment • Influence of security training • Influence of company vision • Poor digital mindset

5 Discussion and Implications

When linking perspectives from Cameroon and Switzerland on the influence of national culture, several common elements emerged, including state regulatory influences, attitudes toward trust and sharing, and fear of the unknown. Both sides emphasised the pivotal role of the government in shaping people's cybersecurity behaviour, particularly in high power distance cultures. The presence of cybersecurity policies and their stringent enforcement can drive positive cybersecurity practices.

The identified factor of trust aligns with the study by [30], which concluded that people's trust is often rooted in their cultural backgrounds and can lead to risky cybersecurity behaviour. Additionally, sharing experiences of cyberattacks fosters a stronger cybersecurity culture, but individuals must remain cautious of blind trust.

The relationship between collectivism and cybersecurity behaviour contradicts the findings of [15], who argued that high individualism is positively related to a country's cybersecurity maturity. However, a few interviewees in Switzerland also supported this perspective.

Lastly, fear of the unknown or uncertainty avoidance was a common theme among interviewees from both countries. However, its impact on cybersecurity behaviour depends on how individuals respond. When people question new rules due to their unfamiliarity, they are less likely to fall victim to cyberattacks. Conversely, when individuals entirely avoid new rules or technologies—including cybersecurity measures—due to unfamiliarity, they may increase their exposure to cyber threats.

Turning to organisational cultural elements, key points highlighted by both interview groups included authority and hierarchy, training, objectives, and vision. Like the findings of [15], strong hierarchical structures within organisations can negatively impact employees' cybersecurity behaviour, leading to over-reliance on leaders for decision-making.

In line with [20], our findings suggest that regular cybersecurity training positively influences cybersecurity behaviour. Conversely, the absence of such training leaves employees unable to recognise cyber threats, making them more vulnerable to attacks.

Lastly, having a clear vision and cybersecurity objectives, particularly in highly hierarchical companies, plays a crucial role in steering employees toward positive cybersecurity behaviour. When cybersecurity goals are well-defined, employees are more likely to understand their role in maintaining security within the organisation.

6 Conclusion and Outlook

By synthesising perspectives from Switzerland and Cameroon, this study has highlighted cultural elements that influence human cybersecurity behaviour, considering both national and organisational culture. Additionally, we have successfully linked cybersecurity behaviour to Hofstede's cultural dimensions, an aspect that has been largely overlooked in previous studies.

Still, our study has some limitations. First, the findings are based solely on qualitative interviews, which, while insightful, are inherently subjective and may introduce bias. Second, our interviewees were primarily drawn from specific regions, namely the German-speaking part of Switzerland and the English-speaking region of Cameroon, limiting broader generalisability.

For future research, we recommend exploring the same topic using a quantitative approach to validate our findings on a larger scale. Further studies could also focus on implicit organisational cultural elements that influence cybersecurity behaviour. Additionally, conducting quantitative surveys with participants from diverse regions across Cameroon and Switzerland would provide a more comprehensive perspective on the cultural factors affecting cybersecurity practices.

Acknowledgements. This study was carried out as part of a project funded by the Leading House (LH) Africa Consolidation Grant 2023.

References

1. SentinelOne, Cybersecurity's Defining Moments: 7 lessons from History's OST Infamous Breaches (2024). https://www.sentinelone.com/blog/cybersecuritys-defining-moments-7-lessons-from-historys-most-infamous-breaches/. Accessed 26 May 2024
2. Hancock, J.: Psychology of Human ErrorUnderstand the mistakes that compromise your company's cybersecurity. Tessian Research (2020)
3. Hadlington, L.: Human factors in cybersecurity; examining the link between Internet addiction, impulsivity, attitudes towards cybersecurity, and risky cybersecurity behaviours. Heliyon 3 (2017)
4. Chowdhury, N.H., Adam, M.T., Teubner, T.: Time pressure in human cybersecurity behaviour: Theoretical framework and countermeasures. Comput. Sceur. (2020)

5. Delanoy, W.: What is culture?. In: The cambridge handbook of intercultural communication. cambridge handbooks in language and linguistics, pp. 17–34. cambridge university press (2020). https://doi.org/10.1007/978-3-030-57446-8_2

6. Chatman, J.A., Cha, S.E.: Leading by leveraging culture. Calif. Rev. Manag. **XLV**(4) (2003)

7. Wiley, A., McCormac, A., Calic, D.: More than the individual: examining the relationship between culture and information security awareness. Comput. Secur. **88** (2020)

8. Yeoh, W., Wang, S.C., Popovi, A., Chowdhury, N.H.: A systematic synthesis of critical success factors for cybersecurity. Comput. Secur. (2022)

9. Hall, E.T.: Beyong Culture. Knopf Doubleday Publishing Group, New York (1976)

10. Barczyk, C., Rarick, C., Winter, G.: An exploratory study of the cultural values of cameroon's young, elite, urban population: implications for management and international business. J. Bus. Divers., 11–25 (2021)

11. Djamen, R., Georges, L., Jean-Louis, P.: Understanding the cultural values at the individual level in Central Africa: a test of the CVSCALE in Cameroon. In: International Conference on Advanced Marketing, 2017. The Culture Factor, Country Comparison Tool (2024). https://www.hofstede-insights.com/country-comparison-tool?countries=switzerland. Accessed 18 June 2024

12. The Culture Factor, Country Comparison Tool (2024). https://www.theculturefactor.com/country-comparison-tool?countries=switzerland. Accessed 18 June 2024

13. Hofstede, G., Hofstede, G.J., Minkov, M.: Cultures and Organisations: Software of the Mind. The McGraw Hill Companies (2010)

14. Onumo, A., Cullen, A., Ullah-Awan, I.: An empirical study of cultural dimensions and cybersecurity development. In: IEEE 5th International Conference on Future Internet of Things and Cloud (2017)

15. Jeong, J.J., Chamikara, M., Grobler, M., Rudolph, C.: Fuzzy logic application to link national culture and cybersecurity maturity. In: 2019 IEEE 5th International Conference on Collaboration and Internet Computing (CIC) (2019)

16. Creese, S., Dutton, W.H., Esteve-González, P.: The social and cultural shaping of cybersecurity capacity building: a comparative study of nations and regions. Pers. Ubiquit. Comput., 941–955 (2021)

17. Crespos-Pérez, G.: Factors that influence the cybersecurity behaviour: a cross-cultural study. Universidad Ana G Méndez-Gurabo, Gurabo, Puerto Rico (2021)

18. Crossler, R.E., Andoh-Baidoo, F.K., Menard, P.: Espoused cultural values as antecedents of individuals' threat and coping appraisal toward protective information technologies: study of U.S. and Ghana. Inf. Manag., 754–766 (2019)

19. Halevi, T., et al.: Cultural and psychological factors in cyber-security. In: Proceedings of the 18th International Conference on Information Integration and Web-based Application and Services (2016)

20. Hasan, S., Ali, M., Kurnia, S., Thurasamy, R.: Evaluating the cyber security readiness of organizations and its influence on performance. J. Inf. Secur. Appl. **LVIII** (2021)

21. Onumo, A., Ullah-Awan, I., Cullen, A.: Assessing the moderating effect of security technologies on employees compliance with cybersecurity control procedures. ACM Trans. Manag. Inf. Syst. **12**(2), 1–29 (2021)

22. Solomon, G., Brown, I.: The influence of organisational culture and information security culture on employee compliance behaviour. J. Enterp. Inf. Manag. (2020)

23. Bell, E., Bryman, A., Harley, B.: Business Research Methods. Oxford University Press, Oxford (2022)

24. Flick, U.: An Introduction to Qualitative Research, 6th ed. Sage Publications (2018)

25. Mueller, R.A.: Episodic narrative interview: capturing stories of experience with a methods fusion. Int. J. Qual. Methods, 1–11 (2019)

26. Dawson, S., Manderson, L., Tallo, V.L.: A manual for the use of focus groups. a boston: international nutrition foundation for developing countries (INFDC). In: A manual for the use of focus groups/Susan Dawson and Lenore Manderson and Veronica L. Tallo. (1993)
27. Barbour, R.: Introducing focus groups. In: Doing Focus Groups, pp. 1–14. SAGE Publications Ltd (2018)
28. Bryman, A.: Social Research Methods, 4th edn. Oxford University Press, New York (2012)
29. Miles, M., Huberman, A.M., Saldana, J.S.: Qualitative Data Analysis: A Methods Sourcebook, 3rd edn. Sage Publications Inc., London (2014)
30. Alhasan, I.: Human factors in cybersecurity: a cross-cultural study on trust. doctoral dissertation. Purdue University Graduate School (2023)

Inclusive Education for All: Online Instructional Course Design Guidelines for Curriculum Transformation

Sunet Eybers[✉][iD], Jan H. Kroeze[iD], and Corné J. van Staden[iD]

University of South Africa, Johannesburg, South Africa
`eeyberss@unisa.ac.za`

Abstract. Quality education is one of the United Nations' 17 Sustainable Development Goals (https://sdgs.un.org/goals), vital for South Africa as a Global South nation. It strives to "ensure inclusive and equitable quality education and promote lifelong learning opportunities for all" (https://sdgs.un.org/goals/goal4). In a developing country, such as South Africa, higher education institutions that offer opportunities to study online using an open distance e-learning model provide many learners the chance to work while studying. This study explores how online courses can create an environment of educational inclusivity, considering local, indigenous examples through Africanization as part of curriculum transformation. This study is based on data gathered and analyzed in 2021 as part of another study when interviews were conducted with academic staff members to obtain their perceptions of the Africanization attempt. Thematic analysis was used to identify recurring themes. Using these themes as a starting point, a single case study was described, using the ADDIE model as the primary theoretical lens to propose guidelines for online instructional designers to foster curriculum transformation through localization, promoting inclusive online education. The guidelines contribute instructional design guidelines from an African perspective towards promoting inclusive, sustainable, high-quality education for learners.

Keywords: inclusive education · curriculum transformation · instructional course design principle · ADDIE · ODeL · Africanization · human-computer interaction · business analysis · formative assessment · sustainability

1 Introduction

Quality education is one of the United Nations' 17 Sustainable Development Goals [6], vital for South Africa as a Global South nation. It strives to "ensure inclusive and equitable quality education and promote lifelong learning opportunities for all" [8, 30]. Inclusive education is an environment where all learners can access quality education equally. Unfortunately, in a developing country such as South Africa, where most of the population earns a median income of ZAR 95,770.00 per annum [27], access to inclusive and equitable quality education, notably higher education, is often challenging. As a result, many prospective learners opt for open distance e-learning (ODeL) courses,

© The Author(s), under exclusive license to Springer Nature Switzerland AG 2026
F. Corradini et al. (Eds.): Society 5.0 2025, CCIS 2787, pp. 98–111, 2026.
https://doi.org/10.1007/978-3-032-15463-7_9

where a "study whilst you work" model is adopted, over more expensive, full-time residential higher education institutions (HEIs). Furthermore, the record 2024 matric pass rate of 87.3% [13], of which 47.8% qualified for Bachelor studies [24], sparked an unprecedented demand for learner registrations at residential HEIs. Given the limited availability of seats at these institutions, many learners fail to get admission, making ODeL institutions a viable alternative.

Whilst residential HEIs adopted an online learning approach during the COVID-19 pandemic, most HEIs have returned to face-to-face classes. However, in ODeL institutions, the need to deliver quality online content via Learning Management Systems (LMS) remains a high priority. Although many instructional design models assist with course design and development, for example, Analysis, Design, Development, Implementation, and Evaluation (ADDIE) [4], Successive Approximation Model (SAM) [2], and the Dick and Carey Model [9], it is uncertain how these instructional design models facilitate curriculum transformation.

Despite the requirement for new-generation learners to master academic content, they should also acquire the necessary "cognitive and social skills that enable them to deal with the complex problems of our age" [23]. Computer Science and Informatics-related subjects face even more challenges. These include the pressure to keep up with rapidly changing concepts and technologies and the need for curriculum transformation. Curriculum transformation is a strategic goal of many South African HEIs to address previous inequalities and work towards socio-economically relevant education. With Computer Science- and Informatics-related subjects, prescribed work is often presented from a Western society background, increasing the need to present content in a more localized or Africanized context, referred to as Africanization.

To create an environment of educational inclusivity, the paper explores online instructional design guidelines for curriculum transformation based on a dataset from a previous study that attempted to instill Africanization in two undergraduate models. This follow-up study uses the ADDIE model as the primary theoretical lens. It aims to compile a list of guidelines for online instructional designers to foster curriculum transformation through Africanization, promoting inclusive online education.

The paper's outline is as follows: A literature review section focuses on inclusive education, Africanization, curriculum transformation, and instructional course design, including the ADDIE model adopted for this study. The research approach and methodology section describes the adopted case study approach, followed by the data analysis. The case study section contextualizes the environment and presents the study's findings, after which the paper concludes.

2 Inclusive Education, Africanization, and Curriculum Transformation

As the introduction mentions, inclusive education is an environment that allows all learners equal access to learning opportunities. It promotes a feeling of acceptance and aids learning through the development of social and critical thinking skills.

One approach to promote inclusivity and a sense of acceptance and belonging is Africanization. This is achieved by revising traditional Western-led science by infusing constructs from African cultures and knowledge systems. Regarding curriculum transformation, Mendy and Madiope [17] define Africanization as "a renewed focus on using the curriculum to transform Africa". According to Eybers [10], "it is essential to develop curricula which enable methods that bring into lecture halls the histories, cultures, traditions, challenges and aspirations of Africans."

Africanization can be regarded as a specific form of decolonization often used in curriculum transformation. However, according to Sadiki and Steyn [25], decolonization and transformation are not mere synonyms. While transformation "is responsive to the social context and prioritises previously marginalized narratives, voices and knowledge systems", decolonization in the African context aims to integrate African ways of knowing into the mainstream epistemological approaches used in a specific discipline. African cultural traditions must take a central place in the curriculum.

According to Maringe [16], transformation is also interchangeably used with 'change' and 'reform'. When a curriculum is transformed, it entails taking cognizance of social context, and prioritizing marginalized narratives, knowledge systems, and learner voices. In this study, the Human-Computer Interaction (HCI) and Business Analysis (BA) modules have been transformed to acknowledge social context, and learners were sensitized towards Africanization. Maringe [16] also claims that indigenization, decolonization, and Africanization are used interchangeably as well. However, Africanization relates to culture and identity. As Louw [15] indicated, Africanization is not about excluding Europeans and their cultures but about affirming the African culture and its identity. This is an imperative approach to fostering curriculum transformation and creating inclusive education for all.

Mendy and Madiope [17] used psychosocial theory and psychosocial identity development theory to guide the development of their framework of curriculum transformation in ODeL HEIs in Africa. However, it should be noted that Africanization does not imply that current Western systems are swapped out for traditional African ideas. Samuel [26] warns against inbreeding in syllabi that do not consider that modern Africans have developed broader horizons than the traditional, local knowledge systems.

Mheta, Lungu, and Govender [20] provide a valuable list of aspects that should be considered while embarking on the Africanization of a syllabus. The list includes the nature of decolonization and its necessity; the content of the taught material and how it is presented; finding a balance between the localization process and international standards and requirements; the role of Indigenous languages; and the specific institution's role and identity.

2.1 Instructional Course Design

Instructional course design is an organized process adopted when creating course content to enhance learner performance through improved learning [3]. A well-designed course considers unique learner characteristics and needs, contains clear academic objectives, and includes appropriate strategies and resources [32]. Instructional course design models assist developers in developing well-designed courses through their guidance of the course design process by specifying a clear purpose of the intended course outcomes [21]. Other benefits of instructional course design models include uniformity of institutional course design since they can be reused to increase collaboration between developers, designers, stakeholders, and subject matter experts, and to increase learner engagement since they guide developers to follow a structured approach to adopt engaging methods catering to the needs of learners [21].

Many instructional course design models exist, for example, the ADDIE model (which refers to Analysis, Design, Development, Implementation, and Evaluation) [4]; Successive Approximation Model (SAM) [1, 2]; Merrill's Principles of Instruction (MPI) [19]; Task-Centered Learning [18]; Rapid Instructional Design (RID) model [5]; Gagne's Nine Events of Instruction [12]; and the Dick and Carey Model [9]. The appropriate instructional course design model selection largely depends on the institutional environment, the content and level of the module under development, and the learner profile.

The ADDIE model [4] was selected after the data was collected to provide a lens for analyzing it due to its popularity, high citation rate, adaptability, flexibility in various environments, and suitability for course design in e-learning environments, specifically in the HCI and BI modules. The model covered the analysis of the entire course design and development process.

The ADDIE model was introduced in 1975 by the Center for Educational Technology at Florida State University for the US Army [4]. It consists of five phases, namely:

- Analysis: What are learners' characteristics and background, what subject will be taught, and in which environment will the subject be taught?
- Design: A plan focusing on learning objectives, content, activities, and assessments.
- Development: Creating instructional material, including supplementary content.
- Implementation: Delivering/making material available to learners.
- Evaluation: Effectiveness of instruction, identification, and implementation of improvements.

3   Research Approach and Methodology

The research adopted a single exploratory case study approach, suitable for studying and reporting phenomena in their real-world context. In this instance, the goal is to identify online instructional design guidelines for curriculum transformation after attempting to instill Africanization in two undergraduate models, namely HCI and BA, during a study conducted in 2021. Secondary documentation, such as institutional documentation relevant to the curriculum, was consulted. Thematic analysis of data from the previous study, where semi-structured interviews were conducted with academic staff, was used. In that study, purposive sampling was applied due to the eligibility criteria for the study, namely, their academic involvement in at least one of the two modules. Although 12 participants were identified and approached, only five agreed to participate in the online MS team interviews. Interviews were recorded and consisted of 20 predefined questions, which consisted of 3 main themes, namely:

1) Feedback and support of academic staff.
2) Syllabus and practical examples included in the academic content.
3) Formative module assessments set at the applicable level of the National Qualifications Framework (NQF) for the various modules (HCI on NQF-level 7 and BA on NQF-level 6), using one scenario and two case study assignments with essay-type

questions in each module, tools, and feedback to learners, all pitched at the appropriate cognitive level according to Bloom's taxonomy. The African cases used for the formative assessments, with the assignment questions and selected model answers, are available at: https://doi.org/10.6084/m9.figshare.28917614.v1.

The original objective of the interviews was to explore academics' perceptions about using Africanization in the context of teaching and learning in HCI and BA undergraduate modules. However, the in-depth feedback that was received could be harnessed in this study to explore and identify online instructional design guidelines for curriculum transformation. According to Creswell and Creswell [7], particularity, rather than generalizability, is the defining feature of qualitative research. Themes are developed in the context of a specific case leading to a nuanced understanding of the situation. A detailed description of the research process and its interview protocols, however, to ensure the confirmability and trustworthiness of the results [22].

4 Data Analysis

During the study conducted in 2021, on which this research is based, an independent qualitative research statistician conducted a thematic analysis. As prescribed by Clarke and Braun [6], the coding process enabled thematic analysis of the unstructured transcribed interview data. An inductive process was followed using ATLAS.ti v23. In addition to identifying themes during the inductive process, additional open codes were assigned where necessary to match similar feedback from participants. Once the coding process was complete, the research statistician grouped together codes with similar meanings after considering general research objectives. As mentioned previously, the perceptions of academic staff were evaluated, and information about implementing the Africanization attempt in the two modules was provided. The analyzed dataset was reused in this study.

5 Case Study

The higher education institute (HEI) where the study was conducted was one of its kind in Africa, with hundreds of thousands of learners from many countries worldwide enrolled for qualifications ranging from certificates to higher degrees. Academic offerings from nine colleges were available through an ODeL model, enabling learners to study online. At the time of the data-gathering phase, which was performed in 2021, the two modules under investigation resided in a Computing department housed in the institute's science faculty. The undergraduate HCI module was offered as a third-year NQF-level 7 module as part of the BSc Computer Science, BSc Informatics, and BCom Informatics qualifications. The module on BA was provided as a second-year NQF-level 6 module in the Diploma in Information Technology. At the institution, all exit level modules are annually quality assured using the inputs of external moderators.

The results of the original study were reported in Eybers et al. [11], reporting on the perceptions of the academic staff involved. (Also compare Kroeze et al. [14] and Van Staden et al. [31] for related work, which report on feedback gathered from the students in the same study.) Two African case studies were used to demonstrate the relevance and applicability of important theoretical constructs in an undergraduate Business Analysis and a Human-Computer Interaction course. The findings suggested that "the Africanization of content, using local and Afrocentric examples, can assist learners in acquiring relevant knowledge and skills and be useful in cross-cultural teaching and learning, as learners can relate the theory to their local context. However, the concept should be presented to learners before introducing new academic content." [11] The richness of the in-depth data obtained enabled an additional study, reusing the same data set in this study to retrospectively consider the analyzed data by using ADDIE as a theoretical lens to identify instructional design guidelines, therefore expanding on previous work.

5.1 ADDIE Analysis Phase

The first phase of ADDIE refers to the analysis phase. One way to reform the curriculum is to consider indigenous learners' backgrounds to promote cultural inclusivity. The ODeL institution provided an online platform delivering synchronized and asynchronous learning. The two modules under investigation, HCI on NQF-level 7 and BA on NQF-level 6, attracted diverse learners. Although learner demographic statistics are not available for 2020 when the data was gathered, in 2025, students who study at the institution from 110 countries outside South Africa were primarily based in the Southern African Development Community (SADC), which includes Angola, Botswana, Comoros, Democratic Republic of the Congo, Eswatini, and other African countries [29]. Registering for the two modules had no prerequisites, with university entrance being the only requirement.

As part of the seven themes identified during the data analysis phase, technological issues were identified as a very strong sub-theme as part of the overall theme of the "issues in the application of Africanization to context" theme (some of the sub-codes of this theme were grouped together as part of the implementation phase). Technological issues refer to challenges experienced by learners in accessing technological platforms as prescribed by the assignment instructions. Learners were unfamiliar with the prescribed platform and experienced internet access, availability issues, and "load shedding" (i.e., regular, scheduled power cuts). As interview participants mentioned:

> *"In rural areas also, technology should be available to all the people for example, most of [the] people are using [the] WhatsApp and only [a] few people know [the] Telegram and WeChat."*

> *"Some learners had internet data problems and access to devices was constricted during load shedding, but there were no learners who outright could not complete the module."*

It was, therefore, imperative to consider the residential environment of learners during the analysis phase.

5.2 ADDIE Design Phase

The second phase of ADDIE refers to the design phase, which involves planning the curricula and course delivery while considering the learning objectives. One central aspect of this study was the focus on using Africanization to foster learners' understanding of theoretical constructs, mainly through an essay-type assessment. One central theme that emerged from the interviews with the academic members was the relevance and interpretation of practical examples in the case scenarios presented to learners. The following sub-themes emerged, which created the foundation of valuable lessons for the design of online courses fostering inclusivity:

Suitability of Eurocentric examples: When assessments are planned, cognizance should be taken that practical examples in textbooks are often Eurocentric rather than speaking to an Africanization context. Therefore, the learners involved in this project often found applying theory in a local context challenging.

Africanization case application: The academic team agreed that using Africanization case studies based on locally relevant examples helped learners understand and apply the concept of Africanization with real-life examples due to their familiarity with their surroundings and upbringing within the African context:

"Yes, practical application works very well for learners to understand the assignments. It gives more information to learners."

Augmenting the current study material with African constructs rather than replacing completely: The interview participants indicated that curriculum material and course structure should be augmented, rather than replaced, to add more African examples, as the concept was still in its infant phase, which made it challenging to apply it to universal examples. Using practical local examples assisted learners in grasping concepts from a practical viewpoint they could relate to and recall.

Local examples are more practical: It was felt that learners tended to understand and apply the theoretical aspects related to the theory more easily when local business cases related to Africa with which they were familiar were presented. Using case studies and essay-type questions was a good way to engage learners with the theory of the coursework and apply it to real-life situations. However, some learners expressed frustration with Africanization and wanted to focus on completing the assignments quickly. The African context was believed to make it easier for learners to apply the concepts to design applications:

"Whilst the contextualization ... I thought it would excite learners or feel ownership; that we are doing this thing for ourself, for ourselves. I think that was the essence of contextualizing the case study within the African context."

More concerned with passing: The academic team felt that learners were mainly focused on passing the subjects and not necessarily focused on grasping the theory and practical applications in the cases presented. A good example was frequent questions about the assignment structure and length restriction. Perhaps one solution would be to find methods during the design phase of the module to contextualize content in the bigger context of successful module completion.

Preparation with practical African examples: The academic team indicated that using local and Afrocentric examples seemed more effective as learners grasped the theoretical aspects surrounding the concept of Africanization and the relevant theories associated with the task, such as the HCI aspects of the assignment. It seems learners were more satisfied with understanding and applying local Afrocentric examples than following the textbook's Eurocentric approach to practical examples. Additionally, it was mentioned that the teaching team sent additional reading material to learners to better grasp the theoretical component through academic papers that also apply African-centered examples. More relevant African case studies could make it easier for learners to understand and engage with the course content, as it aligns with their familiar cultural context.

5.3 ADDIE Development Phase

The third phase refers to the <u>development phase</u>. The learning objectives of the two modules were as follows: The HCI module aimed to enable students to apply their theoretical knowledge to evaluate existing interactive system and prototypes using a variety of evaluation techniques. The purpose of the BA module was to empower students to grasp business processes from the client's perspective; analyze a business from a financial and business process perspective; and propose a business solution. During the development phase, the objective was to create instructional material to meet the learning objectives. African case studies were developed and used to explain theoretical concepts as part of this objective. Additional reading was provided as part of the learner study material. Learners were expected to complete a practical assessment after considering the material. Three central themes were identified during the ADDIE design phase: "assessment and application of theory"; "preparation of material and assessment processes"; and "application of Bloom's taxonomy".

As part of the assessment and application of the theory theme, five sub-themes were identified:

<u>Difficulty in theory application</u>: Interview participants indicated that learners experienced issues when answering assignment questions, particularly when applying theoretical aspects to Africanized case studies, was required. Although the academic team sensed that learners understood the theory, they didn't understand the context in which it should be applied. Overall, the learners had a mixed understanding of the theory and struggled to apply it to practical examples. One suggested solution to this challenge is that the concept of Africanization and the theoretical constructs of the modules should be split into smaller sections and introduced systematically, on separate occasions, to learners.

<u>Good foundational grasp</u>: The academic team felt that the model examples and memorandum provided to learners after the assignment were sufficient and contributed to their understanding of the theoretical constructs. It was indicated that the assignment instructions could have been more explicit. Pre-assignment reading could have prepared learners in the HCI module to understand the context of Africanization and theoretical constructs in the discipline.

> *"… yes, the model answers and memos were sufficient, although I might say that additional, for example, additional theory or articles would have been of benefit in preparation."*

<u>Regurgitation of textbook material</u>: Many learners merely repeated material in the prescribed textbook. Interview participants felt that learners used this assignment as a

"memory testing" exercise rather than an actual application of the theoretical material to the presented cases. This refers to the issue of learners having trouble implementing them in the context of a case's instruction. One proposed solution might be to prepare learners for the upcoming assessments by providing mock assessment opportunities.

Sufficient understanding and application of theory: The academic team indicated that some learners grasped the theory and related concepts, answered the questions, and completed the expected assignment tasks. Various teaching team members mentioned that the learners understood what was expected of them and applied this sufficiently. Learners felt that they gained much information from theory and e-tutoring sessions, which helped them understand concepts. The assignment questions became more demanding but also nurtured critical thinking skills. There was a significant improvement in the assignments, as learners showed they had grasped the concept.

The preparation of material and the assessment process's theme focused on presenting academic material to teach theoretical concepts to learners by fostering understanding. Learners should be equipped with knowledge and skills that can be implemented in real-life scenarios, which is a requirement for both NQF-levels 6 and 7. Five sub-themes were identified and are discussed in the following paragraphs.

Instructional design: Respondents felt that the instructional design of both courses should have catered to the dichotomy of attending to two tasks in one assignment without confusing learners. This referred to the instruction to compile a report, a foreign concept to learners, whilst considering the Africanization case study. This was one of the aspects the academic team noticed and subsequently recommended that the teaching team pay more attention to it. It was also suggested that clear instructions should be part of the course design, focusing on implementing the concept of Africanization and HCI:

> "… is to actually go and be very clear on what's expected in assignments and not create that duality of a report and a theory assignment."

Lack of focus on theoretical implementation: Respondents indicated that learners were so focused on applying the Africanization concept that they lost track of applying theory within the assignment context. They thought an overemphasis on Africanization threw learners off the idea of HCI in completing tasks. One solution might be to introduce concepts individually and systematically before combining them into one assignment.

Lack of time and word count: Like the previous theme, respondents indicated that learners were focused on the word count restriction of the assignment and the unique report structure rather than the implementation of the theory of HCI and how the concept of Africanization is implemented in a particular case.

Learning components dealing with metaphors: HCI learners constantly struggled to apply metaphors in one of their assignments regarding the concept of Africanization. The respondents felt that there was a lack of understanding about the idea of metaphors in the context of the question.

Sharing of assignment answers among learners: Respondents indicated a tendency for learners to share assignment answers. The academic staff noticed that some learners worked in groups to complete their assignments. This became problematic as they shared their assignment answers, presenting similar results on assignments. Although the issue was not blatant plagiarism, but similar answers, it warranted the question of academic staff if the learners even immersed themselves in the study material to learn something from the process by applying assignment tasks. Perhaps one solution would be to allow learners to work in groups, enabling peer learning.

The third and final theme of the ADDIE development phase was the application of Bloom's taxonomy. Using Bloom's taxonomy in course design is critical, given the NQF-levels of the two modules [28]. The following sub-themes were identified:

Application and evaluation component, knowledge component and NQF-standard: Bloom's taxonomy is a model that classifies the complexity levels of learning objectives. The model comprises six levels: remember, understand, apply, analyze, evaluate, and create. Depending on the NQF-level of the qualification, learning objectives should focus on higher levels of the model. Typically, the two modules under investigation required students to acquire knowledge and display their understanding in solving problems, apply concepts to real-life situations, or demonstrate practical skills in new contexts. The African case study was used as an example to teach higher-order thinking skills. The assignment questions focused more on learning activities involving application, analysis, evaluation, and synthesis, rather than merely remembering, repeating and understanding "facts". As a result, learners were prompted to apply their knowledge and reasoned judgment, focusing on how technology should be modified to fit African culture. The course encouraged critical thinking about cultural acceptance and how technology should be adapted to African culture. Including practical, application-type questions and scenarios is imperative to online instructional design.

5.4 ADDIE Implementation Phase

The implementation phase of ADDIE refers to delivering and implementing learning material to learners. During the implementation phase, learners had many inquiries about the Africanization tasks during the two assignments, including the main theme identified during data analysis. Sub-themes included:

Additional reading on Africanization where learners and academic staff members asked for further material to upskill themselves on the topic.

The assignment structure and format were queried by many students, as writing a report as part of the assignment was a foreign assessment type to many.

Many learners requested copies of previous assignments, which can be used as examples when completing their tasks.

As proposed above, it is suggested that instructional course designers include additional reading of foreign concepts into their curriculum development to prepare learners for assessment opportunities and unique assignment structures. It can also be beneficial to provide learners with examples of assignments.

5.5 ADDIE Evaluation Phase

The last phase of ADDIE is the evaluation phase, which refers to the effectiveness of instructions and identifying and implementing improvements. One central theme emerged, focusing on the learner and academic staff support during assessments. Although tutors facilitated smaller learner groups, the academic team felt they required additional reading and further support from the lecturers. Online instructional designers should consider mechanisms for ongoing educational support, such as academic and student discussion forums.

Table 1 provides a summary of the online instructional course design guidelines.

Table 1. Summary of online instructional course design guidelines.

ADDIE Phase	Theme and sub-themes	Online instructional course design guidelines
Analysis	<u>Issues in the application of Africanization to context</u> ○ Technological issues	○ Access to internet ○ Availability of electricity ○ Technology platforms providing knowledge and skills
Design	<u>Relevance and interpretation of practical examples</u> ○ Eurocentric examples not fitting ○ Africanization case application ○ Augment material with African constructs rather than replacing existing material ○ Local examples were more effective ○ More concerned with passing ○ Preparation with practical African examples	○ Customize case studies ○ Use locally relevant examples ○ Augment existing curriculum material in support of the Africanization concept ○ Contextualize content in the bigger context of successful module completion ○ Include case studies and long questions applicable to real-life scenarios ○ Include additional reading on the concept of Africanization
Development	<u>Assessment and application of theory</u> ○ Difficulty with application of theory ○ Good foundational grasp ○ Regurgitation of textbook material ○ Sufficient understanding and application of theory <u>Preparation of material and assessment processes</u> ○ Instructional design ○ Lack of focus on theoretical implementation ○ Lack of time and word count ○ Components regarding metaphors ○ Sharing assignment answers among learners <u>Application of Bloom's taxonomy</u> ○ Application and evaluation component ○ Knowledge component ○ NQF-standard	○ Break new concepts into manageable pieces ○ Introduce new concepts to learners systematically (for example, unique report structures, the concept of Africanization, and metaphors) ○ Include additional reading of foreign concepts ○ Include extensive model answers to assignments ○ Prepare learners for assessment opportunities and unique assignment structures ○ Incorporate online sessions ○ Include clear instructions ○ Allow learners to work in groups to foster peer learning ○ Include questions and practical scenarios focused on various levels of Bloom's taxonomy according to applicable NQF-level
Implementation	<u>Learner inquiries around Africanization tasks</u> ○ Additional readings on Africanization ○ Assignment structure ○ Format of the assignment ○ Request for past material	○ Include additional reading of foreign concepts (per the development phase) ○ Prepare learners for assessment opportunities and unique assignment structures (per the development phase) ○ Provide learners with examples of assignments
Evaluation	<u>Learner support process during assessment</u> ○ Additional readings provided ○ Lack of preparedness ○ Teaching team support	○ Implement academic support (for example, discussion forums) for learners and academic staff

6 Conclusion

A case study approach was followed to report on thematically analyzed data from a previous study exploring academics' perceptions of Africanization attempts. Here, the themes identified in that study were further analyzed using ADDIE as the primary theoretical lens to identify instructional design guidelines. The study proposes many instructional design guidelines to be considered when embarking on an intervention such as Africanization and fostering inclusive, sustainable, quality education. Most of the design guidelines focus on the design and development phase. The five-course design guidelines that transpired from the empirical study can be summarized as follows:

- Learners should have the digital infrastructure and repositories for their Computing modules.
- Localized case studies, amended by additional reading on the concept of Africanization, may be used to contextualize the theoretical content of Computing courses.
- Formative assessments should include questions covering all Bloom's taxonomy levels to foster higher-order thinking skills.
- Detailed model answers should be provided to students after grading their assignments to self-remediate weak areas in their work.
- Learners should be supported with additional study material (such as similar assignment questions and answers) and online seminars to prepare them to successfully do their formative assignments and write a final summative examination.

Further research efforts should use the design guidelines in online module development to test and refine this paper's recommendations.

References

1. Allen, M.: Leaving ADDIE for SAM: An Agile Model for Developing the Best Learning Experiences. ASTD Press, Alexandria (2012)
2. Allen, M.: The successive approximation model (SAM). In: Reiser, R.A., Carr-Chellman, A.A., Dempsey, J.V., Trends and Issues in Instructional Design and Technology, 5th ed., p.15. Routledge, New York, NY (2024). https://doi.org/10.4324/9781003502302
3. Branch, R., Merrill, M.D.: Characteristics of instructional design models. In: Reiser, R.A., Dempsey, J.V. (eds.) Trends and issues in instructional design and technology, 3rd ed., pp. 8–17 Merrill Prentice Hall, New York, NJ (2011)
4. Branson, R.K., Rayner, G.T., Cox, J.L., Furman, J.P., King, F.J., Hannum, W.H.: Interservice procedures for instructional systems development: technical level workshop, 185 pp. Defense Technical Information Center (1975). https://apps.dtic.mil/sti/pdfs/ADA019486.pdf. Accessed 05 May 2025
5. Burke, W.E.: Rapid Instructional Design: Learning ID Fast and Right. Jossey-Bass/Pfeiffer, San Francisco (1999)
6. Clarke, V., Braun, V.: Thematic analysis. J. Posit. Psychol. **12**(3), 297–298 (2017). https://doi.org/10.1080/17439760.2016.1262613
7. Creswell, J.W., Creswell, J.D.: Research Design: Qualitative, Quantitative and Mixed Methods Approaches. SAGE, London (2022)
8. Department of Economic and Social Affairs, Sustainable Development: United Nations: Sustainable Development Goals (SDG): Goal 4. United Nations Department of Global Communications. https://sdgs.un.org/goals/goal4. Accessed 05 May 2025

9. Dick, W., Carey, L.: The Systematic Design of Instruction, 4th edn. Harper Collins, New York (1996)
10. Eybers, O.: A social realist ontology for developing Afrocentric curricula in Africa. J. Decolonising Disciplines **1**(1), 47–63 (2019). https://doi.org/10.35293/2664-3405/2019/v1n1a4
11. Eybers, S., Kroeze, J.H., Van Staden, C.J.: Enhancing cross-cultural teaching and learning: An instructor's view of Africanization. In: Hinkelmann, K., Smuts, H. (eds.) Society 5.0 2024. Communications in Computer and Information Science, vol. 2173, pp. 98–110. Springer, Cham. https://doi.org/10.1007/978-3-031-71412-2_8
12. Gagne, R.M., Briggs, L.J., Wager, W.W.: Principles of Instructional Design. Harcourt Brace Jovanovich College Publishers, Forth Worth (1992)
13. Government Communications: Government congratulates the matric class of 2024. https://www.gcis.gov.za/newsroom/media-releases/government-congratulates-matric-class-2024. Accessed 03 Feb 2025
14. Kroeze, J.H., Van Staden, C. J., Eybers, S.: Die afrikanisering van voorgraadse kursusse in Mens-rekenaar-interaksie (MRI) en Besigheidsontleding (BO):'n Kwantitatiewe studie oor studente se ervaring [The Africanisation of undergraduate courses in Human-Computer Interaction (HCI) and Business Analysis (BA): A quantitative study of students' experience, English translation available on ResearchGate]. LitNet Akademies **21**(3), 231–269 (2024). https://doi.org/10.56273/1995-5928/2024/j21n3d2
15. Louw, W.: Africanisation: a rich environment for active learning on a global platform. Progressio **32**(1), 42–54 (2010). https://hdl.handle.net/10520/EJC88838
16. Maringe, F.: Transforming knowledge production systems in the new African university. In: Cross, M., Ndofirepi, A. (eds.) African higher education: Developments and perspectives: Knowledge and change in African universities, Volume 2 - Re-imagining the Terrain, pp. 1–18. Sense Publishers, Rotterdam (2017). https://doi.org/10.1007/978-94-6300-845-7_1
17. Mendy, J., Madiope, M.: Curriculum transformation: a case in South Africa. Perspect. Educ. **38**(2), 1–19 (2020). https://doi.org/10.18820/2519593X/PIE.V38.I2.01
18. Merrill, M.D.: A task-centered instructional strategy. J. Res. Technol. Educ. **40**(1), 33–50 (2007). https://doi.org/10.1080/15391523.2007.10782498
19. Merrill, M.D.: First principles of instruction. Educ. Tech. Research Dev. **50**(3), 43–59 (2002). https://doi.org/10.1007/bf02505024
20. Mheta, G., Lungu, B.N., Govender, T.: Decolonisation of the curriculum: a case study of the Durban University of Technology in South Africa. South Afr. J. Educ. **38**(4), 1–7 (2018). https://doi.org/10.15700/saje.v38n4a1635
21. Morrison, G.R., Ross, S.J., Morrison, J.R., Kalman, H.K.: Designing Effective Instruction, 8th edn. Wiley, Hoboken, NJ (2019)
22. Oates, B.J., Griffiths, M., McLean, R.: Researching Information Systems and Computing. 2nd ed. SAGE, Los Angeles, CA (2022)
23. Partnership for 21st Century Skills: Standards: A 21st Century Skills Implementation Guide. https://files.eric.ed.gov/fulltext/ED519427.pdf. Accessed 05 May 2025
24. SA News: Class of 2024 Achieves Historic Pass Rate. https://www.sanews.gov.za/south-africa/class-2024-achieves-historic-pass-rate. Accessed 03 Feb 2025
25. Sadiki, L., Steyn, F.: Decolonising the Criminology curriculum in South Africa: views and experiences of lecturers and postgraduate students. Transf. High. Educ. **7**(0), a150, 1–9 (2022). https://doi.org/10.4102/the.v7i0.150
26. Samuel, M.: Learning and teaching literature: a curriculum development perspective. Alternation: Interdisc. J. Study Arts Human. Southern Afr. **2**(1), 94–107 (1995)

27. Statistics South Africa: Income & Expenditure Survey (IES) 2022/2023. https://www.sta
tssa.gov.za/?p=17995#:~:text=Results%20of%20the%20survey%20further%20show%20t
hat%2C%20on,annum%20compared%20to%20R158%20481%20for%20female-headed%
20households. Accessed 03 Feb 2025
28. Lasley, T.J. II: Bloom's Taxonomy. https://www.britannica.com/topic/Blooms-taxonomy.
Accessed 05 May 2025
29. UNISA: UNISA Fast Facts (Brochure, Feb. 2025). https://www.unisa.ac.za/static/corpor
ate_web/Content/About/Documents/19611_UNISA%20Facts%20Sheets%20Brochure_F
ebruary%202025_D3%20(002).pdf. Accessed 05 May 2025
30. United Nations South Africa: How the UN Is Supporting the Sustainable Development Goals
in South Africa. https://southafrica.un.org/en/sdgs. Accessed 03 Feb 2025
31. Van Staden, C.J., Eybers, S., Kroeze, J.H.: Students question the need for the Africanisation of
information systems education: a qualitative study. In: Nagar, A., Jat, D.S., Mishra, D., Joshi,
A. (eds.) WorldS4 2024. Lecture Notes in Networks and Systems, vol. 1180, pp. 311-321.
Springer, Singapore (2025). https://doi.org/10.1007/978-981-97-9324-2_25
32. Wright, A.C. et al.: Features of high quality online courses in higher education: a scoping
review. Online Learn. **27**(1), 46–70 (2023). https://doi.org/10.24059/olj.v27i1.3411

Beyond the Classroom: Service-Learning as a Mechanism for Social Transformation in IT Education

Rouxan Colin Fouché[(⊠)] [ID] and Wynand Nel[ID]

Department of Computer Science and Informatics, University of the Free State, Bloemfontein, South Africa
`foucherc@ufs.ac.za, wynandn@akademia.ac.za`

Abstract. In the context of current-day South Africa, service-learning presents a unique opportunity to address systemic technological inequalities while developing future IT professionals. This study investigates how serving as technology educators transforms IT students' professional and personal development. This study measured learning outcomes in 40 second-year IT students before and after 10 weeks of delivering computer literacy training to unemployed community members. Using the Service-Learning Outcomes Measurement Scale, we assessed how teaching technology influences knowledge application, professional development, civic engagement, and self-awareness. Utilising pre- and post-intervention surveys, the study reveals significant improvements across multiple dimensions. Participants demonstrated enhanced abilities to translate complex technical concepts for non-technical audiences, develop leadership skills, and deepen their understanding of technology's social impact. Notably, gender-specific insights emerged, with female participants showing more pronounced improvements in civic responsibility and self-perception. Theoretically grounded in Experiential Learning Theory, Social Constructivism, Critical Pedagogy, and Transformative Learning Theory, the research highlights service-learning's potential to develop technical competence and promote social transformation simultaneously. The findings underscore the importance of educational approaches that not only bridge technological divides but also shape socially conscious IT professionals who can effectively address both technical and societal challenges in the digital age.

Keywords: Community engagement · Digital divide · Experiential learning · IT education · Service-learning · Social transformation · Technological empowerment

1 Introduction

In South Africa, technology access and digital literacy are crucial for addressing systemic inequalities [1]. The digital divide deepens socio-economic inequities and limits opportunities for marginalised communities [2]. Addressing these challenges aligns with Society 5.0's vision for a human-centred technological society that promotes inclusivity and sustainability [3, 4].

© The Author(s), under exclusive license to Springer Nature Switzerland AG 2026
F. Corradini et al. (Eds.): Society 5.0 2025, CCIS 2787, pp. 112–123, 2026.
https://doi.org/10.1007/978-3-032-15463-7_10

Higher education institutions (HEIs), like the University of the Free State (UFS), play a vital role in community engagement and socio-economic development [5]. The Information Technology Service-Learning (ITSL) project at the UFS integrates academic knowledge with practical application to address local challenges and foster students' personal, professional, and civic growth [6]. Through the semester module, second-year Information Technology (IT) students deliver free technological skills training to underserved communities (see Fig. 1), focusing on digital literacy [7]. The project, which was implemented face-to-face and presented by 40 s-year students, reached 160 participants in 2024.

Fig. 1. Service-learning students providing computer literacy training.

This study examines how serving as technology educators transforms these IT student presenters' ability to translate complex technical concepts for non-technical audiences, develop leadership skills, and deepen their understanding of technology's social impact. Through delivering weekly computer literacy training, these students engage in experiential learning that bridges classroom knowledge with community needs. The research investigates how this teaching experience influences students' professional competencies, personal development, and social consciousness, particularly in the context of South Africa's broader digital inclusion goals [8].

The study contributes to the growing literature on SL as a sustainable intervention [9], demonstrating how it simultaneously develops technical professionals and addresses societal needs for a more equitable digital society [10].

2   Literature Review and Theoretical Frameworks

SL integrates community service with academic instruction, enabling the practical application of theoretical knowledge while fostering social responsibility [11]. It helps address challenges like the digital divide while transforming both participants and communities [7]. This section explores the theoretical frameworks guiding SL within the South African context.

2.1 Core Theoretical Frameworks in SL

Four key theoretical frameworks inform this study's methodology, offering a comprehensive understanding of SL's educational and societal impact:

Experiential Learning Theory (ELT). Kolb's ELT explains learning as a cyclical process involving concrete experience, reflective observation, abstract conceptualisation, and active experimentation. In SL, students engage with community challenges, reflect on their experiences, form new understandings, and apply insights in subsequent actions. This cyclical process fosters deeper learning, connecting theoretical knowledge with real-world applications [12]. Jarvis [13] emphasises how these interactions between personal experience and social knowledge lead to both technical skill development and transformative growth in understanding social and cultural issues.

Social Constructivism. Vygotsky's Social Constructivism highlights the role of social interaction and cultural tools in shaping cognitive development. In SL, students collaborate with community members, co-construct knowledge, and expand their "zone of proximal development" [14]. These collaborative environments foster collective responsibility and active problem-solving, which are essential for addressing complex challenges like the digital divide.

Critical Pedagogy. Freire's Critical Pedagogy advocates for education that empowers participants through dialogue, critical reflection, and social action. Students and community members are co-learners in SL, collaboratively addressing societal inequalities [15]. The focus on recognising lived experiences and fostering critical consciousness aligns SL with broader social justice and transformation goals.

Transformative Learning Theory. Mezirow's Transformative Learning Theory explores how critical reflection on disorienting dilemmas can shift participants' perspectives [16]. SL provides opportunities for these shifts, encouraging students to question assumptions and develop deeper ethical and cultural awareness.

These frameworks collectively inform this study by offering a lens through which to examine how SL fosters both technical skill development and social transformation, particularly in addressing systemic inequities.

2.2 Addressing the Digital Divide and Social Transformation

The intersection of SL and technology offers a unique opportunity to address the digital divide in South Africa. By equipping communities with technological skills, SL fosters economic empowerment, social mobility, and opportunities [17].

ICT-focused SL interventions empower marginalised communities by bridging technological access and skills gaps. These projects engage students in meaningful work that addresses socio-economic disparities, helping community members navigate the digital world. This approach challenges historical inequities in South Africa while fostering technological citizenship and economic resilience [17].

This integration of theoretical perspectives highlights how SL can transform SL students and communities by promoting technical competence, critical consciousness, and social justice.

3   Methodology

3.1   Research Design and Sampling

This study employed a quantitative approach to investigate the impact of the ITSL intervention on the student presenters. The research design aimed to provide robust insights into the multifaceted outcomes of SL experiences, focusing on immediate student outcomes.

The study targeted 40 students enrolled in the SL module at the UFS during the semester of the ITSL project. The student-presenters committed to delivering weekly three-hour computer literacy training sessions every Friday from 10:00 AM to 1:00 PM over 10 weeks. The ITSL intervention followed a structured pedagogical approach. Students developed targeted lesson plans connecting technical skills to community needs (e.g., CV creation, budget spreadsheets), deliberately positioning them as knowledge facilitators rather than technical experts.

Each presenter was responsible for teaching basic computer skills (including MS Word and MS Excel) to a large group of mostly unemployed community members, requiring them to translate their technical knowledge into accessible instruction while managing real-world teaching challenges. This teaching experience formed the core intervention being studied, with measurements focusing on how this role as a technology educator impacted the students' own development. Purposive sampling was used to select students directly involved in the project. This sampling strategy ensured an in-depth focus on participants' experiences and the intervention's impact on their personal, professional, and civic development. All enrolled students were invited to participate in the study. Pre- and post-intervention surveys were administered to evaluate changes in their learning outcomes. The research population of 40 was determined by the total number of students enrolled in the SL module, which typically has low enrollment due to its elective nature. A total of 30 participants completed both pre- and post-intervention surveys. These participants made up the eventual sample (N = 30).

3.2   Data Collection and Instrumentation

Data was collected using the Service-Learning Outcomes Measurement Scale (S-LOMS), a 56-item questionnaire designed to capture SL interventions' nuanced impacts. The instrument evaluates four critical dimensions of student learning outcomes: knowledge application, personal and professional skills, civic orientation and engagement, and self-awareness [18].

Surveys were administered twice: once before the SL intervention began to assess students' baseline perceptions and readiness for the project, and once after the 10-week project to measure changes in these areas. The surveys were conducted anonymously to encourage honest responses, with informed consent obtained from all participants, according to the ethical clearance obtained from the UFS.

The S-LOMS was selected after a comprehensive review of available tools for its suitability in capturing the multidimensional impacts of SL. Its established reliability and validation in similar educational contexts further supported its use in this study [18].

3.3 Data Analysis

All the data collected through the pre-test and post-test questionnaires were manually captured and numerically coded in an MS Excel spreadsheet. The data was exported to SPSS Statistics for Windows, version 29.0. The data were analysed using descriptive and inferential statistical methods. The primary analysis focused on changes in student outcomes across the four dimensions assessed by the S-LOMS questionnaire (see Sect. 3.2).

Paired data from the pre- and post-surveys were analysed using Wilcoxon signed-rank tests, a non-parametric method to evaluate significant differences in responses across the 5-point Likert scale. To assess whether gender influenced the results, a repeated measures ANOVA was performed to examine outcome differences across the two time points. All analyses were conducted at a 95% confidence level, with statistical significance set at $p < 0.05$.

3.4 Reliability and Validity

The reliability and validity of the study's findings were ensured using the S-LOMS questionnaire, a widely validated tool with demonstrated internal consistency in prior research [18]. The instrument's alignment with the ITSL project's objectives ensured its ability to capture meaningful learning outcomes accurately. The data collection process was standardised, with all participants receiving identical instructions and completing surveys under similar conditions. The pre- and post-test format further supported the comparability and consistency of data. Together, these measures ensured the credibility of the study's findings, offering a reliable reflection of the ITSL project's impact.

4 Results: Overview of Intervention Outcomes

This section presents the findings from the pre- and post-test questionnaires, organised around four critical dimensions of student learning outcomes: knowledge application, personal and professional skills, civic orientation and engagement, and self-awareness. These dimensions are analysed to assess the impact of the intervention on students' development, informed by experiential learning and community engagement frameworks [18].

4.1 Demographics of Participants

The study included 30 participants (SL students) with near-balanced gender representation: 53.3% male (n = 16) and 46.7% female (n = 14). Participants' ages ranged from 19 to 24, averaging 21 years. The linguistic diversity reflected South Africa's multilingual context, with participants speaking Southern Sotho (7), Northern Sotho (6), Tswana (6), Zulu (4), Xhosa (3), Tsonga (2), Venda (1), and Afrikaans (1). This diversity underscores the inclusive nature of the university and the SL intervention, aligning with South Africa's commitment to linguistic and cultural representation in higher education. The sample represents the demographic and cultural richness of second-year IT students in contemporary South African universities.

4.2 Knowledge Application

Participants demonstrated significant improvements in applying classroom knowledge to real-world contexts, as assessed by the Knowledge Application section of the S-LOMS questionnaire. Statistically significant improvements were observed in the categories of (a) real-life problem-solving (M = 3.80 to 4.43, p = 0.001), (b) addressing complex issues (M = 3.90 to 4.30, p = 0.022), and (c) knowledge transfer across settings (M = 3.87 to 4.43, p = 0.001). No gender-based differences were detected, indicating the broad efficacy of the intervention across all participants.

These results align with Kolb's Experiential Learning Theory, particularly the stages of active experimentation and abstract conceptualisation, highlighting the value of experiential learning in fostering practical knowledge application.

4.3 Personal and Professional Skills

The ITSL intervention significantly enhanced participants' personal and professional skills across key areas, including creative problem-solving, interpersonal competencies, self-reflection, and critical thinking.

Creative Problem-Solving: Confidence in addressing problems and adopting new perspectives improved significantly, with mean scores increasing from 3.63 to 4.37 and 3.83 to 4.50, respectively (in both cases p < 0.001). Other dimensions showed modest, non-significant improvements.

Interpersonal Competencies: Statistically significant gains were observed in six out of eight dimensions, including (a) maintaining connections (M = 3.07 to 3.90, p = 0.002), (b) building relationships (M = 3.13 to 4.17, p < 0.001), (c) establishing effective relationships (M = 3.30 to 4.00, p < 0.001), (d) resolving conflicts (M = 3.30 to 3.87, p = 0.004), (e) confidence in leading toward common goals (M = 3.63 to 4.07, p = 0.010), and (f) teamwork (M = 3.63 to 4.27, p = 0.010).

Self-reflection: Statistically significant improvements were noted in (a) task evaluation (M = 3.60 to 4.13, p = 0.045) and (b) reflective consideration of circumstances (M = 3.93 to 4.37, p = 0.040), though the frequency of self-reflection remained unchanged.

Critical Thinking: Participants' ability to (a) analyse issues comprehensively and (b) view complex problems from multiple perspectives improved significantly, with mean scores increasing from 3.70 to 4.20 and 3.83 to 4.27, respectively (p < 0.05).

These findings underscore the intervention's success in fostering practical, interpersonal, and cognitive skills critical for professional and personal growth.

4.4 Civic Orientation and Community Engagement

The SL intervention significantly enhanced participants' civic orientation and community engagement, aligning with Kolb's Experiential Learning Theory (ELT) and Freire's Critical Pedagogy, emphasising active learning and social transformation.

Community Engagement and Resource Identification: Participants demonstrated statistically significant increases in (a) discussing community improvements (M = 2.97 to 3.97, p < 0.001), (b) improved ability to identify community resources (M = 3.47 to 3.90, p = 0.009), (c) identifying important issues for disadvantaged communities (M = 3.80 to 4.23, p = 0.009), (d) recognising social issues (M = 3.77 to 4.33, p = 0.021) and (e) willingness to address social problems (M = 3.77 to 4.33, p = 0.011).

Gender-based differences were evident in civic orientation and community engagement. Females demonstrated more substantial improvements compared to males across various dimensions. For instance, females' scores increased from 2.71 to 4.29 in discussing community improvements, while males' scores rose from 3.19 to 3.69 (p = 0.017). In identifying issues for disadvantaged communities, females improved significantly from 3.57 to 4.50 (p = 0.006), while males showed no change (4.00 to 4.00).

Caring and Respect Dimensions: Minimal changes were noted in caring and respect, with high pre-intervention scores (e.g., considering others' points of view: M = 4.50 and caring about others: M = 4.37). This may reflect the post-apartheid emphasis on reconciliation and empathy, which has cultivated these attitudes in South African society.

Social Responsibility: Statistically significant improvements were observed in civic participation (M = 3.97 to 4.43, p = 0.006) and commitment to helping those in need (M = 3.97 to 4.27, p = 0.029). Females showed a significant improvement in social responsibility (M = 4.00 to 4.71, p = 0.023), while males experienced a slight decline in this dimension (M = 3.94 to 3.88).

Overall, females showed more pronounced improvements in community engagement and social responsibility compared to males, particularly in their ability to discuss community issues and identify resources for disadvantaged communities. These findings highlight the importance of tailoring SL interventions to address diverse demographic needs, particularly gender-based differences in impact. Additionally, the high baseline scores for caring and respect dimensions suggest that societal and educational initiatives in South Africa have fostered empathy and social responsibility. These results reinforce the value of community-focused experiential learning in promoting civic engagement and social transformation.

4.5   Self-awareness and Personal Growth

The SL intervention significantly enhanced participants' self-awareness and personal development, aligning with experiential learning theories and psychological growth, particularly Mezirow's Transformative Learning Theory, which posits that disorienting experiences, like those encountered in SL, prompt critical self-reflection and personal transformation.

Self-efficacy and Achievement: Participants showed statistically significant improvements in (a) satisfaction with achievements (M = 3.30 to 3.90, p = 0.014), (b) recognition of positive qualities (M = 3.83 to 4.33, p = 0.009), and (c) self-positivity (M = 3.83 to 4.27, p = 0.018).

Gender analysis revealed that females experienced significantly more substantial improvements in self-positivity than males. In self-positivity, females' scores increased from 3.64 to 4.50, while males' scores increased slightly from 4.0 to 4.06 ($p = 0.013$). This might be attributed to culture-specific gender roles.

Self-understanding Dimensions: Clarity of self-understanding demonstrated significant growth (M = 3.73 to 4.33, $p = 0.007$), with females showing a more substantial increase in self-understanding compared to males (females: M = 3.36 to 4.50; males: M = 4.06 to 4.19, $p = 0.005$). This gender difference was particularly significant given the lower pre-test scores of females, suggesting that SL may be especially transformative for women in enhancing self-awareness.

Commitment to Self-Improvement: Statistically significant improvements were observed across all dimensions, including (a) commitment to acquiring new skills (M = 4.37 to 4.63, $p = 0.046$), (b) motivation to learn (M = 3.80 to 4.33, $p = 0.009$), and (c) keeping knowledge up-to-date (M = 3.70 to 4.37, $p = 0.003$). These improvements were consistent across genders, indicating the intervention's universal impact on professional development and motivation for ongoing personal growth.

Overall, these findings demonstrate the effectiveness of SL in fostering self-awareness, self-perception, and professional development, with particular benefits for female participants. The results also underscore the importance of designing inclusive SL interventions that acknowledge gender-specific responses to experiential learning while promoting universal growth in self-efficacy and motivation.

4.6 Contextual Interpretation

IT Student Specificity. The participants, all second-year IT students, brought a unique technical perspective to the SL experience. Their background in IT allowed them to apply complex technical knowledge in real-world contexts effectively. The students demonstrated a higher level of intrinsic motivation for community engagement, with a greater understanding of the role of technology in social empowerment. This technical expertise enabled them to bridge the gap between theoretical knowledge and practical application in community settings. Additionally, their familiarity with digital tools fostered both technical proficiency and socio-economic impact, helping to enhance community engagement and further the goals of the ITSL initiative.

South African Socio-historical Context. The outcomes of the intervention must be interpreted within the broader context of South Africa's socio-historical landscape. Given the country's history of educational inequality, technological marginalisation, and the enduring effects of apartheid, the ITSL project was pivotal in equipping participants with essential digital literacy skills. These competencies not only facilitated potential pathways for economic empowerment but also aligned with national efforts to reduce digital disparities and foster more equitable participation in the digital economy [8]. The intervention's emphasis on community engagement was particularly impactful in addressing systemic barriers to technological access. In this regard, the ITSL initiative contributed to broader social transformation by promoting a culture of inclusion and empowerment through technology.

Gender and Empowerment. The ITSL project revealed significant gender-based differences in self-perception, community engagement, and technological confidence among second-year IT students, particularly within South Africa's context of persistent gender inequality. Female students showed notable growth in confidence, leadership, and engagement with technology, demonstrating the SL intervention's effectiveness in enhancing their social agency as educators. By applying their digital skills in real-world teaching scenarios, these students gained self-efficacy and professional growth, addressing gender disparities in technology fields [19]. This focus on empowering female students highlights the potential of SL to foster a more inclusive generation of IT professionals.

5   Conclusion: Transformative Potential of SL in IT Education

This study examined the transformative impact of an ITSL intervention on second-year IT students who served as technology educators in their community. The findings demonstrate that having IT students serve as technology educators creates a powerful dual impact. While community members gain essential digital skills, the student-presenters undergo significant professional and personal transformation.

The pre- and post-intervention measurements revealed significant improvements across multiple dimensions of student development. In terms of knowledge application, students demonstrated enhanced abilities to solve real-world problems and transfer theoretical knowledge to practical situations. Their role as presenters significantly strengthened their capacity to translate complex technical concepts into accessible instruction, a critical skill for IT professionals.

Personal and professional growth was evidenced through significant improvements in creative problem-solving, interpersonal competencies, and critical thinking. Particularly noteworthy was the development of leadership skills and the ability to build effective relationships in professional contexts. These improvements suggest that the experience of teaching technology skills provides unique professional development opportunities that traditional IT coursework alone cannot offer.

The intervention profoundly impacted students' civic orientation and social consciousness. Community engagement scores increased significantly, indicating a deeper understanding of technology's role in social transformation. Gender-specific findings revealed that female participants experienced more pronounced improvements in community engagement and self-perception, suggesting the intervention's potential to address gender disparities in the technology sector. These outcomes have significant implications for IT education and professional development. The findings demonstrate that incorporating SL into IT education develops professionals who:

1. Can effectively translate technical knowledge for non-technical audiences - a critical skill in today's technology-driven workplace;
2. Understand the social impact of digital inclusion, making them more likely to consider accessibility and user needs in their future IT careers;
3. Develop enhanced leadership and communication skills vital for technical team management;

4. Gain practical experience in project management and problem-solving in real-world contexts;
5. Show increased awareness of social responsibility, potentially influencing how they approach future technological developments.

In the context of South Africa, this transformation extends beyond individual student development. By bridging the digital divide through community engagement, these IT students contribute to broader social transformation while developing the professional and personal competencies needed to address both technical and social challenges in their future careers.

This research demonstrates that SL in IT education creates an environment where technical skill development intersects meaningfully with community engagement. The experience of serving as technology educators shapes more competent, socially aware IT professionals who are better prepared to contribute to both technological advancement and social equity. These findings suggest that integrating SL into IT education is not merely an educational approach but a potent strategy for developing technically proficient professionals who understand and can address the societal implications of their work.

6 Limitations

This study at the UFS in South Africa reflects a specific context. It may not be generalisable to other SL projects or communities with differing socio-economic, educational, or cultural backgrounds. Still, key elements of the ITSL model show potential for adaptation elsewhere: (1) combining technical training with reflection, (2) positioning students as educators, and (3) scaffolding translation of technical skills. Adaptation would require tailoring content, duration, and reflection to local needs.

The purposive sampling $(N = 30)$ limits statistical generalisability and may not reflect the full range of student experiences. Nonetheless, effect sizes across various areas indicate meaningful educational outcomes worth exploring in broader studies.

7 Future Research

Future research should expand this work in three critical directions:

1. **International Comparative Analysis:** Cross-cultural studies examining ITSL outcomes across different regions (developing vs. developed nations) could reveal how varying technological infrastructures and cultural contexts influence program effectiveness. Such analysis would be valuable for identifying universal best practices and culture-specific adaptations needed for successful ITSL implementation.
2. **Longitudinal Impact Assessment:** Long-term studies tracking both student presenters' career trajectories and community participants' technological advancement would provide crucial insights into the sustained impact of ITSL interventions.
3. **Gender and Diversity Dynamics:** Given the significant gender-based differences observed in this study, future research should investigate how these patterns manifest across different cultural contexts and explore strategies for maximising ITSL's potential in addressing gender disparities in technology fields.

Acknowledgements. Wynand Nel is affiliated with Akademia, a Christian, classical and independent higher education institution from and for the Afrikaans language and cultural community.

Disclosure of Interests. The authors have no competing interests to declare relevant to this article's content.

Statement on Ethics. Ethical clearance for this study was granted by the General/Human Research Ethics Committee of the UFS (Ethical clearance number: UFS-HSD2023/1745). Informed consent was secured from all participants, ensuring they understood the research objectives and their right to withdraw at any time.

References

1. Aruleba, K., Jere, N.: Exploring digital transforming challenges in rural areas of South Africa through a systematic review of empirical studies. Sci Afr. **16**, e01190 (2022). https://doi.org/10.1016/j.sciaf.2022.e01190
2. Van Dijk, J.: The Digital Divide. John Wiley & Sons, Cambridge (2020)
3. Deguchi, A., et al.: What is society 5.0? In: Society 5.0: A People-Centric Super-Smart Society, pp. 1–23. Springer, Singapore (2020). https://doi.org/10.1007/978-981-15-2989-4
4. Lythreatis, S., Singh, S.K., El-Kassar, A.-N.: The digital divide: a review and future research agenda. Technol. Forecast. Soc. Change **175** (2022). https://doi.org/10.1016/j.techfore.2021.121359
5. Department of Higher Education and Training: Higher Education Amendment Act 9 of 2016 (2016)
6. Fouché, R.C., Nel, L.: Bridging the digital divide: assessing the impact of a community-focused service-learning project. In: Proceedings of the 53rd Annual Southern African Computer Lecturers' Association (SACLA 2024), SACLA 2024 Organising Committee, Gqeberha, South Africa, pp. 17–30 (2024)
7. Fouché, R.C., Nel, W.: Closing the gap: leveraging recorded video lessons for digital inclusion in rural South Africa. In: Hinkelmann, K. and Smuts, H. (eds.) Society 5.0, pp. 111–122. Springer Nature Switzerland, Cham (2024). https://doi.org/10.1007/978-3-031-71412-2_9
8. Ministry of Communication and Digital Technologies: National digital and future skills strategy. Government Gazette, pp. 3–38 (2020)
9. Adarlo, G., et al.: From classroom to community: Service-learning and the sustainable development goals. In: Proceedings of the 18th International Multi-Conference on Society, Cybernetics and Informatics: IMSCI 2024, pp. 23–29. International Institute of Informatics and Cybernetics (2024). https://doi.org/10.54808/IMSCI2024.01.23
10. Balderama, H., et al.: Sustainable and inclusive internationalization: reimagining approaches in higher education in an era of global uncertainties. York University, Toronto (2021). https://doi.org/10.25071/10315/38628
11. Aramburuzabala, P., Cerrillo, R.: Service-learning as an approach to educating for sustainable development. Sustainability (Switzerland) **15** (2023). https://doi.org/10.3390/su151411231
12. Kolb, D.A., Boyatzis, R.E., Mainemelis, C.: Experiential learning theory: previous research and new directions. In: Sternberg, R.J., Zhang, L.F. (eds.) Perspectives on thinking, learning, and cognitive styles, pp. 227–247. Routledge (2001)
13. Jarvis, P.: Towards a philosophy of human learning - an existentialist perspective. In: Jarvis, P., Parker, S. (eds.) Human Learning - An holistic approach, pp. 1–15. Routledge, London and New York (2006)

14. Vygotsky, L.S.: Mind in Society: The Development of Higher Psychological Processes. Harvard University Press, Cambridge (1978)
15. Freire, P.: Pedagogy of the Oppressed. Bloomsbury Academic (2018)
16. Mezirow, J.: Mezirow-transformative-learning. New Dir. Adult Continuing Educ. **74**, 5–12 (1997)
17. Fouché, R.C.: Addressing the South African digital divide through a community-informed strategy for service-learning: a critical utopian action research (CUAR) approach (2022)
18. Snell, R.S., Lau, K.H.: The development of a service-learning outcomes measurement scale (S-LOMS). Metrop Univ. **31**, 44–77 (2020). https://doi.org/10.18060/23258
19. Master, A., Meltzoff, A.N., Cheryan, S.: Gender stereotypes about interests start early and cause gender disparities in computer science and engineering. Proc. Natl. Acad. Sci. **118**, e2100030118 (2021). https://doi.org/10.1073/pnas.2100030118

Transforming Whistleblowing Through Digital Trust: a Comparative Study of South Africa and Switzerland

Hermann Grieder[1]([envelope]) [iD], Petra Maria Asprion[1] [iD], Marié Hattingh[2] [iD], and Alex Norta[2,3] [iD]

[1] University of Applied Sciences and Arts Northwestern Switzerland FHNW, Olten, Switzerland
{hermann.grieder,petra.asprion}@fhnw.ch
[2] University of Pretoria, Pretoria, South Africa
marie.hattingh@up.ac.za, alex.norta.phd@ieee.org
[3] Tallinn University, Tallinn, Estonia

Abstract. This exploratory research investigates digital trust as a framework for whistleblowing, comparing South Africa and Switzerland. Whistleblowing efficacy hinges on trust in political systems, processes, reporting tools, and whistleblower protections. We identify digital trust as transformative for whistleblowing mechanisms across contrasting societal frameworks. The methodology encompasses literature review of digital trust concepts, innovations, and legal frameworks. Preliminary findings show notable differences between South African, Swiss and European Union whistleblowing approaches. This research provides insights for policymakers, technology developers, and civil society organizations to foster secure, trust-based whistleblowing mechanisms.

Keywords: Comparative Analysis · Digital Trust · Ethics · Governance · Privacy · Technology Adoption · Whistleblowing

1   Introduction

Whistleblowing refers to the disclosure of wrongdoing or illegal activities within organizations by individuals with insider knowledge, serving as a critical mechanism for accountability, transparency, and ethical conduct in both public and private sectors (Near & Miceli, 1985) Historically, whistleblowers have played pivotal roles in exposing corruption, fraud, and malpractice, yet they often face significant personal and professional risks, for example retaliation, ostracism, and legal challenges. These risks underscore the need for secure reporting systems that protect those who expose misconduct.

Trust in government and perceptions of corruption vary widely between Switzerland and South Africa, with Switzerland ranking 6th in the world on Transparency International's Corruption Perceptions Index and 1st in the OECD for trust in government at 83.78%, while South Africa ranks 83rd out of 180 countries for corruption (OECD, 2023;

F. Corradini et al. (Eds.): Society 5.0 2025, CCIS 2787, pp. 124–137, 2026.
https://doi.org/10.1007/978-3-032-15463-7_11

Transparency International, 2024). This contrast is reflected in the number of whistle-blower reports received in each country–the Swiss Federal Audit Office received 350 reports in 2023, up from 232 in 2022, while Corruption Watch South Africa received 2,110 complaints in 2023 alone, an average of 11 per day (Corruption Watch, 2024; Swiss Federal Audit Office, 2023).

The effectiveness of whistleblowing mechanisms hinges fundamentally on trust: in the political system, the process, the reporting tools, and the protection afforded to whistleblowers (Near & Miceli, 1985). Whistleblowing in the context of digital trust, as an interdisciplinary research field, examines how digital trusted whistleblowing ecosystems facilitate the safe disclosure of unethical or illegal practices within organizations. This field investigates the interplay between security, privacy, ethics, resilience, robustness and reliability in building and maintaining digital trust. It explores mechanisms that protect whistleblowers–ensuring anonymity and confidentiality–while addressing ethical, legal, and technological challenges (Asprion et al., 2023). The discussion of whistleblowing leads to reporting channels, as well as trustworthy digital solutions, whereby trustworthiness means the five pillars of security, privacy, ethics, resilience, robustness and reliability (Maple et al., 2021).

From an organizational perspective various viewpoints need to be considered, e.g. (1) legal obligations–as a fundamental driver for organizations to act, (2) risks for whistle-blowers–and their need for a trustworthy reporting channel, (3) the concept of digital trust as a relatively new and promising flanking concept, (4) existing digital reporting solutions and their trustworthiness promise, and (5) emerging technologies like for example Distributed Ledgers or Artificial Intelligence (AI) as approaches which potentially support digital trust. Ultimately, the interdisciplinary research around whistleblowing aims to integrate mechanisms within a robust digital trust framework, fostering a trustworthy digital ecosystem (Asprion et al., 2023).

This exploratory research aims to investigate the potential of digital trust as a framework for whistleblowing, through a comparative case study of South Africa and Switzerland. South Africa faces significant challenges with systemic corruption and inadequate whistleblower protections, resulting in a climate of fear and distrust. Although adequate whistleblower protection policies are in place in South Africa (Nortje, 2022), a recent parliament session called for a "robust system that guarantees the safety and anonymity of those who come forward, given the high risks of retaliation and intimidation by criminal syndicates" (Parliament of the Republic of South Africa, 2024). In contrast, Switzerland offers a worldwide valued environment for ethical reporting, though it still encounters issues in areas such as legal regulations and private sector adoption (Hauser et al., 2021; PwC, 2023).

We address two overarching research questions: (1) how can digital trust and related dimensions support whistleblowing in different societal contexts? (2) how could the interplay between organizational culture, technical infrastructure, and human factors be framed for building a digital "trusted whistleblowing ecosystem"? A further objective is to lay the foundation for future research on cross-cultural implementation of trusted whistleblowing ecosystems in different economic, social, and cultural contexts. By exploring these research questions through the lens of South Africa and Switzerland, we seek to provide actionable insights for policymakers, technology developers, and civil society organizations to enable a global shift toward trust-based whistleblowing.

2 Methodology

This research uses an exploratory approach to derive research questions that have not been extensively investigated in the outlined research field. We examine the role of digital trust in whistleblowing ecosystems, with a focus on the contrasting contexts of South Africa and Switzerland. The methodology consists of a comprehensive literature review, encompassing an exploration of digital trust concepts, an analysis of whistleblowing ecosystem innovations, and digital trust initiatives in South Africa, Switzerland and the European Union (EU), contrasting regulatory and market-driven approaches. The review surveys existing research on whistleblowing mechanisms, digital trust dimensions, and the application of emerging technology features that put emphasis on the trustworthiness of digital data. The legal analysis compares South Africa's Protected Disclosures Act (PDA), Switzerland's legal frameworks, and the EU Directive 2019/1937, identifying differences in whistleblower protections, enforcement mechanisms, and the influence of the EU Directive.

3 Comparison Between South Africa, Switzerland and EU

This section analyses the impact of contrasting legal, institutional and technological environments on the application of research mechanisms when reporting wrongdoing in South Africa, Switzerland and the EU. The regions represent a contrast in governance structure and trust context and are as such interesting environments to study how digital trust frameworks may be facilitated–nor impeded–by contextual circumstances. We compare national laws, readiness of institutions, and technologies that promote trust, revealing systemic strengths and remaining weaknesses. Consequently, Sect. 3.1 covers whistleblowing trends and challenges in South Africa, followed in Sect. 3.2 by an overview of institutional and technical preparedness in Switzerland, and finally Sect. 3.3 focuses on EU-level regulatory developments, which entail the Whistleblower Directive and digital trust initiatives.

3.1 Whistleblowing in South Africa

South Africa has a long history of corruption and institutional mistrust (Madonsela, 2019; Nortje, 2022). Despite the enactment of the Protected Disclosures Act (PDA) (Department of Justice and Constitutional Development of South Africa, 2000) to protect whistleblowers from "occupational detriment," whistleblowers often face retaliation, legal challenges, and physical harm (Nortje, 2022; Onyango, 2021; Wright, 2024). High-profile scandals highlight systemic corruption and the lack of effective whistleblowing (protection) mechanisms. Studies have shown that fear of retaliation and a lack of institutional support are significant barriers to whistleblowing in South Africa (Nortje, 2022; Onyango, 2021; Wright, 2024).

Observed shortcomings of the current PDA include lack of effective support for dismissed employees, technical requirements that defeat the Act's purpose, and limited scope (Department of Justice and Constitutional Development of South Africa, 2000).

Proposed reforms include better alignment with international standards, expanded scope "outside the limits of occupational detriment," additional disclosure recipient bodies, enhanced whistleblower trustworthiness guarantees, and establishing specialized courts for whistleblower cases (Department of Justice and Constitutional Development of South Africa, 2023).

3.2 Whistleblowing in Switzerland

As one of the most innovative and trustworthy countries globally (World Intellectual Property Organization, 2024), Switzerland is uniquely positioned to advance digital trust initiatives. Its political system, emphasizing consensus, stability, and citizen involvement, provides a strong foundation for governing digital trust mechanisms in whistleblowing contexts. Switzerland, despite its reputation for innovation, lacks a comprehensive whistleblower protection law mandating internal reporting channels for all organizations (Deloitte, 2023). Nevertheless, many Swiss companies have voluntarily implemented internal whistleblowing systems as part of their compliance strategies, with 63.4% of Swiss organizations maintaining internal reporting channels as of 2021 (Hauser et al., 2021).

Switzerland's revised Federal Act on Data Protection (nFADP) (FDPIC, 2025), effective since September 2023, strengthens individual data protections. Though not specifically targeting whistleblowers, the nFADP provisions on the rights of data subject – including access, rectification, and erasure – allow whistleblowers to exercise control over their personal data and seek recourse if their information is mishandled.

Various Swiss entities are actively developing digital trust initiatives. The Federal Department of Finance and "digitaleschweiz" are working toward a "smart" Switzerland with digital trust as a central pillar (NCSC, 2024). Switzerland has also introduced the world's first Digital Trust Label (Swiss Digital Initiative, 2025), a certification demonstrating commitment to trustworthy digital practices that organizations including UNICEF and Cisco have obtained.

Switzerland's combination of innovation culture, data protection frameworks, and voluntary adoption of whistleblowing channels positions it as a leader in creating environments where whistleblowers can report misconduct with reduced fear of retaliation or data misuse.

3.3 Whistleblowing in the EU

The EU Whistleblower Directive (EU Directive 2019/1937) came into force on December 16, 2019, with the aim of protecting whistleblowers who report breaches of EU law from retaliation such as dismissal, demotion, and other forms of discrimination (European Commission, 2019). Key elements of the directive include: (1) Broad definition of whistleblower that covers current and former employees, job applicants, volunteers, and others; (2) Requirement for organizations with 50+ employees to establish internal reporting channels and procedures; (3) Option for whistleblowers to report internally or externally to competent authorities; (4) Strict timelines for acknowledging receipt of reports and providing feedback; (5) Allowance for public disclosures as a last resort.

Furthermore, the European Commission, the executive body of the EU, has recognized the importance of digital trust and launched numerous initiatives to bolster digital trust across the EU (Table 1). Switzerland's role in this context is special: Switzerland is at the heart of the EU but is not a member of the EU. Therefore, it is not required to implement the EU Directive (EU Directive 2019/1937).

Table 1. Exemplary European Commission's initiatives towards digital trust

Key initiatives	Focus Area	Source
eIDAS Regulation	Framework for electronic identification and trust services, ensuring cross-border recognition and enhancing trust in digital transactions	Commission (2014)
EU Cybersecurity Strategy	A comprehensive plan to protect EU citizens and businesses from cyber threats, promoting resilience and trust in the digital environment	Commission (2020)
Digital Europe Programme	Research funding program aimed at bringing digital technology to businesses, citizens, and public administrations to enhance digital trust	Commission (2021)
Digital Services Act (DSA)	Sets out new rules to create a safer digital space where users' rights are protected, enhancing trust in online platforms	Commission (2022)
Artificial Intelligence Act	Proposes a legal framework to ensure AI systems are safe, transparent, and respect fundamental rights, fostering trust in AI technologies	Commission (2024)

However, Swiss organizations that maintain business relationships in the EU may fall within the scope of the EU Directive. Similarly in South Africa, the PPLAAF recommended that the PDA be aligned with the EU Directive on the protection of whistleblowers who "… Shall not incur liability of any kind in respect to reasonable acts necessary to revelations of a disclosure and to protection of his anonymity as long as they had reasonable reasons to believe that the disclosure fell under the conditions of the PDA" (Department of Justice and Constitutional Development of South Africa, 2023, p. 36). In conclusion, both Switzerland and South Africa, despite neither being members of the EU, recognize the initiatives of the EU in supporting whistleblowers.

4 Contextualizing Digital Trust Within Whistleblowing

To explore how whistleblowing can be securely and effectively integrated into digital ecosystems, it is essential to examine both the conceptual and practical elements of digital trust. This section situates whistleblowing within broader discussions of digital trust, drawing on cross-disciplinary concepts and ecosystem models that inform system development and stakeholder relationships. In Sect. 4.1, we define digital trust through both techno-centric and human-centric lenses, and in Sect. 4.2, present a generic ecosystem model based on ISACA's DTEF framework. Finally, Sect. 4.3 proposes how whistleblowing can be reconceptualized as a potential first killer application for a digitally trustworthy infrastructure.

4.1 Digital Trust Defined

There are different attempts to describe digital trust; as early as 2003, digital trust is described as "an attitude of confident expectation in an online situation of risk that one's vulnerabilities will not be exploited" (Corritore et al., 2003, p. 740). ISACA, a global professional association and learning organization with 185,000 members who work in digital trust fields, designed the Digital Trust Ecosystem Framework (DTEF) in which digital trust is described as "the confidence in the integrity of the relationships, interactions and transactions among providers and consumers within an associated digital ecosystem" (ISACA, 2022). The most recent definition we could find distinguishes between technical trust and human trust and postulates that digital trust "is the foundation determining the confidence in digital ecosystems. It goes beyond integrity, security, authenticity and ethical use of systems and data, to ensure that all participants can interact securely and responsibly. It is ensured by the interplay of the two inseparable parts: Technical Trust and Human Trust" (Swiss Financial Innovation Desk, 2025).

4.2 Digital Trust as Generic Ecosystem

ISACA (2023) highlights that organizations nowadays understand the crucial role of digital trust in strengthening brand reputation and operational resilience with the result that building digital trust is essential for organizations to remain competitive and maintain customer loyalty. ISACA's DTEF provides a generic approach to understand and cultivate digital trust in diverse digital environments (2022). The framework identifies five key elements that form the foundation of a digital trust ecosystem: (1) stakeholders (encompass a wide range of actors, including providers, consumers, third parties, and digital peers), (2) relationships (a spectrum of interactions, from communication and transactions to more complex engagements), (3) relationship mediums (communication technologies that facilitate digital transactions), (4) activities (a hierarchy, ranging from basic digital identity and behavior to more complex interactions and transactions), and (5) ethics, reputation, and privacy. Each of these elements plays a crucial role in shaping the dynamics of digital trust within a digital ecosystem.

ISACA's DTEF model (Fig. 1) addresses three traditional dimensions of Information Technology (people, process and technology) and adds a fourth dimension (organization); all four dimensions (nodes) are interconnected with assigned attributes (culture, human factors, architecture, emergence, enabling and support, and direct and monitor).

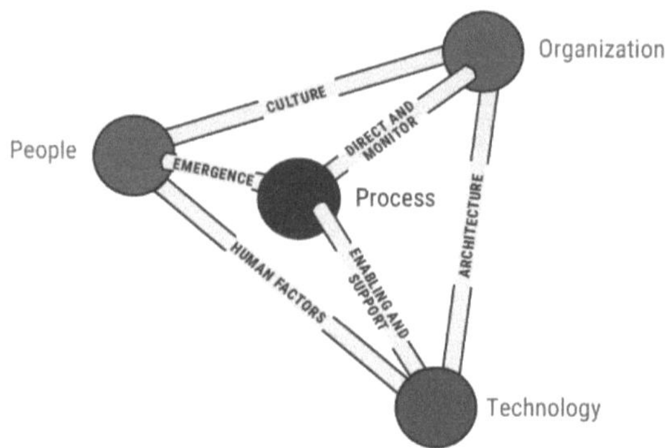

Fig. 1. ISACA's DTEF model, (ISACA, 2022) adopted

The DTEF incorporates a systems thinking approach by acknowledging the interdependence and relationships among the DTEF model nodes.

Consequently, any modification to one node of the model will likely propagate changes throughout the system. Theoretically, a digital ecosystem should be comprehensive and balanced; however, alterations or persistent vulnerabilities can disrupt this equilibrium, ultimately distorting the model's overall integrity. The DTEF model can be mapped with digital trust related requirements and this in turn can be mapped to requirements relevant in whistleblowing contexts. The DTEF offers a comprehensive lens for understanding the interplay of stakeholders, relationships, relationship mediums, activities, ethics, reputation, and privacy in shaping digital trust. Understanding these elements and their interrelationships enables organizations to develop robust strategies that support whistleblowing and create trustworthy reporting ecosystems.

4.3 Digital Trust as a Leading Prospect

By embedding whistleblowing within a digital trust framework, organizations create an environment where individuals feel safer reporting wrongdoing. People – the whistleblowers themselves – represent the focal point of this ecosystem, with technology and organizational structures serving to empower and protect them. This human-centered approach recognizes that even the most advanced technical solutions must align with whistleblowers' psychological safety needs and cultural contexts.

Building upon this foundation, a trusted whistleblowing ecosystem based on digital trust dimensions requires coordination and the involvement of various stakeholders (e.g., stakeholders derived in the DTEF (ISACA, 2022)). A trusted whistleblowing ecosystem which relies on digital trust could be based on ISACA's DTEF or other best practices. The reliance on a framework like DTEF published from a recognized professional association can help organizations proactively identify and mitigate risks, ensuring they align with the (ethical) expectations of all stakeholders.

Incorporating trust dimensions in whistleblowing ecosystems exemplifies digital trust in practice. However, implementing robust digital trust measures requires a multifaceted approach. Focusing solely on technical challenges, various innovations can be

Table 2. Technical Whistleblowing Innovations

System	Key Features and Innovation	Source
Distributed Whistleblowing System	Blockchain, Smart Contracts, IPFS, decentralized architecture and infrastructure to maintain anonymity & security	(Habbabeh et al., 2020)
BB2AR	Ring signature cryptography, anonymous rewarding mechanism, batch verification	(Wang et al., 2020)
Self-Sovereign Identity Integration	Zero-knowledge proofs, verifiable claims, employment credential verification. Enhanced credibility & maintaining anonymity	(Young & Farshadkhah, 2021)
Blockchain-based Whistleblowing Service	Ring signatures, HMAC authentication, Game theory modeling, IPFS integration to create favorable conditions for whistleblowers through decentralized trust and cryptographic anonymity	(Tomaz et al., 2022)
Integrity@Inside	Private blockchain infrastructure; combines regulatory compliance with technical protection of whistleblower anonymity	(Asprion et al., 2023)
Silencing the Risk	LLM-based text sanitization, semi-automated risk assessment, Interactive adjustment, preserves semantic meaning while protecting whistleblower identity	(Staufer et al., 2024)
ARAR	Protection against insider threats, eliminates trusted third parties using smart contracts, Public blockchain timestamping	(Patil & Parmar, 2024)

assessed for their contribution to digital trust. Table 2 highlights recent innovations in whistleblowing.

5 Call for Further Research

We conclude that digital trust is a foundational prerequisite for implementing digitally trustworthy whistleblowing ecosystems, and initial frameworks like ISACA's DTEF (2022) offer a basis for further development. However, to contextualize whistleblowing within digital trust and ensure its applicability across countries such as Switzerland and South Africa, many hypotheses remain unexplored and key research questions unanswered. Table 3 highlights essential questions aligned with the four DTEF dimensions – organizational, technical, people, and process – each representing a critical area for scholarly inquiry. While not exhaustive, these questions aim to encourage researchers to engage with the topic and expand upon it.

Table 3. Proposed research questions and associated research objectives

Research Question	Research Objective
Organizational Perspective	
RQ1: How do digitally trusted whistleblowing ecosystems influence trust and ethical behavior within organizations?	This question examines whether implementing trusted reporting systems creates broader cultural shifts toward transparency and accountability. Research could assess changes in ethical climate and reported misconduct rates through longitudinal studies of organizations adopting digital trust frameworks
RQ2: What are the long-term effects of implementing trusted whistleblowing ecosystems on employee engagement and stakeholder confidence?	Beyond immediate compliance benefits, this question explores how digital trust mechanisms might enhance organizational reputation and employee commitment. Research could measure changes in engagement metrics and stakeholder perceptions to establish the business case for digital trust implementation
RQ3: What factors affect the adoption of trusted whistleblowing ecosystems in organizations across industries?	This question explores traits, leadership factors, and industry contexts that affect the implementation of trusted reporting systems. Comparative studies may reveal key success factors and obstacles to more effective strategies
RQ4: What are the perceived risks or barriers for organizations and whistleblowers in using those trusted whistleblowing ecosystems?	This question explores organizational and individual hesitations that may limit the effectiveness of digital trust solutions. Understanding these barriers is key to designing future interventions and improving digital trust ecosystems
Technical perspective	

(continued)

Table 3. (*continued*)

Research Question	Research Objective
RQ5: How can digital trust elements be integrated into the design of the digital part of trusted whistleblowing ecosystems?	This question explores the practical challenges of implementing security, privacy, and resilience in whistleblowing platforms, focusing on architectural choices and user experience to balance technical robustness with usability
RQ6: What technological innovations (Table 2) would enhance the effectiveness and adoption of trusted whistleblowing ecosystems?	This question explores which emerging technologies best address current limitations in whistleblowing systems. Comparative studies could assess their real-world effectiveness, focusing on anonymity preservation and evidence integrity
RQ7: What role does employee training and awareness play in the success of trusted whistleblowing ecosystems?	This question explores how technical solutions must be accompanied by human understanding to create effective reporting environments. This question bridges technical implementation with human factors essential for system adoption and proper use
People perspective	
RQ8: What are the ethical implications of managing whistleblower reports within a trusted whistleblowing ecosystem?	This question explores the ethical dilemmas of those who process sensitive disclosures. Research could examine decision-making frameworks and the balance between transparency and confidentiality to create ethical guidelines for digital trust systems
RQ9: To what extent do individual factors influence a person's decision to act as a whistleblower via a trusted whistleblowing ecosystem?	This question examines psychological and personal characteristics that affect willingness to report wrongdoing. Understanding these factors could help organizations design systems that address whistleblowers' concerns
RQ10: How does the culture of the whistleblower influence their decision to act within a trusted whistleblowing ecosystem?	This question investigates how cultural backgrounds and societal norms shape whistleblowing behaviors and trust in digital systems. Cross-cultural studies could identify culturally specific barriers and enablers to inform adaptive designs for diverse users
RQ11: How do whistleblowers perceive the protection provided by digital trust measures via a trusted whistleblowing ecosystem?	This question explores the gap between technical protections offered and whistleblowers' subjective sense of safety. Findings could inform improvements in both technical features and communication strategies to increase perceived protection

(*continued*)

Table 3. (*continued*)

Research Question	Research Objective
Process perspective	
RQ12: How can the safety of whistleblowers be ensured if the person the disclosure is made to is potentially corrupt?	This question addresses systemic vulnerabilities in reporting chains that technological solutions alone cannot solve. Research could examine governance structures and oversight mechanisms that ensure report integrity even in compromised organizational environments
RQ13: How to incentivize whistleblowers to blow the whistle?	This question explores ethical and effective ways to motivate reporting of wrongdoing without creating counterproductive consequences. Research could compare different incentive structures and their effects on reporting behavior and quality while minimizing false reports
RQ14: How can organizations (or maybe third parties) securely and in a trustworthy manner monitor the whistleblowing process in a trusted whistleblowing ecosystem?	This question examines governance structures needed to maintain system integrity while respecting confidentiality. Research could investigate audit mechanisms and accountability frameworks that provide transparency in process management without compromising whistleblower protection

6   Key Insights and Implications

This research makes the following key contributions to understanding whistleblowing through the lens of digital trust:

People-Centric Trust Is Foundational. Across both Switzerland and South Africa, the effectiveness of whistleblowing systems depends less on legal provisions or technical sophistication and more on perceived personal safety, anonymity, and cultural norms. Thus, the 'people' node of the DTEF model should be analytically prioritized in whistleblower system design.

Digital Trust Requires Legal Anchoring. While digital trust systems can be technologically robust, they require alignment with national and supranational legal frameworks to achieve institutional legitimacy. The interplay between Switzerland's decentralized trust culture and South Africa's top-down regulatory reform illustrates this dependence.

Emerging Technologies Must Map to Trust Dimensions. Innovations like blockchain, self-sovereign identity, and AI-based anonymization systems show promise in supporting the five pillars of trustworthiness but need contextual embedding. Technologies must be adopted not as end-goals but as instruments of culturally and legally grounded trust design.

Comparative Analysis Reveals Global Design Challenges. The juxtaposition of high-trust Switzerland with low-trust South Africa surfaces a universal challenge: the mismatch between legal affordances, organizational culture, and whistleblower behavior. This reinforces the need for multi-layered trust architectures adaptable to varying societal contexts.

The DTEF Model is Actionable, but Incomplete Without Regulatory Layering. The ISACA DTEF model provides a coherent structure for analyzing digital ecosystems, but in whistleblowing contexts, it must be supplemented with regulatory meta-structures to capture the real-world constraints and enablement mechanisms.

6.1   Conclusion and Future Work

This research introduces the concept of digitally trusted whistleblowing ecosystems and uses the DTEF framework to structure inquiry across four system dimensions. While preliminary, the comparative case study illuminates structural challenges, legal gaps, and technological opportunities. Returning to our two overarching research questions, we can offer initial insights stated below.

- Our comparative analysis reveals that digital trust must be tailored to each country's unique legal, cultural, and institutional context to support whistleblowing. In South Africa, it must prioritize anonymity and protection against retaliation in an environment of institutional mistrust. In Switzerland, it can leverage existing trust to improve reporting efficiency and integration with voluntary compliance systems.
- On the interplay between organizational culture, technical infrastructure, and human factors, our findings suggest a dynamic relationship where technological solutions must be embedded within supportive organizational cultures and aligned with human psychological needs for safety and recognition. The DTEF model provides a promising foundation for conceptualizing these relationships but requires customization for whistleblowing contexts.

In the future, we will address these questions empirically by (1) validating the research propositions developed based on the extant literature (2) prototyping and testing technological renderings of digitally trusted whistleblowing systems within real organizational contexts, and (3) developing a theoretical model of the interplay between legal norms, technological affordances, and trust in user expectations. In pursuing these research directions, we aim to contribute to the re-invention of whistleblowing from a high-stake personal project into a secure, trustworthy and digitally mediated version of civic responsibility.

References

Asprion, P., Grieder, H., Grimberg, F., Moriggl, P.: Building digital trust to protect whistleblowers – A blockchain-based Reporting Channel. Hawaii International Conference on System Sciences 2023 (HICSS-56) (2023). https://aisel.aisnet.org/hicss-56/in/privacy/2

Corritore, C.L., Kracher, B., Wiedenbeck, S.: On-line trust: concepts, evolving themes, a model. Int. J. Hum Comput Stud. **58**(6), 737–758 (2003). https://doi.org/10.1016/S1071-5819(03)000 41-7

Corruption Watch. Corruption Watch Annual Report 2023 (p. 46) (2024)

Deloitte. Are employers taking employee trust for granted? (2023). https://www2.deloitte.com/content/dam/Deloitte/us/Documents/Advisory/data_privacy_info_8-5x11_vF.pdf

Department of Justice and Constitutional Development of South Africa. Protected Disclosures Act 26 of 2000. Government Gazette (2000). https://www.justice.gov.za/legislation/acts/2000-026.pdf

Department of Justice and Constitutional Development of South Africa. Discussion document on proposed reforms for the whistleblower protection regime in South Africa. Republic of South Africa (2023). https://www.stateofthenation.gov.za/assets/scc-legislation-and-reports/20230629-whistleblower-protection-regime_cover.pdf

European Commission. Regulation–910/2014 (2014). https://eur-lex.europa.eu/eli/reg/2014/910/oj/eng

European Commission. Directive (EU) 2019/1937 of the European Parliament and of the Council of 23 October 2019 on the protection of persons who report breaches of Union law (2019). http://data.europa.eu/eli/dir/2019/1937/oj/eng

European Commission. The Cybersecurity Strategy (2020). https://digital-strategy.ec.europa.eu/en/policies/cybersecurity-strategy

European Commission. Digital Europe Programme (2021). https://commission.europa.eu/funding-tenders/find-funding/eu-funding-programmes/digital-europe-programme_en

European Commission. The Digital Services Act (2022). https://commission.europa.eu/publications/legal-documents-digital-services-act_en

European Commission. Artificial Intelligence Act (2024). https://eur-lex.europa.eu/eli/reg/2024/1689/oj/eng

FDPIC. Data protection (2025). https://www.edoeb.admin.ch/en/data-protection

Habbabeh, A., Asprion, P.M., Schneider, B.: Mitigating the risks of whistleblowing-an approach using distributed system technologies. PoEM Workshops, pp. 47–58 (2020)

Hauser, C., Bretti-Rainalter, J., Blumer, H.: Whistleblowing Report 2021: Die umfassende Studie über Whistleblowing in europäischen Unternehmen (2021). . https://www.integrityline.com/de-ch/knowhow/white-paper/whistleblowing-report/

ISACA. The Digital Trust Ecosystem Framework. ISACA (2022). https://www.isaca.org/digital-trust

ISACA. State of Digital Trust Report 2023 (p. 25) (2023). https://www.isaca.org/resources/reports/state-of-digital-trust-2023

Madonsela, S.: Critical reflections on state capture in South Africa. Insight on Africa **11**(1), 113–130 (2019). https://doi.org/10.1177/0975087818805888

Maple, C., Epiphaniou, G., Gurukumar, N.: Facets of Trustworthiness in Digital Identity Systems, Tech. Report (2021). https://www.turing.ac.uk/sites/default/files/2021-05/technical_briefing-facets_of_trustworthiness_in_digital_identity_systems.pdf

NCSC. Federal Council adopts Digital Switzerland Strategy 2025 (2024). https://www.ncsc.admin.ch/ncsc/en/home/dokumentation/medienmitteilungen/newslist.msg-id-103560.html

Near, J.P., Miceli, M.P.: Organizational dissidence: the case of whistle-blowing. J. Bus. Ethics **4**(1), 1–16 (1985). https://doi.org/10.1007/BF00382668

Nortje, J.G.J.: The protection of whistleblowers in South African criminal cases. J. Financ. Crime **30**(6), 1444–1457 (2022). https://doi.org/10.1108/JFC-09-2022-0234

OECD. Trust in government. OECD (2023). https://www.oecd.org/en/data/indicators/trust-in-government.html

Onyango, G.: Whistleblower protection in developing countries: a review of challenges and prospects. SN Bus. Econ. **1**(12), 169 (2021). https://doi.org/10.1007/s43546-021-00169-z

Parliament of the Republic of South Africa. Parliament Session No. 73 – 2024 (p. 223) (2024). [Parliament Session]. https://www.parliament.gov.za

Patil, S., Parmar, K.: Novel mechanism for anonymous reporting and anonymous rewarding using blockchain technology. Int. J. Inf. Secur. **24**(1), 2 (2024). https://doi.org/10.1007/s10207-024-00913-0

PwC. EU Whistleblowing Directive. PwC (2023). https://www.pwc.ch/en/insights/regulation/eu-whistleblowing-directive.html

Staufer, D., Pallas, F., Berendt, B.: Silencing the risk, not the whistle: a semi-automated text sanitization tool for mitigating the risk of whistleblower re-identification. Proceedings of the 2024 ACM Conference on Fairness, Accountability, and Transparency, pp. 733–745 (2024). https://doi.org/10.1145/3630106.3658936

Swiss Digital Initiative. Swiss Digital Initiative. Digital Trust (2025). https://swiss-digital-initiative.org/de/

Swiss Federal Audit Office. Whistleblowing. Swiss Federal Audit Office (SFAO) (2023). https://www.efk.admin.ch/en/whistleblowing/

Swiss Financial Innovation Desk. Pathway 2035 for Financial Innovation (2025)

Tomaz, A.E.B., Nascimento, J.C.do, de Souza, J.N.: Blockchain-based whistleblowing service to solve the problem of journalistic conflict of interest. Ann. Telecommun. **77**(1), 101–118 (2022). https://doi.org/10.1007/s12243-021-00860-0

Transparency International. 2023 Corruption Perceptions Index: explore the results (2024). Transparency.Org. https://www.transparency.org/en/cpi/2023

Wang, H., He, D., Liu, Z., Guo, R.: Blockchain-based anonymous reporting scheme with anonymous rewarding. IEEE Trans. Eng. Manage. **67**(4), 1514–1524 (2020). https://doi.org/10.1109/TEM.2019.2909529

World Intellectual Property Organization. Global Innovation Index 2024: Innovation in the face of uncertainty. World Intellectual Property Organization (2024). https://doi.org/10.34667/TIND.50062

Wright, J.: Encouraging whistleblowers of corruption in South Africa: a critical evaluation of money rewards. J. Anti-Corruption Law **8**, 140–158 (2024)

Young, J.A., Farshadkhah, S.: Improving anonymous whistleblower credibility with self-sovereign identity. Proceedings of the 2021 IFIP, 8(11.13) (2021). https://www.academia.edu/download/75760975/Young_Farshadkhah_2021_Improving_Anonymous_Whistleblower_Credibility_with_Self_Sovereign_Identity.pdf

Factors that Influence the Adoption of AI Fraud Detection Capabilities in the Banking Sector: A Society 5.0 Perspective

Rhulani Hlungwani[1], Hendrik Pretorius[2]($\boxtimes$) (iD), and Yuvraj Sunecher[2] (iD)

[1] Department of Informatics, University of Pretoria, Pretoria 0001, South Africa
`henk.pretorius@up.ac.za`
[2] University of Technology, Port Louis, Mauritius
`lenxh90@gmail.com, ysunecher@utm.ac.mu`

Abstract. This systematic literature review analyses the factors influencing AI adoption for fraud detection in the banking sector from a Society 5.0 perspective. Society 5.0 provides a human-centred framework that emphasizes the integration of advanced technologies to address societal challenges, including financial security.

This paper reviews 31 studies to identify the technological, organizational, and socio-economic factors that influence AI adoption in banking. Key themes emerging from the thematic analysis include: challenges associated with regulatory compliance and legacy systems; the pivotal role of advanced AI techniques, including machine learning and natural language processing; operational advantages such as improved accuracy and cost savings; and the influence of socio-economic factors on AI adoption.

The findings contribute to a strategic framework for integrating AI into fraud detection, aligning technological advancements with societal goals of inclusivity and sustainability. This review highlights both challenges and opportunities, while proposing pathways for future research focused on ethical system design, skill development, and regulatory alignment. These insights offer a roadmap for effective AI adoption, fostering a secure and equitable financial ecosystem.

Keywords: AI Fraud Detection · Banking Sector · Society 5.0 · Technological Adoption · Regulatory Compliance

1 Introduction

The financial sector faces growing threats from sophisticated fraudulent activities that evolve with technological advancements [1, 2], challenging traditional fraud detection methods [3]. These methods, relying on static rules and manual processes, struggle to counter the innovative tactics employed by cybercriminals [4]. This highlights the urgent need for more effective fraud detection solutions [5]. Moreover, the banking industry faces increasing pressure from regulatory frameworks like Know Your Customer (KYC) and Anti-Money Laundering (AML) to enhance transparency and strengthen fraud prevention measures [6]. This challenge is amplified within the Society 5.0 context.

© The Author(s), under exclusive license to Springer Nature Switzerland AG 2026
F. Corradini et al. (Eds.): Society 5.0 2025, CCIS 2787, pp. 138–150, 2026.
https://doi.org/10.1007/978-3-032-15463-7_12

Society 5.0 is a human-centred framework integrating AI and other advanced technologies to address societal challenges by merging cyber-space with physical space. It promotes digital transformation focused on human welfare, inclusivity, and sustainability, goals highly relevant to the financial sector [7]. Through cyber-physicalsocial systems (CPSSs), Society 5.0 aims to revolutionize human interactions, improve societal functions, and foster economic resilience [8].

AI plays a pivotal role in fraud detection, offering advancements in real-time data processing and adaptive security [9]. AI-driven systems can enhance banking security, reducing fraud and improving operational efficiency [10]. This review explores the factors influencing AI adoption for fraud detection in banking, aligned with the goals of Society 5.0, aiming to propose a secure, inclusive banking environment.

The central research question driving this review is: *What factors influence the adoption of fraud detection AI capabilities in the banking environment from a Society 5.0 perspective?*

2 The Role of Artificial Intelligence in Banking

2.1 AI in Fraud Detection

AI has revolutionized fraud detection by moving beyond traditional rule-based systems to machine learning and neural networks, enabling real-time analysis of vast datasets to spot irregularities that may signal fraud [9]. These adaptive systems not only detect current threats but also learn from new data to anticipate emerging fraud tactics [10], a critical capability as fraudulent methods become more sophisticated [11]. However, inconsistent implementation across institutions due to a lack of standardization can impact detection reliability and performance.

In banking, AI boosts operational efficiency by enhancing decision-making, cutting costs, and improving profitability. It enables smarter, safer financial services— especially during economic disruptions—by forecasting trends, automating tasks, and optimizing resources [12]. While AI supports compliance through encryption and secure data handling, its reliance on extensive datasets raises privacy concerns, necessitating strong governance, encryption, and access controls [13]. Balancing efficiency, security, and regulatory compliance remains a core challenge [13].

Economically, AI strengthens stability by reducing risk and bolstering consumer confidence. Its ability to detect anomalies in transactional data helps prevent financial losses [14]. Yet, the accuracy of AI systems hinges on the quality of training data, including transaction histories and customer behaviour patterns [15]. Building a robust data infrastructure is therefore essential to maximizing AI's potential for economic resilience and public trust.

2.2 The Role of AI in Society 5.0

Integrating AI within Society 5.0 seeks to tackle societal challenges by incorporating human-centred technologies into banking. AI facilitates financial inclusion, helping to reduce economic disparities and democratize access to financial services [7]. Society

5.0 envisions a seamless integration of digital and physical spaces to improve quality of life through innovation and inclusivity, with a focus on equitable resource distribution and sustainable development [16]. As financial institutions adopt AI, they contribute to economic stability and promote fairer resource distribution. However, a gap in AI literacy exists, which could hinder the full achievement of Society 5.0's objectives. AI literacy is crucial for effectively understanding and leveraging AI technologies. Enhancing AI literacy can empower individuals to engage with AI across sectors, including banking, and drive societal progress [17].

AI acts as a catalyst for innovation, enabling banks to create anti-fraud solutions that align with Society 5.0's vision of an advanced, technological ecosystem [7]. Predictive analytics provides a competitive edge by forecasting market trends [9]. However, the successful adoption of AI technologies in the banking sector, particularly for future societies, must address key factors such as ethical considerations and decision-making processes [10].

3   Research Method

A Systematic Literature Review (SLR) is a rigorous approach to collecting and critically analysing research studies and literature on a specific topic. Using predefined criteria, SLRs aim to minimize bias and enhance the reliability of conclusions by evaluating and synthesizing relevant studies. The process includes systematic searching, selection, data extraction, and synthesis of findings, ensuring transparency and reproducibility [18]. SLRs are vital for identifying research gaps and guiding future investigations, particularly in fields that require evidence-based conclusions [19]. This section outlines the SLR methodology used to address the research question.

3.1   Data Sources and Search Terms

The following data sources were selected to gather information relevant to the research question and topic The databases and corresponding search strings derived from these sources are summarized in Table 1.

Table 1. Summary of Data Sources and Search Terms.

Database source/Data	
Search Terms/Search Strings	
Google Scholar, Emer-	((fraud detection AI) OR (AI adoption in banking)) AND ((Soald Insight ciety 5.0) AND (banking fraud prevention))
Wiley Online Library	((banking fraud prevention) AND (AI capabilities)) OR ((fraud detection) AND (AI in banking) AND Society 5.0)
ACM Digital Library,	

(continued)

Table 1. (*continued*)

Database source/Data	
ScienceDirect, EBSCOhost	((Artificial intelligence in banking)) OR ((AI adoption in financial systems) AND (Society 5.0 implications) OR (AI-driven fraud prevention))
IEEE Xplore® Digital OR Library, SpringerLink,	((AI innovation in banking) AND (Society 5.0 framework)) ((Machine learning in fraud detection) AND (Society 5.0 goals)
Library	AND (financial inclusion))
Google Scholar, Emer-	((fraud detection AI) OR (AI adoption in banking)) AND ((Soald Insight ciety 5.0) AND (banking fraud prevention))

3.2 Selection Criteria and Quality Assurance

The selection and quality assurance criteria were as follows: 1) Studies must be relevant to AI applications in fraud detection, specifically within the banking sector. 2) Only peer-reviewed articles are considered. 3) Articles published between 2018 and 2024 are included. 4) The language of publication must be English. 5) Research that highlights societal impacts, aligning with Society 5.0 goals, and focuses on AI's role in fostering human-centred innovation and sustainable development is included.

3.3 Prisma Flowchart

The PRISMA flowchart (Fig. 1.) provides a visual representation of the systematic steps taken to identify, screen and select studies for inclusion in this SLR (Fig. 1).

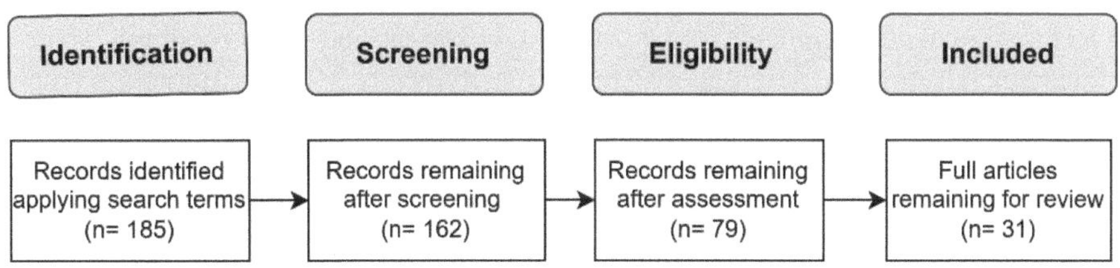

Fig. 1. Prisma Flowchart

The PRISMA flowchart illustrates the systematic review process, from identification to inclusion. Initially, a search across academic databases resulted in 185 records, with an additional 35 identified from other sources. After removing duplicates, and after screening titles and abstracts, 162 unique records remained, leading to the exclusion of 83 records due to irrelevance to AI in banking or Society 5.0. An eligibility assessment of the remaining 79 full texts resulted in the exclusion of 48 for reasons such as lack of relevance, missing peer review, or unavailable full texts. Ultimately, 31 studies were included in the qualitative synthesis, with 10 contributing to the quantitative synthesis, enriching the review's analysis and conclusions.

3.4 Data Analysis

Thematic Analysis was selected as the data analysis method for this systematic literature review. This structured qualitative approach is well-suited for organizing and analysing complex datasets [21]. Thematic analysis involves six key steps: familiarizing oneself with the data, generating initial codes, searching for themes, reviewing themes, defining and naming themes, and producing the final report [20].

Categories were created by organizing the articles into specific areas of interest, including AI techniques, regulatory challenges, and socio-economic impacts. This categorization provided a clear view of how these factors collectively influence the adoption of AI in banking fraud detection. The criteria and thematic codes used were essential for synthesizing insights and drawing meaningful conclusions from this systematic literature review.

4 Findings and Discussion

The review highlights four interconnected themes (Fig. 3) that influence the adoption of AI for fraud detection, examining how technological, organizational, and socioeconomic factors collectively shape its implementation. These themes align with Society 5.0's focus on human-centred, secure, and efficient technological progress, while also addressing the practical challenges and opportunities within banking systems.

4.1 Discussion of Themes

The analysis of themes from the reviewed literature on AI for fraud detection in banking revealed several critical insights. These themes underscore the complex interplay of technological advancements, organizational dynamics, and socio-economic contexts influencing AI adoption. Aligning with the vision of Society 5.0, this exploration emphasizes a human-centred approach, integrating secure and efficient AI technologies into banking systems, e.g. RPA [22]. The discussion provides valuable insights into the challenges, methodologies, and strategic benefits of AI, as well as the contextual factors shaping its implementation. By examining these themes, we aim to uncover the nuanced factors that collectively impact AI utilization, offering a comprehensive perspective vital for navigating the complexities of modern financial ecosystems.

4.1.1 Challenges in AI Adoption

AI adoption in banking faces intertwined challenges, including workforce resistance, integration with legacy systems, and regulatory complexities. Employee resistance and a lack of AI-specific skills emphasize the need for workforce training programs to promote collaboration with AI systems. These initiatives should be supported by infrastructural investments to ensure seamless integration of AI technologies with existing legacy systems [23–25].

Data and availability of data remain significant barriers to AI adoption. AI systems rely on high-quality, labelled datasets, yet variability in data availability can undermine model accuracy. Standardized data-sharing frameworks and equitable access are essential to address this challenge. Moreover, unchecked algorithmic biases can lead to unfair outcomes, highlighting the need for rigorous testing and auditing practices to ensure inclusivity and fairness [23, 24, 26].

Regulatory demands, such as POPIA and GDPR, complicate AI adoption but are crucial for ensuring ethical governance. Society 5.0 emphasizes the need to balance regulatory compliance with technological progress to enable equitable adoption. Cross departmental collaboration and interdisciplinary partnerships are key strategies to overcome these barriers while promoting an inclusive, human-centred approach [24, 27, 28].

Regulatory demands, such as POPIA and GDPR, pose challenges to AI adoption but are essential for maintaining ethical governance. Society 5.0 stresses the importance of balancing regulatory compliance with technological advancement to ensure equitable adoption. Cross-departmental collaboration and interdisciplinary partnerships are vital strategies to address these challenges while fostering an inclusive, human-centred approach [24, 27, 28].

Finally, as AI technologies permeate the banking sector, there is an impending alteration in employment trends, potentially leading to job displacement. Banks must adapt by becoming "AI-first" organizations, shifting towards AI-driven models and refining their core technological infrastructures [3, 33].

4.1.2 AI Techniques for Fraud Detection

Machine learning, deep learning, and natural language processing play a crucial role in advancing fraud detection capabilities. These techniques offer predictive analytics that outperform traditional methods in accuracy and flexibility, effectively identifying anomalous transaction patterns and minimizing human error. For example, machine learning models can detect fraud in real-time, providing quicker and more reliable insights to safeguard banking systems [3, 4, 15].

AI's adaptability ensures that systems can evolve in response to emerging fraud tactics, making them both scalable and robust. These capabilities directly address fraud detection challenges while aligning with Society 5.0's vision of a data-driven society that prioritizes security and operational efficiency. However, embedding ethics and transparency into AI system design is essential to achieving societal goals of fairness and accountability [17, 24].

By enabling real-time fraud detection, these advanced techniques contribute to broader societal objectives, such as fostering economic stability and enhancing public trust in financial systems. The integration of AI techniques thus serves as both a solution to operational challenges and a key enabler of societal resilience [14, 24, 28].

Advanced AI techniques, including anomaly detection, pattern recognition, and risk mitigation, have demonstrated significant effectiveness in identifying financial fraud. For example, anomaly detection algorithms enable the identification of complex fraud schemes that conventional systems may overlook, improving both speed and reliability in fraud prevention efforts [34, 35]. The use of real-time machine learning models enhances the security of payment systems by integrating these models into transaction monitoring processes, allowing for continuous learning and adaptation to evolving fraud tactics [36, 37].

AI-driven approaches not only strengthen real-time transaction monitoring but also facilitate the interpretation and transparency of fraud detection models. This emphasis on transparency helps ensure that machine learning and anomaly detection techniques comply with regulatory standards, ultimately boosting trust in digital transaction systems [38–40].

4.1.3 Operational and Strategic Benefits.

AI provides substantial operational and strategic benefits to banking systems, significantly improving accuracy and reducing false positives. These advancements streamline operations, enhance response times, and foster public trust, supporting Society 5.0's goal of economic resilience and sustainability [23, 25, 28].

A specific example of this is the automation of repetitive tasks, which reduces operational costs and frees resources for strategic priorities. For instance, fraud detection workflows can be automated to minimize manual intervention, enhancing productivity and allowing organizations to focus on innovation. Additionally, AI improves customer experience by reducing false positives, fostering trust in banking systems, and promoting human-centred service delivery [3, 24].

AI's scalability further reinforces its strategic importance. Its ability to adapt to evolving fraud tactics ensures its long-term relevance and supports financial institutions in achieving operational stability. These benefits not only strengthen organizational resilience but also align with Society 5.0's vision of efficient resource utilization and inclusive progress [23, 28].

AI introduces efficiencies that transform banking operations, particularly through advanced automation and process optimization. These advances not only streamline workflows but also improve service delivery in financial markets, offering strategic advantages such as enhanced risk management and performance evaluation [41].

In the context of strategic agility, AI's role in real-time risk assessment and decision making is crucial. Using AI, banks can dynamically respond to changes in fraud tactics and market conditions, thus maintaining competitive advantage. This adaptability is facilitated by AI's machine learning algorithms, which continuously learn from new data, thereby reinforcing a bank's strategic positioning within the financial ecosystem [32, 42].

4.1.4 Contextual Influences on Adoption

The adoption of AI for fraud detection is heavily influenced by socio-economic factors and regulatory frameworks. Laws such as POPIA and GDPR impose strict data privacy and ethical governance requirements, compelling financial institutions to implement strong safeguards for AI systems. While these regulations are essential for ethical governance, they can also create challenges that may hinder innovation if not managed properly [25, 27].

Collaboration across sectors is crucial to balancing compliance with technological innovation. Policymakers, financial institutions, and technology developers must join forces to establish guidelines that foster responsible AI adoption. Integrating ethical principles—such as transparency, fairness, and accountability—into AI systems ensures that technological advancements align with societal goals [17, 24, 28].

AI enables financial institutions to tackle regulatory and socio-economic challenges by reducing costs, enhancing scalability, and adapting to evolving fraud tactics. However, achieving these benefits requires ongoing collaboration and governance to ensure AI implementations align with Society 5.0's focus on sustainable and equitable technological adoption [23, 24, 28].

5 A Framework for AI Adoption in Fraud Detection in the Banking Sector Aligned with Society 5.0

Building on the thematic analysis of AI's role in fraud detection, a framework (Fig. 4) was developed to provide a structured pathway for the successful and sustainable adoption of AI in the banking sector. Guided by the insights from the identified themes, the framework addresses the multifaceted challenges and opportunities highlighted in the review. It aligns with the principles of Society 5.0, which emphasize human- centred, secure, and efficient technological progress, aiming to optimize AI integration in ways that maximize benefits while overcoming potential barriers [3, 23, 24].

This framework outlines four interconnected phases to guide financial institutions through the complexities of AI adoption in fraud detection. Each phase is tailored to address specific aspects of the implementation process, ensuring the sustainable integration of AI capabilities. By following this structured approach, banks can enhance operational efficiency while also supporting broader societal goals, fostering a secure and inclusive ecosystem.

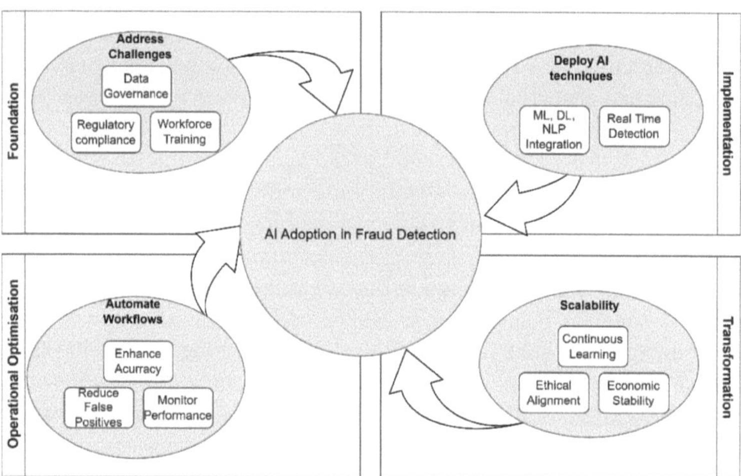

Fig. 2. Framework for AI Adoption in Fraud Detection the Banking Sector

- Foundation Phase: Address Challenges

The Foundation Phase addresses the initial challenges of AI adoption by focusing on critical infrastructural and organizational issues. Establishing a strong foundation ensures seamless integration and optimal utilization of AI capabilities.

– **Data Governance:** Implement quality control measures and standardized data practices to ensure reliable and consistent data inputs [24.
– **Regulatory Compliance:** Ensure AI implementations comply with legal requirements, such as POPIA and GDPR, to maintain ethical standards [27].
– **Workforce Training:** Provide staff with essential AI skills through targeted training programs to overcome resistance and foster collaboration [25].
– **Implementation Phase: Deploy AI Techniques**

The Implementation Phase introduces core AI technologies tailored to enhance fraud detection capabilities within banking systems. This includes Machine Learning and Natural Language Processing. The technologies are applied for real life proactive and timely fraud prevention, ensuring swift responses to potential threats [3].

- **Operational Optimization Phase: Automate Workflows**

This phase seeks to optimize operations through AI-driven automation and improved workflows. This includes **Enhancing Accuracy** to continuously improve AI systems to reduce errors and increase fraud detection precision [3]. Also. **Reducing False Positives** to build customer trust by minimizing false alarms, thereby enhancing user experience and satisfaction [23]. Finally, to **Monitoring Performance** to conduct regular evaluations to maintain system effectiveness and adaptability to changing conditions.

- **Transformation Phase: Scalability and Societal Alignment**

The Transformation Phase focuses on achieving long-term scalability and aligning AI capabilities with broader societal goals. This includes **Continuous Learning**, to ensure AI systems adapt to evolving fraud tactics, maintaining relevance and robustness [23]. **Ethical Alignment** for embed transparency and fairness into AI systems to ensure ethical integrity and build public trust. Also, **Economic Stability** to support broader societal objectives, including financial inclusion and economic resilience [27].

By systematically addressing each stage, this framework enables banks to effectively adopt AI for fraud detection. The approach not only enhances operational efficiencies but also aligns with Society 5.0's emphasis on sustainable progress and human- centred innovation.

6   Conclusion

This systematic literature review explores the research question: What factors influence the adoption of fraud detection AI capabilities in the banking sector from a Society 5.0 perspective? To address this question, 31 articles were analysed using thematic analysis, leading to the identification of four key themes: challenges in AI adoption, AI techniques for fraud detection, operational and strategic benefits, and contextual factors influencing adoption. These themes contributed to the development of a framework that guides the strategic integration of AI in fraud detection.

The implications of this research are substantial for financial institutions aiming to leverage AI's potential. It provides a roadmap for aligning AI strategies with sustainable and ethical principles, promoting resilience and efficiency in banking operations. The framework acts as a tool for navigating technological adoption in ways that support broader societal objectives.

Future research could focus on the long-term impacts of AI adoption in banking, addressing gaps in AI literacy, and refining ethical considerations in AI system design. This work lays the foundation for continued exploration into the responsible integration of AI technologies in financial services, in line with the principles of Society 5.0.

References

1. H.K., S.: Analyzing the Bank scam's financial fraud and its technological repercussions using data mining. In: 2023 Second International Conference on Electronics and Renewable Systems (ICEARS), pp. 1553–1559 (2023). https://doi.org/10.1109/ICEARS56392.2023.10085354
2. Biswas, A., Deol, R.S., Jha, B.K., Jakka, G., Suguna, M.R., Thomson, B.I.: Automated Banking fraud detection for identification and restriction of unauthorised access in financial sector. In: 2022 3rd International Conference on Smart Electronics and Communication (ICOSEC), pp. 809–814 (2022). https://doi.org/10.1109/ICOSEC54921.2022.9951931
3. Daliri, S.: Using harmony search algorithm in neural networks to improve fraud detection in banking system. Comput. Intell. Neurosci. **2020**, 6503459 (2020). https://doi.org/10.1155/2020/6503459
4. Sarma, D., Alam, W., Saha, I., Alam, M.N., Alam, M.J., Hossain, S.: Bank Fraud Detection using Community Detection Algorithm. In: Proc. 2nd Int. Conf. Inven. Res. Comput. Appl. ICIRCA 2020, pp. 642–646(2020). https://doi.org/10.1109/ICIRCA48905.2020.9182954

5. Ranjan, N., Jhajharia, A.: Analysis of fraud credit transaction and its detection. In: 2022 Fourth International Conference on Emerging Research in Electronics, Computer Science and Technology (ICERECT), pp. 1–5 (2022). https://doi.org/10.1109/ICERECT56837.2022.10060262

6. Beniiche, A., Rostami, S., Maier, M.: Society 5.0: internet as if people mattered. IEEE Wirel. Commun. **29**(6), 160–168 (2022). https://doi.org/10.1109/MWC.009.2100570 7

7. Gladden, M.: Understanding the cyber-physical-social-intentional Workforce 4.0. Nowocz. Syst. Zarządzania **14**(3), 15–26 (2019). https://doi.org/10.37055/nsz/132723

8. Lu, M., Han, Z., Zhang, Z., Zhao, Y., Shan, Y.: Graph neural networks in realtime fraud detection with lambda architecture (2021). Available at: http://arxiv.org/abs/2110.04559

9. Muhamed, S.J.: Detection and prevention WEB-Service for fraudulent ETransaction using APRIORI and SVM. Al-Mustansiriyah J. Sci. **33**(4), 72–79 (2022). https://doi.org/10.23851/mjs.v33i4.1242

10. Pandey, A., Jaiswal, H., Vij, A., Mehrotra, T.: Case study on online fraud detection using machine learning. In: 2022 2nd International Conference on Advance Computing and Innovative Technologies in Engineering (ICACITE), pp. 48–52 (2022). https://doi.org/10.1109/ICACITE53722.2022.9823538

11. Jain, R.: Role of artificial intelligence in banking and finance. J. Manag. Sci. **13**(3), 1–4 (2023). https://doi.org/10.26524/jms.13.27

12. Mittal, S., Jindal, P., Ramkumar, K.R.: Data privacy and system security for banking on clouds using homomorphic encryption. In: 2021 2nd International Conference for Emerging Technology (INCET), pp. 1–6 (2021). https://doi.org/10.1109/INCET51464.2021.9456345

13. Reddy, G.D., Saxena, S., Eliza, K.R., Isabels, G., Rathnakar, G., Turar, U.: Utilization of AI for streamlining and optimizing credit decision process and security in banking sector. In: 2022 Sixth International Conference on I-SMAC (IoT in Social, Mobile, Analytics and Cloud) (I-SMAC), pp. 715–721 (2022). https://doi.org/10.1109/ISMAC55078.2022.9987389

14. Priya, G.J., Saradha, S.: Fraud detection and prevention using machine learning algorithms: a review. In: 2021 7th International Conference on Electrical Energy Systems (ICEES), pp. 564–568 (2021). https://doi.org/10.1109/ICEES51510.2021.9383631

15. Carayannis, E.G., Morawska-Jancelewicz, J.: The futures of europe: society 5.0 and Industry 5.0 as driving forces of future universities. J. Knowl. Econ. **13**(4), 3445–3471 (2022). https://doi.org/10.1007/s13132-021-00854-2

16. Kelley, P.G., Woodruff, A.: Advancing explainability through AI literacy and design resources. Interact. **30**(5), 34–38 (2023). https://doi.org/10.1145/3613249

17. Snyder, H.: Literature review as a research methodology: an overview and guidelines. J. Bus. Res. **104**, 333–339 (2019). https://doi.org/10.1016/j.jbusres.2019.07.039

18. Lame, G.: Systematic literature reviews: An introduction. Proc. Int. Conf. Eng. Des. ICED, pp. 1633–1642 (2019). https://doi.org/10.1017/dsi.2019.169

19. Clarke, V., Braun, V.: Thematic analysis. J. Posit. Psychol. **12**(3), 297–298 (2017). https://doi.org/10.1080/17439760.2016.1262613

20. Vaismoradi, M., Snelgrove, S.: Theme in qualitative content analysis and thematic analysis. Forum Qual. Sozialforsch. **20**(3) (2019). https://doi.org/10.17169/fqs20.3.3376

21. Castleberry, A., Nolen, A.: Thematic analysis of qualitative research data: is it as easy as it sounds? Curr. Pharm. Teach. Learn. **10**(6), 807–815 (2018). https://doi.org/10.1016/j.cptl.2018.03.019

22. Mamede, H.S., Gonçalves Martins, C.M., Mira da Silva, M.: A lean approach to robotic process automation in banking. Heliyon **9**(7), e18041 (2023). https://doi.org/10.1016/j.heliyon.2023.e18041

23. Liang, W., et al.: Advances, challenges and opportunities in creating data for trustworthy AI. Nat. Mach. Intell. **4**(8), 669–677 (2022). https://doi.org/10.1038/s42256-02200516-1

24. Horani, O.M., Al-Adwan, A.S., Yaseen, H., Hmoud, H., Al-Rahmi, W.M., Alkhalifah, A.: The critical determinants impacting artificial intelligence adoption at the organizational level. Inf. Dev. (2023). https://doi.org/10.1177/02666669231166889

25. Mehrotra, A.: Artificial Intelligence in financial services-need to blend automation with human touch. In: 2019 Int. Conf. Autom. Comput. Technol. Manag. ICACTM 2019, pp. 342–347 (2019). https://doi.org/10.1109/ICACTM.2019.8776741

26. Jana, V.L.M., Chitimira, H., Torerai, E., Jana, V.L.M., Lisa, V., Jana, M.: Leveraging artificial intelligence money laundering and related crimes in the South African Banking sector money laundering remains a persistent threat that is posing significant. **2024**, 27 (2024)

27. Mehndiratta, N., Arora, G., Bathla, R.: The use of Artificial Intelligence in the banking industry. In: 2023 International Conference on Recent Advances in Electrical, Electronics & Digital Healthcare Technologies (REEDCON), pp. 588–591 (2023). https://doi.org/10.1109/REEDCON57544.2023.10150681

28. Moharrak, M., Mogaji, E.: Generative AI in banking: empirical insights on integration, challenges, and opportunities in a regulated industry. Int. J. Bank Mark. (2024). https://doi.org/10.1108/IJBM-08-2024-0490

29. Lazo, M.P., Ebardo, R.A.: Artificial Intelligence adoption in the banking industry: current state and future prospects. J. Innov. Manag. **11**(3), 54–74 (2023). https://doi.org/10.24840/2183-0606_011.003_0003

30. Ghandour, A.: Opportunities and challenges of Artificial Intelligence in Banking: systematic literature review. TEM J. **10**(4), 1581–1587 (2021). https://doi.org/10.18421/TEM104-12

31. Rahman, M., Ming, T.H., Baigh, T.A., Sarker, M.: Adoption of artificial intelligence in banking services: an empirical analysis. Int. J. Emerg. Mark. (2022). https://doi.org/10.1108/IJOEM-06-2020-0724/FULL/XML

32. Ashta, A., Herrmann, H.: Artificial intelligence and fintech: an overview of opportunities and risks for banking, investments, and microfinance. Strateg. Chang. **30**(3), 211–222 (2021). https://doi.org/10.1002/jsc.2404

33. Mucsková, M.: Transforming banking with artificial intelligence. Trends Econ. Manag. **18**(42), 21–37 (2024). https://doi.org/10.13164/trends.2024.42.21

34. Lin, A.K.: The AI revolution in financial services: emerging methods for fraud detection and prevention. J. Galaksi **1**(1), 43–51 (2024). https://doi.org/10.70103/galaksi.v1i1.5

35. Gayam, S.R.: Artificial intelligence for financial fraud detection: advanced techniques for anomaly detection, pattern recognition, and risk mitigation. African J. Artif. Int. Sust. Dev. **1**(2), 377–411 (2021)

36. Potla, R.T.: AI in fraud detection: leveraging real-time machine learning for financial security. J. Artif. Intell. Res. Appl. **3**(2), 534–549 (2019)

37. Kasaraneni, B.P.: Advanced AI techniques for fraud detection in travel insurance: models, applications, and real-world case studies. **5**, 455–512 (2019)

38. Bello, O.A., Olufemi, K.: Artificial intelligence in fraud prevention: exploring techniques, applications, challenges, and opportunities. Comput. Sci. IT Res. J. **5**(6), 1505–1520 (2024). https://doi.org/10.51594/csitrj.v5i6.1252

39. Chaudhary, P.R.M.N., Kumar, A.K., Chotrani, A.K.: AI in fraud detection: Evaluating the efficacy of artificial intelligence in preventing financial misconduct. J. Electr. Syst. **20**(3s), 1332–1338 (2024). https://doi.org/10.52783/jes.1508

40. Chikwarti, D.K.: AI-enhanced data mining techniques for large-scale financial fraud detection. San Francisco Bay University (2024)

41. Doumpos, M., Zopounidis, C., Gounopoulos, D., Platanakis, E., Zhang, W.: Operational research and artificial intelligence methods in banking. Eur. J. Oper. Res. **2022**, 04 (2023). https://doi.org/10.1016/j.ejor.2022.04.027
42. Al-Ababneh, H.A., Borisova, V., Zakharzhevska, A., Tkachenko, P., Andrusiak, N.: Performance of artificial intelligence technologies in banking institutions. WSEAS Trans. Bus. Econ. **20**, 307–317 (2023). https://doi.org/10.37394/23207.2023.20.29

Rethinking Cars for Sustainable Mobility: How Large Language Models Can Leverage Change

Stephan Jüngling[1]([⊠]), Said M. Easa[2], Dominik Wörner[1], and Gordana Kierans[3]

[1] University of Applied Sciences and Arts Northwestern, Basel, Switzerland
{stephan.juengling,dominik.woerner}@fhnw.ch
[2] Toronto Metropolitan University, Toronto, Canada
seasa@torontomu.ca
[3] MGT OPEN, Grižane, Croatia
gordana.kierans@mgtopen.com

Abstract. Autonomous driving cars, powered by advancements in artificial intelligence (AI), sensor technology, and enhanced communication capabilities of 5G, are set to revolutionise transportation, promising significant improvements in safety, efficiency, and accessibility. The transition to fully autonomous vehicles should align with the shift to Society 5.0, where vehicles are zero-emission and fully integrated into a circular economy. This shift requires a radical change not only in the automotive industry but also among car users, who are moving from being car owners to car users with shared autonomous electric vehicles becoming a more sustainable public mobility service. This transition is a complex endeavour in a socio-technical system and needs a coordinated effort from many different stakeholders. We conducted qualitative research that included a human survey and prompts for Large Language Models (LLMs) focused on sustainable mobility. This human-focused survey comprised questions about participant expertise, public-private partnerships, policies, stakeholders, consumers, and standards. We carefully crafted the prompts for the LLMs to elicit more accurate, relevant, and contextually appropriate responses. Based on the insights gained from both the final human responses and those generated by the LLMs, we proposed a hybrid methodology that integrates findings from both approaches. This hybrid methodology combines insights, reflecting the current literature and representing an integrated view among all stakeholders to achieve the transition to SAEV and CE implementation. This approach could serve as a reference process for combining LLM-generated responses with real-life human expertise to collaboratively conduct questionnaires, and extend qualitative research methods, especially for complex domains with many different stakeholder interests. Our findings reveal that LLMs offer scalability and speed, complementing human expertise which is often difficult to access and limited in speed. We provide a particular example to illustrate similarities and differences in the process steps and combine the strengths and weaknesses of experts and LLG-generated responses to leverage the insights from different stakeholder perspectives and accelerate the transition toward more sustainable mobility.

Keywords: Shared Autonomous Electric Vehicles (SAEVs) · circular economy (CE) · large language models (LLMs) · process redesign · sustainable mobility · qualitative methods · public-private partnerships (PPP)

© The Author(s), under exclusive license to Springer Nature Switzerland AG 2026
F. Corradini et al. (Eds.): Society 5.0 2025, CCIS 2787, pp. 151–167, 2026.
https://doi.org/10.1007/978-3-032-15463-7_13

1 Introduction

According to Ursula von der Leyen, the President of the European Commission (EC), the European automotive industry is at a critical juncture [18]. This shift is driven by the need to tackle environmental challenges and promote sustainability. The ongoing deinnovation and European Union (EU) emphasises the urgency of transitioning to a circular economy (CE), resulting in an Action Plan focusing on key areas, such as talent and resource access, technological innovation, and establishing a predictable regulatory framework. This strategic initiative aims to enhance the industry's resilience and competitiveness while facilitating both a clean transition and addressing social considerations. The Draghi Report [7] noted that the industry is undergoing a significant transformation and emphasised that scale, standardisation, and collaboration will be vital for EU manufacturers to compete in the markets for small, affordable European EVs, software-defined vehicles, and autonomous driving solutions, as well as in the circularity value chain.

This urgent need for more sustainable transportation is also reflected in the future technology trends published by the World Intellectual Property Organization (WIPO) of the United Nations. Their latest report about the future of transportation [24] categorises transportation innovations into four main domains: land, sea, air, and space, and identifies four key families of patent publications: Sustainable Propulsion, Automation and Circularity, Communication and Security, and Human-Machine Interface. These categories highlight the diverse technological advancements driving the future of transportation. Notably, the growth trend for patents in land transportation is significant, with a 13.1% increase in Automation and Circularity. This rate is the highest among all categories, equal to the growth rate for Communication and Security in space transportation. This trend reflects the rapid advancements and increasing focus on sustainable and automated solutions in these areas. The McKinsey Report about the 18 next big arenas of competition [6] also highlights that from 2010 to 2021, more than 400 companies reported a total of more than $100 billion in investment in robo-taxis and robo-shuttles. These were mainly venture capital and private equity firms, followed by big tech and automotive OEMs. While in the United States, this investment has dropped since its peak in 2019, overall investments are still increasing. In their scenarios, SAEVs could capture 25 to 51 percent of the shared mobility industry's revenues by 2040. The big range results in uncertainty related to the pace of technological development and adoption of SAEVs.

Although the goals and benefits are clearly defined, the complexity of the transition involving all stakeholders is exceptionally high. Moreover, moving toward new circular business models, as discussed in our previous paper on rethinking cars [17], poses significant challenges. What should be the next steps to effectively support the transition to SAEVs and facilitate creating new business processes that leverage existing stakeholders' roles and responsibilities? What activities and insights are currently being shared among various stakeholders? Are we on track to achieve sustainable mobility and CO2 neutrality in the transportation sector by 2040? How can we accelerate this transition, and what questions should we ask to ensure efficient and effective implementation?

To address this gap, we raise the question whether insights from LLMs can leverage the necessary change for the transition to SAEVs and the implementation of CE principles and how the insights compare to those from experts. Research comparing large language models (LLMs) to individual experts in these fields remains largely unexplored. We begin with a brief literature review on current trends in SAEVs, focusing on sustainable mobility and global public-private partnerships (PPP). Next, we analyse the application of LLMs in empirical research methods, such as interviews and questionnaires. We propose a process for conducting interviews and questionnaires, emphasising the differences between human and AI actors to identify the next steps for advancing sustainable mobility.

2 Literature Review

In our literature review, we first shed some light on recent trends, policies, and stakeholder initiatives of sustainable mobility, and then on existing approaches employing LLMs as AI participants in qualitative research. The diverse range of startups, from electric autonomous shuttles to smart drones and underwater vehicles, highlights the rapid growth and innovation in the autonomous vehicle sector [1]. The review paper by McKinsey [22] highlighted the following key insights for advancing shared autonomous mobility: (1) achieving a balance between affordability and profitability is crucial, as shared autonomous electric vehicles (SAEVs) must be cost-effective for users while ensuring profitability for businesses along the value chain, (2) improving safety and building consumer trust are essential, with ongoing advancements in SAEV hardware and software, and establishing dedicated safety organisations and better governance mechanisms, and (3) sustainability remains a significant focus, with shared SAEVs primarily being electric and can reduce emissions, though potential issues like road congestion and "deadhead" miles must be addressed to maximise environmental benefits.

Volkswagen Group [22] is intensifying its commitment to electrification by encouraging its employees to adopt EVs and significantly expanding its charging infrastructure, powered by renewable energy from the company's solar plant. This initiative aims to position Spain as a hub for EVs in Europe while promoting a cultural shift toward sustainable mobility within the organisation.

During the World Economic Forum in 2023, it was emphasised that the automotive industry, with vehicles comprising over 30,000 components, requires strong PPPs to effectively address the increasing number of sustainability regulations and achieve comprehensive lifecycle management [23]. The authors identify three key areas for collaboration and stress the importance of PPPs. They advocate for the adoption of a sustainability footprint compass to visualise and expedite the transition to net zero emissions, and the development of a toolkit to enhance value chain transparency. This approach underscores the significance of non-competitive collaborations to identify disruptions in the global value chain and achieve sustainability goals. Additionally, during WEF 2024, the necessity for the automotive industry to transition to a CE throughout its entire product lifecycle was further underscored [2]. This transition is essential to further reduce direct emissions and will require a coordinated, systemic effort from the EU, China, and the USA.

Most existing studies comparing human responses to those generated by LLMs have primarily focused on fields such as health and medicine, law and legal research, social sciences and psychology, as well as business and marketing [20]. These studies typically assess the accuracy, coherence, bias, and effectiveness of LLMs in comparison human responses. For example, Gibson and Beattie [14] showed that LLMs can produce humanlike responses, but they fell short in replicating the richness of human-generated affect and embodiment. Their study highlighted the challenges posed by AI in qualitative research, emphasising the importance of theoretical frameworks to discern the nuanced differences between actual human and AI-generated data. The authors argued that AI, despite its advancements, could not fully capture the subjective human experience central to qualitative research. Thus, the authors are raising significant ethical and methodological concerns.

On the contrary, Dillion et al. [7] argue that while AI models will not entirely replace human participants, they can complement human-based data in certain conditions. They suggest that comparing and analysing AI-generated data with expert-generated data can provide better insights into human vs. machine judgments. Anis and French [4] recommend using AI with small data sets in qualitative research, emphasising its advantages regarding efficiency, explanatory power, and equity.

3   Qualitative Research Methods – Results and Analysis

Interviews and surveys are well-established methods in qualitative research, providing valuable insights from human experience and expertise. However, they often face challenges such as limited access to experts, potential biases, and time-consuming processes, particularly in complex domains like the intersection of SAEVs and CE. New approaches that leverage LLMs could help overcome these limitations by offering scalable access to diverse perspectives, broadening the range of data collected, and reducing the time required for analysis.

3.1   A Human Survey Questionnaire

The transition to sustainable mobility requires rapid and effective solutions. However, formulating the right questions and selecting experts or survey participants without introducing bias can be quite difficult. It is crucial to choose interviewees, and the preparation of the structured, semi-structured, and open-ended questions that can gain insights into the individual experiences and viewpoints. These elements are essential for gaining a deep understanding of the topics at hand. Initial insights can be drawn from the literature review and then can be iteratively refined using different methods, such as grounded theory, action research, or the Delphi method [13]. The Delphi method involves multiple rounds of questionnaires given to experts. After each round, the responses are summarised and the questions are refined, repeating until a consensus emerges.

Our set of questions is relatively brief and not yet mature to address the entire complexity of the underlying socio-technical system, which includes various economic and social dimensions. However, it can be used to compare different approaches. The questions are presented in Table 1. The first three questions are designed to identify the areas of expertise of the survey participants. The following questions focus on key areas that support the adoption of CE principles and SAEVs, including PPP, policies, stakeholders, consumers, and standards. These areas address important stakeholder needs to help create a cohesive ecosystem.

Table 1. Questions asked to various domain experts

Context	Question
Background	Please provide your current role, position, and location
SAEVs	How are you involved in the field of sustainable mobility?
CE	What is your experience or involvement within the circular economy?
PPP	How can PPP (e.g., EU's SHOW project) address SAEV infrastructure gaps?
Policies	What policies best incentivize circular design (e.g., modular design and recycling of batteries, communication components, AI components, sensors, materials)?
Stakeholders	Which stakeholders could play a key role in adopting circular economy principles from the beginning into the SAEV ecosystem?
Consumers	Which consumer segments most resist SAEV adoption, and how can trust be built?
Standards	How can standardization bodies (e.g., IEEE) accelerate AV component interoperability?

3.2 Results of the Human Survey

The insights from the responses reflect the perceived problems caused by the wide scope of the complex problem domain. The first three questions are easy to answer and provide valuable insights into the different areas of expertise from past projects. However, the responses in Table 2, addressing the long-term transition process which needs a systematic and coordinated approach shared among stakeholders with quite diverse sets of goals, remain very short and the questionnaire would require much further investigation using the qualitative research design methods mentioned earlier.

However, the insights from the experts are often not as deep as they could be, because the accessibility of the experts is quite limited. This problem is more pronounced if the inquiry includes many different topic domains. For example, electric vehicles consist of batteries and vehicle hulls, and the design of these is completely separated. Plus, the CE with its reverse logistics and Extended Producer Responsibility (EPR) adds a complexity layer, without even mentioning business models and smart city infrastructure development.

Table 2. Responses and insights from human experts

Context	Responses and Insights
Background	R&D departments; Universities; Transportation engineering; no responses from car manufacturers yet
SAEVs	Projects from numerous sustainability and mobility projects; mobility as a service; personal experience being an EV driver; Traffic impact studies, city infrastructure planning

(continued)

Table 2. (*continued*)

Context	Responses and Insights
CE	CE-consultancy; sustainability topics, in general, e.g. DMA, ESG etc.; Circular jobs; Circular Gap Reports (CGR); reports for countries (e.g. Ireland) and sectors (textiles); Circle Economy Foundation (CEF); institutional clients (EU, EC, UN, multilateral banks) and cities/regions that have in common that besides that they develop policies, they have a responsibility in implementing these policies; NA
PPP	No infrastructure exists without government involvement and no government activity without societal demand. Mobilising society is required to accelerate the development of relevant infrastructure. Enhance the impact of programs by addressing a broader audience. Providing infrastructure for the city and awareness campaigns
Policies	Storytelling, everybody wants to live in a better world Standards regarding the modular design and regulations regarding recycling. Recycling of batteries and other goods for the transition to sustainable cities and net zero emission goals
Stakeholders	(Future) users of SAEV have the key role. SAEV providers and manufacturers as well as battery OEMs. Waste management companies, insurance companies, financial investors
Consumers	Focus on early adopters and willing minorities. When the advantages become clear, the rest will follow. Open a low-level access to SAEVs to test them without subscriptions. Adults, low-income people, women and drivers
Standards	Second-life batteries; Vehicle-to-Home V2H; use of communication protocols and access to infrastructure components. Adopting worldwide best practices, increasing safety awareness, certification courses, promotion of sustainability

3.3   Results of LLMs

LLM Prompt

One key difference from traditional surveys is that researchers must establish their expectations for the LLM using prompt engineering. Well-crafted prompts can guide the models to produce more accurate, relevant, and contextually appropriate responses. By designing prompts thoughtfully, researchers can fully leverage the LLM capabilities to gain valuable insights. The following prompt was used, followed by the questions shown in Table 1.

"We strive to achieve net zero CO2 emissions, by integrating CE principles and pushing SAEVs which can reduce the total number of cars produced, which is most promising. I am seeking advice on how to advance these fields effectively. Specifically, I would like to understand:

(a) *What are the key strategies for implementing CE practices in the transportation sector, particularly in the context of SAEVs?*

(b) *How can we enhance the design, production, and end-of-life management of SAEVs to align with CE principles?*
(c) *What policy measures and incentives can governments introduce to support the adoption of CE and SAEVs?*
(d) *How can stakeholders, including automotive manufacturers, technology companies, and mobility service providers, collaborate to drive innovation and overcome challenges in these areas?*
(e) *What are the best practices for engaging the public and raising awareness about the benefits of CE and SAEVs in reducing carbon emissions?*

Your insights will be invaluable in guiding our efforts to create a sustainable and efficient transportation system that contributes to our net zero CO2 emission goals. "

Responses and Insights: Copilot

The responses from Copilot are summarised in Table 3. Further facts and figures can be found in the additional comments and references afterwards.

Table 3. Responses from Copilot

Context	Response
PPP	By leveraging the strengths of both the public and private sectors and PPP can effectively address infrastructure gaps and accelerate the deployment of SAEVs, contributing to a more sustainable and efficient transportation system
Policies	To incentivise circular design, policies such as EPR, eco-design regulations, and subsidies, can encourage manufacturers to create products that are durable, repairable, and recyclable. Also, research and development grants, PPP and consumer awareness campaigns can drive innovation and promote sustainable practices across industries
Stakeholders	Automotive manufacturers, technology companies, government agencies, PPP, mobility service providers, recycling companies, research institutions, and consumers
Resistant Consumers	Consumer segments of older adults, rural residents, and lower-income groups are identified. Strategies, such as education and awareness campaigns, pilot programs and demonstrations, subsidies and financial incentives, enhanced safety features, and reliable infrastructure are listed, which can build trust in SAEVs that can lead to broader adoption and contribution to the goal of net zero CO2 emissions
Standards	Mentions strategies of standardisation bodies (e.g., IEEE): Developing comprehensive standards, promoting collaboration, ensuring transparency and openness, facilitating testing and certification, updating standards regularly

The following are some insights regarding each context:

- **PPP:** This summary of PPP includes several important insights, referring to additional examples such as the study from Austin, Texas [21] investigating the benefits of co-locating fleet-owned chargers with public charging stations. Their cord-sharing practices demonstrated a cost reduction of 12% and lowered SAEV wait times to about 25% by the sharing model compared to a fleet-owned operation of EV charging stations.
- **Policies:** The LLM outlines several policies such as the EPR which requires the manufacturers to take over the responsibility for waste management from governments and to incentivise them to design products including end-of-life management [24].

This policy promotes sustainable product design and helps reduce the environmental impact of waste by ensuring that manufacturers are accountable for their products' entire lifecycle. Important regulations, such as EU's Ecodesign for Sustainable Products Regulation [8] are mentioned, setting requirements for energy efficiency and material recovery for the product design.

- **Stakeholders:** The list of stakeholders is evident, including their responsibilities as well as their potential influencing activities (e.g., government agencies: enforce regulations, provide funding). The additional references point out the importance of engagement and collaboration between stakeholders with diverse interests in such a socio-technical ecosystem [18].
- **Resistant Consumers:** While SAEVs offer a cost-effective alternative to personal car ownership, reducing costs by $0.20 to $0.50 to approximately $0.80 per mile [23], there are concerns about privacy, safety, and technology reliability. Also, the emotional attachment to personal vehicle ownership and the perceived inconvenience of shared transportation options can further hinder widespread acceptance. Nevertheless, the significantly lower CO2 emissions, enhanced road safety, and the convenience of shared transportation might be more convincing in the long run.
- **Standards:** strategies and general hints about standardisation processes (e.g., compatibility and interoperability of components across different manufacturers) are mentioned but a list of existing standards is missing. However, a follow-up question refers to the IEEE standards relevant to SAEVs and CE, including IEEE P2030.1 for electric grid infrastructure, IEEE 2413.3–2024 for IoT integration, IEEE 1573–2003 for electronic power subsystems, and IEEE 2686–2024 for battery management systems.

Responses and Insights: DeepSeek

The responses from DeepSeek are summarized in Table 4.

Table 4. Responses from DeepSeek

Context	Response
PPP	PPPs like the EU's SHOW project are critical for bridging SAEV infrastructure gaps by pooling resources, expertise, and funding. Key strategies include Co-developing Charging/Energy Infrastructure, Shared Data Platforms, and Policy Alignment
Policies	Policies are listed directly: Extended Producer Responsibility, Tax Breaks/ Subsidies, Design Standards, and R&D Grants
Stakeholders	Automakers, Battery Recyclers, Tech Firms, City Planners, Material Suppliers
Resistant Consumers	Older generations, rural population, car enthusiasts are listed as consumers and transparency, Incentives, and education as trust-building strategies
Standards	Specific hints to global standards, modular interfaces, circularity frameworks, and collaborative platforms

The following are some insights regarding each context:

- **PPP:** Additional facts related to different strategies are mentioned, including the integration of SAEVs into a bidirectional vehicle-to-grid charging infrastructure (V2G) and reusing retired EV batteries for energy storage, the creation of an open-access data ecosystem for traffic patterns, energy demand, and fleet optimisation, which first requires SAVE's deployment and testing to validate infrastructure needs, like smart signals, and the policy alignment of the governments for regulatory sandboxes and private investors for scalable solutions (e.g., charting stations).
- **Policies:** Focus on recyclable components for batteries and sensors such as the EU's Battery Regulation of the European Parliament and Council [12] which sets a recycling target of 70% for lithium recovery by 2030. Rewarding companies for using recycled materials (e.g., aluminium, rare earth metals) or modular designs (e.g., Sweden's tax cuts for circular businesses), the required modularity (e.g., ISO 20887 for disassembly) as well as interoperability (e.g., standardised battery connectors), and fund projects such as Circularise from the EC [10], using blockchains for material traceability in close loop supply chains are pointed out.
- **Stakeholders:** The following stakeholder responsibilities are pointed out: Automakers: Design vehicles for longevity (e.g., upgradable AI hardware) and recyclability; Battery Recyclers: Partnering with OEMs (e.g., Redwood Materials) to recover critical minerals; Tech Firms: Developing AI for predictive maintenance and component reuse (e.g., NVIDIA's AV platforms); City Planners: Integrating SAEVs with circular infrastructure (e.g., shared hubs with repair facilities); Material Suppliers: Providing low-carbon, recyclable materials (e.g., bio-based composites).
- **Resistant Consumers:** Mentioning the reasons (Scepticism about AV safety, Limited SAEV coverage, and Preference for ownership), strategies (Share safety data, like disengagement rates), and third-party certifications (e.g., Euro NCAP for AVs), subsidized SAEV rides in underserved areas or offering loyalty programs, and immersive demos (e.g., AR simulations) to showcase reliability and environmental benefits.
- **Standards:** Mentioning protocols for V2X communication (e.g., IEEE 802.11bd for low-latency vehicle networks) and sensor calibration, standardised connectors for batteries, lidar, and AI chips to simplify repairs and upgrades (e.g., USB-C-like universality), metrics for component reuse (e.g., IEEE P2851 for battery health tracking) and industry alliances (e.g., Autoware Foundation) to align SAEV architectures with CE principles.

4 Proposed Methodology

4.1 Human-LLM Integration Process

Our preliminary experiment demonstrates some key differences between human and LLM responses. Both have strengths and weaknesses, but a process that does focus on combining both responses seems more promising. The new process combines qualitative insights from humans and AI. Specifically, it involves a series of steps for human and LLM interactions, as illustrated in Fig. 1.

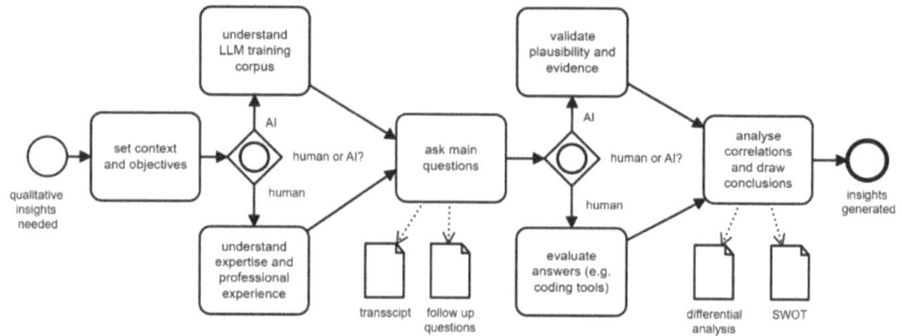

Fig. 1. Proposed methodology: Combining insights from humans and LLMs

These steps are designed to effectively leverage the strengths of both sources of information while ensuring that the quality, accuracy, and relevance of the results are maintained. For traditional expert interviews/questionnaires, people's opinions and expertise are influenced by their business domain context. The researchers choose them because of their roles in their organisations. However, this might introduce some contextual bias, and researchers must pay attention to an appropriate selection. This differs significantly from the functioning of LLMs. They generate responses using probabilistic algorithms, that integrate stakeholder perspectives across the entire text corpus from their training data.

Consequently, the LLM responses are based on their knowledge base and are characterised by similarity measures between the prompt & query and the topic clusters in the knowledge base, as illustrated in Fig. 2. The figure shows a distribution of the number of relevant text documents in the different topic clusters along the x-axis, on an arbitrary normalised y-axis.

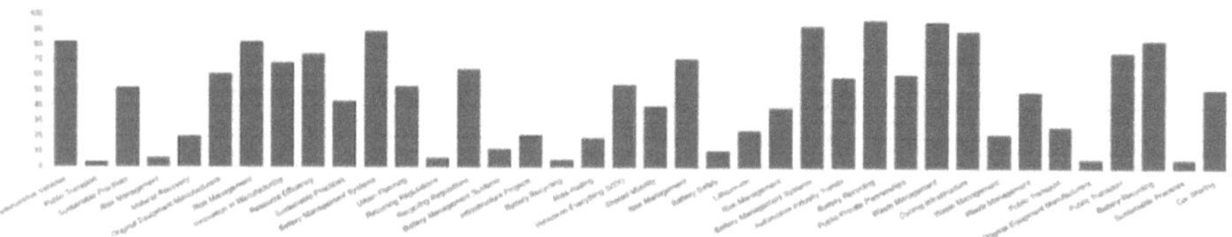

Fig. 2. Knowledge Base from the training data in LLM

The distribution is fictitious and does not represent accurate distributions of a text corpus. It also incorporates information from various stakeholders. As previously stated, the responses from the LLMs reflect the overall opinions and facts gathered from different stakeholders' documents, though any potential bias inherent in the selection of training data remain obscured. This highlights two important AI-related activities in Fig. 1 that follow the 'Inclusive AND' gateway (a decision-making point in a process flow). Unlike the well-known 'Exclusive OR' gateway, where either the AI or the human sequence flows are selected, the proposed process allows both flows to be combined simultaneously. In the case of LLMs, the two critical steps involve understanding the training corpus and validating the plausibility and evidence of the LLM's responses. These steps correspond to comprehending human experience and expertise, followed by coding the responses either manually or with the assistance of tools like ATLAS.ti [15]. Such tools enable researchers to efficiently organise, code, and analyse large unstructured data to identify themes and insights relevant to their research. However, this task—often automated by various tools—seems somewhat redundant since LLM responses conduct a similar analysis implicitly as a hidden process.

4.2   Analysis of a LLM Knowledge Base

The number of different LLMs and their capabilities is growing rapidly. However, even for open-source LLMs, the training data and knowledge base are not fully transparent. However, it is quite intriguing to observe how the responses of different LLMs are structured when asked about their respective knowledge bases. Table 5 summarises several responses to the following question: "What types of sources did you use to collect information for training as an LLM, concerning CE and SAEVs?".

Table 5. Responses of LLMs concerning their knowledge base of the training text corpus

LLM	Characteristics of the Response
Copilot	States that the training corpus is unknown. Provides a list of general sources in both areas (CE: Academic Journals and Research Papers, Industry Reports, Government and NGO Publications, Newspapers and Media Reports, Books and Educational Materials, Conferences and SAEVs: Academic Journals and Research Papers, Industry Reports, Government and NGO Publications, Newspapers and Media Reports, Books and Educational Materials, and Conferences)
DeepSeek	Thinks for 23 s and explores sources for both topics (CE, SAEVs) first. After categorising the content of retrieved documents, it searches for the intersection of both topics, followed by a ranking based on the query. It recognizes key sources and categorises them into different contributions (*CE perspectives in transportation* with, *SAEVs*, with participatory planning for Shared Automated Electric Mobility Systems and Energy-Mobility synergy; and *interdisciplinary integration* with stakeholder dynamics & infrastructure and business models) followed by a conclusion
Claude 3.5 Sonnet	States that the training corpus is unknown. Explains, that it can discuss the topic based on its training data, help to find relevant academic and industry sources, and can also help to analyse additional sources, which could be uploaded

(continued)

Table 5. (continued)

LLM	Characteristics of the Response
Gemini 2.0 Flash Thinking	States that it has been trained on a massive dataset of text and code, and points out SAEVs specifically, while this corpus has been selected, gathered, and processed by its developer teams, followed by the structure of the topics CE and SAEVs (CE: Academic Literature, Industry and Business Publications, Government and Policy Documents, News and Media, Standards and Guidelines; SAEVs: same categories, replacing Standards and Guidelines by Forums and Communities). Adds important considerations (Scale and variety, constantly evolving data, not reflecting the "truth" and referring to potential bias, knowledge is based on pre-processing)
Olama Tülu 3405B	States that the exact corpus of training data is proprietary, but refers to (CE: Academic Journals and Research Papers, Government and NGO Reports, Industry Reports and White Papers, Books and Monographs, Newspapers and Blogs and SAEVs: Academic Journals and Conference Proceedings, Market Research Reports, Policy Documents and Legislation, Industry Publications, Educational Resources, News Outlets, and Technology Blogs)

While all models mention that they do not have explicit knowledge about their training text corpora, there are notable differences in the responses. DeepSeek implicitly references its corpus knowledge, which can be linked to an expert's claim of expertise. Interacting with the LLM resembles interviewing an expert who evaluates the questions before the interview. The responses are compiled from the most relevant sources during the retrieval augmented generation (RAG) step. These sources include EVs examined from lifecycle and CE perspectives, SAEVs interacting with microgrids from an energy resilience standpoint, and methodological aspects, such as the Delphi method. This method is a structured communication technique, developed as a systematic, interactive forecasting method that relies on a panel of experts. These experts respond to questionnaires in multiple rounds, where a facilitator provides an anonymised summary of the experts' forecasts and reasons after each round. This process continues until the group reaches a consensus.

4.3   Consolidation of Findings

Based on the insights from our questionnaire, we conclude that the responses from the LLMs are most beneficial and should be considered to extend the insights from human experts. However, to what extent do the responses from LLMs differ from human responses? Drawing on our experience with human experts and LLM-generated questionnaire responses, we performed a SWOT analysis (Strengths, Weaknesses, Opportunities, and Threats). The results of the analysis for exclusively human experts and LLMs are presented in Tables 6 and 7, respectively.

The insights provided by experts may be limited compared to interactions with LLMs. However, there is a distinct advantage in terms of stimulating activities and embedding ideas into the minds of opinion leaders, who have the authority to implement changes based on the communication and insights gathered from the surveys and interviews. Moreover, incorporating LLMs into the process ensures that various aspects of our socio-technical system are considered from the diverse perspectives of automotive engineering, environmental science, urban planning, and economics.

What are the advantages of considering both? Researchers are increasingly exploring the use of LLMs for urban sustainability assessments. A recent study comparing the use of LLMs and human experts in these assessments reached similar conclusions.

Table 6. SWOT Analysis of using human experts

Strengths	Weaknesses
• Real-world experience and understanding • Understanding of needs and consequences • Awareness of historical & political contexts • Practical reasoning skills • Ability to initiate and develop initiatives	• Prone to bias based on work habits • Dependence on organisational strategies • Specialisation can lead to silo-thinking • Unavailability due to many inquiries • A tendency to remain in linear thinking patterns
Opportunities	Threats
• Prompting specific stakeholder perspectives • Encouraging innovation and fresh thinking • Fostering collaboration among different stakeholders	• Insufficient cross-domain oversight • Experts may have conscious or unconscious biases • Over-enthusiasm for technology may overshadow the purpose of SAEV and its role in Society 5.0

LLMs can efficiently conduct standardised sustainability assessments, resulting in significant time savings and consistency compared to traditional methods that rely solely on human input. This approach also encourages a holistic perspective on urban development projects, fostering collaboration across various sectors and helping to break down barriers. However, integrating human expertise is essential for interpreting nuanced, context-specific factors, and for addressing ethical considerations.

Table 7. SWOT Analysis of using LLMs

Strengths	Weaknesses
• Speed and breadth of expertise • Comprehensive policy identification and references • Many diverse examples • In-depth analysis and integration of facts	• Lack of understanding of implications • Misinterpretation due to language usage • Disclosed training data • Requires evidence and plausibility checking • Challenges in probabilistic reasoning

(continued)

Table 7. (*continued*)

Strengths	Weaknesses
Opportunities	Threats
• Addressing specific stakeholder perspectives • Agentic AI by leveraging existing potentials • Greater data availability might enhance "Connecting the dots" • Enhancing perspectives by combining human expertise with AI, as illustrated in this article	• A misleading belief that LLMs can answer any question • The reliability of historical data may be questionable • The accuracy of responses is not assured, which could adversely affect user trust

5   Conclusions and Outlook

This paper emphasises the urgent need for transformation in the automotive industry, which is facing significant challenges. We explored the collaboration between humans and machines to address key questions about sustainable mobility and CE. As highlighted in a previous paper [17], the stepwise transition to SAEVs and CE requires a new set of infrastructure, processes and business models. Based on this study, the following comments are presented:

1. Our literature review revealed that comparing the use of LLMs to actual experts in the field of sustainable mobility has not been extensively studied. Therefore, we aimed to address the complex issues surrounding the transition design of SAEVs and the implementation of CE principles for a sustainable Society 5.0. Our analysis of incorporating LLMs in empirical research methods demonstrated that LLMs can gather data and compile a more comprehensive list of policies, standards, and PPPs than a limited number of experts.
2. SAEVs represent a logical step toward achieving a more sustainable e-mobility, as they could help reduce the material footprint of millions of cars on the road. However, this journey is not without its challenges.
3. We found that human expertise is vital in areas requiring technical knowledge and strategic decision-making, such as sustainable mobility and the circular economy. However, a hybrid approach that uses LLM responses as a complementary perspective to human expert insights is essential for effective sustainability practices. At this stage, we believe that humans innovate while LLMs provide responses based on historical datasets.
4. As we illustrate, one key difference from traditional research is that the researcher must establish expectations for the LLM through prompt engineering. The prompts can guide the models to generate more accurate, relevant, and contextually appropriate responses. Posing the right questions and specifying the correct prompts will be more important in the future, than collecting and coding the answers in human-centred processes in the past.
5. We propose a process focusing on the collaboration between humans and AI in qualitative research that covers complex topics such as the transition to SAEV and CE.

6. Further transparency of LLM training corpora would be necessary to choose LLMs according to their area of expertise, like the selection of human experts based on their background.

Conducting LLM-human surveys is an emerging field, particularly in sustainable mobility. Future research should investigate how LLMs and human insights can be integrated to design and implement innovative transportation policies and solutions as a more systematic approach between all stakeholders involved. Our proposed hybrid qualitative research process could also be validated in case studies about current implementation of CE principles or existing autonomous driving pilot areas.

This paper highlights several weaknesses, one of which is the very small number of experts available to respond to the questions. Due to the complexity of the topic, there is no dedicated group of specialised experts who can provide insights, as was the case with combustion engine designers. As previously mentioned, vehicle hull manufacturers operate independently from battery producers. Furthermore, the infrastructure requirements for SAEVs depend heavily on IT infrastructure and AI expertise. Governments must expand and enforce regulatory frameworks for CE practices and autonomous driving, ensuring that they are consistent across regions. Car manufacturers should address cost barriers to make their vehicle more modular and sustainable, allowing for updates related to V2X communication with the necessary smart vehicle platforms. Finally, consumers should consider changing their behaviors to support these advancements and turn away from owning cars towards more sustainable mobility in a Society 5.0. As stated by one of the experts, the acceptance will grow with the winning minority of early adopters. When the advantages become clear, the rest will follow.

References

1. Adarsh, R.: 30 top autonomous vehicle startups and companies to watch in 2025. StartUs Insights (2025). Accessed February 20, 2025: https://www.startus-insights.com/blog/mobility/30-top-autonomous-vehicle-startups-and-companies-to-watch-in-2025/
2. Allgood, K., Na, N.: Automotive industry circularity: how the EU, China and the US are revving up sustainability. World Economic Forum (2024). Accessed February 20, 2025: https://www.weforum.org/agenda/2024/03/automotive-industry-circularity/
3. Anis, S., French, J.A.: Efficient, explicatory, and equitable: why qualitative researchers should embrace AI, but cautiously. Bus. Soc. 62(6), 1139-1144 (2023). https://doi.org/10.1177/00076503231163286
4. Bradley, C., Chui, M., Russell, K., Ellingrud, K., Birshan, M., Chettih, S.: The next big arenas of competition. McKinsey Global Institute (2024). https://www.mckinsey.com/~/media/mckinsey/mckinsey%20global%20institute/our%20research/the%20next%20big%20arenas%20of%20competition/the-next-big-arenas-of-competition_final.pdf
5. Dillion, D., Tandon, N., Gu, Y., Gray, K.: Can AI language models replace human participants? Trends Cogn. Sci. 27(7), 597–600 (2023). https://doi.org/10.1016/j.tics.2023.04.008
6. ESPR: Ecodesign for Sustainable Products Regulation (2024). Accessed 20 Feb 2025. https://commission.europa.eu/energy-climate-change-environment/standards-tools-and-labels/products-labelling-rules-and-requirements/ecodesign-sustainable-products-regulation_en
7. European Commission: Address by Mr. Mario Draghi at the presentation of the report on the Future of European competitiveness in the European Parliament (2024). Accessed 20 Feb 2025. https://commission.europa.eu/topics/eu-competitiveness/draghi-report_en

8. European Commission: Circularize: circular economy through innovative recycling and reuse strategies. Horizon 2020 Research and Innovation Programme (Grant Agreement No. 101003491) (2021)

9. European Parliament and Council: Regulation (EU) 2023/1542 of the European parliament and of the council of 12 July 2023 concerning batteries and waste batteries, amending directive 2008/98/EC and regulation (EU) 2019/1020 and repealing Directive 2006/66/EC. Official J. Eur. Union L **191**, 1–117 (2023)

10. Fish, L.S., Busby, D.M.: The Delphi method. In: Sprenkle, D.H., Moon, S.M. (eds.), Research Methods in Family Therapy, pp. 469–482 (1996)

11. Gibson, A.F., Beattie, A.: More or less than human? Evaluating the role of AI-as-participant in online qualitative research. Qual. Res. Psychol. **21**(2), 175–199 (2024). https://doi.org/10.1080/14780887.2024.2311427

12. Hecker, J., Kalpokas: Auto-coding & smart-coding in research. ATLAS.ti (n.d.). Retrieved 26 Feb 2025. from https://atlasti.com/guides/qualitative-research-guide-part-2/auto-coding-smart-coding

13. Jonveaux, L.: Using Large Language Models for a standard assessment mapping for sustainable communities (2024). arXiv. https://arxiv.org/html/2411.00208v2

14. Jüngling, S., Kierans, G., Easa, S.M., Wörner, D.: Rethinking cars for sustainable mobility – shared-autonomous vehicles and circularity. Zenodo (2024). https://doi.org/10.5281/zenodo.11617425

15. Kaipainen, J., Uusikartano, J., Aarikka-Stenroos, L., Harala, L., Alakerttula, J., Pohls, E.L.: How to engage stakeholders in circular economy ecosystems: the process. In: Kujala, J., Heikkinen, A., Blomberg, A. (eds.) Stakeholder Engagement in a Sustainable Circular Economy. Palgrave Macmillan, Cham (2023). Accessed 20 Feb 2025. https://doi.org/10.1007/978-3-031-31937-2_7

16. Kelkar, A., Heineke, K., Kellner, M., Kampshoff, P., Tolstinev, D., Mañas Pont, E.: Getting on board with shared autonomous mobility. McKinsey & Company (2025). Accessed 20 Feb 2025. https://www.mckinsey.com/industries/automotive-and-assembly/our-insights/getting-on-board-with-shared-autonomous-mobility

17. Mittelstädt, J.M., Maier, J., Goerke, P., et al.: Large language models can outperform humans in social situational judgments. Sci. Rep. **14**, 27449 (2024). Accessed 20 Feb 2025. https://doi.org/10.1038/s41598-024-79048-0

18. PubAffairs Bruxelles: President von der Leyen launches strategic dialogue on the future of the automotive industry and announces action plan. PubAffairs Bruxelles (2025). https://www.pubaffairsbruxelles.eu/eu-institution-news/president-von-der-leyen-launches-strategic-dialogue-on-the-future-of-the-automotive-industry-and-announces-action-plan/

19. Sinha, A., Gustafsson, N.: How the automotive industry is gearing up into sustainability's fast lane. World Economic Forum (2023). https://www.weforum.org/stories/2023/01/automotive-industry-sustainability-davos2023

20. Stena Recycling: Designing batteries for circularity (2025). Accessed 20 Feb 2025. https://www.stenarecycling.com/news-insights/insights-inspiration/guides-articles/designing-batteries-for-circularity/

21. Su, L., Gurumurthy, K.M., Kockelman, K.M.: (2024). Siting and sizing of public-private charging stations with impacts on household and private electric vehicle fleets. Transportation Research Part A. Currently Under Review. Accessed 20 Feb 2025: https://www.caee.utexas.edu/prof/kockelman/public_html/TRB25PublicPrivateChargingStations.pd

22. Volkswagen Group: Leading by example: SEAT S.A. strengthens its commitment to electrification in 2025 (2025). Accessed 20 Feb 2025: https://www.volkswagenag.com/en/news/2025/02/leading-by-example-seat-sa-strengthens-its-commitment-to-electrification.html

23. Wegscheider, A.K., Hagenmaier, M., Bert, J., Collie, B., Palme, T., Rose, J.: Shared, autonomous, and electric: an update on the reimagined car. Boston Consulting Group (2022). Accessed 20 Feb 2025. https://www.bcg.com/publications/2022/update-on-shared-autonomous-electric-vehicles-market
24. World Intellectual Property Organization: WIPO technology trends report 2025: the future of transportation. WIPO (2025). https://doi.org/10.34667/tind.57963

Bridging the Skills Gap for an Inclusive Society 5.0: Hard Skills, Digital Literacy, and Entrepreneurial Pathways for Rural Youth

Sean Kruger$^{(\boxtimes)}$ and Isak van der Walt

University of Pretoria, Pretoria 0002, GT, South Africa
sean.kruger@up.ac.za

Abstract. With the increasing emphasis on inclusive workforce development towards a Society 5.0, the need for an integrated approach to hard skills training, digital literacy, and entrepreneurial pathways for rural youth in developing countries has been highlighted. Despite policy interventions, these youth remain marginalised from traditional industries and emerging digital economies, largely due to sectoral skill gaps and a lack of structured training frameworks. This study employs a Systematic Quantitative Literature Review (SQLR) to assess the evolution, key trends, and thematic gaps in youth skills development research within rural contexts. A bibliometric analysis was conducted, incorporating 2,083 peer-reviewed studies filtered through the SPAR-4-SLR framework to ensure systematic evaluation. Findings reveal a shift towards interdisciplinary and digital competency research. Keyword co-occurrence and co-citation analyses highlight five dominant thematic clusters: education and workforce readiness, digital transformation and entrepreneurship, rural healthcare systems, social determinants of employability, and sustainability-oriented training. Despite progress, fragmentation in skill-building initiatives, limited integration of digital and industrial skills, and a low citation impact of recent research indicate the need for localised, cross-sectoral training solutions. This study proposes a review of centres as multidisciplinary hubs that can integrate hard skills training, entrepreneurial incubation, green talent and digital literacy education to bridge the urban-rural employment divide. Future studies could explore implementation strategies for such centres and evaluate their impact on long-term economic sustainability in rural economies, with attention on how integrated models can address psychosocial readiness, promote human–AI collaboration, and strengthen inclusive ecosystems.

Keywords: Digital Literacy · Entrepreneurship Ecosystems · Rural Employment · Society 5.0 · Youth Skills Development

1 Introduction

The persistence of high youth unemployment in South Africa has necessitated a re-evaluation of traditional workforce development strategies. As of 2025, unemployment in the country reached 59.6% for youth aged 15–24. 25–34 stood at 39.4% [1]. This disproportionately affects rural communities where economic opportunities remain scarce

F. Corradini et al. (Eds.): Society 5.0 2025, CCIS 2787, pp. 168–180, 2026.
https://doi.org/10.1007/978-3-032-15463-7_14

[2]. The barriers to employment are complex, encompassing a lack of access to quality education, insufficient vocational training, and digital exclusion [3]. The Fourth Industrial Revolution (4IR) and Society 5.0, a concept that integrates technology with sustainable, human-centred development, offer new pathways for economic participation [4]. However, without the necessary skill development, rural youth risk being further marginalised from emerging employment opportunities [5].

Efforts to address this challenge have traditionally focused on vocational training and entrepreneurial initiatives. However, many existing programmes fail to integrate sector-specific hard skills development with digital competencies, limiting their effectiveness in preparing youth for both traditional workforce participation. For example, agriculture, mining, infrastructure and digital entrepreneurship [6]. Moreover, existing research has emphasised the fragmentation in skills training ecosystems, where rural youth are trained for specific industries but lack cross-sectoral competencies that would enable them to transition between employment opportunities or launch technology-driven enterprises [7]. While industries remain crucial for employment, they are rapidly evolving with the introduction of automation, data analytics, and AI-driven management systems, requiring upskilled labour forces that can adapt and innovate in this new technological landscape [7, 8]. Despite growing recognition of digital transformation in rural employment, division in training frameworks has resulted in sector-specific knowledge that does not equip young people with multi-sectoral adaptability [6].

Furthermore, rural youth often lack access to structured digital literacy education, further exacerbating the skills gap between urban and rural workforces [9]. In urban areas, technological integration is increasingly embedded into education and workforce training, whereas rural communities continue to experience digital exclusion due to poor internet access, limited technical training programmes, and a lack of investment in ICT-driven learning environments [3, 10]. If unaddressed, these disparities will result in an increasingly divided labour market where rural youth are excluded from high-value economic opportunities in technology-driven industries.

A key gap in existing research is the lack of an interdisciplinary approach to skills development. While vocational education has long been studied as a pathway to youth employment, the intersection between technical workforce training, digital competency building, and entrepreneurship ecosystems remains underexplored [3, 9–12]. This study addresses this gap by assessing the existing body of knowledge on rural youth skills development, examining key thematic trends and knowledge deficits. The study builds on a Systematic Quantitative Literature Review (SQLR) methodology to analyse 2,083 peer-reviewed studies from the Scopus database, ensuring a comprehensive evaluation of youth skills research in rural contexts. Through bibliometric analysis, the study attempts to answer the following research questions. RQ1. How has the publication productivity and citation impact of research on skills in rural and youth employment contexts evolved? RQ2. Who are the most productive and impactful contributors to research on hard skills and competencies in rural youth employment? RQ3. What are the major knowledge foundations that underpin research on hard skills and competencies in rural and youth employment? RQ4. What are the future directions for advancing hard skills and competencies in rural and youth employment?

The remainder of this paper is structured as follows. Section 2 presents the methodology, outlining the SQLR approach, bibliometric techniques, and data analysis process. Section 3 reviews findings, highlighting key research gaps. Section 4 offers discussions and implications, with Sect. 5 noting conclusions drawn.

2 Methodology

To address the research questions a SQLR methodology is used to provide an objective evaluation of youth skills in rural contexts [13]. To systematically examine the literature and identify emerging themes and trends based on scientific knowledge, bibliometric techniques are utilised. In alignment with bibliometric analysis methodologies proposed by Aria and Cuccurullo (2017), Block and Fisch (2020), and Donthu et al. (2021), a Scientific Procedures and Rationales for Systematic Literature Reviews (SPAR-4-SLR) framework is applied [14–16]. Developed by Paul et al. (2021), SPAR-4-SLR facilitates the systematic identification, evaluation, and synthesis of relevant literature, enhancing both reproducibility and comprehensive quantitative analysis. This approach aligns with the researchers' pragmatic stance in systematically assessing cognitive technologies, particularly youth and hard skills in rural (non-urban) contexts [17].

Research outputs from 2010 to 2025 are used as it is a period marked by significant advancements in skills development, focal research on youth and an increasing adoption in entrepreneurial practice [18]. The Scopus database was used due to its comprehensive coverage and access to high-quality academic literature, facilitating data retrieval for bibliometric analysis. The peer-review process and high editorial standards of Scopus minimise the risk of incorporating predatory journals. Additionally, Scopus is recognised as a reputable academic database, indexing ISI-listed outlets, academic publications, summaries, and citation records [19]. Scopus is also a preferred database in bibliometric studies within management research due to its bibliographic metadata, including indexed documents, article titles, publication types, authors' institutional affiliations, keywords, abstracts, citation counts, journal names, publisher details, publication years, volumes, issue numbers, and cited references [20]. This coverage ensures that the bibliometric analysis incorporates a wide range of high-quality research outputs, thereby maintaining analytical rigor and integrity. To compile a comprehensive set of studies a search string as noted in the annexure was applied using the "OR" and "AND" operator to create the final search string. The search covered titles, abstracts, keywords, and publications.

The initial search retrieved 2833 documents from the Scopus database. These documents were filtered using specific selection criteria to focus on relevant research articles. (i) Limiting terms used per search string. (ii) Inclusion in one of the following domains: The study encompasses the fields of Business, Management and Accounting, Engineering, Computer Science, Social Sciences, Decision Sciences, Economics, Econometrics and Finance, Multidisciplinary, Energy and Psychology. (iii) Documents categorised as either articles, conference papers or book chapters, in English, and published between 2010 and 2025. Conference proceedings were incorporated into the analysis due to their role in disseminating new and emerging research, predominantly within rapidly evolving and interdisciplinary fields such as skills development and the role of technology [21]. In emerging disciplines and those that bridge multiple fields, conference proceedings are particularly valuable as they often showcase cutting-edge research and novel insights. Following the application of selection criteria, the dataset was refined to 2,086 documents.

Data pre-processing was conducted using OpenRefine 3.8.2 to ensure accuracy and consistency in the dataset. This step involved cleaning and formatting the data to eliminate errors and duplicates. The Metaphone 3 algorithm was employed to identify and correct minor inconsistencies, while the Daitch-Mokotoff algorithm was used to handle variations in names and spellings. This process resulted in a clean dataset ready for bibliometric analysis, resulting in a final data set of 2083.

Performance analysis was conducted to identify publication productivity and impact as well as key contributors (journals, authors, countries) to youth skills development in rural contexts (RQ1). Science mapping was performed in three ways: first, keyword co-occurrence analysis in VOSviewer was executed to clarify nomological networks that present the state of the field; second, bibliographic coupling and co-citation analysis in VOSviewer was conducted to locate knowledge foundations and developments in the field (RQ2 & 3); third, a density-centrality four quadrant analysis in Bibliometrix in R was utilised to identify future directions (RQ 4), thereby presenting ways forward in a data-driven manner [22]. The results were interpreted using a sensemaking approach that involved scanning of trends, sensing for insights, and substantiating with rationales [16, 23].

Visual tools provided a clear depiction of the relationships and trends within the dataset, aiding in the comprehensive analysis of youth skills development in rural contexts. Post pre-processing, the cleaned data set of 2083 records were analysed using Bibliometrix, a comprehensive tool for bibliometric analysis based on the R programming language, specifically R-4.4.0-arm64.pkg [14]. To interact with the user interface, RStudio/2024.12.0 + 467 was then used.

3   Findings

3.1   Performance Analysis: Publication Productivity (RQ1)

The annual rate growth rate of publications on youth skills in rural contexts was found to be 20.35% as shown in Fig. 1. The publications had a high degree of collaboration, where 90.64% of the documents were internationally co-authored. Only 195 documents (9.36%) were single authored, indicating that research in this field is highly collaborative. In terms of document types, 1,865 were journal articles, 113 book chapters, and 105 conference papers, signalling a maturing but still evolving research area. On average, each publication received 13.96 citations, reflecting moderate impact across the corpus. Research output increased significantly over the years. In 2010, only 69 publications were recorded. By 2024, the number of publications peaked at 240. A noticeable decline in 2025 (23 publications) suggests a temporary lag in data indexing. This upward trajectory reflects the growing importance of equipping youth in rural settings with relevant skills for employment and entrepreneurship. The expansion of research output can be attributed to multiple factors, including increased policy focus on rural youth employment initiatives globally, advancements in training frameworks and skill development programmes, and rising engagement from academic and industry stakeholders.

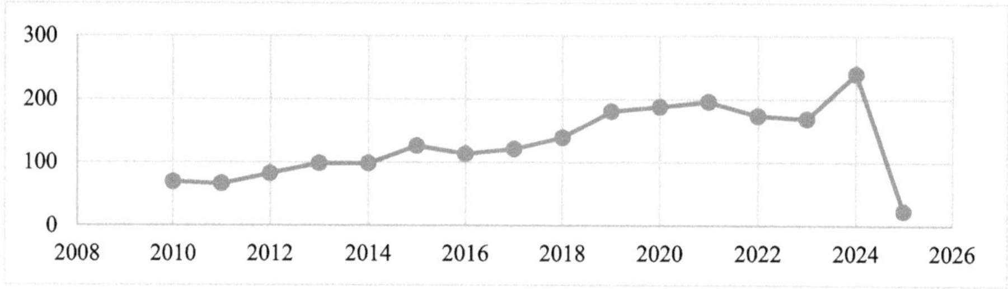

Fig. 1. Publication trends in youth skills in rural areas

3.2 Performance Analysis: Impactful Contributors (RQ2)

The academic landscape surrounding hard skills and competencies in rural youth is shaped by a diverse range of contributors spanning various disciplines and geographies. Key readings in this domain are informed by highly cited research, which serves as a foundation for scholarly discourse. For this corpus, Table 1 offers an overview of the top ten authors, institutions, authors and countries where articles are counted by their number (n). At the institutional level, the University of California (82 articles), the University of Georgia (68 articles), and Monash University (57 articles) represent key intellectual hubs. Their sustained engagement with issues related to youth employment and rural skills development underscores their research focus to tackling contemporary socio-economic challenges. This demonstrates a mixed dispersion between institutions based in developing countries. The geographical distribution of research contributions reveals a concentration in leading academic nations. The United States (2636 articles), Australia (894 articles), and India (643 articles) are dominant players, reflecting their research infrastructure and policy-driven focus on skills development. This global engagement highlights the increasing recognition of rural employment as a critical issue warranting scholarly attention. Moreover, South Africa (399 articles) and Nigeria (185 articles) contribute meaningfully, demonstrating active research engagement from the Global South.

Table 1. Most productive contributors on youth skills development in rural settings

Panel A. Journals	Articles (n)	Panel B. Authors	Articles (n)	Panel C. Institutions	Articles (n)	Panel D. Countries	Articles (n)
Plos One	54	Zhang, Jie	13	University of California	82	USA	2636
Bmc Public Health	39	Kogan, Steven M	12	University of Georgia	68	Australia	894
	39	Brody, Gene H	11	Monash University	57	India	643
BMC Health Services Research	28	Jr., [Full Name Not Found]	10	University of Kwazulu-Natal	43	China	621

(continued)

Table 1. (*continued*)

Panel A. Journals	Articles (n)	Panel B. Authors	Articles (n)	Panel C. Institutions	Articles (n)	Panel D. Countries	Articles (n)
BMJ Open	25	Li, Xiaoming	10	University of North Carolina At Chapel Hill	40	UK	478
Sustainability (Switzerland)	25	Wang, Yuchen	10	Emory University	38	Canada	476
BMC	22	Helm, Stephen	8	University of Saskatchewan	37	South Africa	399
Australian Journal of Rural	20	Okamoto, Scott K	8	The University of Sydney	36	Nigeria	185
Rural And Remote Health	20	Liu, Yang	7	University of the Witwatersrand	34	Uganda	163

3.3   Science Mapping: Co-Occurrence Analysis Based on Keywords (RQ3)

The co-occurrence network shows thematic clusters providing an overview of how interdisciplinary themes interconnect. Each is reviewed in Table 2.

Table 2. Co-occurrence network clusters thematic area and impact

Cluster	Thematic Area
1: Education, Skills, and Workforce Readiness (Blue)	Focuses on curriculum design, digital literacy, professional training, and education's role in socio-economic mobility. Examines workforce readiness, skill development, and leadership programs
2: Psychology, Adolescent Development, and Behavioural Studies (Green)	Examines cognitive and emotional development, self-concept, mental health, and youth psychology. Emphasises the role of psychosocial factors in learning outcomes and adolescent well-being
3: Rural Healthcare, Maternal & Child Health Services (Yellow)	Covers healthcare service access, maternal and newborn health, emergency health services, and rural medical training. Highlights disparities in medical care and healthcare workforce distribution

(*continued*)

Table 2. (*continued*)

Cluster	Thematic Area
4: Social Determinants of Health & Risk Factors (Red)	Explores the impact of poverty, economic status, social structures, food security, and environmental conditions on public health and education. Examines socio-economic factors influencing policy decisions
5: Early Childhood Development & Epidemiology (Orange)	Focuses on early childhood education, nutritional interventions, epidemiological studies, and child health trends. Highlights the importance of preschool learning, motor development, and health surveillance

3.4   Science Mapping: Co-Citation Analysis (RQ3)

Using a co-citation analysis, key knowledge foundations underpinning research on hard skills, competencies, and rural youth employment have been identified across distinct thematic clusters. These clusters highlight significant intellectual contributions that have shaped the field, with foundational works anchoring research trajectories in education, psychology, healthcare, and public policy.

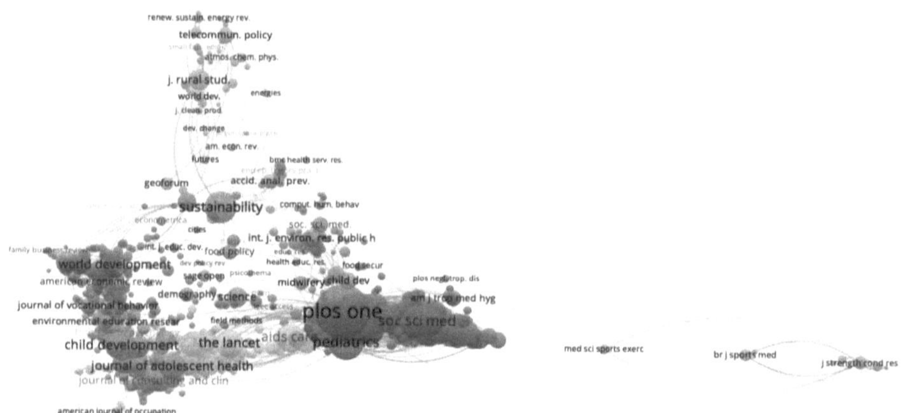

Fig. 2. Co-citation analysis of major themes. Notes. Red (Medical and public health), Green (Qualitative Research and Methodology).

The co-citation network (Fig. 2) visually maps the intellectual lineage of these research domains, demonstrating the interdisciplinary nature of scholarly engagement in this space.

Psychological and behavioural research has significantly shaped our understanding of youth development, motivation, and skill acquisition, particularly in rural employment. The frameworks underscore how self-efficacy influences entrepreneurial tendencies and vocational preparedness, forming a key foundation for competency-building interventions in education and workforce development [24]. This thematic structure suggests that psychological frameworks, methodological rigour, entrepreneurial education, and digital transformation are shaping rural youth employment research. The resulting clusters and thematic themes are shown in Table 3. These insights provide a roadmap for future inquiry, promoting interdisciplinary engagement with emerging paradigms in education, employment, and policy planning.

Table 3. Major themes revealed through keyword co-citation analysis

Cluster	Themes
1: Red (Medical & Public Health Sciences)	Represents high-impact medical and public health research, influencing policy decisions, healthcare interventions, and global health strategies
2: Blue (Development, Sustainability & Economic Studies)	Focuses on economic development, sustainability, and social mobility, shaping policies on education, employment, and environmental governance
3: Green (Child Development & Adolescent Health)	Addresses youth well-being, psychological development, and learning environments, informing education and health interventions for children
4: Yellow (Healthcare Systems & Midwifery Research)	Examines maternal and child health, healthcare accessibility, and nutrition, guiding maternal healthcare policies and community-based health initiatives
5: Purple (Social Sciences, Environment & Risk Studies)	Intersects social determinants of health, environmental policy, and risk assessment, supporting evidence-based social and ecological interventions
6: Orange (Sports & Exercise Science)	Focuses on sports medicine, physical activity, and athletic performance, influencing public health and fitness policies

3.5 Science Mapping: Bibliographic Coupling

In the context of hard skills and competencies in rural and youth employment, bibliographic coupling enables the classification of studies into distinct but interrelated thematic clusters. Figure 3 presents the bibliographic coupling network. The Healthcare

Systems & Service Delivery works argue that beyond technical training, workforce sustainability is contingent on access to quality healthcare services, mental health support, and community-based health initiatives.

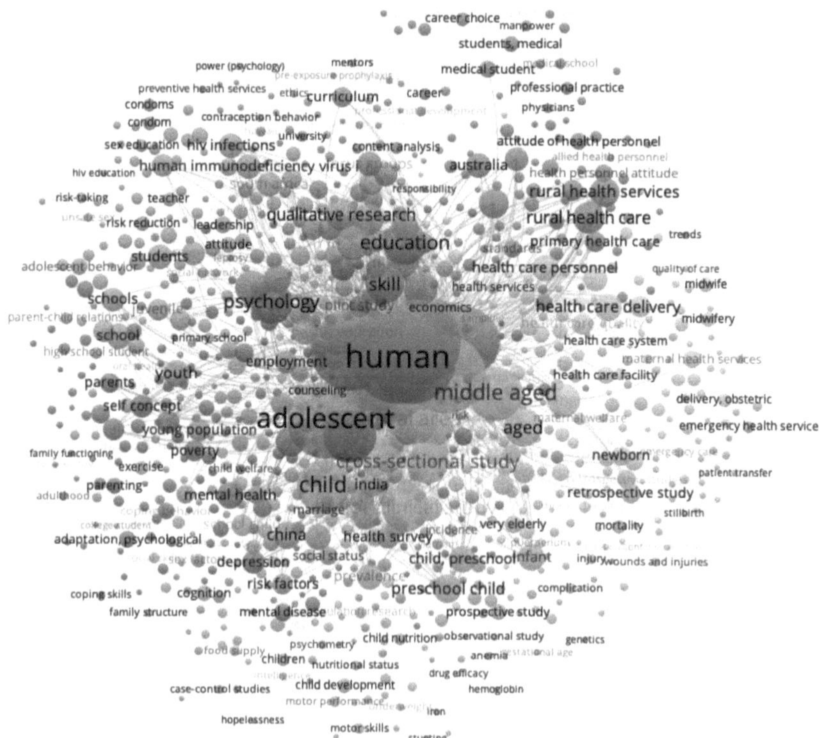

Fig. 3. Bibliographic coupling analysis. Note: Green (Education, Skills & Workforce Development), Red (Healthcare Systems & Service Delivery), Purple (Digital Transformation & Entrepreneurship), Blue (Maternal & Child Health), Yellow (Social Sciences & Sustainability)

The Education & Workforce Development cluster highlight that access to quality education alongside skill-oriented training is a crucial determinant of economic integration, particularly for young individuals in rural and underserved regions [25, 26]. The centrality of this cluster within the network highlights its strategic role in shaping broader workforce development policies [27, 28].

The Social Sciences & Sustainability cluster reviews the role of ecological awareness in vocational training programs is highlighted, accenting the growing significance of sustainability-linked skill development in rural employment [29]. Additionally, the network uncovers a strong intersection between sustainability research and education-focused studies, suggesting that environmental literacy is becoming an integral component of workforce development strategies [30, 31]. The Digital Transformation & Entrepreneurship cluster reveals that this cluster is strongly interconnected with education and workforce development research, reinforcing that digital competency is now a fundamental pillar of employability. This highlights the importance of innovation hubs, startup ecosystems, and micro-entrepreneurship programs in empowering young professionals and rural workers. The positioning of this cluster within the network underscores its increasing relevance as industries move toward automation and digital economy models. The Maternal & Child Health cluster indicates that while maternal and child health remain somewhat peripheral to broader employment research, their influence on long-term economic outcomes is steadily increasing.

3.6   Thematic Mapping (RQ4)

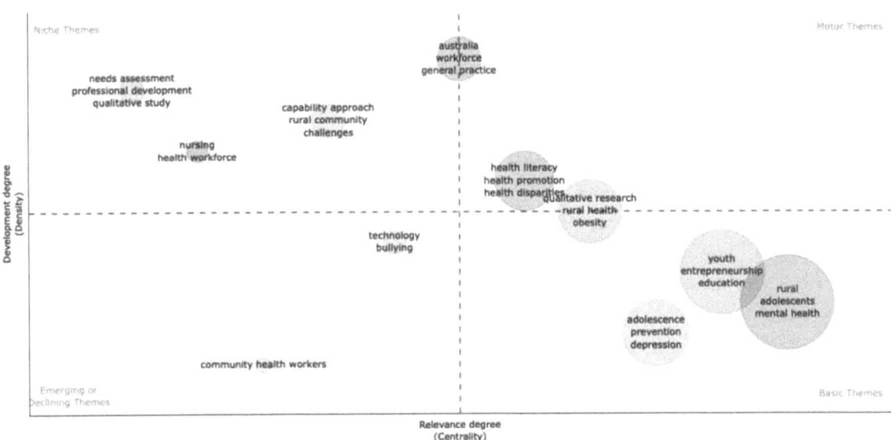

Fig. 4. Clustering centrality of keywords

Thematic mapping identifies knowledge gaps and positions future research within established streams by analysing centrality (theme relevance) and density (internal development). Thematic maps classify research into basic, motor, niche, and emerging or declining themes. In this study, as shown in Fig. 4, basic themes like "youth entrepreneurship" and "education" are foundational but underdeveloped, needing further research on their interaction with skills and social mobility. Motor themes, such as "health literacy" and "qualitative research," dominate the field, highlighting the intersection of health and employability. Niche themes, including "nursing" and "capability approach," are specialised but not widely integrated into employment discourse. Emerging themes like "technology" and "community health workers" show growth potential, necessitating further exploration into their impact on rural employment and workforce resilience.

4   Discussion

The bibliometric analysis conducted in this study offers a systematic evaluation of the knowledge foundations underpinning research on hard skills and competencies in rural and youth employment. An analysis of publication output and citation trends reveals a steady increase in scholarly contributions, reflecting a growing recognition of the role of hard skills and competencies in youth employability.

The findings contribute to existing theoretical domains, including human capital theory, capability theory, and workforce analytics. This study broadens these models by integrating psychological, social, and environmental determinants of employability, supporting the call by Habiyaremye et al. (2022) to address labour market mismatches through inclusive, multi-dimensional skill development. The emphasis on psychosocial factors resonates with Baloyi, Wale, and Chipfupa (2024), who found that behavioural attributes influence rural youth's engagement in non-primary agribusiness, reinforcing the need for interventions that build both technical and psychological readiness. Furthermore, the integration of sustainability and digital competencies responds to Tomczyk's (2024) insights into the digital competency gaps between rural and urban youth, and the imperative to equip marginalised groups for a rapidly digitising world. Finally, the growing role of AI and analytics in workforce forecasting aligns with Kruger and Steyn (2024), who argue for innovation ecosystems underpinned by data-driven planning and adaptive skill-building to prepare youth for dynamic labour markets shaped by the 4IR.

From a practical perspective, the findings suggest that policymakers should integrate mental health frameworks into workforce strategies, ensuring that psychosocial resilience is embedded in employment readiness initiatives. This aligns with Wilkinson et al. (2017), who found that youth in rural South Africa face complex psychosocial barriers including stress, limited access to support systems, and low self-efficacy which impact their employment prospects and learning outcomes. Similarly, Kour and Sharma (2020) highlight the importance of self-efficacy and self-regulation in shaping entrepreneurial intentions. Education systems should also expand digital and AI-driven skill-building programmes to equip youth for the demands of the 4IR as highlighted by Tomczyk (2024). Additionally, ICT training that enables green skills should be embedded in workforce policies to align employment strategies with sustainability goals, as noted by Salemink et al. (2017). Workforce analytics should be leveraged to inform evidence-based employment policies, ensuring that training programmes remain adaptable to evolving labour market conditions. Based on these findings, this study proposes Central Communities of Excellence (CCEs) as a transformative approach to youth skills development in rural contexts. Unlike existing vocational training programmes, CCEs can offer multi-sectoral skill-building ecosystems, integrating technical training, entrepreneurship incubation, and digital literacy education under one framework. These hubs can function as regional innovation centres, providing youth with adaptable career pathways that connect traditional industries with emerging opportunities.

5 Conclusion

This study reviewed key areas and expanded human capital and capability theories, adding psychosocial and technological factors to workforce strategies. Policy recommendations include integrating mental health into employment programs, expanding digital training, embedding sustainability skills, and using workforce analytics for decision-making. As labour markets shift, future research should prioritise assessing development practices of integrated, cross-sectoral training models such as CCEs, noting how to combine hard skills, digital literacy, and entrepreneurial education for rural youth. Within this there is a need to examine the role of psychosocial factors, such as mental health, behavioural readiness and cyber-bullying in enhancing employability and readiness for the workforce. Finally, further inquiry is needed into the effectiveness of entrepreneurship ecosystems tailored to rural realities particularly those engaging in green economies, and the policy frameworks that foster inclusive, cross-sectoral collaboration. This includes exploring how human-AI collaboration can enhance these ecosystems to support sustainable development in the Global South aligned with the values of Society 5.0.

Disclosure of Interests. The authors have no competing interests to declare that are relevant to this research study. Funding for this study is attributed to the University Capacity Development Programme (UCDP).

References

1. Statistics South Africa: Stats SA, http://www.statssa.gov.za/. Last accessed 28 October 2018
2. Geza, W., Ngidi, M.S.C., Slotow, R., Mabhaudhi, T.: The Dynamics of Youth Employment and Empowerment in Agriculture and Rural Development in South Africa: A Scoping Review (2022). https://doi.org/10.3390/su14095041
3. Wilkinson, A., et al.: The employment environment for youth in rural South Africa: a mixed-methods study. Dev. South. Afr. **34**, 17–32 (2017)
4. Carayannis, E.G., Morawska-Jancelewicz, J.: The futures of Europe: society 5.0 and industry 5.0 as driving forces of future universities. J. Knowl. Econ. **13**, 3445–3471 (2022)
5. Srivastava, A.K., Logar, B., Sanghvi, S., Vaghela, A., Adwani, M.: Vocational training and employability: a study in reference to skill development program from Gujarat, India. Eval. Program Plann. 110 (2025)
6. Tomczyk, Ł.: Digital transformation and digital competences of urban and rural polish youths. Politics and Governance 12, (2024)
7. Baloyi, R., Wale, E., Chipfupa, U.: The impact of behavioral attributes on rural youth's propensity to participate in non-primary agribusinesses: Evidence from KwaZulu-Natal. South Africa. Local Develop. Soc. **5**, 394–409 (2024)
8. Kruger, S., Steyn, A.A.: Developing breakthrough innovation capabilities in university ecosystems: a case study from South Africa. Technol. Forecast Soc. Change 198, (2024)
9. Habiyaremye, A., Habanabakize, T., Nwosu, C.: Bridging the labour market skills gap to tackle youth unemployment in South Africa. Econ. Labour Relat. Rev. **33**, 786–805 (2022)
10. Mohamad, Z., et al.: The impact of digital entrepreneurial competencies, digital literacy and government support on digital entrepreneurship using regression analysis. Innovat. Econ. Res. J. (2025)
11. Majee, W., Conteh, N., Jacobs, J., Wegner, L.: Needs ranking: a qualitative study using a participatory approach. Health Soc. Care Community **30**, e5095–e5104 (2022)
12. Welman, L.: The resurgence of service-learning as a social impact tool for youth confidence-building and learning: the untapped latent capital of the Saldanha area. SN Social Sciences 3 (2023)
13. Tranfield, D., Denyer, D., Smart, P.: Towards a Methodology for Developing Evidence-Informed Management Knowledge by Means of Systematic Review (2003)
14. Aria, M., Cuccurullo, C.: Bibliometrix: An R-tool for comprehensive science mapping analysis. J. Informetr. **11**, 959–975 (2017)

15. Block, J.H., Fisch, C.: Eight tips and questions for your bibliographic study in business and management research (2020)
16. Donthu, N., Kumar, S., Mukherjee, D., Pandey, N., Lim, W.M.: How to conduct a bibliometric analysis: An overview and guidelines. J. Bus. Res. **133**, 285–296 (2021)
17. Paul, J., Lim, W.M., O'Cass, A., Hao, A.W., Bresciani, S.: Scientific procedures and rationales for systematic literature reviews (SPAR-4-SLR). Int. J. Consum. Stud. (2021)
18. Kruger, S., Steyn, A.: A conceptual model of entrepreneurial competencies needed to utilise technologies of Industry 4.0. Int. J. Entrepren. Innov. **22**, 56–67 (2020)
19. Goodell, J.W., Kumar, S., Lim, W.M., Pattnaik, D.: Artificial intelligence and machine learning in finance: Identifying foundations, themes, and research clusters from bibliometric analysis. J. Behav. Exp. Fin. **32**, 100577 (2021)
20. Del Vecchio, P., Secundo, G., Garzoni, A.: Phygital technologies and environments for breakthrough innovation in customers' and citizens' journey. A critical literature review and future agenda. Technol. Forecast Soc. Change 189 (2023)
21. Huang, C.C.: Cognitive factors in predicting continued use of information systems with technology adoption models. Info. Res. 22 (2017)
22. Mukherjee, S.P.: A Guide to Research Methodology: An Overview of Research Problems. Tasks and Methods. CRC Press, New york (2020)
23. Mukherjee, D., Lim, W.M., Kumar, S., Donthu, N.: Guidelines for advancing theory and practice through bibliometric research. J. Bus. Res. **148**, 101–115 (2022)
24. Kour, S., Sharma, M.: Impact of self-efficacy on entrepreneurial intentions: Role of self-regulation and education. In: Sustainable Business Practices for Rural Development: The Role of Intellectual Capital, pp. 169–189. Palgrave Macmillan (2020). https://doi.org/10.1007/978-981-13-9298-6_10
25. Jones, D.E., Greenberg, M., Crowley, M.: Early social-emotional functioning and public health: the relationship between kindergarten social competence and future wellness. Am. J. Public Health **105**, 2283–2290 (2015)
26. Salemink, K., Strijker, D., Bosworth, G.: Rural development in the digital age: a systematic literature review on unequal ICT availability, adoption, and use in rural areas. J. Rural. Stud. **54**, 360–371 (2017)
27. Ameyaw, E.K., et al.: Prevalence and determinants of unintended pregnancy in sub-Saharan Africa: a multi-country analysis of demographic and health surveys. PLoS One. 14 (2019)
28. Kuravackel, G.M., Ruble, L.A., Reese, R.J., Ables, A.P., Rodgers, A.D., Toland, M.D.: COMPASS for hope: evaluating the effectiveness of a parent training and support program for children with ASD. J. Autism Dev. Disord. **48**, 404–416 (2018)
29. Rockers, P.C., et al. Two-year impact of community-based health screening and parenting groups on child development in Zambia: follow-up to a cluster-randomized controlled trial. PLoS Med. **15** (2018)
30. Karim, A.M., et al.: Effect of ethiopia's health extension program on maternal and newborn health care practices in 101 rural districts: a dose-response study. PLoS One 8 (2013)
31. Tao, F., Huang, K., Long, X., Tolhurst, R., Raven, J.: Low postnatal care rates in two rural counties in Anhui Province, China: Perceptions of key stakeholders. Midwifery **27**, 707–715 (2011)

A Blockchain-Based, Semantics-Driven, Modular Implementation of BPMN Choreographies

Nawaz Abdullah Malla[1(✉)], Alessandro Marcelletti[1], Andrea Morichetta[1], and Francesco Tiezzi[2]

[1] University of Camerino, Camerino, Italy
`nawaz.malla@unicam.it`
[2] University of Florence, Florence, Italy

Abstract. Blockchain technology is nowadays a prominent solution to ensure trustworthiness in the enactment of multi-party business processes, typically described in terms of BPMN choreography models. These blockchain-based enactment approaches are based on the translation of choreographies into smart contracts. However, existing proposals aim at optimizing the execution costs, resulting in smart contract code that does not intuitively reflect the behavior of the corresponding choreography, thus hindering its understandability. To overcome this issue, we propose a translation approach that is modular and semantics-driven. The aim is to generate smart contracts that have a one-to-one correspondence with the elements of the originating BPMN choreographies, thus increasing the trust in the overall solution. Our approach is agnostic about the language used to write the smart contracts, which makes the approach general and applicable to different blockchain platforms. To assess the feasibility of our proposal, and the execution costs that it induces, we experimented with Solidity and PyTeal smart contracts resulting from the translation of a choreography from the healthcare application domain.

Keywords: BPMN · Blockchain-based enactment · Modular implementation

1 Introduction

For some years now, in the Business Process Management (BPM) community the blockchain technology has become a prominent solution to support the enactment of multi-party business processes [10]. Such processes consist of structured interactions among distributed participants to achieve their goals collaboratively. The BPM community provided a standard modeling notation, the Business Process Modelling Notation (BPMN) [17], which is nowadays largely adopted by the industry and academia. BPMN permits the representation of multi-party business processes with different perspectives. In particular, we rely on *choreography*

F. Corradini et al. (Eds.): Society 5.0 2025, CCIS 2787, pp. 181–193, 2026.
https://doi.org/10.1007/978-3-032-15463-7_15

diagrams, as they allow to describe how the exchange of messages should happen among different parties without exposing their internal behavior.

In this context, **blockchain technology** has emerged as a key platform for executing choreographies. One of the main challenges in such distributed environments is establishing trust, as participants typically cannot rely on trust assumptions. Blockchain addresses this issue by providing a decentralized infrastructure where data is stored immutably and transparently. Choreography models are typically translated into smart contracts, which enforce interactions between parties, ensuring adherence to the initial model [4,11]. This approach offers secure, verifiable records of past activities, enabling auditing of the process execution.The current existing proposals have cost optimization as a major aim. Indeed, the transaction fees to be paid for the execution of the smart contract were one of the major limitations of these kinds of proposals until a few years ago. The reference blockchain platform of such solutions was primarily Ethereum [9,18], which required costs for executing choreographies that were not negligible for certain application domains. This led to optimized smart contracts for reducing costs, which however did not intuitively reflect the behavior of the originating choreography models.This undermines the understandability of the resulting smart contracts for humans, even technicians.This lack of intuitive understanding can limit trust in the overall system, as users might question the reliability and security of contracts they cannot fully comprehend.

To overcome such issues, we propose a novel translation approach for implementing BPMN choreographies in terms of smart contracts that are modular and semantics-driven. The translation approach is *modular* in the sense that the structure of a generated smart contract follows the structure of the choreography from which it originates. This is the key contribution of this work, as it ensures a one-to-one correspondence between BPMN choreography elements and smart contract functions. Modularity is achieved by resorting to a compositional characterization of the syntax and semantics of BPMN choreography models. To this aim, the translation definition is *driven by a BPMN choreography formalization*, given in terms of Backus Normal Form (BNF) syntax and operational semantics, whose nature is intrinsically compositional.Altogether, the modularity and the formal basis of our approach aim to make closer the correspondence between the choreography model and the generated smart contract, hence reducing the perceived uncertainty in the produced code.Overall, as envisioned in [14,16], this would make the proposed blockchain-based execution approach more trustworthy for users. In addition, our modular approach would foster flexibility, which requires choreographies to change to react to internal or external needs. Specifically, modularity permits confining, and easily identifying the parts of the smart contract code that are affected by a change in the choreography model.

To make our approach applicable to different blockchain technologies, we defined it in an agnostic way. Specifically, the translation does not produce code written in a specific smart contract language, but it resorts to a pseudocode that can be straightforwardly rendered in a mainstream smart contract language. To demonstrate the feasibility of our proposal, we evaluate how a choreography model can be rendered in Solidity and PyTeal.This also permits us to evaluate the proposal in terms of execution costs, by executing the contracts in an EVM-based platform (i.e., Polygon) and the Algorand blockchain, respectively. The experiment results state that our approach is promising, as it achieves modularity with affordable execution costs in recent, yet popular, blockchain platforms.

The rest of the paper is organized as follows. Section 2 provides an overview of BPMN choreography diagrams and presents our running example. Section 3 illustrates the formalization at the basis of our translation. Section 4 presents translation from BPMN choreographies to smart contract pseudocode. Section 5 reports on the experiments we conducted with Solidity and PyTeal contracts to evaluate our proposal. Section 6 discusses the closest related works. Section 7 concludes the paper by touching upon directions for future work.

2   BPMN Choreographies

BPMN choreography diagrams [17, Ch. 11] provide an intuitive means for describing the interactions occurring among the participants of a distributed scenario. We illustrate the most relevant choreography elements by resorting to the model in Fig. 1, drawn from [5]. This model, used throughout the paper as a running example, represents a healthcare process that a patient must follow to schedule and do an X-ray analysis. In this scenario, blockchain is relevant to increase trust in the healthcare system and enable auditability of its processes.

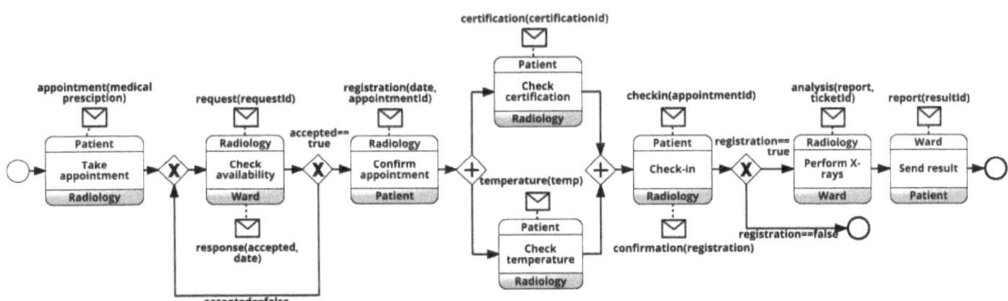

Fig. 1. X-ray exam choreography.

The starting point of the choreography is represented by the *start* event, which is drawn as a circle with an outgoing edge. Edges (called *sequence flows*) are used to specify the execution flow by connecting choreography elements. In this case, the start event is connected to a *task* element describing the interaction where the patient, owning a medical prescription, asks for an appointment with the radiology department. A *one-way choreography task* allows defining a message exchange between two participants involved in the choreography. Tasks are represented as rectangles divided into three bands: the central one contains the task's name, while the others refer to the involved parties (the white band is the initiator, and the grey one is the recipient).

The execution flow of the choreography is controlled by using *gateways*. Gateways act as split nodes (forking into outgoing edges) or join nodes (merging incoming edges). An *exclusive (XOR) gateway*, drawn with a diamond marked with the × symbol, represents conditional choices. In particular, a XOR-split gateway is used to introduce branches to be selected on the basis of the conditions labelling the outgoing edges; when executed, it activates exactly one outgoing edge. A XOR-join gateway acts as a pass-through, meaning that its outgoing edge is activated each time the gateway is reached. In the running example, two XOR gateways are used to specify a sort of do-while loop: the radiology department checks the availability of the ward for the X-ray exam; if there is a free date, the appointment is confirmed; otherwise, the availability is checked again. Notably, the request-response interaction between the radiology department and the ward is modeled by a *two-way choreography task*, in which both participants send a message. In case the X-ray analysis request is accepted, the response is sent to the patient. Before performing the physical check-in, due to pandemic-related entry restrictions, the patient must check his/her temperature and vaccine certification. These checks are performed in parallel, which is specified by using two *parallel (AND) gateways* (drawn with diamonds marked with the + symbol): the AND-split gateway activates all the outgoing edges simultaneously, while the join one has to wait to be reached by all its incoming edges to be activated. The patient then performs the physical check-in, by providing the appointment identifier that is controlled by the radiology department, which returns the confirmation response. If the appointment is not confirmed, the choreography terminates. In this case the execution flow is directed by an XOR-split gateway to an *end* event, which is drawn as a circle with an incoming edge and denotes an ending point of the choreography. If instead the appointment is confirmed, the X-ray exam is done and the results are provided to the ward that compiles a final report, then sent to the patient.

3   BPMN Choreography Formalization

This section presents the formalization of BPMN choreographies we rely on. This formalization results from the extension of the one presented in [7] with additional features inspired by the formalization in [8].

The graphical notation of BPMN choreographies makes unhandy the definition of the formal semantics. Therefore, the formalization is based on an alternative textual representation of choreographies, whose syntax is defined by the BNF grammar in Fig. 2. In the grammar, the non-terminal symbol C represents *Choreography Structures*, while the terminal symbols, denoted by the sans serif font, are the considered elements of a BPMN model, i.e. events, gateways and tasks. Non-terminal symbols X and T represent expression lists and event-based task lists, respectively; when convenient, we shall regard these lists simply as sets. As a matter of notation, let $\mathbb{E}$ be the set of *sequence edge* names, in the

$$C ::= \mathsf{start}(\mathsf{id}, \mathsf{e}_0, \mathsf{e}_1) \mid \mathsf{end}(\mathsf{id}, \mathsf{e}) \mid \mathsf{andSplit}(\mathsf{id}, \mathsf{e}, E) \mid \mathsf{andJoin}(\mathsf{id}, E, \mathsf{e}) \mid \mathsf{xorSplit}(\mathsf{id}, \mathsf{e}, X)$$
$$\mid \mathsf{xorJoin}(\mathsf{id}, E, \mathsf{e}) \mid \mathsf{task}(\mathsf{id}, \mathsf{e}_1, \mathsf{p}_1, \mathsf{m}, \mathsf{p}_2, \mathsf{e}_2) \mid \mathsf{eventBased}(\mathsf{id}, \mathsf{e}, T) \mid C_1 \mid C_2$$
$$X ::= (\mathsf{e}, \mathsf{exp}) \mid X_1, X_2 \qquad T ::= (\mathsf{p}_1, \mathsf{m}, \mathsf{p}_2, \mathsf{e}) \mid T_1, T_2$$

Fig. 2. Syntax of BPMN Choreography Structures.

following $\mathsf{e} \in \mathbb{E}$ denotes an edge, while $E \in 2^{\mathbb{E}}$ a set of edges. Notice that the set $\mathbb{E}$ also includes spurious edges for denoting the enabled/disabled status of start events. Moreover, the set $\mathbb{M}$ of *messages* is ranged over by m, while the set $\mathbb{V}$ of *values* is ranged over by v. Notation p ranges over names uniquely identifying *participants*, while id ranges over *element identifiers* (these unique identifiers are not visualized in the graphical representation of the diagram, but are included in the underlying XML file). We also use a set $\mathbb{EXP}$ of *expressions*, ranged over by exp, whose precise syntax is deliberately not specified; we just assume that expressions contain message parameters and values. Such a design choice has been influenced by the fact that the expression language operating on data is left unspecified even by the BPMN standard. Notably, we are not proposing a new modeling formalism, but we are only using a textual notation for the BPMN elements. With respect to the graphical notation, the textual one is more manageable for supporting the formal definition of the semantics and its implementation. The one-to-one correspondence between the graphical notation of BPMN and the syntax used here is straightforward. We will only consider terms of the textual syntax that are derived from BPMN models. Notice that two-way tasks are rendered in our formal framework as pairs of one-way tasks, hence they are not explicitly included in the syntax.

To achieve a *compositional definition*, each sequence edge of the BPMN model is split in two parts: the part is outgoing from the source element, and the part is incoming into the target element. The two parts are correlated by means of unique sequence edge names in the BPMN model.

The operational semantics we propose is given in terms of configurations of the form $\langle C, \sigma, \gamma \rangle$, where C is a choreography structure, $\sigma : \mathbb{E} \to \mathbb{N}$ is an *execution state function* mapping sequence edges to numbers of tokens ($\mathbb{N}$ is the set of natural numbers), and $\gamma : \mathbb{M} \to \mathbb{V}$ is a *message state function* mapping messages to values. The execution state obtained by updating in the state σ the number of tokens of the edge e to n is written as $\sigma \cdot \{\mathsf{e} \mapsto \mathsf{n}\}$. The message state obtained by updating in γ the value of a message m to v, written as $\gamma \cdot \{\mathsf{m} \mapsto \mathsf{v}\}$, is defined similarly. The *initial* states of a choreography, where all sequence edges are unmarked (but for the spurious ones that are marked by one token) and all message values are undefined, are denoted respectively by σ_0 and γ_0.

The operational semantics is defined by means of a labelled transition system (LTS) on choreography configurations, formalising the execution of a choreography in terms of marking evolution and message exchanges. Labels l of the LTS represent computational steps and are defined as: τ, denoting movements of tokens; and $\mathsf{p}_1 \to \mathsf{p}_2 : \mathsf{m}$, denoting an exchange of message m from participant

p_1 to p_2. The transition relation over choreography configurations is defined by the rules in Fig. 3. We refer to our companion technical report [13] for a complete discussion of our BPMN choreography formalization.

$$\langle \mathsf{start}(\mathsf{id}, \mathsf{e}_0, \mathsf{e}_1), \sigma_0, \gamma_0 \rangle \xrightarrow{\tau} \langle inc(dec(\sigma_0, \mathsf{e}_0), \mathsf{e}_1), \gamma_0 \rangle \qquad \sigma(\mathsf{e}_0) > 0$$

$$\langle \mathsf{end}(\mathsf{id}, \mathsf{e}), \sigma, \gamma \rangle \xrightarrow{\tau} \langle dec(\sigma, \mathsf{e}), \gamma \rangle \qquad \sigma(\mathsf{e}) > 0$$

$$\langle \mathsf{andSplit}(\mathsf{id}, \mathsf{e}, E), \sigma, \gamma \rangle \xrightarrow{\tau} \langle inc(dec(\sigma, \mathsf{e}), E), \gamma \rangle \qquad \sigma(\mathsf{e}) > 0$$

$$\langle \mathsf{andJoin}(\mathsf{id}, E, \mathsf{e}), \sigma, \gamma \rangle \xrightarrow{\tau} \langle inc(dec(\sigma, E), \mathsf{e}), \gamma \rangle \qquad \forall \mathsf{e}' \in E \ . \ \sigma(\mathsf{e}') > 0$$

$$\langle \mathsf{xorSplit}(\mathsf{id}, \mathsf{e}', \{(\mathsf{e}, \mathsf{exp})\} \cup X), \sigma, \gamma \rangle \xrightarrow{\tau} \langle inc(dec(\sigma, \mathsf{e}'), \mathsf{e}), \gamma \rangle \qquad \sigma(\mathsf{e}') > 0 \ \wedge \ eval(\mathsf{exp}, \gamma)$$

$$\langle \mathsf{xorJoin}(\mathsf{id}, \{\mathsf{e}\} \cup E, \mathsf{e}'), \sigma, \gamma \rangle \xrightarrow{\tau} \langle inc(dec(\sigma, \mathsf{e}), \mathsf{e}'), \gamma \rangle \qquad \sigma(\mathsf{e}) > 0$$

$$\langle \mathsf{task}(\mathsf{id}, \mathsf{e}_1, \mathsf{p}_1, \mathsf{m}, \mathsf{p}_2, \mathsf{e}_2), \sigma, \gamma \rangle \xrightarrow{\mathsf{p}_1 \to \mathsf{p}_2 : \mathsf{m}} \langle inc(dec(\sigma, \mathsf{e}_1), \mathsf{e}_2), upd(\gamma, \mathsf{m}) \rangle \qquad \sigma(\mathsf{e}_1) > 0$$

$$\langle \mathsf{eventBased}(\mathsf{id}, \mathsf{e}', \{(\mathsf{p}_1, \mathsf{m}, \mathsf{p}_2, \mathsf{e})\} \cup T), \sigma, \gamma \rangle \xrightarrow{\mathsf{p}_1 \to \mathsf{p}_2 : \mathsf{m}} \langle inc(dec(\sigma, \mathsf{e}'), \mathsf{e}), upd(\gamma, \mathsf{m}) \rangle \qquad \sigma(\mathsf{e}') > 0$$

$$\frac{\langle C_1, \sigma, \gamma \rangle \xrightarrow{l} \langle \sigma', \gamma' \rangle}{\langle C_1 | C_2, \sigma, \gamma \rangle \xrightarrow{l} \langle \sigma', \gamma' \rangle} \qquad \frac{\langle C_2, \sigma, \gamma \rangle \xrightarrow{l} \langle \sigma', \gamma' \rangle}{\langle C_1 | C_2, \sigma, \gamma \rangle \xrightarrow{l} \langle \sigma', \gamma' \rangle}$$

Fig. 3. Semantics of BPMN Choreographies.

4   From Choreographies to Smart Contracts

We present here the translation of BPMN choreography models into smart contracts. The main challenge is providing a smart contract implementation that is modular in the structure of choreography models (i.e., the smart contract that implements a choreography model follows the structure of the choreography itself). This aspect, which we call 'modular blockchain-based choreography implementation', is one of the main technical aspects that characterizes this work. It is worth noticing that our approach is agnostic to the blockchain technology used for enacting the choreographies, meaning that it is not based on specific features of the smart contract language supported by the blockchain platform used. In fact, we provide a translation of a smart contract pseudocode, which can then be easily rendered in most mainstream smart contract languages.

The translation of BPMN choreography elements in smart contract terms exploits the translation functions $\langle\!\langle \cdot \rangle\!\rangle$ and $[\![\cdot]\!]$. The former function generates the contract header, containing the definitions of data types and variables, auxiliary functions, and the model-independent code triggering the execution. The latter function, instead, is defined by induction on the syntax of choreographies (see Fig. 2) and transforms each element of the BPMN model into a corresponding function of the smart contract that faithfully implements the element's semantics.

The definition of the translation functions $\langle\!\langle \cdot \rangle\!\rangle$ is shown in Listing 1.1, where we assume that the input choreography C involves n parties, m edges (named e_i with $i \in \{1..m\}$, while e_0 denotes the spurious edge), k messages (named msg_j with $j \in \{1..k\}$), and h BPMN elements (with identifiers id_w with $w \in \{1..h\}$).

```
1  ⟪C⟫ =
2    enum MsgStatus {DISABLED,ENABLED}
3    enum ChoreographyState {INIT, RUNNING, MSG_WAITING, COMPLETED, DEADLOCKED}
4    private address party₁ = 0x...; ...; private address partyₙ = 0x...;
5    private ChoreographyState chorState = ChoreographyState.INIT;
6    private int e₀ = 1; private int e₁ = 0; ...; private int eₘ = 0;
7    private int enabledMessages = 0;
8    private MsgStatus status_msg₁ = MsgStatus.DISABLED;
9    private Type₁₁ payload_msg₁_param₁, ..., Type₁ᵣ payload_msg₁_paramᵣ;
10   private MsgStatus status_msgₖ = MsgStatus.DISABLED;
11   private Typeₖ₁ payload_msgₖ_param₁, ..., Typeₖₜ payload_msgₖ_paramₜ;
12   ⟦C⟧
13   private int getMarking(){ return e₀+e₁+...+eₘ; }
14   private boolean executeOneRule() { return id₁() || ... || idₕ(); }
15   public void execute() {
16     chorState = ChoreographyState.RUNNING;
17     while (executeOneRule()) {}
18     if (enabledMessages > 0) { chorState = ChoreographyState.MSG_WAITING; } else {
19       if (getMarking()>0){ chorState = ChoreographyState.DEADLOCKED; }
20       else { chorState = ChoreographyState.COMPLETED; }
21   } }
```

Listing 1.1. Top-level translation function $\langle\!\langle \cdot \rangle\!\rangle$.

This translation generates the smart contract code that, once deployed in the blockchain, deals with the execution of a specific choreography instance. The code must be instantiated with the addresses of the parties participating in the given choreography instance (see variables $\mathtt{party}_i$, line 4). In this respect, more dynamic solutions could be realized, but this is out of the scope of this work. The smart contract variables store the state of the choreography instance. The execution state function σ is rendered by the variables $\mathtt{e}_i$ (line 6), while the message state function γ is rendered by the variables $\mathtt{payload\_msg}_j\mathtt{\_param}_k$ (lines 8–11). For each message, in addition, a variable (lines 8 and 10) keeps track of whether the reception of the message is ENABLED or DISABLED.

The execution of the choreography instance is carried out by the execute() function (lines 15–21). This is the public function that one has to invoke to activate the choreography instance once the smart contract has been deployed in the blockchain. It iteratively executes one semantic rule at a time on the choreography's elements, thus implementing the interleaving semantics given in Sect. 3 (see rules Int_1 and Int_2). This behavior is realized by resorting to the private function executeOneRule() (line 14), which sequentially invokes the execution of each choreography's element (using functions $\mathtt{id}_i()$ generated by translation function $\llbracket \cdot \rrbracket$) until one element is successfully executed. If all elements of the choreography cannot be executed, the instance execution stops, and the motivation underlying this termination is checked. If there are enabled messages, the execution is suspended and will be resumed when the waited message is delivered. Otherwise, the instance terminates successfully (if the marking is empty) or unsuccessfully (if there are deadlocked tokens).

The definition of the translation functions $\llbracket \cdot \rrbracket$ is shown in Listings 1.2 and 1.3 (due to space limitations, the translation of event-based gateway is omitted here). Each choreography element is translated into a function according to the semantics given in Fig. 3 and returns a boolean value indicating whether the element is executed or not. In other words, invoking function `id()` corresponds to try to apply the corresponding semantic rule to the choreography element identified by id; if the rule is applicable, the state of the choreography is modified accordingly and the function returns `true`, otherwise it returns `false`.

```
1  [[start(id, e_0, e)]] = private boolean id() {
2                 if (e_0 > 0) { e_0--; e++; return true; } else return false; }
3
4  [[end(id, e)]] = private boolean id() {
5                 if (e > 0){ e--; return true; } else return false; }
6
7  [[andSplit(id, e, {e_1, ..., e_n})]] = private boolean id() {
8            if (e > 0) { e--; e_1++; ...; e_n++; return true; } else return false; }
9
10 [[andJoin(id, {e_1, ..., e_n}, e)]] = private boolean id() {
11                if (e_1 > 0 && ... && e_n>0) { e_1--; ... e_n--; e++; return true;
12                } else return false; }
13
14 [[xorSplit(id, e, {(e_1, exp_1), ..., (e_n, exp_n)})]] = private boolean id() {
15                if (e > 0 && exp_1) { e--; e_1++; return true;
16                } else ...
17                } else if (e > 0 && exp_n) { e--; e_n++; return true; }
18                else return false; }
19
20 [[xorJoin(id, {e_1, ..., e_n}, e)]] = private boolean id() {
21                if (e_1 > 0) { e_1--; e++; return true; } else ...
22                } else if (e_n > 0){ e_n--; e++; return true; } else return false; }
```

Listing 1.2. Inner translation function $[\![\cdot]\!]$: start/end events, AND/XOR gateways.

```
1  [[task(id, e_1, p_1, msg(param_1, ..., param_n), p_2, e_2)]] =
2     private boolean id() {
3        if (e_1 > 0) {
4           e_1--; status_msg = MsgStatus.ENABLED;
5           enabledMessages++;
6           emit MessageEvent(p_1,p_2,msg);
7           return true;
8        } else return false;
9     }
10    public void msg(Type_1 param_1, ..., Type_n param_n){
11       if (status_msg == MsgStatus.ENABLED && msg.sender==p_1) {
12          payload_msg_param_1 = param_1; ...; payload_msg_param_n = param_n;
13          status_msg = MsgStatus.DISABLED;
14          enabledMessages--;
15          e_2++;
16          execute();
17    } }
18
19 [[C_1 | C_2]] = [[C_1]]  [[C_2]]
```

Listing 1.3. Inner translation function $[\![\cdot]\!]$: tasks and elements composition.

As an example, the function corresponding to a start event (lines 1–2 in Listing 1.2) checks if the spurious edge of the event is marked; in the negative case it returns `false`, because the condition $\sigma(e_0) > 0$ of the semantic rule is not satisfied and hence the rule is not applicable, otherwise the function moves one token from the spurious edge to the outgoing edge and returns `true`.

The most interesting case of the translation definition is one of the task elements (lines 1–18 in Listing 1.3), which generates two functions. The private function (lines 2–9), if the incoming edge is marked, consumes the incoming token, enables the exchange of the message, and notifies the involved parties by emitting an event (which contains the same information as the transition label produced by the *Task* rule). The public function (lines 10–17), instead, is invoked by the sending party to send the message, whose payload is stored in the contract variables representing the message state function γ (line 12). Then, the message is disabled, the outgoing edge is marked, and the choreography instance execution is resumed. Notably, the message function can be successfully executed only if it is invoked by the expected sending party and if the message exchange for that specific type of message is enabled (line 11). Finally, the translation of the composition of elements (i.e., $C_1|C_2$) is simply rendered as the juxtaposition of the functions resulting from the translations of the composition arguments (line 19). The pseudocode resulting from the translation of the X-ray exam choreography is available as a text file in our artifacts repository [1].

5   Evaluation

In this section, we report the evaluation of our translation approach presented in Sect. 4. To this purpose, we considered two different blockchain platforms, Algorand and an EVM-based one (i.e., Polygon). Following the approach, we implemented the smart contracts of the X-ray exam BPMN choreography described in Sect. 2. The source code of the implemented smart contracts is available together with the execution logs at [1].

Experiments and Performance Analysis. For each considered platform, we deployed the X-ray smart contract on a public testnet and executed relevant paths. The choreography execution can be described through four distinct paths based on the values assigned to the variables *accepted* and *registration*, influencing the decision points (i.e., XOR gateways). In the first path, the choreography is executed with both accepted and registration set to true. In the second path, accepted is set to true, while registration is false. The third path has two iterations of the loop, where accepted is initially set to false and then changed to true, while registration remains true. Finally, in the fourth path, the choreography undergoes two loop iterations but terminates with registration set to false. The execution performances of each path were analyzed in terms of gas used for Polygon and cost for Algorand, compared then with the fiat currency.

Polygon Experiments. The first experiments were made on the Solidity implementation of the smart contract using the Polygon Amoy testnet. For each executed path, we analyze the performance in terms of units of gas used for the *deployment, execution,* and the *total* sum. Considering the experiments, all the deployments consumed 3,131,321 units of gas as the smart contract logic remains the same for all the cases. The execution cost instead, depends on the followed path as demonstrated by the resulting performance. Indeed, the lowest amount of gas used is 816,986 and corresponds to the shortest path where there is no loop and the choreography terminates on the registration task. On the contrary, the highest amount of gas used is 1,204,517 and it corresponds to the execution of the choreography with the first performed loop and the termination on the longest path. Of course, the other paths that perform more iterations of the loop have an increasing cost (i.e., 145,109 units of gas per iteration).

Algorand Experiments. Considering the Algorand experiments, the results are reported as follows. In this case, it is worth noticing that Algorand has a fixed transaction fee of 0.001 ALGO for every transaction, regardless of the type. This leads to the deployment costs of 0.001 ALGO for each path, and the execution only depending on the number of executed messages. Indeed, the lowest execution cost is 0.009 ALGO, corresponding to the shortest path without any loop in the choreography. The highest cost is 0.013 ALGO refers to the longest execution path with the initial loop and the termination on the last task.

Discussion. To provide an evaluation of the feasibility of the proposed approach, we report here the comparison between the two implemented translations and executed paths. Considering Polygon, the execution of the four paths costs an average of 0.125187 POL corresponding to 0.0504 USD (according to the exchange value at the time of writing). For Algorand instead, the average cost is 0.001475 ALGO corresponding to 0.000179 USD. These results highlight the feasibility of the implemented choreography transformation, as the smart contracts deployed and executed exhibit strong performance. It is important to consider that the chosen blockchain platform determines the execution costs, which can vary significantly from one platform to another. For example, using Ethereum could increase the costs. However, this variance is independent of the proposed approach and can be mitigated by selecting the appropriate platform. Another important factor is the size of the choreography, which directly affects the size of the implemented smart contract. As the number of elements in the choreography increases, the size of the smart contract linearly grows, leading to higher costs. However, given the obtained results, small increases in the choreography model size are likely not to result in significant variations in the performance of the smart contract. Anyway, in practice, large increases in the choreography size are not frequent and the considered case study is part of the average cases [3].

6   Related Works

Over the years, many works have explored the creation of trustworthy blockchain-based applications [18]. Many languages, such as UML, BPMN, or domain-specific ones, have been employed to support the automatic generation of blockchain code [9]. In particular, the BPMN standard has obtained relevance, as blockchain was recognized as an enabling technology driven by the need for trustworthiness in multi-party business processes [10]. With its immutability and decentralized nature, blockchain offers a promising solution for ensuring integrity, transparency, and trust in such processes.

Caterpillar, introduced in the seminal work [11], has been the reference model-driven solution for implementing BPMN collaboration models via translation into Solidity code. Indeed, initially, the blockchain was used by commercial BPM systems (e.g., Bizagi and Camunda) only for auditing purposes, i.e., parties record their activities on a blockchain so that all other parties can check that they respect the process. This was achieved by adapters offered by the BPM systems to record transactions in a blockchain. In this way, however, the task of monitoring the execution of the process was entirely on the shoulders of the parties, and any deviation from the process requires the involved parties to participate in a conflict resolution procedure. To overcome these issues, [11] introduces the compliance-by-design approach, where the compliance of the process execution with respect to the process model (which, in this case, is a BPMN collaboration diagram) is enforced by invoking a Solidity smart contract running on the blockchain. Caterpillar was extended by the Pupa approach [15], where the authors proposed a solution to translate BPMN models into Solidity smart contracts. In this case, the approach focuses on supporting the timer event and inclusive gateway elements. Lorikeet [19] is a solution specifically devised to deal with the execution of business processes that manage non-fungible assets (e.g., cars, houses, supply chain goods). Thus, besides automatically producing Solidity smart contracts from business process models (again, BPMN collaboration diagrams), Lorikeet also generates a registry data schema used to create asset data stores in the blockchain. ChorChain [4,6] is still based on translation to Solidity code, but considers choreography diagrams as source models, as in our case. In addition, ChorChain offers a complete framework supporting the whole lifecycle of choreographies: from modeling to execution and auditing. For each choreography instance, ChorChain generates a Solidity smart contract, specifying the involved participants and implementing the message exchange as executable functions. Similarly to the aforementioned works, the smart contract is used to enforce the workflow specified in the choreography. Differently, TABS [2] aims at generating a set of methods of smart contract(s) using Discrete EventâĂŞHierarchical State Machine (DE-HSM) modeling. With this approach, the original model is divided into patterns that can be deployed and executed on a sidechain. Additionally, the translation supports both Ethereum and Hyperledger Fabric as target smart contract implementations.

Our proposal shares with the above works the translational approach for the blockchain-based implementation of multi-party business processes. However, it differs from all of them, as it specifically focuses on the modularity of generated smart contracts, achieved by relying on a formal-driven approach. In fact, none of the other solutions relies on a model-to-code translation that has been designed following a formal semantics, and none of them generates smart contracts that enjoy the modularity property. Finally, our approach is agnostic about the target smart contract language.

7　Concluding Remarks

This paper proposes an implementation of BPMN multi-party business processes for execution on blockchain platforms. Processes are expressed as BPMN choreography diagrams, which are translated, following a formal-driven and modular approach, into smart contracts. We experimented with Solidity and PyTeal contracts to assess the feasibility and the costs of our proposal.

As future work, we aim to enhance our translation approach into a multilanguage automatic translator tool capable of generating smart contracts in various target languages, including Solidity and PyTeal. Moreover, an interesting direction of work is the definition of formal techniques to verify properties of choreographies, ensuring a correct-by-design generation of the corresponding smart contracts. Finally, we intend to take advantage of the modularity of our translation by using it to support different forms of flexibility techniques [5,12].

Acknowledgment. This work was partially supported by project SERICS (PE00000014) under the MUR National Recovery and Resilience Plan funded by the European Union - NextGenerationEU and partially funded by Ministero dell'Università e della Ricerca (MUR), issue D. M. 351/2022 "Borse di Dottorato" - Dottorato di Ricerca di Interesse Nazionale in "Blockchain & Distributed Ledger Technology", under the National Recovery and Resilience Plan.

References

1. Online artifacts repository (2025). https://github.com/nawaz-malla/bpmn-to-blockchain
2. Bodorik, P., Liu, C.G., Jutla, D.: Tabs: transforming automatically bpmn models into blockchain smart contracts. BCRA **4**(1), 100115 (2023)
3. Compagnucci, I., Corradini, F., Fornari, F., Re, B.: A study on the usage of the bpmn notation for designing process collaboration, choreography, and conversation models. Bus. Inf. Syst. Eng. **66**(1), 43–66 (2024)
4. Corradini, F., Marcelletti, A., Morichetta, A., Polini, A., Re, B., Tiezzi, F.: Engineering trustable and auditable choreography-based systems using blockchain. ACM Trans. Manag. Inf. Syst. **13**(3), 31:1–31:53 (2022)
5. Corradini, F., Marcelletti, A., Morichetta, A., Polini, A., Re, B., Tiezzi, F.: A flexible approach to multi-party business process execution on blockchain. Future Gener. Comput. Syst. **147**, 219–234 (2023)
6. Corradini, F., Marcelletti, A., Morichetta, A., Polini, A., Re, B., Tiezzi, F., et al.: Chorchain: a model-driven framework for choreography-based systems using blockchain. In: ITBPM@ BPM, pp. 26–32 (2021)
7. Corradini, F., Morichetta, A., Polini, A., Re, B., Tiezzi, F.: Collaboration vs. choreography conformance in BPMN. Log. Methods Comput. Sci. **16**(4) (2020)
8. Corradini, F., Morichetta, A., Re, B., Tiezzi, F.: Walking through the semantics of exclusive and event-based gateways in BPMN choreographies. In: Alvim, M.S., Chatzikokolakis, K., Olarte, C., Valencia, F. (eds.) The Art of Modelling Computational Systems: A Journey from Logic and Concurrency to Security and Privacy. LNCS, vol. 11760, pp. 163–181. Springer, Cham (2019). https://doi.org/10.1007/978-3-030-31175-9_10

9. Curty, S., Härer, F., Fill, H.: Design of blockchain-based applications using model-driven engineering and low-code/no-code platforms: a structured literature review. Softw. Syst. Model. **22**(6), 1857–1895 (2023)
10. Jan Mendling et al.: Blockchains for business process management - challenges and opportunities. ACM Trans. Manag. Inf. Syst. **9**(1), 4:1–4:16 (2018)
11. López-Pintado, O., García-Bañuelos, L., Dumas, M., Weber, I., Ponomarev, A.: Caterpillar: a business process execution engine on the ethereum blockchain. Softw. Pract. Exp. **49**(7), 1162–1193 (2019)
12. López-Pintado, O., Dumas, M., García-Bañuelos, L., Weber, I.: Controlled flexibility in blockchain-based collaborative business processes. IS **104**, 101622 (2022)
13. Malla, N.A., Marcelletti, A., Morichetta, A., Tiezzi, F.: A Blockchain-based, Semantics-driven, Modular Implementation of BPMN Choreographies – Technical Report (2025). https://github.com/nawaz-malla/bpmn-to-blockchain/blob/main/ Society_5.0__Algorand__Technical
14. Müller, M., Ostern, N., Rosemann, M.: Silver bullet for all trust issues? Blockchain-based trust patterns for collaborative business processes. In: Asatiani, A., et al. (eds.) BPM 2020. LNBIP, vol. 393, pp. 3–18. Springer, Cham (2020). https://doi. org/10.1007/978-3-030-58779-6_1
15. Naha, R.T., Zhang, K.: Pupa: smart contracts for BPMN with time-dependent events and inclusive gateways. In: BPM Blockchain, RPA, and CEE Forum. LNBIP, vol. 459, pp. 21–35. Springer, Heidelberg (2022)
16. Mohammadi, N.G., et al.: Trustworthiness attributes and metrics for engineering trusted internet-based software systems. In: CLOSER. CCIS, vol. 453, pp. 19–35. Springer, Heidelberg (2013)
17. Object Management Group: Business Process Model and Notation (BPMN V 2.0). OMG Standard document (2011). http://www.omg.org/spec/BPMN
18. Stiehle, F., Weber, I.: Blockchain for business process enactment: a taxonomy and systematic literature review. In: BPM Blockchain, RPA, and CEE Forum. LNBIP, vol. 459, pp. 5–20. Springer, Heidelberg (2022)
19. Tran, A.B., Lu, Q., Weber, I.: Lorikeet: a model-driven engineering tool for blockchain-based business process execution and asset management. In: BPM Demo and Industrial Track. CEUR-WS Proceedings, vol. 2196, pp. 56–60 (2018)

The Impact of AI Integration in Dating Apps on User Trust

Sfiso Ntuli and Machdel Matthee[(✉)] [iD]

Department of Informatics, University of Pretoria, Pretoria, South Africa
`u24021742@tuks.co.za, machdel.matthee@up.ac.za`

Abstract. In this research, the effect of AI implementation in dating applications on trust among users is investigated by conducting a structured literature review. Trust is a vital aspect for the success and acceptance of dating apps, therefore this problem is particularly significant as AI brings both benefits and issues to the table. Major results indicate that AI promotes trust through improved matching algorithms, user safety and information verification while simultaneously challenging data privacy, algorithmic transparency and biases. These findings are in line with prior work on trust for general IS applications and extends this understanding to dating applications. This has important implications for research and practice, pointing towards the necessity of providing further empirical validation in relation to trust issues, investigating new dimensions of trustworthiness (that appeals to transparency) as well as designing more transparent and user-friendly dating applications. Therefore, further research is needed across cultures, generations and regions to mitigate the limitations pointed out. The knowledge from this research can be used by service providers to create user centric and reliable dating applications.

Keywords: Artificial intelligence (AI) · user trust · Impact · dating apps · structured literature review

1 Introduction

Online dating has evolved from being seen as a niche pastime to a commonplace aspect of modern life, with a multitude of services available to assist individuals in finding romantic partners [1]. Hinge, Bumble, and Tinder (all apps provided by Match Group), are a few of the well-known mobile dating apps. There are currently over 381 million users in the online dating sector [2], and AI is increasingly used to improve the efficiency of the services such as matching potential romantic partners according to compatibility, hobbies, and preferences [3]. Despite the notable decline in usage of dating apps [4], there are projected to be 470.0 million users in the online dating sector by 2029 [2]. Algorithms can have an important impact on people's decisions which makes them helpful in the process of locating possible partners [5]. By using machine learning to analyze and decode data, draw on their experiences, and adjust to fresh scenarios, AI-powered dating apps may be able to continually improve and learn from their matching

© The Author(s), under exclusive license to Springer Nature Switzerland AG 2026
F. Corradini et al. (Eds.): Society 5.0 2025, CCIS 2787, pp. 194–204, 2026.
https://doi.org/10.1007/978-3-032-15463-7_16

algorithms [6]. Apart from matchmaking, AI chatbots in dating apps are sometimes used as love coaches. Some AI systems even suggest restaurants and clubs for physical dates [7]. AI is also used in dating apps to maintain security and safety in the online dating space [8]. For instance, Tinder uses an AI algorithm to check private messages for inappropriate language in order to make users feel safe and increase their trust in the system [9].

Match Group recently announced the launching of an AI assistant in March 2025 which will "transform" online dating. According to Bernard Kim, CE of Match Group "This technology is revolutionary for dating, and we're bringing it to life across our entire portfolio. I envision AI to be felt through the entire experience, influencing everything from profile creation to matching and connecting for dates, literally everything." [4]. It is clearly important to comprehend the dynamics of technology in this setting, particularly AI.

Trust is difficult to define, even though it is present in almost every element of people's lives. Chiu and Pan [10] define trust in technology as "a social-technical construct and reflects an individual's willingness to be vulnerable to the actions of another, irrespective of the ability to monitor or control these actions."

Wang et al. [11], highlight the relationship between the trustor and trustee in building "online trust": An individual perusing an online store is the trustor in the context of online trust. The online retailer (the one the website represents) is the trustee. Any online transaction carries some risk, for instance, customers are particularly exposed and vulnerable to certain breaches of trust in online trades, such as financial loss and invasion of personal information [12]. Users have two options when they visit a website: "just browsing" or "engage in service." To get individuals to engage with them, suppliers need to ensure that they are certain they will gain more than lose. Online trust is intrinsically subjective because individuals have varying perspectives and attitudes towards technology [13].

Given the inherent risk in using dating apps, dating apps service providers know that they need to earn the trust of users in order for it to be used [14]. Already it appears that the use of AI in dating apps impact the trust of users: A study looking into perceptions of AI engagement in profile generation in dating apps found a significant decline in user belief in the trustworthiness of the systems, informing the complex interplay between AI integration and trust [15]. A study conducted in 2021 by Gillath [16] examined the relationship between AI trust and attachment, highlighting the emotive aspects of trust development. The work of Gillath [16] also sheds light on the complex interplay between psychological constituents and consumer trust within AI-driven dating systems with respect to how attachment security affects AI trust.

This research will therefore focus on the impact of the use of AI in dating apps on user trust. A number of researchers work on the issue of online trust in AI-enabled systems [16–18], but less so on user trust in AI-enabled dating apps. The aim of this systematic literature review is therefore to determine the status quo of research on user trust in AI-enabled dating apps also drawing from research on user trust and AI- enabled systems in general. The research question is therefore: What is the effect of the use of AI in dating apps on user trust? A future research agenda on this topic is provided as well as a list of potential trust factors to take into account by dating app service providers.

2 Literature Background

Yang et al. [18] present a comprehensive conceptual framework for the understanding of user's trust in AI. They show the different approaches followed in literature to explore this issue. Their conceptual framework summarises the factors influencing user trust in AI to include technological, organizational, contextual, social and personal factors. The quality of the system, information, service and design of AI influences trust. Furthermore, the reputation and characteristics of the AI-enabled service-provider also play a role. The context and reason for the use of these AI-enabled systems also have an effect. It is expected that systems carrying greater risks in terms of privacy violations or leaving users vulnerable, will ask for more trust. Social norms and natural culture appear to play a role on trusting behaviour of users. Users' prior experiences, familiarity with technology, personality and perceptions influence the formation of trust in AI-enabled systems [7].

It is assumed that the same factors influence users' trust in AI-enabled dating apps, but the unique context of dating apps could highlight some factors or introduce others. Chiu and Pan [10] highlight the uncertainty of the dating app transactions as one such a unique feature: users may date several times before they find the right one. Also, they cannot return a "product" if not satisfied and renew trust in that sense. Chiu and Pan [10] developed a trust-inducing model for dating apps experience with dimensions corporate trust, matching trust, risk trust, system trust, and information trust. They considered these dimensions across pre-and post-engagement with dating apps. Although Chiu and Pan [10] did not take the effect of AI integration into account, their research remains valuable.

Each of these dimensions of trust according to Chiu and Pan [10] is discussed in the Table 1 below:

Table 1. Trust-inducing framework for dating apps [10]

Before interaction	
Company trust dimension 1 Branding and marketing 2. Indirect experience	Consumers' trust in an online business is shaped by its branding and marketing efforts in addition to its size and reputation [19, 20]. Users' trust will also be influenced by app reviews and their friends' experiences before they interact with dating app systems [19]
After interaction	

(continued)

Table 1. (*continued*)

System trust dimension 1 UI design (Layout, color) 2 UX design (Content, features)	Prior user experience studies on trust concentrated on graphic design [19, 21]. The dating app's UI design includes its colour scheme and layout. [22] demonstrated that dating apps will have higher levels of trust if their layouts resemble those of chat services. For instance, the earlier study shown a favourable correlation between users' trust in the registration procedure of dating apps and their ability to connect with social networking service accounts, such as Facebook [23]
Information trust dimension 1 Personal information 2 Identity verification	Uncertainty about the authenticity of an individual's details on dating apps leads to distrust and concerns about safety [10]. Match Group upgraded its security procedures in 2020 and included a method for artificial intelligence-powered photo integration and verification within its application [22]. These two characteristics confirm the legitimacy of a match. According to studies, users' SNS account identity verification and detailed personal information can boost trust [23]
Matching trust dimension 1 Matching success rate 2 Matching experience	Good matches bring good experiences and builds trust. Matches with inactive users decrease trust in the dating apps [10]
Risk trust dimension 1 Privacy management 2 Safety management	Security (safety) and privacy comprise this dimension. For example, the safety tips can be included in a report system. The privacy section should contain a transparent privacy policy. Continued app use is adversely impacted by perceived privacy risk [24]

3 Research Method

This study was carried out by utilizing a systematic literature review as proposed by Boland, Cherry, and Dickson [25]. The purpose of this study is to investigate the impact of AI in dating applications on user trust. To achieve this, the research question was framed: What is the effect of the use of AI in dating apps on user trust?

ScienceDirect, SpringerLink and Tandfonline were used to gather research papers that are relevant to the research question.

The search terms used for each database were as follows:

- ScienceDirect: ("AI" OR "Artificial intelligence") AND ("Dating apps") AND ("User trust" OR 'Trust')
- SpringerLink: ("Artificial intelligence" OR "AI") AND ("trust") AND ("dating apps")
- Tandfonline: ("Trust" OR "User trust") AND ("AI" or "Artificial intelligence") OR ("dating apps")

To conduct this systematic literature review, the following criteria was used to choose from the papers retrieved by the search terms:

- Date of Publication: Research papers published between 2019 and 2024.
- Language of Publication: Research papers published in English only.
- Research Method used: Papers that use both quantitative and qualitative methods were used.
- Publication type: Review articles, research articles and journal articles (from academic journals).
- Papers focusing on trust in AI-enabled systems as well as papers focusing on trust in AI enhanced dating apps.
- Full text availability: Research papers accessible by means of Institutional Access.

The Preferred Reporting Items for Systematic Reviews and Meta-Analyses process was followed to make the selection of the final number of articles [26]. The literature search found 1048 articles from the databases used (ScienceDirect, SpringerLink and Tandfonline) and 7 additional articles were found through forward chaining (citation chaining). As multiple databases were used, several articles were included two or more times in this number. These duplicates (206 articles) were removed leaving 849 unique articles. These articles were then reviewed for relevance based on titles and abstracts leading to the exclusion of 687 articles. 162 full text articles were assessed for eligibility using the inclusion criteria resulting in 117 exclusions. A total of 45 articles successfully met the inclusion criteria and its data was analysed in a data extraction table. Inductive thematic analysis was used to determine themes. Thematic analysis is a method for assessing qualitative data such as papers to find themes and relationships within the data [27]. Using the data extraction table, significant data units were labelled to create preliminary codes. After grouping these codes to find possible themes, the accuracy of the findings was checked. After themes have been refined, clarified, and given names, a narrative describing each theme was written (Sect. 4). After this, the findings per theme were mapped to the framework of [10] (Sect. 5).

4 Findings

Three main themes were identified from the articles that included factors influencing user trust in AI enabled dating apps. They were categorized as individual related factors, technology related factors and organizational factors. This section will discuss these factors.

4.1 Individual Related Factors

This encompasses factors like user attributes and past experiences. Age and gender appear to influence the willingness to use dating apps, indicating trust in dating apps.

Sumter et al. [28] claim that males use dating apps at a higher rate than females. The study conducted by Paul and Ahmed [29] indicated that young male respondents more strongly believed in the effectiveness of dating algorithms.

Also, in 2020, young people between ages 18–30 were the most likely to use dating applications [30]. Four years later and the demographics of users shifted: According to a Statista survey in 2023, 61% of people in the USA using dating apps are millennials whereas GenZ makes up 26% of users [31].

Favourable past experience with dating apps influence trust. According to Hu and Wang's [32] study, it is claimed that high usage of dating applications will make the users more open to the action of algorithmic matching, which could lead to an increase in trust. Paul and Ahmed [29], on the other hand, illustrate how the sheer volume of relationship-starting encounters on dating apps might offset unfavourable perceptions (such as unfairness) of dating algorithms.

In addition, according to Ma, Song, and Chong [33], users of dating apps would be motivated to use them again based on their own perceptions of their autonomy. Users must have a sense of freedom and control over the interactions they have on dating apps. If users believe AI is making judgements without consulting them or their understanding, they may become uncomfortable and be less likely to utilize the app. Ensuring users comprehend AI and have the ability to impact its functioning is crucial [7].

Detrimental effects of dating apps can have an influence on trust: Dating apps often tend to emphasize physical attraction and appearance, which may encourage harmful results regarding body image, including body shaming. Negative perceptions related to nutrition and body image, remain a concern for the mental health of users [30, 34]. Another influence is social risk, which refers to potential status loss within one's social network based on the belief held by some that those who use dating apps are socially awkward [35]. Another concern associated with using dating apps is the detrimental impact they have on one's peace of mind, for instance, too much unsolicited messages and requests can ruffle one's peace of mind and create emotional strain [35].

Users may experience anxiety if they depend on AI to make emotional and sensitive decisions, like choosing a love partner. It can be uncomfortable when the intensely personal aspect of dating and the impersonal nature of AI collide. According to research, people's emotional reactions to AI differ greatly, with many of them finding it unsettling that AI will make decisions in such intimate situations [7].

4.2 Technological Factors

Castro and Barrada [30] emphasise that dating apps should be simple, secure, and offer an effective matching mechanism that provides matches between users according to their preference and interests. According to Chiu and Pan [10], a positive matching experience and a higher matching rate boost user trust.

The configuration of dating apps plays an important role in inducing trust [30]. This includes privacy concerns and security risks, as these might give rise to worries about losing control over personal data and the ease of localization. Second, there are safety hazards associated with dating apps, like romance scams and meeting people without doing a trustworthy background check [35]. Users also have concerns about tracking of data and evaluation, sharing of data to other organizations and government agencies [29].

Trust in dating algorithms determines to a large extent trust in dating apps. The use of embedded AI (black-boxed AI) contributes to the perception of a lack of openness and validity of dating algorithms [29]. When it comes to explaining the underlying workings of their algorithms, online dating sites tend to be evasive, claiming that they use sophisticated algorithms for matchmaking. Consumers are not provided with an easy way to confirm the algorithm's "ever-evolving" nature or even to understand the algorithm's basic operation [29].

Recently, online dating services have tried to increase their algorithmic transparency. Dating services like Tinder created tech blogs on which they put up posts that deal with their technological advancements such as simple explanations of the ways their algorithms work, ways to deal with data privacy and user protection against misuse and fraud [29]. Unfortunately, the higher order explanations of the algorithmics remain opaque. [29] show that online dating platforms are not transparent with the calculations the algorithms perform using users' personal information to determine compatibility. Because of this, it is impossible to determine if the matchmaking algorithms recommendations are compatible or the result of pure chance. Ensuring that algorithms are impartial, equitable, and transparent is crucial in addressing algorithm aversion [6]. In addition, users should be provided some context and information on how the algorithmic matchmaking process works [3]. By doing this, people are more likely to stick with it and are kept from losing trust in the algorithm in the case that it makes an incorrect choice or recommendation.

Algorithm design is yet another component to consider, since it may eventually institutionalize social and cultural bias [34]. The architecture of algorithms may contain biased perceptions programmed by algorithm designers. Algorithmic profiling and recommendation could amplify these prejudiced impressions, further solidifying the reality of biased social norms and culture [34]. Another element is system design, the more diverse the design is, the more trustworthy the system is perceived to be [10]. Increasing user trust additionally relies on the AI system's verification of user profiles. It's important to evaluate the matching algorithms' efficacy as well.

4.3 Organizational Factors Influencing User Trust on Dating Apps.

The trust-inducing framework for dating apps established by Chiu and Pan [10] included the corporate trust dimension, as was previously mentioned. The reputation and scale of the business, as well as its branding and marketing, all affect user's trust. Marketing should include how matching algorithms are used and how security and privacy are ensured. Third-party endorsement also plays a vital role in reinforcing trust to validate the credibility of the platform.

5 Discussion

The research question for which the current study answers was: "What is the effect of AI use in dating apps on user trust?" The results show that the effects of AI on user trust in dating applications are highly nuanced and depend on organizational, individual, and technology-related factors. The research of individual-related factors demonstrates that background, attitudes, and previous experience have a significant effect on user trust both before and after engaging with the dating app. Positive previous experience with AI systems increases trust while the negative ones diminish it. This is consistent with other research that holds the view that successful contacts and familiarity with technology increase trust [17, 36, 37]. Moreover, demographic variables that may affect knowledge and willingness to understand the dating app are age, gender and educational level [38].

Building confidence in technology-related aspects requires a focus on the perceived quality of AI systems in dating applications. High-quality, personalized content, safe systems, and transparent and accurate AI algorithms all contribute to users' trust [39–41]. To improve perceived system quality and user trust, the mechanisms of security have to be firm, errorless, and user-friendly [42, 43]. User trust is impacted by organizational elements such as the service provider's reputation, ethical standards compliance, and social responsibility commitment. Positive perceptions of AI-enabled dating apps can increase acceptability and confidence in them. These perceptions can be strengthened by ethical treatment of data and third-party endorsements [36, 44, 45]. It is also important to observe user autonomy, fairness and unbiased interactions [17, 46].

Understanding these aspects, can help focus the development of more trustworthy forms of artificial intelligence systems within dating apps. An emphasis on safety, openness, and user control encourages trust among users. The findings align with previous research emphasizing the value of ethical, security, and transparent factors in building user confidence in AI systems [41, 43]. The factors influencing user trust in AI enabled dating apps are mapped to the trust dimensions (see Table 2) in dating app experience of Chiu and Pan [10].

Table 2. Summary of trust factors influencing AI enabled dating app use

Before interaction	
Personal: User-related and social factors	Indirect experience [10], attitude [10], age [30], gender [28, 29], previous experience [32]
Organisational: Company trust dimension	Branding, marketing, corporate reputation [29]
During interaction	
Personal: User-related and social factors	Indirect experience [10], attitude [10], age [30], gender [28, 29], previous experience [32], perceived risk (body image, mental health) [30, 34, 35], emotional impact [7]
Technology: System trust dimension	UI design (Layout, color), UX design (Content, features), diverse elements [10], user autonomy [33], user control [33]
Technology: Information trust dimension	Personal information, Identity verification of users [30], data protection [29, 30], algorithmic transparency [3, 29]
Technology: Matching trust dimension	Matching success rate [30], Matching experience [35], algorithmic fairness [34], algorithmic transparency [29]
Technology: Risk trust dimension	Privacy management [30] Safety management [30, 35]

6 Conclusion

This research aimed to explore the impact of AI integration in dating apps on user trust through a structured literature review. The methodology involved systematically reviewing 45 articles to identify and analyze studies that examined trust factors related to AI in dating apps and apps in general. By looking through relevant literature, we discovered that the use of AI to improve matchmaking algorithms, increase user safety and validate user information has a positive effect on trust. However, issues with algorithmic transparency, data privacy, and potential biases were revealed as major challenges. Previous research has highlighted openness, data privacy, dependability of systems, and relevance of information in building trust amongst the users. This review deepens our understanding of these aspects in the context of dating apps, underlining the particular challenges and potential given by AI in this sector.

The identification of specific trust dimensions supports previous research on trust frameworks and adds depth to our knowledge of how trust works in AI-enabled dating apps. The systematic approach and categorization of trust factors into dimensions are the strengths of this review, although it is limited by the scope and quality of available studies and the rapidly evolving nature of AI. Only three databases were considered. The systematic review clearly touches on ethical considerations, including data privacy, algorithmic bias, lack of algorithmic transparency and the potential harm to mental health. However, the scope of this study did not allow an in-depth discussion of the ethics of AI integrated dating apps. Furthermore, given how quickly AI technologies are developing, some insights might quickly become out of date.

This extended trust-inducing framework can be used by the service providers to enhance the user's trust based on key dimensions such as corporate trust, system trust, information trust, matching trust, and risk trust that would in turn help them build more reliable and user-friendly AI-enabled dating apps. Future researchers can use it in empirical studies on how different trust dimensions evolve with emerging technologies like AI across diverse cultural contexts and geographic locations, especially the Global South. Most of the papers that were reviewed in this report were from Asia, North America and Europe, further limiting its generalizability to other settings. In addition, the trust dimensions could provide some insight to service providers in how the trust of younger users such as genZ can be earned to encourage usage of dating apps. In conclusion, while AI integration provides considerable benefits, resolving issues of transparency, privacy, and bias is critical to the continued use of dating apps. More thorough investigations of the ethical implications of AI integrated dating apps are needed.

References

1. Zytko, D., Grandhi, S.A., Jones, Q.: Frustrations with pursuing casual encounters through online dating. In: Proceedings of the 33rd annual ACM conference extended abstracts on human factors in computing systems, pp. 1935–1940. (2015)
2. Statista: Online Dating - worldwide (2024). Statista Market Forecast. https://www.statista.com/outlook/372/100/online-dating/worldwide. Accessed 22 Apr 2024
3. Van der Linde, L.: Algorithmic Trust and Matching Score in Online Dating. Unpublished Masters dissertation. Tilburg University (2023)

4. Boyd, R.: Dating apps prepare to launch AI features to help users find love. The Guardian, 30 December 2024. (2024). Accessed online 13 February 2025 at https://www.theguardian.com/technology/2024/dec/30/dating-apps-prepare-to-launch-ai-features-to-help-users-find-love

5. Montal, T., Reich, Z.: I, robot. You, journalist. Who is the author? Authorship, bylines and full disclosure in automated journalism. Digital Journalism 5, 829–849 (2017)

6. Cabiddu, F., Moi, L., Patriotta, G., Allen, D.G.: Why do users trust algorithms? a review and conceptualization of initial trust and trust over time. Eur. Manag. J. 40, 685–706 (2022)

7. Wang, H.: Algorithmic colonization of love: the ethical challenges of dating app algorithms in the age of AI. Techne: Res. Philos. Technol. 27 (2023)

8. ItechnoLABS.: AI in Dating Apps (2024). https://itechnolabs.ca/ai-in-dating-apps/. Accessed 12 Apr 2024

9. Rivero, N.: Tinder is using AI to monitor DMs and tame the creeps. Quartz (2021). https://qz.com/2011998/tinder-is-using-ai-to-monitor-dmsand-tame-the-creeps/. Accessed 12 Apr 2024

10. Chiu, E.Y., Pan, Y.H.: The impact of trustworthiness in the dating app experience: A trust-inducing model proposal. J. Next-generation Converg. Info. Ser. Technol. 9, 327–340 (2020)

11. Wang, Y.D., Emurian, H.H.: An overview of online trust: concepts, elements, and implications. Comput. Hum. Behav. 21, 105–125 (2005)

12. Friedman, B., Khan, P.H., Jr., Howe, D.C.: Trust online. Commun. ACM 43, 34–40 (2000)

13. Grabner-Kraeuter, S.: The role of consumers' trust in online-shopping. J. Bus. Ethics 39, 43–50 (2002)

14. Bach, T.A., Khan, A., Hallock, H., Beltrão, G., Sousa, S.: A systematic literature review of user trust in AI-enabled systems: An HCI perspective. Int. J. Human-Comp. Interact. 40, 1251–1266 (2024)

15. Wu, Y., Kelly, R.M.: Online dating meets artificial intelligence: how the perception of algorithmically generated profile text impacts attractiveness and trust. In: Proceedings of the 32nd Australian conference on human-computer interaction, pp. 444–453 (2020)

16. Gillath, O., Ai, T., Branicky, M.S., Keshmiri, S., Davison, R.B., Spaulding, R.: Attachment and trust in artificial intelligence. Comp. Hum. Behav. 115, 106607 (2021)

17. Qin, F., Li, K., Yan, J.: Understanding user trust in artificial intelligence-based educational systems: Evidence from China. Br. J. Edu. Technol. 51, 1693–1710 (2020)

18. Yang, R., Wibowo, S.: User trust in artificial intelligence: a comprehensive conceptual framework. Electron. Mark. 32, 2053–2077 (2022)

19. Egger, F.N.: Affective design of e-commerce user interfaces: how to maximise perceived trustworthiness. In: Proc. Intl. Conf. Affective Human Factors Design, pp. 317–324. Citeseer (2001)

20. Morrison, D.E., Firmstone, J.: The social function of trust and implications for e-commerce. Int. J. Advert. 19, 599–623 (2000)

21. Kim, J., Moon, J.Y.: Designing towards emotional usability in customer interfaces—trustworthiness of cyber-banking system interfaces. Interact. Comput. 10, 1–29 (1998)

22. Lee, H.-J., Choi, Y.-H., Lee, B.Y., Lee, J.-W.: Analysis and Design on Mobile Application Based Social Dating Contents. The J. Korea Contents Ass. 14, 336–345 (2014)

23. An, H.-J., Kim, S.-I.: Evaluation for user experience about social dating mobile application service in Korea-Focusing on I-um and noondate. J. Digit. Converg. 15, 335–341 (2017)

24. Wang, E.S.-T., Lin, R.-L.: Perceived quality factors of location-based apps on trust, perceived privacy risk, and continuous usage intention. Behav. Info. Technol. 36, 2–10 (2017)

25. Boland, A., Dickson, R., Cherry, G.: Doing a systematic review: a student's guide (2017)

26. Moher, D., Liberati, A., Tetzlaff, J., Altman, D.G.: Preferred reporting items for systematic reviews and meta-analyses: the PRISMA statement. PLoS Med. 6, e1000097 (2009)

27. Braun, V., Clarke, V.: Using thematic analysis in psychology. Qual. Res. Psychol. 3, 77–101 (2006)

28. Sumter, S.R., Vandenbosch, L.: Dating gone mobile: Demographic and personality-based correlates of using smartphone-based dating applications among emerging adults. New Media Soc. **21**, 655–673 (2019)
29. Paul, A., Ahmed, S.: Computed compatibility: examining user perceptions of AI and matchmaking algorithms. Behav. Info. Technol. **43**, 1002–1015 (2024)
30. Castro, Á., Barrada, J.R.: Dating apps and their sociodemographic and psychosocial correlates: a systematic review. Int. J. Environ. Res. Public Health **17**, 6500 (2020)
31. Battle, M.: Why GenZ is ditching dating apps. Time, 29 February 2024 (2024). Accessed online 17 February 2025 at https://time.com/6836033/gen-z-ditching-dating-apps/
32. Hu, J., Wang, R.: Familiarity breeds trust? The relationship between dating app use and trust in dating algorithms via algorithm awareness and critical algorithm perceptions. Int. J. Human-Comp. Interact. **40**, 4596–4607 (2024)
33. Ma, Z., Chong, W.K., Song, L.: How arousing benefits and ethical misgivings affect AI-based dating app adoption: The roles of perceived autonomy and perceived risks. In: International Conference on Human-Computer Interaction, pp. 160–170. Springer (2022)
34. Yang, K.: A technoethical exploration of online dating algorithms: a systematic literature review. Unpublished Masters dissertation. University of Ottawa (2021)
35. Chen, Q., Yuan, Y., Feng, Y., Archer, N.: A decision paradox: benefit vs risk and trust vs distrust for online dating adoption vs non-adoption. Internet Res. **31**, 341–375 (2021)
36. Lobschat, L., et al.: Corporate digital responsibility. J. Bus. Res. **122**, 875–888 (2021)
37. Zhou, J., Luo, S., Chen, F.: Effects of personality traits on user trust in human–machine collaborations. J. Multimodal User Interfaces **14**, 387–400 (2020)
38. Araujo, T., Helberger, N., Kruikemeier, S., De Vreese, C.H.: In AI we trust? Perceptions about automated decision-making by artificial intelligence. AI & society **35**, 611–623 (2020)
39. Foehr, J., Germelmann, C.C.: Alexa, can I trust you? Exploring consumer paths to trust in smart voice-interaction technologies. J. Ass. Consumer Res. **5**, 181–205 (2020)
40. Glikson, E., Woolley, A.W.: Human trust in artificial intelligence: review of empirical research. Acad. Manag. Ann. **14**, 627–660 (2020)
41. Hsiao, K.-L., Chen, C.-C.: What drives continuance intention to use a food-ordering chatbot? an examination of trust and satisfaction. Library Hi Tech **40**, 929–946 (2022)
42. Felzmann, H., Villaronga, E.F., Lutz, C., Tamò-Larrieux, A.: Transparency you can trust: Transparency requirements for artificial intelligence between legal norms and contextual concerns. Big Data Soc. **6**, 2053951719860542 (2019)
43. Triberti, S., Durosini, I., Curigliano, G., Pravettoni, G.: Is explanation a marketing problem? the quest for trust in artificial intelligence and two conflicting solutions. Public Health Genomics **23**, 2–5 (2020)
44. Nguyen, N., Pervan, S.: Retailer corporate social responsibility and consumer citizenship behavior: The mediating roles of perceived consumer effectiveness and consumer trust. J. Retail. Consum. Serv. **55**, 102082 (2020)
45. Nordheim, C.B., Følstad, A., Bjørkli, C.A.: An initial model of trust in chatbots for customer service—findings from a questionnaire study. Interact. Comput. **31**, 317–335 (2019)
46. Ryan, M.: In AI we trust: ethics, artificial intelligence, and reliability. Sci. Eng. Ethics **26**, 2749–2767 (2020)

Adoption of FinTech by Young Adults in Mauritius: Integrating Technology Acceptance Model with Perceived Risk, Attitude and Trust

Kiran Odit Dookhan

University of Technology Mauritius, Port Louis, Mauritius
`koditdookhan@utm.ac.mu`

Abstract. The adoption of financial technology (FinTech) among young adults in Mauritius is increasingly modelled by various psychological and contextual factors, prominently illustrated by the Technology Acceptance Model (TAM). In line with the model, aperceived ease of use and perceived usefulness are substantial determinants of acceptance of a technology. However, with FinTech, it is intertwined with additional considerations such as perceived risk, attitude, and trust, above all among those youth. An online survey was conducted with a sample of 271 young adults in Mauritius and analysed with SPSS version 26, highlighting essential considerations for realizing adoption of FinTech. Perceived usefulness and ease of use had less of an impact on attitudes toward FinTech, compared to expectations. Instead, a demographic perspective had a strong impact on levels of trust. The study suggests that stakeholders should focus in their strategies on reducing risk and establishing trust to encourage young adults to adopt FinTech. Recommended actions include targeted education campaigns, increased security measures, and tailored financial offerings based on the various demographic groups.

Keywords: FinTech Adoption · Perceived Ease of Use · Attitude · Perceived Usefulness · Perceived Risk · Trust

1 Introduction

In general, the FinTech innovations provide user-friendly digital interfaces for the customer's transactions, thus providing cost-effective solutions and allowances for their use. The online payment includes PayPal, stock broking applications, as well as cryptocurrency exchanges such as Coinbase. FinTech aims to enhance efficiency and speed compared to traditional methods, leveraging global internet connectivity to meet customer expectations and address market gaps in a highly competitive landscape.

With the global advancement in technology and the adoption of financial services, the usage of FinTech has dramatically increased [1]. Also, there is a rise in the use of FinTech because of the increased use of the internet and mobile phones [2]. Mauritius is actively attempting to establish itself as a FinTech powerhouse in Africa.

F. Corradini et al. (Eds.): Society 5.0 2025, CCIS 2787, pp. 205–215, 2026.
https://doi.org/10.1007/978-3-032-15463-7_17

The present study investigates the intricate interplay between technological advances and consumer behaviours, given the context of the banking sector in Mauritius The study will analyse in-depth the preparedness and adaptability of the Mauritian population relative to such technological advances. The study of customer trust-inducing characteristics regarding the launch of FinTech products may provide essential information to businesses, politicians, and financial institutions. Focus on Mauritius, being a small island developing nation, makes the research valuable in providing important text to emerging countries on the individual challenges and prospects regarding FinTech in the digital banking ecosystem. The research thus aims at providing an insight into the implications of FinTech transition in Mauritius, which hopefully will illuminate areas to guide future improvement activities in this line.

2 Review of Literature

FinTech implies the inventive technology applications in the financial services ecosystem. Technology thus does help to increase efficiency in service delivery, while an improvement is seen in the automation and speed to be achieved. Financial technology encompasses diverse facilities and technologies that disrupt the financial space, including mobile payments, online banking, artificial intelligence (AI), robots, forex trading, peer-to-peer lending, wealth management services, blockchain technology, cryptocurrencies, digital currencies, and crowdfunding [3, 4].

The majority of FinTech innovations deliver positive benefits to the financial sector [5]. Current FinTech services go beyond e-banking and digital transformation of traditional financial offerings by focusing on consumer needs to efficiently implement innovative technologies that address client financial demands. The research indicates that FinTech services will not lead to the abrupt disappearance of banks, yet they will impact bank revenues and alter traditional perspectives on financial intermediation [5].

The transformative impact of technology on the financial sector, suggesting that FinTech has the potential to enhance consumer trust in banks, bolster data security, and improve overall service quality [6]. They contended that FinTech not only promotes competition within the finance industry but also reshapes regulatory frameworks for banks. Furthermore, FinTech simplifies operations for businesses and owners by effectively addressing consumer market demands [7]. The adoption of FinTech can significantly elevate service quality and efficiency by harnessing innovations in the delivery of financial services [8].

In current society, the widespread use of mobile phones has been linked to a significant increase in young people' digital literacy. The global financial crisis of 2008 had a substantial impact on the younger demographic's spending patterns [9]. Several factors contributing to the rise of FinTech, including a youthful and digitally engaged populace, barriers to obtaining financial services, a thriving commercial sector [10], as well as a public sector prepared for development and innovation. In contrast, some claimed [11] that the expansion of FinTech is likely attributable with progress in digital technology, shifts in consumer behavior driven by needs and expectations, the impact of the COVID-19 pandemic, diminished entry barriers, and increased investment in the FinTech arena. Additionally, the expansion of e-commerce and governmental support for FinTech initiatives [12].

2.1   The Advancement of Technology

Smartphone usage has increased dramatically in recent years, having a huge impact on the FinTech business. The global mobile internet traffic ratio climbed from 31.16% in 2015 to 58.33% in 2023's first quarter [13]. Currently, 91.21% of the global population owns a cell phone, with 86.11% owning a smartphone, which can efficiently handle and store data for purposes other than interaction, enjoyment, and internet surfing [14]. FinTech's advancement is largely due to the advanced technology included in phones [12]. Mobile payment platforms have simplified and accelerated financial transactions, promoting the use of emerging technologies [15]. The negative consequences of technology on the financial services sector, resulting in disruptions in areas such as payment systems, data measurement, data valuation, and trading within the securities market [16].

2.2   Fintech Awareness Among the Young Adults

Young adults represent a demographic particularly vulnerable to the influence of technology and the internet [17]. This group is characterized by its receptiveness to diverse innovations. Young adults exhibit heightened engagement with social networks and technological reliance, thereby optimally embracing technological innovations in the financial sphere. As kids gain basic economic understanding and develop distinct financial habits, they appear as a desirable population for financial services firms to aim at as potential customers.

FinTech encompasses a diverse array of innovations that are significantly reshaping the financial services landscape. Acquaintance with innovations involving Blockchain, Cryptocurrencies, as well as other FinTech innovations is critical since they can provide young individuals with a competitive edge in financial management and future economic planning. Most young individuals are aware of FinTech and its uses, indicating a high level of financial technology consciousness [18]. Moreover, young adults asserted that FinTech is the cheapest way to transact online and believed they have requisite access to resources for using FinTech applications, showing their preparedness to engage with such technologies. They agreed almost unanimously that FinTech would be helpful in preventing fraud, citing the safety advantages in using it. Young adults likewise showed a strong inclination toward adopting FinTech in the future, reflecting a positive attitude toward its uptake [18].

2.3   Adoption of Fintech by Young Adults

This demand for Fintech services and products goes beyond mere digitalization of financial services, or ordinary electronic banking [19]. Other theories [20] explain this relationship wherein the adoption of FinTech depends on perceived risks and benefits. The technology acceptance model stands out as a framework of dominant theoretical weight to explain FinTech adoption [21].

The Technology Acceptance Model (TAM) and its various adaptations have been used, amongst others, to explain the adoption of new technologies in the banking sector [22]. Moreover, it has proved to be useful in analyzing the phenomenon of FinTech [23, 24]. Several researchers [6, 25] have made it known that the distinct features of FinTech significantly affect the application of the TAM framework in explaining technology adoption in this domain contrasted to more fields like e-commerce. While TAM remains the most researched aspect of FinTech's consumer acceptance towards user adoption, [24] added that other than the TAM model, several works in FinTech also study the effect of demographic, social, and economic variables [26, 27], or perceived risk [27], or some combinations of these with selected variables from various theoretical frameworks. Although not new, FinTech is gaining momentum in the financial sector [28].

However, defining FinTech in a generic way remains a difficult job. Perceived ease of use and perceived utility became the first inputs that impacted the consumer acceptance of a new system [29]. The respective variables are indeed positively correlated with attitudes towards the adoption of FinTech [30]. Furthermore, trust and security issues are very much an important factor for adoption. The three main factors-trust, transparency, and financial literacy-are of considerable weight in decisions concerning FinTech usage [31]. The safety and the extent of trouble experienced while using FinTech need to be weighed when adopting such platforms and their subsequent usage [32]. In addition, it is observed that FinTech adoption incurs risks associated with privacy concerns and data security [33].

Largely, the investigations into factors determining the adoption of FinTech amongst the youth have received limited attention, for example within Mauritius as a small island economy. Hence, there still exists a significant gap in understanding the determinants of FinTech adoption amongst this segment of the age paradigm in Mauritius. A theoretical framework of technology acceptance model (TAM) is set to study five critical determinant factors affecting the adoption of FinTech products and services under this study: perceived usefulness, perceived ease of use, attitude, self-efficacy, and perceived risk. The suggested study model, shown in Fig. 1, aims to identify the causes of such variables that influence the uptake of FinTech services and products with younger adults in Mauritius.

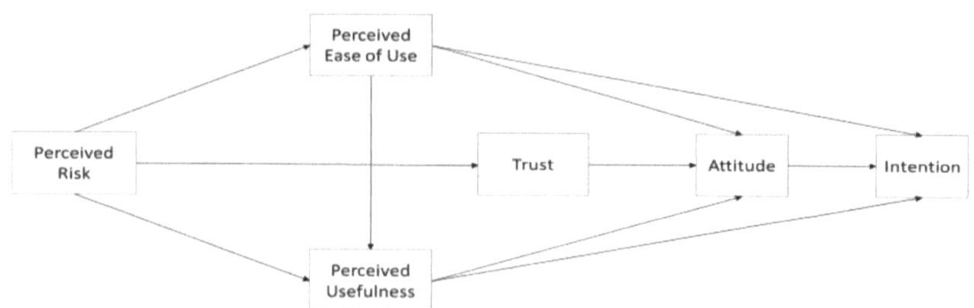

Fig. 1. Conceptual Framework

3   Methodology

The research employed a quantitative technique of cross-sectional research design to determine the study examines the association amid independent variables—namely perceived usefulness, perceived ease of use, attitude, trust, and perceived risk—and the dependent variable, intention, within a demographic of young individuals. Data were gathered through a self-administered questionnaire designed to assess the fundamental constructs outlined in the theoretical framework and ensure consistency in responses. The questionnaire was a structured form containing a series of questions aligned with the research objectives and theoretical framework. To ensure validity and reliability, the questionnaire included the demographic items (e.g., age, gender, education level), construct items that measure theoretical variables (e.g., attitudes, trust, behaviors, intentions), likert scales questions to quantify responses, clear instructions to aid respondent understanding and pilot-tested items for clarity and relevance. Young people residing in Mauritius during last quarter of the year 2024 was considered as the sampling frame for the study. This study used the convenience sampling which is a technique for collecting data by selecting participants based on their availability [34, 35]. This sampling technique was chosen due to time and resource limitations which necessitated the use of easily accessible participants. Also, Mauritius has a relatively small and localized population, and the study aimed at testing the theoretical framework before broader application, making convenience sampling more viable than in large, diverse nations [36]. 300 valid questionnaires were circulated among the young adults from different TEIs, private institutions, polytechnic, vocational institutions, sports clubs and youth centers, which improved trust and compliance. Reminders and follow-up messages encouraged completion, with a response rate of 90%, 271 respondents returned questionnaires were finally approved and included in the data analysis which reduced the likelihood of non-response bias.

To accurately measure the theoretical constructs, the instrument used pre-validated scales from previous studies to ensure content validity. Appropriate changes were made to fit the context of young people's adoption of fintech. The questionnaire for this study had seven sections. In addition to demographic information, the questionnaire assessed perceived risk, perceived utility, attitude, perceived ease of use, reliability, and desire to use fintech. Respondents were asked to rate the extent of consensus or disagreement regarding the measuring questions on a scale made up of five Likert scales, with one representing "strongly disagree" and five representing "strongly agree.". Data analysis was conducted utilizing SPSS version 26 statistical software. To assess the reliability of the obtained data for each scale, a Cronbach's Alpha test was used, as shown in Table 1 below. Cronbach's Alpha values in each dimension exceeded the acceptable threshold of 0.7, indicating a reliable model [37].

Table 1. Reliability Test for the Dimensions with Number of Items

Dimensions	Items Number	Cronbach's Alpha
Perceived risk	5	0.907
Perceived Ease of Use	5	0.934
Perceived Usefulness	6	0.837
Attitude	4	0.801
Trust	2	0.759
Intention	7	0.818

4 Result and Discussion

The study presents an analysis of the demographic characteristics and financial literacy of the survey respondents. As shown in Fig. 2, the sample was composed of 56% male respondents and 44% female respondents, indicating a good representation of both genders. The gender representation (56% male, 44% female) is balanced enough for basic gender-based inference.

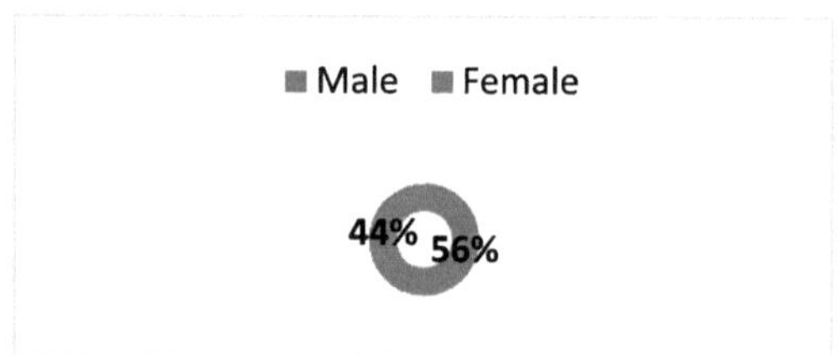

Fig. 2. Participants' Gender

As depicted in Fig. 3 with regards to educational qualification, 22.5% had primary school education, 27.5% had School Certificate, 23.2% Higher School Certificate, 17.7% had Bachelor's degree while the remainder had Master's degree which comprised 8.9% of the total respondents. 47.6% of respondents were employed compared to 18.5% who were students. The demographic breakdown offers a heterogeneous sample with varied education statuses, which increases the richness of the analysis and potential explanatory power.

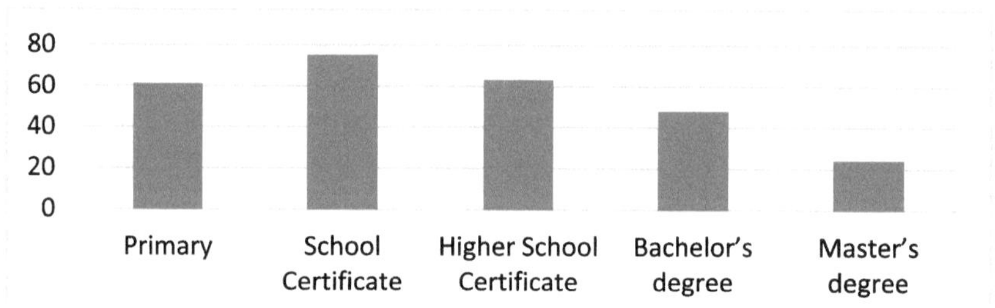

Fig. 3. Participants' Educational Attainment

Out of all respondents the financial literacy assessment shows 19.9% of respondents said they are not at all financially literate, 22.1% said they are slightly financially literate, while 34.7% said they are moderately financially literate, 14.8% said they are very financially literate, and 8.5% said they are extremely financially literate. Financial literacy was self-assessed, which is common in survey-based studies but could be improved with objective tests in future research.

A review of the data shows generally positive views toward the technology in question. Trust, with mean and standard deviation of 21.45 ± 1.301, and the positive attitude, mean 18.19 ± 2.247. The low variability in both trust and attitude suggests a consensus among the participants regarding their confidence in the technology, thereby positing trust as a robust predictor of behavioural intention. This observation corroborates existing scholarly literature that emphasizes the fundamental role of trust in alleviating perceived risks, particularly within the realm of technology adoption that involves data security or financial transactions.

For perceived usefulness with an average of 23.20 (STD. Dev. of 4.356, and ease of use measured with mean of 17.52, with SD of 4.411, indicate moderate levels of acceptance; however, the presence of variability in these metrics suggests that user experiences may differ significantly. This divergence may be influenced by demographic factors or previous encounters with technology. These outcomes are consistent with the foundational principles of the TAM, which asserts that both perceived utility and usability are fundamental in influencing user attitudes and intentions around technology.

Furthermore, they perceived moderate levels of risk (mean score 3.49, standard deviation 1.16). Nevertheless, it doesn't seem that this notion significantly hinders adoption, potentially due to the compensatory influence of high trust levels. The relatively low standard deviation suggests that perceptions of risk were consistent across the participant pool. The moderately high intention to use, measured at 19.63, further implies that perceived risk does not significantly obstruct adoption, with trust and perceived usefulness likely mitigating these concerns. The given findings hold implications for devising risk management strategies, implying that building trust could effectively lower concerns over the perceived risks. A positive attitude toward the technology together with higher levels of trust and perceived usefulness suggest that attitude may serve as a mediating variable between the constructs, such as perceived ease of use and intention to adopt.

Finally, the behavioural intention mean score of 19.63 with SD of 3.962 shows a moderate level of intention to adopt. The finding is somewhat in favour; however, the higher SD reflects the variability among the participants in terms of their readiness. This variability points to the existence of certain sub-sets in the sample that could exhibit different levels of technology acceptance and may require targeted interventions like training programs or customized onboarding programs. To summarize, the results show that trust, perceived usefulness, and positive attitudes serve as key facilitators of technology acceptance, while the perceived risks appeared to play a lesser role in shaping participants' intention about accepting the technology. The constructs such as trust, attitude, perceived usefulness, ease of use, and perceived risk were measured with appropriate mean and standard deviation values, showing internal consistency. Notably, trust had a high mean and low SD (21.45 ± 1.301), suggesting a consensus on this construct's importance. Additionally, moderate SDs in ease of use and usefulness (4.411 and 4.356, respectively) reflected diverse respondent experiences, signaling potential sub-group differences that could be explored further via cluster analysis or moderation effects.

Table 2. Hypotheses testing

The intention of FinTech use at last relates with financial literacy	Supports	< 0.01
There is direct and negative effect on actual use of FinTech	Supports	< 0.001
Perceived Usefulness influences adoption intention of FinTech	Supports	< 0.01
Perceived Risk influence the intention to adopt FinTech	Supports	< 0.01
Attitude positively impacts FinTech adoption	Supports	< 0.01
Perceived trust influences the intention to use FinTech	Supports	< 0.01

As evident from Table 2, investigation clearly shows that the intention to adopt and the actual use of FinTech services are based upon quite a number of determinants. It means that there is a positive relation between financial literacy and intention to adopt, which proved to be significant at the statistical level ($p < 0.01$). This implies that those knowledgeable enough in finance are more inclined to adopt FinTech solution. Then the perceptions about utility and ease of use are prominent indicators in the context of adoption behavior. More specifically, it is strongly supported by empirical results that perceived ease of use had a strong influence ($p < .001$), whereas perceived usefulness only focused on its influence on the intention to adopt ($p < .01$). On the flip side, perceived risk shows a negative influence ($p < 0.01$) on the intention of adopting a service, hence suggests an attempt towards trust building in mitigating insecurities related to FinTech services. Also, trust plays a significant role in augmenting the adoption capability, proving significantly) at the statistical level ($p < .01$) for contributing in helping to mitigate risk. Incipient interest in FinTech is also recognized as having a considerable role as an impetus in the adoption behaviour and is thereby proven significantly statistically.

5   Conclusion

These findings provide empirical evidence in keeping with theoretical models of technology acceptance, affirming that usability, trust, risk management, and financial education are crucial factors driving users towards adopting FinTech services. FinTech has radically changed the face of financial service provision in Mauritius by offering almost instant paperless services, upgraded with digital technological innovation combined with changing consumer behavior, the COVID-19 pandemic, and investments into the sector. Despite the use of convenience sampling, the large sample size ($n = 271$) and high response rate (90%) enhance the robustness of the dataset. The investigation reveals that FinTech has achieved reasonable awareness, with 83.4% of respondents having used it in the last six months. More generally, respondents feel that FinTech is fairly easy to use and somewhat beneficial in daily transactions. Perceived ease of use and perceived usefulness of FinTech correlated with greater trust and greater adoptability, whereas risk, however, continues to remain a concern. Despite concerns regarding risks, there is an increasing interest among Mauritian youngsters towards achieving a cashless system, albeit with opinions varying across respondents on the basis of their financial literacy.

Awareness campaigns should thus find a wider target audience, especially among older people, to stimulate further adoption of FinTech. Improving user interfaces and navigation can further encourage adoption. Trust should be built by improving security measures and by communicating them clearly since security concerns now constitute one of the primary barriers. Cooperation between financial institutions and FinTech providers should go a long way towards enhancing the reach and engagement of customers.

This study provides credible initial findings on FinTech adoption among Mauritian youth, grounded in established theory (TAM and its extensions) and supported by statistically significant relationships. While convenience sampling poses a limitation, the high response rate, theoretical alignment, and detailed construct measurement render the results replicable and credible, especially if future work addresses sampling bias and expands statistical modeling. Some respondents displayed negative attitudes toward FinTech, notwithstanding the positive assessment of usability, indicating the necessity for qualitative research, e.g., interviewing or open-ended surveys, to ascertain the reasons behind this inconsistency. Replication of this study could be enhanced by using stratified or quota sampling in future studies to improve external validity. Future studies could also include multivariate analysis or path modelling to control for these and explore complex relationships more fully.

References

1. Setiawan, B., Nugraha, D.P., Irawan, A., Nathan, R.J., Zoltan, Z.: User innovativeness and Fintech adoption in Indonesia. J. Open Innov.: Technol. Mark. Complex **7**(3), 188 (2021)
2. Boot, A., et al.: The coronavirus and financial stability 2.0: Act jointly now, but also think about tomorrow. SAFE Policy Letter 79 (2020)
3. Earls, E.M.: Preparing students for a future in fintech: The role of Massachusetts public universities. White Paper No. 194. Pioneer Institute for Public Policy Research (2019)
4. Kuzmina-Merlino, I., Saksonova, S.: The knowledge and competencies required for the fintech sector. In: New Challenges of Economic and Business Development—2018: Productivity and Economic Growth, pp. 387–95. Univ Latvia, Riga (2018)
5. Jarvis, R., Han, H.: Fintech innovation: review and future research directions. Int. J. Bank. Fin. Ins. Technol. **1**(1), 79–102 (2021)
6. Hu, Z., Ding, S., Li, S., Chen, L., Yang, S.: Adoption intention of Fintech services for bank users: an empirical examination with an extended technology acceptance model. Symmetry **11**(3), 340 (2019)
7. Mention, A.L.: The future of FinTech. Res. Technol. Manag. **62**(4), 59–63 (2019)
8. Gai, K.K., Qiu, M.K., Sun, X.T.: A survey on FinTech. J. Netw. Comput. Appl. **103**, 262–273 (2018)
9. Anyfantaki, S.: The Evolution of Financial Technology (FinTech). Economic Bulletin, Bank of Greece, issue 44, December, pp. 47–62 (2016)
10. Arner, D.W., Barberis, J.N., Buckley, R.P.: The evolution of fintech: a new post-crisis paradigm? J. Fin. Technol. **14**(3), 187–204 (2015)
11. Elsaid, H.: Drivers of fintech's growth in the FSI sector, Qatar National Bank (QNB Group) (2023) from: https://www.linkedin.com/. Accessed 26 November 2024
12. Arora, S., Madan, P.: Conceptual Framework Depicting the Drivers for the Fintech Growth: An Outlook for India (2023)
13. Statista: Investments into Fintech Companies Globally (2023). https://www.statista.com/statistics/719385/investments-into-fintech-companiesglobally. Accessed: 11 November 2024
14. Candy, C., et al.: Fintech in the time of COVID-19: Conceptual Overview, Jurnal Akuntansi, Keuangan, dan Manajemen (Jakman) **3**(3), 253–262 (2022)

15. Kumar, A., Adlakaha, A., Mukherjee, K.: The effect of perceived security and grievance redressal on continuance intention to use M-wallets in a developing country. Int. J. Bank Mark. **36**(7), 1170–1189 (2018)
16. Duffie. D., Foucault. T., Veldkamp. L., Vives. X.: The future of Banking. CEPR Press, Paris (2022)
17. Krupa, D., Buszko, M.: Age-dependent differences in using FinTech products and services—Young customers versus other adults. PLoS ONE **18**(10), e0293470 (2023)
18. Kadam, D.S., Shalini, R.: An empirical study on the awareness of FinTech and its applications among students. Int. Res. J. Moderniz. Eng. Technol. Sci. **5**(4) (2023)
19. Singh, S.K., Sahni, M.M., Kovid, R.K.: What drives FinTech adoption? a multi-method evaluation using an adapted technology acceptance model. Manag. Decis. **58**(8), 1675–1697 (2020)
20. Tewogbade, S.: Discussion on fintech adoption research. Global J. Manage. Bus. Res. **22**(A1), 19–26 (2022)
21. Suzianti, A., Haqqi, F.R., Fathia, S.N.: Strategic recommendations for financial technology service development: a comprehensive risk-benefit IPA-Kano analysis. J. Model. Manag. **17**(4), 1481–1503 (2022)
22. Szopiński, T.S.: Factors affecting the adoption of online banking in Poland. J. Bus. Res. **69**(11), 4763–4768. Elsevier (2016)
23. Nangin, M.A., Rasita, I., Barus, G., Wahyoedi, S.: The effects of perceived ease of use, security, and promotion on trust and its implications for fintech adoption. J. Cons. Sci. **5**(2), 124–138 (2020)
24. Solarz, M., Swacha-Lech, M.: Determinants of the Adoption of Innovative Fintech Services by Millennials. E+M. Ekonomie a Management **24**(3), 149–166 (2021)
25. Stewart, H., Jürjens, J.: Data security and consumer trust in FinTech innovation in Germany. Info. Comp. Secur. **26**(1), 109–128 (2018). https://doi.org/10.1108/ICS-06-2017-0039
26. Carlin, B., Olafsson, A., Pagel, M.: Fintech adoption across generations: financial fitness in the information age. National Bureau of Economic Research, No. w23798 (2017)
27. Diana, N., Leon, F.M.: Factors affecting continuance intention of fintech payment among millennials in Jakarta. European J. Bus. Manage. Res. **5**(4), 1–9 (2020)
28. Lee, I., Shin, Y.J.: Fintech: ecosystem, business models, investment decisions, and challenges. Bus. Horiz. **61**(1), 35–46 (2018)
29. Kim, Y.S., Park, J.S., Yeon, S.H.: Determinants of user acceptance of technology: an empirical study on mobile banking. J. Internet Bank. Commer. **20**(3), 6–18 (2015)
30. Ardiansah, M.N., Chariri, A., Januarti, I.: Empirical study on customer perception of e commerce: mediating effect of electronic payment security. J. Dinamika Akuntansi **11**(2), 122–131 (2019)
31. Jünger, M., Mietzner, M.: Banking goes digital: The adoption of FinTech services by German households. Financ. Res. Lett. **34**, 101260 (2020)
32. Mahmuh, M., Joarder, M.H., Sakib, M.: Security and difficulty in Fintech adoption: a comprehensive review. J. Fin. Technol. **8**(2) (2022)
33. Suryono, R.R., Budi, I., Purwandari, B.: Challenges and trends of financial technology (Fintech): a systematic literature review. Information **11**(12), 590 (2020)
34. Bougie, R., Sekaran, U.: Research methods for business: A skill building approach: John Wiley & Sons. (2019)
35. Etikan, I., Musa, S.A., Alkassim, R.S.: Comparison of convenience sampling and purposive sampling. Am. J. Theor. Appl. Stat. **5**(1), 1–4 (2016)
36. Bornstein, M.H., Jager, J., Putnick, D.L.: Sampling in developmental science: Situations, shortcomings, solutions, and standards. Dev. Rev. **33**(4), 357–370 (2013). https://doi.org/10.1016/j.dr.2013.08.003

37. Hair, J.F., Hult, G.T. M., Ringle, C.M., Sarstedt, M.: A Primer on Partial Least Squares Structural Equation Modelling (PLS-SEM), 3rd ed. SAGE Publications Inc. (2022)

Using a GenAI Chatbot to Facilitate Personalized Learning: a Case Study in Online Higher Education

Corna Olivier$^{(\boxtimes)}$ and Lizette Weilbach

University of Pretoria, Pretoria, South Africa
Corna.olivier@gmail.com

Abstract. The integration of Generative AI (GenAI) chatbots in education is transforming personalized learning, yet their effectiveness in online distance learning remains underexplored. This study investigates how a GenAI chatbot tutor facilitates personalized learning in an online higher education setting, using the Community of Inquiry (CoI) framework. A qualitative case study approach was adopted, analyzing chat logs, chatbot platform analytics, and a semi-structured interview. The study included four voluntary participants who engaged with the chatbot as a learning support tool, while one participant was interviewed to provide deeper insights. Findings indicate that the chatbot contributed to cognitive presence by scaffolding inquiry and promoting adaptive knowledge construction, social presence by enhancing engagement and fostering an inclusive learning space, and teaching presence through context-aware responses and real-time learning insights. However, technological constraints, inconsistent response accuracy, and limited handling of complex queries were identified as challenges. These results suggest that while GenAI chatbots enhance personalized learning, they should be integrated as supplementary tools rather than standalone tutors. Ethical considerations, including data privacy, transparency, and AI reliability, must also be addressed. Future research should focus on refining AI-generated responses, investigating long-term learning outcomes, and optimizing human-AI collaboration in education.

Keywords: Generative AI in Education (GenAIED) · Personalized learning · GenAI chatbot tutor · Intelligent Tutoring Systems (ITS) · Community of Inquiry (CoI) · online distance learning · higher education

1 Introduction

The integration of Generative AI (GenAI) in education, particularly through Intelligent Tutoring Systems (ITS), represents a significant advancement in personalized learning. Traditionally, ITSs have leveraged artificial intelligence (AI) to provide tailored educational experiences, adapting to the unique needs and learning styles of individual students. This adaptability is essential, as previous research has demonstrated that personalized instruction leads to improved learning outcomes compared to traditional

F. Corradini et al. (Eds.): Society 5.0 2025, CCIS 2787, pp. 216–227, 2026.
https://doi.org/10.1007/978-3-032-15463-7_18

classroom settings [1–3]. With the increasing accessibility of GenAI technologies, educators are now exploring how AI-driven chatbot tutors can be integrated into learning environments to enhance student engagement and support individualized learning paths.

This study examines the implementation of a GenAI chatbot tutor within an online distance learning module, focusing on its role as an ITS and its alignment with the Community of Inquiry (COI) framework. By providing students with interactive, real-time feedback and adapting responses based on learner interactions, the chatbot is expected to facilitate a more personalized learning experience. From the educator's perspective, the study evaluates both the chatbot's effectiveness in supporting students and the challenges associated with its design and training.

As educational institutions increasingly integrate AI-driven tools, it is imperative to assess their pedagogical value, potential limitations, and broader implications for teaching and learning. To this end, this study seeks to answer the following primary research question: "How does a GenAI chatbot tutor facilitate personalized learning in an online distance learning environment?".

By investigating this question, the study contributes to the ongoing discourse on AI-driven pedagogy, student engagement, and the responsible implementation of GenAI tutors in higher education. The findings offer valuable insights into optimizing chatbot integration to enhance personalized learning experiences while addressing potential design and ethical considerations.

1.1 Background

The development of ITSs has evolved significantly over time, shaping how personalized learning is facilitated through AI. Early ITSs were primarily based on behaviorist principles, focusing on reinforcement and direct instruction. These systems operated on pre-programmed responses, offering limited adaptability to individual learning need. However, advancements in artificial intelligence have led to more sophisticated models that align with constructivist and inquiry-based learning approaches, providing students with more interactive and meaningful learning experiences [4–6].

Modern ITSs leverage machine learning and natural language processing to provide real-time, adaptive support to learners. Affective Tutoring Systems (ATS), for example, not only provide instructional content but also recognize and respond to students' emotional states, further enhancing engagement and learning outcomes [6]. In addition, ITSs assist generating data-driven insights into student performance, enabling timely pedagogical interventions and the refinement of instructional strategies [7, 8]. This dual benefit underscores the critical role of ITSs as tools that support both student learning and instructor decision-making. In the context of online distance learning, where personalized support is often absent, ITSs can serve as vital learning companions [9]. The emergence of GenAI chatbots as ITSs presents new opportunities for facilitating adaptive learning experiences in digital education environments. Unlike traditional ITSs, which rely on predefined algorithms, GenAI chatbots use probabilistically generated responses, allowing for dynamic, flexible interactions. However, this introduces concerns related to consistency, accuracy, and pedagogical effectiveness, raising questions about how well these chatbots can fulfill the role of a tutor in structured learning environments.

This study builds upon prior research by examining the role of a GenAI chatbot tutor in an online distance learning module, focusing on its capacity to provide personalized learning support within the framework of the Community of Inquiry (CoI). By analyzing student-chatbot interactions, chatbot-generated performance data, and educator reflections on chatbot training, the study aims to explore the pedagogical value of GenAI-driven tutoring and the broader implications of its integration into higher education.

2 Literature Review

2.1 Chatbot Alignment with Community of Inquiry (CoI) Elements

The CoI framework [10] provides a theoretical foundation for understanding online learning experiences. It conceptualizes effective online learning environments as emerging from the interaction of three core elements: cognitive presence, social presence, and teaching presence.

Cognitive presence refers to the extent to which students can construct meaning and engage in critical thinking. GenAI chatbots contribute to this by providing immediate feedback, guiding inquiry-based discussions, and promoting problem-solving skills [11]. By facilitating deeper engagement with course content, these chatbots can support learners in developing higher-order thinking skills.

Social presence is the ability of students to project themselves as real and engaged participants in an online learning environment. Research suggests that students' psychological responses to GenAI tutors are comparable to their interactions with human tutors, fostering a sense of connection and engagement [12]. This indicates that well-designed chatbot interactions may enhance the social dimension of online learning, reducing isolation and increasing motivation.

Teaching presence encompasses the design, facilitation, and direction of learning. Studies have shown that AI tutors can effectively support this presence by structuring learning activities, guiding discussions, and adapting instructional approaches based on student needs [13]. The ability of GenAI chatbots to assist in facilitating structured learning experiences aligns with this aspect of the CoI framework.

Given these elements, the CoI framework provides a valuable lens for analyzing the role of a GenAI chatbot tutor in an online distance learning module. This study examines how such a chatbot functions within this framework, supporting personalized learning through cognitive, social, and teaching presences while addressing potential challenges in chatbot-facilitated learning environments.

2.2 Intelligent Tutoring Systems (ITS) Theory

In addition to the CoI framework, this study also draws upon research from Intelligent Tutoring Systems (ITSs), a field within Artificial Intelligence in Education (AIEd) that focuses on designing AI-driven tools to simulate human tutoring [14]. ITS theories emphasize personalized feedback, adaptive learning pathways, and data-driven instruction, which align with the role of the chatbot as a virtual tutor. Traditional ITS models are designed to diagnose learner needs, provide scaffolding, and deliver tailored instructional support based on predefined rules. These systems operate through structures algorithms that analyze student responses and adjust the instructional approach accordingly. The GenAI chatbot in this study shares many of these features, as it aims to personalize learning experiences by responding dynamically to students' queries. However, unlike rule-based ITSs, which rely on explicit programming, GenAI-powered chatbots generate responses probabilistically using large-scale language models. This introduces complexities regarding consistency, accuracy, and pedagogical effectiveness, as responses may vary based on context, training data, and model limitations.

By situating the chatbot's role within the frameworks of CoI and ITS, this study critically examines the pedagogical value, strengths, and limitations of using GenAI in creative teaching and online distance learning. It explores how AI-driven chatbots can contribute to student engagement, personalized learning, and instructional support, while also addressing potential design and implementation challenges in AI-enhanced education.

3   Research Methodology

This study employs a qualitative case study approach, which is well-suited for an in-depth exploration of a GenAI chatbot tutor in an online distance learning environment. A case study methodology enables researchers to examine a phenomenon within its real-world context, allowing for a rich, contextualized understanding of how the chatbot facilitates personalized learning [15]. Given that the study seeks to explore the experiences, interactions, and perceptions of both students and the educator, a qualitative approach provides thematic depth and interpretative flexibility [16]. To gain deeper insight into students' experiences and the educator's reflections on chatbot training, the study incorporates Interpretive Phenomenological Analysis (IPA). IPA is an established qualitative research method that prioritizes the subjective experiences of participants, making it particularly relevant for studies exploring learning processes and technological interactions in education [17]. This approach allows for a detailed examination of how students perceive and engage with the chatbot, as well as how the educator interprets its pedagogical effectiveness.

3.1   Participants

Approval for the study was obtained from the relevant institutional gatekeeper, ensuring compliance with ethical guidelines. Following this, online distance learning students were invited to participate in the study by engaging with a GenAI chatbot tutor as part of their learning experience. Four students voluntarily participated in the chatbot interactions, and one participant was interviewed to provide deeper insights into the learning experience. All students were provided with detailed information regarding the study's purpose, procedures, and their rights as participants.

Ethical considerations were strictly upheld, including informed consent, data protection, and participant confidentiality. Prior to participation, students were required to provide explicit consent, acknowledging their understanding of how their interaction data, chatbot-generated insights, and feedback would be used for research purposes. Additionally, all collected data was anonymized to protect participants' identities and ensure compliance with research ethics and data privacy regulations.

3.2   Implementation of the GenAI Tutor

The GenAI chatbot developed by Mindjoy [18], was integrated as a supplementary learning tool designed to support cognitive, social, and teaching presence, as outlined in the CoI framework. Its primary function was to enhance personalized learning experiences within the online distance learning module by providing adaptive, interactive, and structured academic support.

To ensure alignment with course content, the chatbot was trained using module learning materials, assessment details, deadlines, and structured inquiry-based learning guidelines. Instead of offering direct answers, the chatbot was programmed to encourage critical thinking by guiding students through discussions, prompting deeper inquiry, and reinforcing key concepts.

3.3   Data Sources

Multiple data sources were utilized to assess the GenAI chatbot tutor's effectiveness in facilitating personalized learning. These sources provided qualitative and quantitative insights into student engagement, learning progress, and chatbot adaptability within the online distance learning module.

- **Chat logs:** Records of student-chatbot interactions were analyzed to examine how the chatbot responded to individual learning needs, facilitated engagement, and addressed recurring challenges encountered by students.
- **Interview transcripts**: A semi-structured interview with a student participant was conducted to capture firsthand experiences and perceptions regarding the chatbot's effectiveness in supporting personalized learning.
- **Chatbot platform analytics:** Data from the chatbot platform, including usage metrics, interaction patterns, and response accuracy, provided both quantitative and qualitative insights into students' learning progress, difficulties, and engagement levels. This data helped to assess the chatbot's impact on student learning.

3.4   Analytical Approach

To analyze the collected data, this study employed a thematic analysis approach [19] to identify patterns and themes in student interactions with the chatbot, as well as insights from the semi-structured interview transcript. Thematic coding was used to explore emerging themes related to personalized learning, with a particular focus on cognitive, social, and teaching presence, as outlined in the CoI framework.

In addition, content analysis was applied to the chatbot-generated data, examining trends in student queries, response accuracy, and the chatbot's adaptive learning capabilities. This quantitative and qualitative examination provided insights into how the chatbot adjusted its responses based on student engagement patterns and the effectiveness of its instructional support.

4   Results

4.1   Results from the Thematic Analysis of Chatlogs and the Interview Transcript

The thematic analysis of chat logs and the interview transcript revealed six key themes that align with the CoI framework, supporting the GenAI chatbot's role in facilitating personalized learning in an online distance learning environment. These themes are categorized under the three CoI presences: Cognitive Presence, Social Presence, and Teaching Presence (see Table 1).

The findings indicate that the chatbot functioned as an interactive learning agent, prompting deeper engagement, knowledge construction, and student-centred interactions. Additionally, while the chatbot demonstrated context-aware and adaptive responses, participants encountered technological limitations that occasionally affected their engagement.

Table 1. Personalized Learning in the Community of Inquiry.

CoI	Theme	Description	Supportive evidence (Quotes)
Cognitive Presence	Scaffolded inquiry and reflection	The chatbot encouraged deeper engagement with content by prompting students to ask follow-up questions and refine their understanding	"Sometimes I needed more information or better clarity, so I'd ask it."
	Adaptive knowledge construction	Participants engaged in iterative learning cycles, requesting elaboration on chatbot responses to build understanding	"When I asked a certain question, it gave me an answer, but then there was something in the answer that I wanted to know more about, so I would ask it to elaborate."
Social Presence	Affirmation and student-centered interaction	The chatbot provided encouragement, reinforcing student confidence and motivation in learning	"That's a fantastic idea, [name of student removed]!"
	Creating a personalized inclusive learning space	The chatbot's use of accessible language made content easier to understand, benefiting second- or third-language speakers	"It is so easy, so easy to understand. It's so easy to tell it, give it to me in a simpler way."

(continued)

Table 1. (*continued*)

CoI	Theme	Description	Supportive evidence (Quotes)
Teaching Presence	Context-aware and personalized guidance	The chatbot tailored responses based on curriculum requirements and individual learner input	"It always brought me back to the foundation phase CAPS document without me having to tell it."
	Technological constraints in personalized learning	Participants faced technical challenges when engaging in complex interactions, such as pasting large texts for chatbot analysis	"There were times where it was glitching a bit… I was copying an entire rubric into it."

4.2 Results from the GenAI Chatbot Platform

The Mindjoy chatbot platform [18] provided real-time analytics on student interactions, engagement, and learning progress. These insights offer valuable data for understanding how students interact with the chatbot, engage with course content, and encounter learning challenges. The platform's ability to track individual and class-level engagement helps educators refine personalized learning strategies.

Student Engagement and Interaction Trends. The class average engagement data (see Fig. 1) reveals that students actively engaged with the chatbot for an average of 1 h and 34 min, with a total time of 27 days and 20 h across the cohort. Students asked an average of 17 questions, of which 10 were answered by the chatbot. These figures suggest moderate engagement, with some question possibly remaining unanswered due to limitations in chatbot response capabilities.

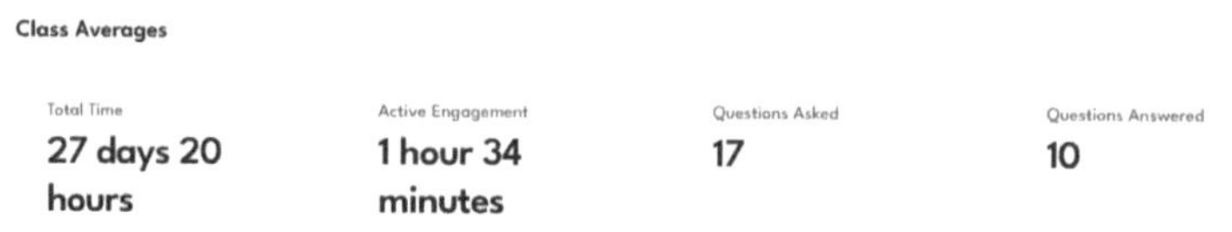

Fig. 1. Chatbot platform tracking student interactions

Tracking Individual Student Sentiment and Engagement. The student engagement dashboard (see Fig. 2) provided individualized insights into sentiment, learning state, and engagement levels. The "Curious" learning state observed among students indicates that the chatbot was effective in stimulating inquiry-based learning. Additionally, engagement scores suggest that students remained actively involved, reinforcing the chatbot's role in maintaining interest and encouraging participation in personalized learning experiences.

Student	Sentiment	Learning	Engagement
	Neutral	Curious	131
	Neutral	Curious	297

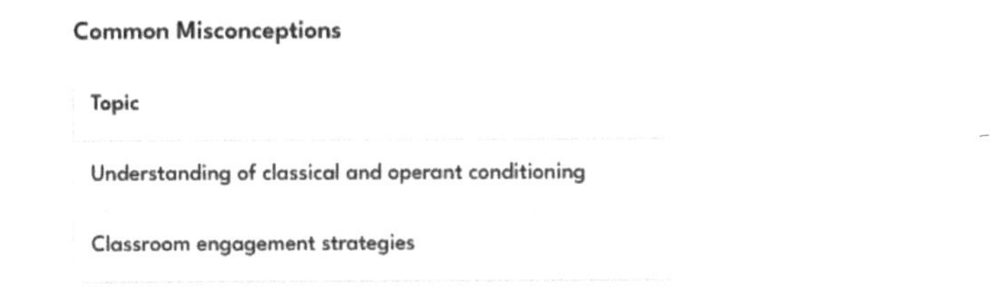

Fig. 2. Chatbot platform data on student engagement (student names removed)

Identifying Learning Challenges and Misconceptions. Analysis of common misconceptions (see Fig. 3) highlights two primary areas of difficulty among students: understanding classical and operant conditioning; and classroom engagement strategies. These findings indicate that while students engaged with these topics, conceptual misunderstandings persisted, suggesting a need for additional instructional support in these areas. This insight allows educators to target interventions more effectively, reinforcing the chatbot's role in diagnosing learning gaps.

Common Misconceptions

Topic
Understanding of classical and operant conditioning
Classroom engagement strategies

Fig. 3. Chatbot platform data on specific areas of weakness

Using Analytics for Personalized Learning Pathways. The chatbot's ability to track misconceptions and engagement trends (see Fig. 4) provides actionable data for educators. By downloading a CSV file (see Fig. 5), instructors can analyze longitudinal data to assess how students' understanding evolves over time and implement data-driven instructional adjustments.

Fig. 4. Chatbot platform analytics on causes of misconceptions

Fig. 5. Excerpt from data in csv file

5   Discussion of the Findings

The findings suggest that the chatbot played a valuable role in facilitating personalized learning by providing real-time feedback, adapting to student inquiries, and tracking learning progress. However, limitations in response accuracy, technological constraints, and ethical considerations highlight areas for refinement. The discussion below explores how the chatbot facilitated personalized learning through the CoI framework, while also addressing potential design improvements and ethical implications for future chatbot integration.

5.1   Cognitive Presence: Facilitating Adaptive Learning

The chatbot contributed to cognitive presence by promoting adaptive learning and iterative knowledge construction. Students engaged in scaffolded inquiry, using the chatbot to clarify concepts and seek deeper explanations (Table 1). The chatbot's ability to prompt reflection and encourage further questioning aligns with prior research on AI-driven cognitive presence in online learning environments [11]. However, chatbot analytics (Fig. 3) revealed persistent misconceptions in topics such as classical and operant conditioning and classroom engagement strategies, suggesting that while the chatbot encouraged inquiry, it did not always provide sufficient conceptual depth. This underscores the need for chatbot designs that integrate supplementary learning resources to support deeper conceptual understanding and minimize the risk of reinforcing misconceptions. Furthermore, the reliability of chatbot-generated explanations is an ethical concern, as students relying solely on AI responses may unknowingly adopt inaccurate or incomplete information. Educators should maintain active oversight and provide guidance on verifying chatbot responses to ensure students develop critical evaluation skills rather than unquestioning reliance on AI.

5.2 Social Presence: Enhancing Engagement and Interaction

The chatbot played a significant role in fostering social presence, particularly in student-centred interactions. Sentiment analysis (Fig. 2) indicated that students exhibited curiosity, suggesting a positive and engaging learning experience. Additionally, chatbot-generated affirmations and encouragement (e.g., "That's a fantastic idea!") reinforced student motivation and engagement (Table 1). Students also highlighted the chatbot's accessible language, which facilitated inclusive learning, particularly for second-language speakers. These findings support existing research suggesting that AI tutors can enhance social presence by simulating human-like interactions [12]. However, to further optimize chatbot engagement, adaptive personalization features could be introduced to recognize individual learning styles and communication preferences, allowing the chatbot to adjust its tone and complexity accordingly. Although AI-driven social interaction enhances engagement, it is important to consider whether students might become over-reliant on chatbot interactions at the expense of human collaboration. AI-generated social presence should not replace peer discussions and instructor feedback, as overuse of chatbot interaction could reduce opportunities for meaningful peer engagement and collaborative learning. Educators should encourage blended AI-human interaction models, ensuring that AI complements rather than replaces human social engagement in learning.

5.3 Technical Presence: Personalized Support and Technological Limitations

The chatbot successfully demonstrated teaching presence by providing context-aware guidance and aligning responses with learning objectives (Table 1). Chatbot analytics (Figs. 1, 4) revealed that it effectively tracked engagement trends, allowing educators to make data-driven instructional adjustments. Students reported that the chatbot referenced curriculum materials effectively, often directing them to relevant learning resources without explicit prompts. However, technological limitations affected its ability to fully personalize learning. Some students experienced difficulties when pasting large texts for chatbot analysis, and chatbot analytics (Fig. 1) showed that some student questions remained unanswered, suggesting gaps in adaptive response capabilities. Improving chatbot performance requires refining natural language processing (NLP) models, enabling the chatbot to better interpret and respond to complex queries. A key consideration in chatbot design should be the inclusion of a feedback mechanism, allowing students to flag inaccurate responses, which could help improve chatbot accuracy over time. Another critical ethical consideration is the chatbot's ability to track student engagement and learning progress. While real-time analytics provide valuable insights for educators, data privacy and security concerns must be addressed. AI-driven learning tools should prioritize transparency in data collection and comply with privacy regulations such as GDPR. Additionally, students should have autonomy over their learning data, including the ability to opt-out of tracking features or access their own analytics.

Without such safeguards, students may feel monitored rather than supported, potentially reducing trust in GenAI learning environments.

5.4 Limitations

While this study provides valuable insights into the role of GenAI chatbots in facilitating personalized learning in online distance education, several limitations must be acknowledged. Firstly, the study is limited to a single case study with a small sample size, which may affect the generalizability of the findings. Further research with larger and more diverse student populations is needed to confirm broader applicability. Secondly, while chatbot-generated data provides useful indicators of student engagement and learning needs, it does not fully capture the depth of students' cognitive and emotional processes or long-term learning outcomes. Additionally, the evolving nature of GenAI models means that chatbot responses may vary over time due to external updates beyond the educator's control, affecting response consistency and accuracy. Finally, student perceptions of GenAI tutoring may be shaped by their prior technology experiences and digital literacy, influencing their engagement and trust in AI-driven learning.

Despite these limitations, this study offers key insights into optimizing GenAI-driven personalized learning in higher education, paving the way for future research on its long-term effectiveness and broader implementation.

6 Conclusion

This study explored how a GenAI chatbot tutor facilitates personalized learning in an online distance learning environment, drawing on the CoI framework. The findings highlight that the chatbot effectively supports cognitive, social, and teaching presence by providing adaptive feedback, fostering student engagement, and offering context-aware guidance. However, design limitations and ethical considerations, such as response accuracy, data privacy, and potential over-reliance on AI, underscore the need for human oversight and continuous refinement of AI-driven educational tools. While GenAI chatbots cannot replace human instruction, they serve as valuable supplementary tools that, when thoughtfully integrated, enhance personalized learning experiences. Future research should focus on refining AI-generated responses, investigating long-term learning outcomes, refining student-chatbot interaction models, and ensuring ethical and transparent AI implementation in education.

References

1. Alkhatlan, A., Kalita, J.: Intelligent tutoring systems: a comprehensive historical survey with recent developments (2018). arXiv preprint arXiv:1812.09628
2. Alobaidi, O.G., Crockett, K., O'Shea, J.D., Jarad, T.M.: The application of learning theories into Abdullah: an intelligent Arabic conversational agent tutor. In: International Conference on Agents and Artificial Intelligence, pp. 361–369. SCITEPRESS (2015)
3. Elkins, S., Kochmar, E., Belfer, R., Serban, I., Cheung, J.C.: Question Personalization in an Intelligent Tutoring System. In: International Conference on Artificial Intelligence in Education, pp. 586–590. Springer (2022)

4. Du Boulay, B.: Escape from the Skinner Box: the case for contemporary intelligent learning environments. Br. J. Edu. Technol. **50**, 2902–2919 (2019)
5. Kahn, K., Winters, N.: Constructionism and AI: a history and possible futures. Br. J. Edu. Technol. **52**, 1130–1142 (2021)
6. Zatarain-Cabada, R., Barrón-Estrada, M.L., García-Lizárraga, J., Muñoz-Sandoval, G., Ríos-Félix, J.M.: Java tutoring system with facial and text emotion recognition. Res. Comput. Sci. **106**, 49–58 (2015)
7. He, G., Huang, C., Yang, S., Ouh, E.L., Ju, R., Chen, Y., Zhu, X.: Predicting Students' Progress in Intelligent Tutoring Systems (2023)
8. Laaziri, M., Benmoussa, K., Khoulji, S., Larbi, K.M.: Outlining an intelligent tutoring system for a university cooperation information system. Eng. Technol. Appl. Sci. Res. **8**, 3427 (2018)
9. Carmona-Guzman, M.E., Enríquez-Gómez, M.D.P., Aguilarcanseco, E.: The function of the academic tutor in virtual modality postgraduate studies. In: Reyes-Monjaras, M.E., Rejón-Jiménez, Y., González-Hernández, D. (eds.) Resilience from the Practice of Mentoring to Contribute to the Permanence of Students, vol. 2, pp. 101–117. ECORFAN Handbooks, Mexico (2023)
10. Garrison, D.R., Anderson, T., Archer, W.: Critical thinking, cognitive presence, and computer conferencing in distance education. Am. J. Dist. Educ. **15**, 7–23 (2001)
11. Fiock, H.: Designing a community of inquiry in online courses. Int. Rev. Res. Open Distrib. Learn. **21**, 135–153 (2020)
12. Kim, J., Merrill, K., Jr., Xu, K., Kelly, S.: Perceived credibility of an AI instructor in online education: the role of social presence and voice features. Comput. Hum. Behav. **136**, 107383 (2022)
13. Wang, X., Pang, H., Wallace, M.P., Wang, Q., Chen, W.: Learners' perceived AI presences in AI-supported language learning: a study of AI as a humanized agent from community of inquiry. Comput. Assist. Lang. Learn. **37**, 814–840 (2024)
14. VanLehn, K.: The relative effectiveness of human tutoring, intelligent tutoring systems, and other tutoring systems. Educ. Psychol. **46**, 197–221 (2011)
15. Yin, R.K.: Case Study Research and Applications: Design and Methods. Sage publications (2017)
16. Tisdell, E.J., Merriam, S.B., Stuckey-Peyrot, H.L.: Qualitative Research: a Guide to Design and Implementation. John Wiley & Sons (2025)
17. Smith, J.A., Larkin, M., Flowers, P.: Interpretative phenomenological analysis: theory, method and research (2021)
18. The AI-powered platform for learning STEM. Accessed 24 Feb. 2024
19. Braun, V., Clarke, V.: Using thematic analysis in psychology. Qual. Res. Psychol. **3**, 77–101 (2006)

Human Behavior Analysis
via Attention-Based LSTM and Process Mining

Sara Pettinari[1], Lorenzo Rossi[2], and Massimiliano Sampaolo[2(✉)]

[1] Gran Sasso Science Institute, L'Aquila, Italy
sara.pettinari@gssi.it
[2] School of Science and Technology, University of Camerino, Camerino, Italy
{lorenzo.rossi,massimiliano.sampaolo}@unicam.it

Abstract. The analysis of human behavior is a complex and evolving research field that enables a holistic understanding of daily activities and habits. Existing approaches focus on classifying individual activities, struggling to provide a clear and structured representation of behavioral patterns. Differently, process mining offers a way to create structured and easily interpretable representations of complex behavioral sequences. In this work, we propose a novel approach that leverages a Long Short-Term Memory network and an attention mechanism to abstract high-level activities from fine-grained sensor data in smart environments. The attention layer enhances explainability by clarifying the inference process during activity recognition. These activities are then transformed into structured event logs for process mining analysis. We evaluate our approach using the CASAS Cairo dataset, demonstrating its effectiveness in extracting meaningful activity sequences and supporting structured behavior analysis.

Keywords: Human Behavior Analysis · Activity Recognition · Long Short-Term Memory · Attention · Process Mining

1   Introduction

The analysis of human behavior is a growing research field, aiming at understanding human activities and habits which by nature are flexible and unstructured [20]. Existing approaches for behavior analysis often rely on statistical modeling or machine learning techniques focused on classifying individual activities [5, 10]. However, these methods often fail to provide a clear and structured representation of human behavior, making it challenging to extract meaningful insights from complex activity sequences. Additionally, traditional approaches tend to focus on isolated aspects of behavior, such as frequency, duration, or classification, without capturing the broader context in which activities occur. This limitation restricts their ability to offer a holistic understanding of behavioral patterns.

F. Corradini et al. (Eds.): Society 5.0 2025, CCIS 2787, pp. 228–240, 2026.
https://doi.org/10.1007/978-3-032-15463-7_19

In recent years, the spread of smart environments, comprising multiple inter-connected devices that capture and store behavioral data from human interactions, has led to the application of process mining techniques as an effective approach for extracting, representing, and analyzing human activities through process models [15]. Process mining offers a set of techniques for discovering, monitoring, and optimizing processes based on event logs [2]. An event log, in turn, is a structured collection of events corresponding to a specific process, typically including a case identifier, which represents a process instance; an activity, which describes an operation, action, or task; and a timestamp indicating when the event occurred.

However, within a smart environment, devices do not record the high-level activity a human is performing, but they collect fine-grained data. Therefore, since process mining techniques require a structured event log, data collected by devices first require extensive preprocessing to abstract corresponding human activities, be shaped in the form of an event log, and then analyzed with process mining techniques.

To permit human behavior analysis, we propose an approach to construct event logs from fine-grained sensor data and consequently discover the underlying process model. To this, we leverage Human Activity Recognition (HAR) techniques to infer high-level activities. Specifically, we utilize a Long Short-Term Memory (LSTM) network with an attention layer to process sensor data and abstract it into structured activities. These are then used to generate an event log suitable for process mining analysis. With the event log constructed, we apply process discovery deriving a model of human behavior in the smart environment. We evaluate the proposed approach in a realistic setting using the CASAS Cairo dataset [7], a publicly available dataset that contains sensor-based activity recordings collected from a smart home.

The rest of the paper is structured as follows. Section 2 provides an overview of process mining, LSTM, and the attention mechanism. Additionally, it discusses approaches from the literature that apply process mining techniques to analyze human behavior in smart environments. Section 3 illustrates the proposed approach for analyzing human behavior using sensor data collected from a smart home. Section 4 evaluates the approach on the CASAS Cairo dataset. Finally, Sect. 5 concludes the work and touches upon future directions.

2   Background

This section provides an overview of process mining, followed by a discussion of LSTM networks and attention mechanisms. Together, these topics form the core of our approach. Additionally, we present related work on the application of process mining in smart environments.

2.1   Process Mining

Process mining [25] is a collection of techniques for analyzing event data generated from the execution of a business process, typically recorded in an IT system.

These techniques are categorized into three main types: discovery, conformance, and enhancement. Process discovery [1] enables the automatic extraction of process models out of recorded event data. Conformance checking [6] identifies deviations from standard process flows by comparing process models with event data, while process enhancement [19] involves enriching process models with quantitative information from other process perspectives (e.g., cost, duration) gathered from the data.

Process mining relies on the assumption that systems record events corresponding to the actual execution of their processes, generating the so-called event logs. An event log consists of events that represent the execution of system activities, each described by a set of attributes. Events are grouped into cases, where each case corresponds to a single execution of the process (i.e., a process instance). The most common attributes of an event include the activity name and timestamp, though additional information, such as the monetary cost associated with the event, can also be recorded. The sequence of events related to a specific case is referred to as a trace.

Sometimes, as in the context of smart environments, there is no IT system that logs events in a structured manner or at a high level of abstraction. Nevertheless, fine-grained data produced by various types of sensors can be used to infer ongoing activities. By applying activity recognition techniques, high-level activities can be extracted from fine-grained data collected through sensors, video, or other sources. These inferred activities can then be organized into an event log by identifying a case ID, assigning timestamps to events, and incorporating any available resource information. Bridging the gap between fine-grained data and high-level activities expands the range of scenarios where process mining can be applied.

2.2 LSTM and Attention

LSTM networks are a special kind of recurrent neural network (RNN) designed to handle sequences of data more effectively than traditional RNNs [14]. The key challenge with standard RNNs is the vanishing gradient problem, which makes it difficult for them to retain information over long sequences. LSTMs address this issue by introducing a memory cell and a set of gates that regulate the flow of information. These three important gates are:

1. **Forget gate** – This decides what information from the past should be discarded. If certain details are no longer relevant, they are "forgotten".
2. **Input gate** – Determines what new information should be added to the memory cell.
3. **Output gate** – Controls how much of the stored information is passed on to the next time step.

These gates use activation functions to ensure smooth and selective information flow. This ability to regulate memory updates makes LSTMs particularly well-suited for tasks involving sequential data, such as time-series forecasting.

Moving to the attention mechanism, it is a key concept in neural networks that enables a model to determine which parts of an input sequence are most relevant for making predictions [13]. Instead of processing every element of the sequence with equal importance, the mechanism computes weights that reflect how much each element should contribute to the final decision. It does so by comparing a representation of the current processing focus with representations of each input element, thereby generating scores that indicate relevance. These scores are then used to form a weighted sum of the input information, ensuring that the model can efficiently capture important long-range dependencies. This dynamic way of allocating focus allows for more flexible and effective learning, addressing some of the challenges faced by traditional sequential models.

2.3 Related Work

Several studies have explored the application of process mining in smart environments. Many of these studies use event abstraction or activity recognition to generate event logs from fine-grained data, facilitating process analysis.

In healthcare, [24] proposes a framework for analyzing human activities and identifying patterns and disorders with the use of process mining and unsupervised learning. [16] leverages wearable sensors to monitor isolated individuals, identifying anomalous behaviors. [22] assumes prior activity recognition and applies process mining for behavior representation and analysis. Differently, from these approaches, [12] focuses on multimodal data. This work proposes a multimodal attention network that integrates verbal transcripts and environmental audio to detect activities during trauma resuscitation.

In smart home environments, [23] uses conditional random fields to infer high-level activities from smart home sensors, to then process models of the inhabitants' behavior. [11] proposes an event abstraction technique based on motifs, i.e., recurring event sequences representing contextualized activities, validated using the CASAS dataset. Similarly, [9] extends this approach to smart offices, using sensor data to infer daily routines as workflow models.

Considering the manufacturing domain, [21] clusters low-level data from programmable logic controllers to derive human-interpretable activities analyzed via process discovery. [17] presents a prototype workstation with cameras recognizing operator activities and logging detected events.

Summing up, abstracting and analyzing human activities is a widely explored field. However, the diversity of data produced by smart environments, including sensor data and multimodal data, along with the unpredictability of human behavior, makes it challenging to establish a universal solution for activity abstraction and analysis.

3 Human Behavior Analysis

This section presents our approach to human behavior analysis. Figure 1 illustrates the steps involved in the proposed method, which consists of two phases.

The *processing phase* aims at abstracting human activities to produce an event log, while the *analysis phase* uses the event log to discover a process model describing the behavior of one or multiple humans.

The approach is designed for structured environments. It leverages sensor data to infer high-level activities and their corresponding timestamps. Subsequently, the approach determines the case identifier, constructing an event log that serves as input for process discovery algorithms.

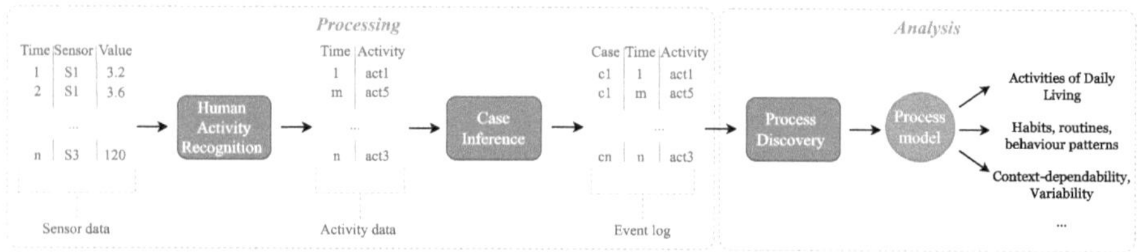

Fig. 1. Steps of the approach.

Processing. The processing phase starts with the activity recognition step. Although HAR is often used to understand and monitor human behavior [10], in our approach, we leverage it as the first step for processing data. This choice has been driven by the necessity of providing a human-interpretable semantic layer to sensor values, and to reduce the complexity of the discovered models. As depicted in Fig. 2, we leveraged activity recognition to group multiple sensor data and interpret them with semantic meaning. Specifically, the blue dots represent sensor data, which are abstracted into green dots corresponding to recognized activities. Notably, during the application of HAR, we also identified and filtered out noise from sensor data that was not directly associated with any activity, represented as yellow dots in the figure. For instance, a temperature sensor may introduce noise by recording frequent variations even unless significant environmental changes or human activities. More in detail, we propose an approach that employs an LSTM neural network for HAR, leveraging its capability to learn both long- and short-term spatiotemporal dependencies in time series data. Additionally, we incorporated an attention layer into the model architecture to address the class imbalance, as some activities are more frequently performed than others in a structured setting. The attention mechanism enables the model to focus on a subset of elements and decompose the problem into a sequence of attention-based reasoning tasks [13]. Furthermore, it generates weights that indicate which parts of the input sequence contribute most to the output, providing valuable insights into the explainability of the results.

The trained model predicts an activity based on a sequence of sensor measurements. To generate predictions, we split the original dataset into overlapping

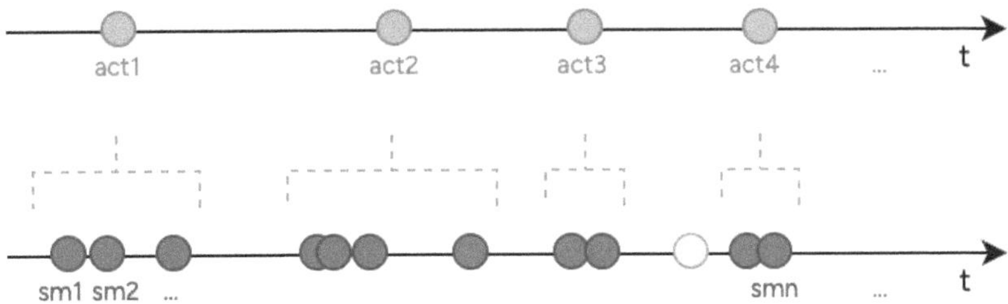

Fig. 2. Activity recognition from sensor data.

subsequences of fixed length. For each subsequence, the model outputs a predicted activity. We assign the start timestamp from the first measurement and the end timestamp from the last measurement in the subsequence. Once all activities have been inferred, consecutive predictions of the same activity are merged, and their timestamps are adjusted accordingly.

To apply traditional process mining techniques, a case identifier must be inferred. The selection of the case identifier depends on several factors, including the available data, the domain, and contextual considerations. Notably, the choice of the case identifier directly impacts the resulting process model, providing different analysis perspectives. Therefore, this step should align with the specific objectives of the analysis. For example, a case can be defined based on a specific time window, such as a day, or it can be associated with an individual human. Once the case identifier is determined, it is assigned to the abstracted activities along with their respective timestamps. This step ultimately generates an event log, making it suitable for process mining-based analysis.

Analysis. The analysis phase of the proposed approach employs process discovery techniques to reconstruct human behavior as a process model [1]. By relying on the same input, that is the event log, the discovery step can use various algorithms from the literature to extract the process model with different algorithms e.g., the Alpha algorithm [26], the Heuristic Miner [27], the Inductive Miner [18], and the Split Miner [3]; and in different notations, e.g., Directly-Follows Graph (DFG), a Petri net, or a BPMN model. The choice of the discovery algorithm depends on the analysis objectives, as each representation provides distinct insights into the structure and flow of activities. In our approach we used a DFG, i.e., a directed graph whose nodes represent the human activities and the arcs indicate a directly-follows relation [1]. Once the process model is extracted, various human behavioral aspects can be analyzed.

Based on the work in [4], we highlight several types of analysis enabled by our approach:

- *Identification of Frequent Patterns.* This analysis identifies recurrent behaviors, routines, or habits, often linked to specific contextual conditions (e.g., the activities a user typically performs in the morning between 08:00 and 10:00).

- *Human Collaboration in Activities of Daily Living (ADLs).* ADLs are groups of human actions with the environment that contribute to achieving a final goal (e.g., cleaning the house). However, the fulfillment of ADLs may also involve collaborative actions by multiple individuals, and the activities themselves can overlap, with individuals performing different tasks simultaneously or sequentially.
- *Human Behavior Variability.* This analysis explores how context can influence behavior, to identify how external factors, such as time of day or environment, affect human behavior patterns. Notably, this aspect requires the discovery of process models capable of expressing the flexibility of human behavior.

4   Evaluation

In this section, we evaluate the processing and analysis steps of the approach using the CASAS Cairo dataset; then we discuss the obtained results. Code and instructions to replicate the experiment are available online[1].

The CASAS Cairo dataset provides a rich source of real-world data. It contains sensor data that was collected in the home of a volunteer adult couple. The residents included a man, a woman, and a dog, with occasional visits from the couple's children. The layout of the sensors in the home is shown in Fig. 3. The dataset includes annotations for various daily activities, such as breakfast, laundry, and lunch. Additionally, some activities are annotated separately for R1 and R2, representing the two individuals in the couple.

Processing. Before training the model, we preprocessed the dataset. Specifically, we constructed a list of consecutive sequences of sensor measurements, each of the same length. For each sequence, we assigned the most frequent activity as the target label. If no activity was annotated, we assigned the label *none* indicating that these sensor changes were not caused by a performed activity but rather by environmental noise. The extracted features included the sensor name, the value measured by the sensor (with motion sensors represented as 0 or 1), and time components such as hours, minutes, and seconds.

For training, we used TensorFlow and Keras, leveraging their flexibility and efficiency for deep learning tasks. During training, we employed accuracy and loss as evaluation metrics to monitor the model's performance over time, using categorical cross-entropy as the loss function. The model was trained for 20 epochs with an 80-20 data split, i.e., 80% for training and 20% for validation. At the end of training, we achieved an **accuracy of 84.1% and a loss of 0.41**. While there is still room for improvement, these results indicate that the model is capable of effectively recognizing human activities from sensor data, demonstrating its ability to learn relevant spatiotemporal patterns. Figure 4 displays the weights assigned by the attention mechanism to one of the fixed lenght sequences of sensor measurements in order to infer the corresponding activity, in

---

[1] https://bitbucket.org/proslabteam/human_behaviour_analysis.

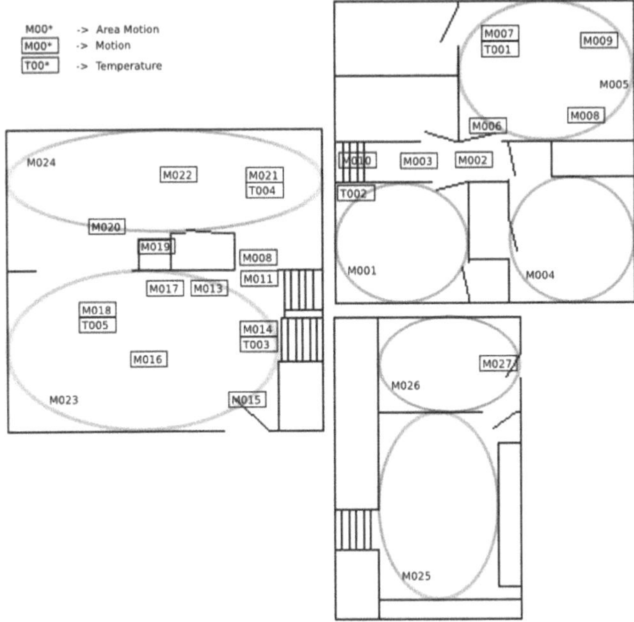

Fig. 3. CASAS Cairo dataset sensor layout.

this case, breakfast. In the sequence of 50 sensor measurements, we can see that a few measurements are more prominent compared to the others. This type of representation is very useful for explainability, helping analysts understand why the model makes good or bad predictions.

After training, we selected 100,000 sensor measurements from the test set and used the model to infer the corresponding activities. These measurements were collected over approximately nine days. This process allowed us to construct a CSV file with four columns: start, end, day, and activity. The start and end columns represent the beginning and end of each activity, respectively. The activity column contains the labels of the performed activities, while the day column stores the concatenation of the day and month. The generated file still requires refinement before applying the discovery algorithm. Specifically, activities predicted from consecutive sensor measurement sequences may be identical. To address this, we merged all consecutive occurrences of the same predicted activity, adjusting the start and end columns accordingly. In our context, we chose the day as the case identifier, aiming to infer the daily dynamics of individuals living in the house.

Analysis. The resulting DFG provides a summary of the various human activities recorded in the event log. Each path from the start to the end node represents a sequence of activities performed within a day. Additionally, the labels on the arcs indicate how many times the connected activities occurred in succession.

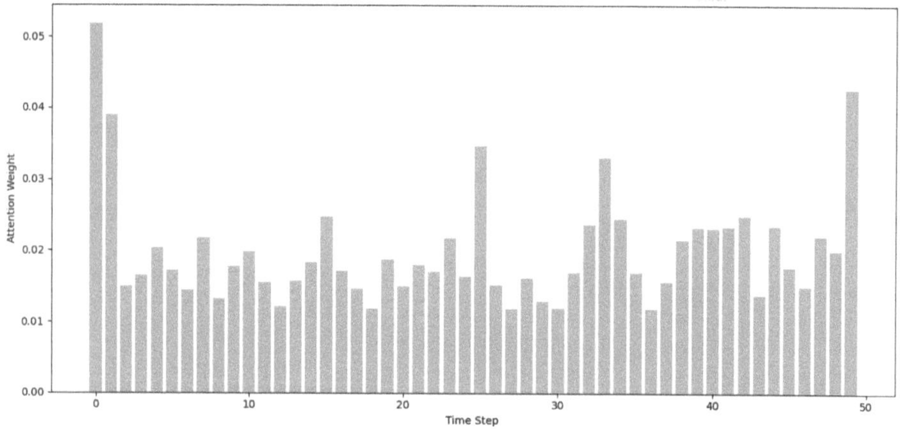

Fig. 4. Attention weights for a sequence of sensor measures.

The nodes not only display the activity name but also report the number of times that activity was performed.

Figure 5 shows the DFG discovered from the event log generated during the processing phase. For process discovery, we used Disco, applying filtering to remove less common paths. The DFG clearly represents the dynamics of daily life in the house, making it easy to identify different phases of the day, from night to morning, midday, and finally evening.

The choice of using the day as the case ID affects the obtained model: it begins with nighttime activities, such as night wandering or bed-to-toilet transitions, and ends with evening activities, such as R1 and R2 going to sleep. The model includes 10 of the 14 activities present in the dataset; this is because our test data does not include all possible activities.

Even though the model demonstrates the potential and effectiveness of our approach in understanding the main dynamics of human behavior in a household, it also highlights some limitations. The frequency of wake-up activities for both R1 and R2 is unexpectedly high, considering that the analysis is performed over just nine days. In many cases, the activity recognition task alternates between R1 wake and R2 wake, misclassifying them. This demonstrates how inaccuracies in the processing step can influence the final analysis of human behavior.

Notably, having most of the activities associated with a general human prevents a more detailed analysis of individual behaviors. Indeed, associating each activity with the specific human performing it would allow for the application of algorithms that could uncover both individual processes and collaborative behaviors [8].

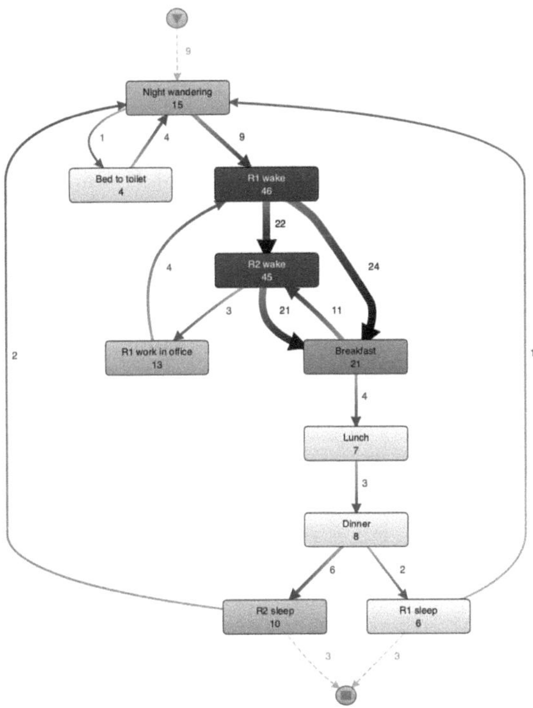

Fig. 5. DFG discovered from the CASAS dataset.

5 Conclusions and Future Work

In this work, we proposed an approach that combines HAR with process mining to analyze human behaviour in smart environments. By leveraging an attention-based LSTM, we were able to classify daily activities based on sensor activation sequences, achieving an accuracy of 84.1%. The extracted activities were then used to generate an event log, which allowed us to apply process mining techniques and construct a directly follows graph representing the residents' daily routines.

This combination of HAR and process mining proved effective in capturing the dynamics of human behavior, including the identification of distinct phases of the day and recurring activity patterns. The discovered process model highlighted not only the expected routines, such as morning wake-up and evening rest periods, but also interesting behavioral characteristics, such as variations in the wake-up and sleep times of different individuals. These insights demonstrate the potential of our approach for understanding and modeling human behavior in smart environments, providing a structured way to analyze how people interact with their surroundings over time.

The ability to model and understand human behavior in smart environments has significant societal implications. By recognizing daily routines and behavioral patterns, our approach can enable the development of more adaptive and personalized services, such as intelligent home automation that improves comfort and energy efficiency. In residential settings, this could translate into optimized heating, cooling, and lighting systems that reduce costs and environmental impact. In industrial and public environments, similar techniques could support more sustainable energy management, improve safety, and enhance user-centered design.

However, our evaluation also revealed a limitation: inaccuracies in HAR have direct repercussions on the final behavioral analysis. Errors in activity recognition propagate through the process mining pipeline, affecting the structure and reliability of the discovered models. This highlights the importance of improving HAR performance to ensure that process mining techniques can generate accurate and meaningful representations of human routines.

This limitation provides a starting point for future work. We will further investigate our HAR approach to enhance performance by exploring different network architectures or incorporating post-processing refinements informed by domain knowledge. Another key direction for future work is the integration of additional contextual information in both the processing and analysis phases. For instance, in the CASAS dataset, we could identify the individuals performing each task. While we currently do this for person-related tasks, it is not applied to more general activities such as lunch, dinner, or night wandering. By enriching the event log with resource annotations, we could enable the use of object-centric process mining, allowing for an analysis of household dynamics from the perspective of each individual actor.

References

1. van der Aalst, W.M.P.: Foundations of process discovery. In: Process Mining Handbook, LNBIP, vol. 448, pp. 37–75. Springer, Heidelberg (2022). https://doi.org/10.1007/978-3-031-08848-3_2
2. van der Aalst, W.M.P.: Process mining: a 360 degree overview. In: Process Mining Handbook, LNBIP, vol. 448, pp. 3–34. Springer, Heidelberg (2022). https://doi.org/10.1007/978-3-031-08848-3_1
3. Augusto, A., Conforti, R., Dumas, M., La Rosa, M., Polyvyanyy, A.: Split miner: automated discovery of accurate and simple business process models from event logs. Knowl. Inf. Syst. **59**(2), 251–284 (2019)
4. Bertrand, Y., den Abbeele, B.V., Veneruso, S., Leotta, F., Mecella, M., Serral, E.: A survey on the application of process discovery techniques to smart spaces data. Eng. Appl. Artif. Intell. **126**, 106748 (2023)
5. Brdiczka, O., Langet, M., Maisonnasse, J., Crowley, J.L.: Detecting human behavior models from multimodal observation in a smart home. IEEE Trans. Autom. Sci. Eng. **6**, 588–597 (2009)
6. Carmona, J., van Dongen, B., Weidlich, M.: Conformance Checking: Foundations, Milestones and Challenges, pp. 155–190. Springer, Heidelberg (2022). https://doi.org/10.1007/978-3-031-08848-3_5
7. Cook, D.: Learning setting-generalized activity models for smart spaces. IEEE Intell. Syst. **27**, 32–38 (2012)

8. Corradini, F., Pettinari, S., Re, B., Rossi, L., Tiezzi, F.: A technique for discovering BPMN collaboration diagrams. Softw. Syst. Model. **23**(6), 1323–1343 (2024)
9. De Carolis, B., Ferilli, S.: Learning daily routines in smart office environments. Front. Artif. Intell. Appl. **298**, 122–139 (2017)
10. Debes, C., Merentitis, A., Sukhanov, S., Niessen, M., Frangiadakis, N., Bauer, A.: Monitoring activities of daily living in smart homes: understanding human behavior. IEEE Signal Process. Mag. **33**, 81–94 (2016)
11. Di Federico, G., Burattin, A.: Cvamos - event abstraction using contextual information. Future Internet **15**(3), 113 (2023)
12. Gu, Y., et al.: Multimodal attention network for trauma activity recognition from spoken language and environmental sound. In: International Conference on Healthcare Informatics, pp. 1–6. IEEE (2019)
13. Hernández, A., Amigó, J.M.: Attention mechanisms and their applications to complex systems. Entropy **23** (2021)
14. Hochreiter, S., Schmidhuber, J.: Long short-term memory. Neural Comput. **9**, 1735–1780 (1997)
15. Janssen, D., Mannhardt, F., Koschmider, A., van Zelst, S.J.: Process model discovery from sensor event data. In: Process Mining Workshops. LNBIP, vol. 406, pp. 69–81. Springer, Heidelberg (2020). https://doi.org/10.1007/978-3-030-72693-5_6
16. Khowaja, S.A., Khuwaja, P., Dev, K., Jarwar, M.A.: Prompt: process mining and paravector tensor-based physical health monitoring framework. IEEE Sens. J. **23**(2), 989–996 (2023)
17. Knoch, S., Ponpathirkoottam, S., Fettke, P., Loos, P.: Technology-enhanced process elicitation of worker activities in manufacturing. In: Business Process Management Workshops. LNBIP, vol. 308, pp. 273–284. Springer, Heidelberg (2017). https://doi.org/10.1007/978-3-319-74030-0_20
18. Leemans, S.J.J., Fahland, D., van der Aalst, W.M.P.: Discovering block-structured process models from event logs containing infrequent behaviour. In: Lohmann, N., Song, M., Wohed, P. (eds.) BPM 2013. LNBIP, vol. 171, pp. 66–78. Springer, Cham (2014). https://doi.org/10.1007/978-3-319-06257-0_6
19. de Leoni, M.: Foundations of Process Enhancement, pp. 243–273. Springer, Heidelberg (2022)
20. Leotta, F., Mecella, M., Mendling, J.: Applying process mining to smart spaces: perspectives and research challenges. In: Persson, A., Stirna, J. (eds.) CAiSE 2015. LNBIP, vol. 215, pp. 298–304. Springer, Cham (2015). https://doi.org/10.1007/978-3-319-19243-7_28
21. Maier, J.B., Gram, J., Weisbarth, M., Hennebold, C., Huber, M.F.: Unsupervised event abstraction for automatic process modeling of plc-controlled automation systems. Procedia CIRP **120**, 631–636 (2023)
22. Sztyler, T., Carmona, J., Völker, J., Stuckenschmidt, H.: Self-tracking reloaded: applying process mining to personalized health care from labeled sensor data. Trans. Petri Nets Models Concurr. **11**, 160–180 (2016)
23. Tax, N., Sidorova, N., Haakma, R., van der Aalst, W.: Mining Process Model Descriptions of Daily Life Through Event Abstraction, pp. 83–104. Springer, Heidelberg (2017). https://doi.org/10.1007/978-3-319-69266-1_5
24. Theodoropoulou, G., Bousdekis, A., Voulodimos, A., Ghazanfarpour, D., Miaoulis, G.: Human activity recognition with unsupervised learning of event logs. J. Comput. Inf. Syst. 1–27 (2024)
25. van der Aalst, W.: Process Mining: Data Science in Action. Springer, Heidelberg (2016)

26. van der Aalst, W., Weijters, T., Maruster, L.: Workflow mining: discovering process models from event logs. IEEE Trans. Knowl. Data Eng. **16**(9), 1128–1142 (2004)
27. Weijters, A., van Der Aalst, W., De Medeiros, A.: Process mining with the heuristics miner-algorithm. TU/e, Technical Report WP **166**, 1–34 (2006)

The Underrepresentation of Women in ICT – a Society 5.0 Perspective: A Systematic Literature Review

Nikkesha Pillay[1], Hendrik Pretorius[1(✉)] ⓘ, Shireen Panchoo[2] ⓘ, Needesh Ramphul[2] ⓘ, and Marie Hattingh[1] ⓘ

[1] Department of Informatics, University of Pretoria, Pretoria, South Africa
`u21427900@tuks.co.za`, `henk.pretorius@up.ac.za`
[2] University of Technology, Port Louis, Mauritius

Abstract. Women remain significantly underrepresented in the Information Communication and Technology (ICT) industry. This study employs a Systematic Literature Review (SLR) to explore the challenges that women experience in the ICT environment and strategies that can be implemented with a Society 5.0 perspective. A PRISMA approach was used. Relevant academic sources were identified from ACM Digital Library, Web of Science, IEEE Xplore, and ScienceDirect databases. Women face many different challenges within the ICT field. Some of these challenges faced by women in ICT are common across the global scale. Other challenges are unique to certain environments or cultural factors within a country. The findings reveal that the common challenges experienced by women can be categorised into professional challenges, socio-cultural challenges, and educational barriers. From the perspective of Society 5.0, where technological advancements are linked to societal needs, it is important to promote an inclusive and diverse ICT work environment. This will foster innovation, creative solutions, and improved problem-solving, which is pivotal to Society 5.0. Various stakeholders can be leveraged to address the barriers of women in ICT. Some of these stakeholders include ICT companies, other women who are actively pursuing ICT careers and have successfully navigated the challenges that arise, and educational institutions. The research conducted in this systematic literature review can be used to implement solutions to encourage and empower women to pursue ICT careers.

Keywords: Women · ICT · Society 5.0 · Career Development · Inclusivity

1 Introduction

Society 5.0 is a concept introduced by the Japanese government in 2016 [1]. Society 5.0 refers to a society driven by developments in technology where the gap between the physical world and the digital world merge through the utilisation of Information and Communication Technology (ICT) to create a "super smart society" [2]. Within such a society the focus is on the human and the associated social problems experienced by human beings characterized through the sustainable development goals (SDGs) [1]. Technologies such as Artificial Intelligence (AI) and Internet of Things (IoT) are utilized to solve these social problems from a new perspective [1].

© The Author(s), under exclusive license to Springer Nature Switzerland AG 2026
F. Corradini et al. (Eds.): Society 5.0 2025, CCIS 2787, pp. 241–251, 2026.
https://doi.org/10.1007/978-3-032-15463-7_20

Technological innovations are breaking boundaries. However, the advancement and inclusion of women in the field of ICT are overlooked. Women face several challenges from gender biases, lack of representation, and unequal opportunities, to stereotypes that hinder women's progress in the ICT field [3].

Addressing the underrepresentation of women in ICT is key to achieve the full capabilities of Society 5.0 [4]. A study by Hyrynsalmi, Islam and Ruohonen highlights that there is a need for a diverse set of competencies to drive innovation [4]. Women can bring unique perspectives and skills to the ICT field to generate creative solutions [4].

Despite the challenges they face, women in ICT have made history and continue to shape society with their remarkable achievements. There have been women who have played a pivotal role in the advancement of technology. Ada Lovelace, renowned as the world's first computer programmer, made groundbreaking contributions to the field of computing [5]. Adele Goldberg's impactful work in user interface design faced skepticism but paved the way for modern graphical user interfaces (GUI), despite gender-based obstacles [6]. Katherine Johnson, a NASA computer scientist, challenged racial and gender discrimination to play a vital role in space exploration achievements [7]. These are just a few examples of women who have excelled in the technology field and who inspire future generations to pursue careers in ICT.

This systematic literature review will explore the research question of challenges women experience in the ICT field and how they can overcome these challenges considering Society 5.0.

The paper is structured as follows: Sect. 2 describe the systematic literature review method employed in this study. Section 3 presents the findings and discussion of the findings. Section 4 concludes the paper by answering the research question and presenting avenues for future research.

2   Research Method

The approach adopted in this study is a systematic literature review. The approach aims at identifying, analysing, and compiling relevant studies to provide a thorough overview of a topic [8].

Google Scholar was used as a search engine to select the data sources for the relevant articles. The following data sources were selected based on their relevance to the study:

ACM Digital Library, Web of Science, ScienceDirect, and IEEE Xplore.

Search terms used for Google Scholar:

("Embracing technologies" OR "Empowerment" OR "Diversity" OR "Gender Equality" OR "Strategies") AND ("Women" OR "Feminism" OR "Females") AND ("Senior Positions" OR "Career" OR "Development" OR "Leadership" OR "Mentorship") AND ("Challenges" OR "Barriers" OR "Glass Ceiling" OR "Attitudes" OR "Stereotypes") AND ("Technology" OR "ICT" OR "IT" OR "New Technology") AND "Society 5.0".

The inclusion and exclusion criteria guided the selection process of the papers resulting from the search terms above. Only papers published between 2019 and 2024 were included, papers that were published in English, and papers that have been published in peer-reviewed conference proceedings and academic journals. Duplicate papers and papers whose full text were not available were excluded.

The systematic literature review process, illustrated in Fig. 1 using a Prisma Flowchart, involved the phases of Identification, Screening, Eligibility and Inclusion. This thorough process determined the number of papers to be included in the systematic literature review.

The initial search from the search terms outlined above yielded 1678 results from Google Scholar and the databases specified above. An additional record of the Basic Plan for Science, Technology and Innovation was included to be assessed for relevance to the research as it served as the introduction of Society 5.0. Duplicates were identified and removed, resulting in 1468 records to be screened. The next step involved applying the inclusion and exclusion criteria detailed above, to assess the relevance of the records. This rigorous process resulted in 1304 records excluded. The 164 remaining records were assessed in its relevance to the study. This assessment resulted in 27 records remaining. These 27 records included in this systematic literature review represents the relevant literature according to the objectives and scope of this study.

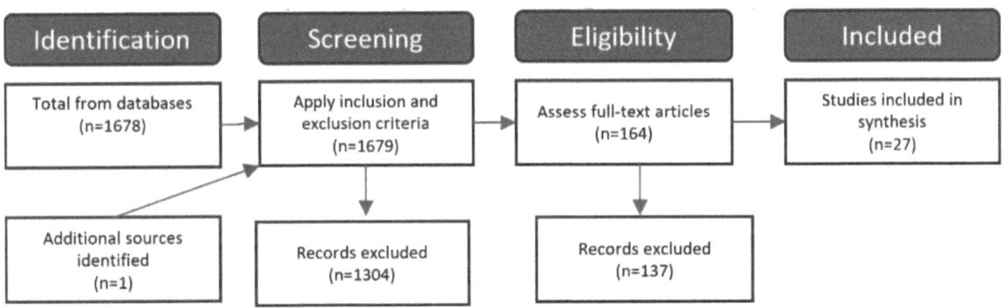

Fig. 1. PRISMA Flowchart.

The data extraction process involved searching for themes that addressed the research question of the underrepresentation of women in the ICT industry and how women can embrace new technologies despite the challenges that they face in ICT. For each paper, the following was documented: the type of paper (journal article, conference paper, book, book chapter or thesis), the journal or conference name, the main concepts or themes of the paper and the comments or notes from the paper.

The data were analysed using thematic analysis. Thematic analysis is a technique used for qualitative data to identify key themes within the data by segmenting the data into three broad areas: general information on the subject matter, themes associated with answering the research question and finally looking for patterns or connections between the themes [8].

3   Findings and Discussion

In answering the first research question, the data analysis revealed three main challenges emerged: professional challenges, socio-cultural challenges, and educational challenges that women experience in ICT. In answering the second research question three themes associated with initiatives that are in place to combat the challenges women face to advance in the ICT industry were identified: company policies, mentorship support and academic and education initiatives. Figure 2 illustrates the sub themes associated with each challenge and strategy.

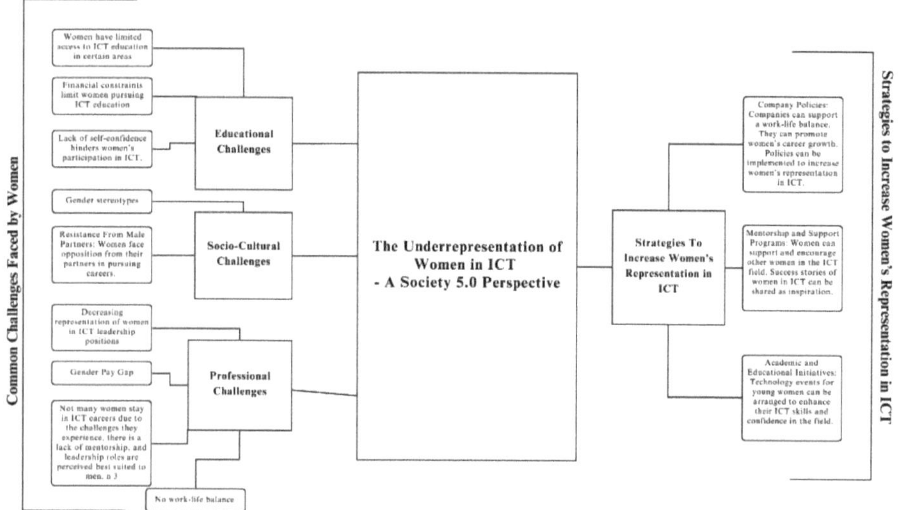

Fig. 2. Conceptual Model

Table 1 details the main themes and sub themes of the challenges women experience in the ICT industry per country and article referenced.

Table 2 details the themes associated with the strategies used to improve women underrepresentation in the ICT industry, the countries where these strategies are employed and the referenced articles.

Each of these themes is discussed in the sections to follow.

3.1 Challenges Faced by Women in ICT

From the examination of the challenges women face in ICT in different regions. There are common challenges that surface. Although each country may have its unique re-gional and cultural context, women in ICT share some common challenges.

The common challenges that women in ICT share are categorized into three main areas: professional challenges, socio-cultural challenges, and educational challenges. The common challenges faced by women in ICT are detailed below.

Professional Challenges Faced by Women in ICT. Women in the ICT environment encounter various professional obstacles. Work-life balance issues impact women more negatively than their male counterparts [26].

Women feel that there are no boundaries set between their work life and their personal life [3]. With the long hours of work, women feel stressed and have difficulty disconnecting from work [3]. Women often have responsibilities in caring for their families. Women

Table 1. Main themes and sub-themes per region

Main Theme	Sub-theme	Country	Sources
Professional challenges	Pipeline problems	Uruguay, New Zealand, Hong Kong	[9–11]
	Gender pay gap	United Kingdom, Spain, Nordic countries, European union	[12–18]
	Sexism and discrimination	United Kingdom, Spain, Bangladesh	[12–14, 19–21]
	Career progression barriers	Spain, New Zealand	[12, 14]
	Work life balance	All countries	[9–18, 22–24]
Socio-Cultural challenges	Gender stereotypes	All countries	[9–18, 22–24]
	Resistance from male partners	South Africa	[24]
Educational challenges	Access to education	Zimbabwe, South Africa, Indonesia, Pakistan	[22, 24, 25]
	Economic barriers to pursue education	South Africa, Indonesia	[23, 24]
	Confidence in pursuing ICT careers	South Africa, Nordic countries, Hong Kong	[9, 10, 15–17, 24]

Table 2. Strategies to Increase women's representation in ICT industry

Main theme	Country	Reference
Company policies	Spain, Nordic Countries, Hong Kong, Uruguay, Bangladesh	[3, 10, 16, 19, 26, 27]
Mentorship and Support Programs	Spain, Nordic Countries, Hong Kong, Uruguay, Bangladesh	[9–18, 22, 23]
Academic and Educational Initiatives	Hong Kong, Uruguay, Bangladesh	[9, 10, 19]

working in the ICT field face extreme pressure to fulfill their family responsibilities and their demanding work responsibilities [26].

Women have expressed that in the ICT industry one is always expected to be learning new things [3]. The ICT industry is constantly evolving. This means that those who work within this industry must continually acquire new knowledge on the latest trends and technologies that impact their work [26]. Women who have parenting or caretaking responsibilities, find this particularly challenging. Women who have these responsibilities have expressed that there is a lack of support and time to accomplish all these tasks [3].

Mothers working in the ICT field are often perceived as "failing at motherhood" because of their demanding work schedules [17]. As a result, these mothers find themselves missing crucial moments in their children's upbringing.

There is a difference in the remuneration of women and men in similar roles in the ICT sector [14]. The ICT field is male-dominated [26]. Women have related that they do not feel that their voices are heard during technical discussions. Women experience comments made by men that are degrading. It is perceived that women cannot adequately fulfil a technical position and that men can yield better technical results [15].

The male-orientated culture that exists in the ICT field creates a structure that favours men in leadership roles [26]. It is difficult for women to advance in their careers. The "Glass Ceiling" hinders many women from entering leadership roles. The glass ceiling, in this context, is a concept where women's access to high management positions is restricted because of work cultures [3]. In this investigation conducted, it is expressed that women are seen as ambitious in a negative way when they strive for high-management positions [3].

In the workplace, women have a feeling of "Imposter Syndrome". Imposter syndrome refers to feelings of self-doubt and inadequacy. It is a feeling of having a sense of not belonging or being able to fit in. Women who experience imposter syndrome feel unworthy of their capabilities and qualifications in the ICT environment [3]. Women mentioned that they must put in extra work and effort to be recognized. This contributes to the imposter syndrome that many women experience. The achievements and skills that a woman has are undervalued when compared to her male counterpart. Women feel that they need to constantly prove their worth to earn recognition and respect in their work environment [26].

Socio-Cultural Challenges Faced by Women in ICT. The ICT field is often characterized as having a "geek" or "nerd" culture [13]. The stereotypes and biases that exist deter women from pursuing careers in ICT [16]. Society perceives that careers that are technical and analytical, such as careers in the ICT field, are best suited to men [15]. Women are perceived to be more suited to roles such as motherhood or other domestic responsibilities [9]. These stereotypes lead many women to doubt their abilities to enter the ICT field [10]. For women who do enter the ICT field, these biases can lead to unequal treatment in the workplace [3].

Kenny and Donnelly's study highlights that women have related they have been excluded from events or activities that require decision-making [13]. This is because women are not perceived as having decision-making capabilities. Their findings further highlight that in the male-dominated ICT field, some women feel that they need to conform to the dress and behaviours of men to fit into the industry [13].

In certain countries, the traditional gender roles expect women to take care of the families and household while men can pursue a career [24]. Women face resistance to pursue careers as it is not seen as a women's role in society [21]. Triyono and Nuariyani found that because of the domestic responsibilities that women are expected to fulfil, these women don't have time to educate themselves [23].

Mentorship and role models play a significant role in providing inspiration and support. In the ICT field, there are a lack of female role models to encourage women to enter the field [22]. With the absence of mentors and role models that understand the challenges women in ICT face, many women miss out on the opportunities in the field [11].

Educational Challenges Faced by Women in ICT. ICT is not a career of choice for many young women [9]. From an early age, young women encounter gender biases that can discourage them and their interest in ICT [27]. With ICT being a male-dominated field, women are unable to identify with the field [13]. Ahmed, Urmi, and Tasmin additionally brings out that young women who are ICT students lack support and encouragement from academic institutions [20]. There is a lack of incentives and programs to support women who do choose to study ICT [9].

According to Tam, Chan and Lai, some young women who studied technology related disciplines did not intend in going into the industry [10]. The study elaborates that this is a result of the lack of confidence these women have and the stereotype that men are best suited and skilled in the technology field. With the lack of women in the industry, there are limited role models that young women can look up to inspire them to pursue ICT [20].

Women from marginalised communities, lack the financial support and awareness of the ICT field [23]. With limited income for families in these communities, funds are used for the basic needs of the family and not education [24]. Women living in marginalised communities have limited access to ICT education [22].

3.2 Strategies to Increase Women's Representation in ICT

The underrepresentation of women is a global issue. It is crucial to foster inclusivity and diversity in the ICT field by attracting women to the field. In combatting the underrepresentation of women in ICT, efforts from organisations and various role players, including women themselves, are needed [27].

Companies can publish success stories of women. Recognising women's achievements in ICT, it can attract more women to the field. By increasing visibility of successful women in the field, it can challenge the biases and empower women in ICT [26]. It is important to associate women with the ICT field to break the stereotypes of ICT being a field for men [27].

Some companies have introduced policies to promote female representation in ICT jobs [14]. Companies can also support women in maintaining a work-life balance, embracing equality, and promoting women's career growth. Companies can do this by offering childcare facilities, maternity leave and flexible work hours and location [3].

Organisations can promote a culture of helping and inspiring one another [28]. A study by Naseviciute and Juceviciene points out that mentorship programs and support initiatives can play a significant role in helping women advance their careers in ICT [26]. These mentorship initiatives will help inspire young women to pursue ICT. It will also help to expose them to the wide variety of career options that are available in ICT [26].

Academic institutions can have technology events and programs designed for young women to enhance their ICT skills [10]. This can aid in an increased confidence of these young women in pursuing ICT. These programs will empower young women by providing opportunities to explore ICT, improve their skills and reduce the gender stereotypes in the industry [10].

A study conducted by Jamal, Hasan, and Sultana speaks about arranging initiatives such as technology boot camps to introduce students to ICT [19]. Female ICT leaders can host Career Talks to share their experiences and inspire young women to choose ICT as their career [19]. Jamal, Hasan, and Sultana further speak about programming contests for female students that can be held. The study goes on to also speak about sessions where issues like sexual harassment can be discussed and educate young women on how to deal with these issues [19].

One study challenges women to break the glass ceiling by sharing their narratives, educating other women, and sharing techniques for navigating the ICT field [3]. Women are encouraged to invest in themselves and their education [27]. In a book authored by Corneliussen, it highlights that women need to be ambitious and brave in breaking away from stereotypes that are attached to ICT [27].

4 Conclusion

From the perspective of Society 5.0, it is crucial for companies to adopt practices to increase women's visibility and recognition in the ICT field. Equal opportunities should be provided for women in their career advancement in ICT. These methods will break through the biases and stereotypes that exist in the ICT industry [26]. Additionally, women in the ICT environment play a pivotal role in making efforts to engage with other women and encourage them to pursue ICT. Women can help and guide other women on navigating the ICT field and share their stories as inspiration [27]. By creating this supportive environment, it coincides with the vision of Society 5.0 [1].

In this systematic literature review, it was determined that the challenges women experience can be categorized into three broad areas. These areas are professional challenges, socio-cultural challenges, and educational challenges. The research also revealed that there are various strategies that can be implemented to increase the representation of women in the ICT field. These strategies include policies that companies can introduce to support a work-life balance and to promote women's career growth. In addition, mentorship and support programs can be arranged where women support and encourage one another in the ICT field. Through these programs, success stories of women in ICT can be shared to inspire other women to navigate the ICT field and grow their careers in this dynamic and fast-paced industry. Academic institutions can further implement initiatives to encourage young women to enhance their skills and confidence in the ICT field.

Previous research on the topic of the underrepresentation of women in ICT outlined barriers that women have experienced in the industry. Such research has recommended possible suggestions to address these barriers. This systematic literature review provides a synthesis of the findings of these papers in the perspective of Society 5.0. In this study it further defines ways women can encourage and empower other women in the ICT field.

This systematic literature review provides a comprehensive overview of challenges experienced and strategies to implement in a global context. Research papers from various countries have been collected to determine the common and unique challenges that women in ICT experience. However, from the suggestions in these research papers, there has not been a wide adoption of these in the ICT industry.

It is crucial to address the challenges that women experience in the ICT industry to create an inclusive workplace environment [4]. By doing so, all talents, regardless of gender can thrive and have access to equal opportunities. When all talent in ICT can reach their full potential, there is an increase in diverse perspectives [4]. These diverse perspectives lead to an innovation, creative solutioning, improved problem solving and an enhancement in meeting the ICT needs [4]. By addressing the obstacles of women in ICT, a forward-looking ICT Sector can be created that is aligned to the principles in Society 5.0.

Prior researchers have focused on the challenges women in ICT experience and strategies that various stakeholders can put into place to help support and encourage women to pursue ICT. However, according to the research conducted, as the technological field grows, the underrepresentation of women in the field is still persistent.

To address this ongoing challenge, it is recommended that further research be done on the effectiveness of the suggested strategies. Research can also be done on the adoption of these suggested strategies by stakeholders. Based on how well the research reveals that the strategies are being implemented in addressing the underrepresentation of women in ICT, additional research can be done on how these strategies can be refined and improved. Continuous improvement of these strategies is imperative to increase the representation of women in ICT.

There can also be future research conducted on the influence of emerging technologies (such as AI, IoT, Cloud Computing, etc.) and how it affects gender diversity in the ICT field. This research can explore the extent of these technologies offering more opportunities for women in ICT or if it re-enforces the underrepresentation of women in ICT. These technologies play a crucial role in future of Society 5.0. Therefore, research can be conducted on the alignment of these technologies to the objectives of Society 5.0 of creating an inclusive ICT environment.

By addressing these areas through research, there can be a measurement on the progress of more women represented in the ICT field. Additionally, research conducted can reveal on the support that technological advancements offer to align to promoting inclusivity and equality in the workplace.

References

1. Narvaez Rojas, C., Alomia Peñafiel, G.A., Loaiza Buitrago, D.F., Tavera Romero, C.A.: Society 5.0: a Japanese concept for a superintelligent society. Sustainability. **13**, 6567 (2021). https://doi.org/10.3390/su13126567
2. Fujii, T., Guo, T., Kamoshida, A.: A consideration of service strategy of Japanese electric manufacturers to realize super smart society (SOCIETY 5.0). In: Uden, L., Hadzima, B., Ting, I.-H. (eds.) Knowledge Management in Organizations, pp. 634–645. Springer International Publishing, Cham (2018). https://doi.org/10.1007/978-3-319-95204-8_53
3. Trinkenreich, B., Britto, R., Gerosa, M.A., Steinmacher: I.: An empirical investigation on the challenges faced by women in the software industry: A case study. In: 2022 ACM/IEEE

4. Hyrynsalmi, S.M., Islam, A.N., Ruohonen, M.: Meaningfulness as a driving force for women in ICT: What motivates women in software industry? In: Empowering Teaching for Digital Equity and Agency: IFIP TC 3 Open Conference on Computers in Education, OCCE 2020, vol. 12345, pp. 107–115 (2020)
5. Rafiq, A.: Ada Lovelace Challenge celebrates women in STEM. Nuclear Future. 20 (2024)
6. Anchan, V.M., Manmohan, R.: Attaining sustainable development goals through gender equality in information and communication technology (ICT). In: ICT as a Driver of Women's Social and Economic Empowerment, pp. 36–50. IGI Global (2023)
7. Andrieu, M.: Getting more girls and women involved in the field of technology: sharing experiences from a pioneering organisation in Luxembourg. In: Gender and Education in Luxembourg and Beyond: Local Challenges and New Perspectives, pp. 230
8. Oates, B., Griffiths, M., McLean, R.: Researching Information Systems and Computing. SAGE, London (2022)
9. Delgado, A., et al.: Bri-ozzo: encouraging girls' involvement in information and communication technologies (ICT) careers in Uruguay. Clei Electron. J. **22**, 1–18 (2019)
10. Tam, H.L., Chan, A.Y.F., Lai, O.L.H.: Gender stereotyping and STEM education: Girls' empowerment through effective ICT training in Hong Kong. Child Youth Serv. Rev. **119**, 105624 (2020)
11. Perera, M.D.: Understanding inclusion: An exploratory study of women ICT employees' experiences (2021)
12. Vergés Bosch, N., Freude, L., Almeda Samaranch, E., Ramos, G.A.M.: Women working in ICT: situation and possibilities of progress in Catalonia and Spain. Gend. Technol. Dev. **25**, 275–293 (2021)
13. Kenny, E.J., Donnelly, R.: Navigating the gender structure in information technology: How does this affect the experiences and behaviours of women? Hum. Relat. **73**, 326–350 (2020)
14. Segovia-Pérez, M., Castro Núñez, R.B., Santero Sánchez, R., Laguna Sánchez, P.: Being a woman in an ICT job: an analysis of the gender pay gap and discrimination in Spain. N. Technol. Work. Employ. **35**, 20–39 (2020)
15. Kurti, E., Ferati, M., Kalonaityte, V.: Closing the gender gap in ICT higher education: exploring women's motivations in pursuing ICT education. In: Frontiers in Education, pp. 1352029. Frontiers Media SA (2024)
16. Corneliussen, H.G. (ed): What brings women to cybersecurity? A qualitative study of women's pathways to cybersecurity in Norway. In: Proceedings of the 2020 European Interdisciplinary Cybersecurity Conference, pp. 1–2 (2020)
17. Seddighi, G., Corneliussen, H.: The illusion of balance: women in ICT working full-time and still having a feeling of opting out. Fem. Encount. J. Crit. Stud. Cult. Polit. **5**, 26 (2021)
18. Gaweł, A., Kapsdorferová, Z.: Women in the ICT sector in European Union states: Facing gender inequalities. Stud. Eur. Aff. **28**, 111 (2024)
19. Jamal, L., Hasan, M., Sultana, M.: Breaking the barriers: empowering girls in information and communication technology education. https://doi.org/10.12783/dtssehs/icedde2019/33686
20. Ahmed, N., Urmi, T., Tasmin, M.: Challenges and opportunities for young female learners in STEM from the perspective of Bangladesh. In: 2020 IEEE International Conference on Teaching, Assessment, and Learning for Engineering (TALE), pp. 39–46 (2020)
21. Mahato, A., Barman: P.: Women Education and Empowerment in India. Women Empowerment (2020)
22. Musungwini, S., Zhou, T.G., Musungwini, L.: Challenges facing women in ICT from a women's perspective: a case study of the Zimbabwean banking sector and telecommunications industry. J. Syst. Integr. **11**, 21–33 (2020)
23. Triyono, A., Nuariyani, N.W.: Information and communication technology (ICT) and women empowerment in Indonesia. Hum. Soc. Sci. Rev. **7**, 255–260 (2019)

24. Pokpas, C.: Exploring the access, usage, and perceptions of ICT of women in marginalized communities in South Africa (2019)
25. Kumari, S., Bhatti, S., Memon, M.A., Umar, A., Kumari, A.: Analysis of women empowerment in ICT institutes of Pakistan. Webology. **19**, 212 (2022)
26. Naseviciute, L., Juceviciene, R.: Overcoming the barriers to women's career in information and communication technology business. Equal. Divers. Incl. Int. J. **43**, 23–40 (2024)
27. Corneliussen, H.G. (ed.): Women Empowering Themselves to Fit into ICT. In: Technology and Women's Empowerment. Taylor & Francis, Location (2021)
28. Benedé, I.A., Díaz, J.C., Gómez-Manzanilla, J.D.B., Dono, E.G., Hernando, S.G., Puértolas, M.T.O.: Encouraging the role of women in the ICT sector. In: 2019 24th IEEE International Conference on Emerging Technologies and Factory Automation (ETFA), pp. 1831–1835 (2019)

A Hybrid AI Approach for Recommending Collaborators in Research Projects

Piermichele Rosati[1,2], Emanuele Laurenzi[1(✉)], and Michela Quadrini[2]

[1] FHNW - University of Applied Sciences and Arts Northwestern Switzerland, Olten, Switzerland
piermichele.rosati@students.fhnw.ch,
piermichele.rosati@studenti.unicam.it, emanuele.laurenzi@fhnw.ch
[2] School of Sciences and Technology, University of Camerino, Camerino, Italy
michela.quadrini@unicam.it

Abstract. The success of research project proposals heavily depends on the consortium, which should be experienced and knowledgeable in the topics outlined in the corresponding calls, e.g., those in the EU's research and innovation programme Horizon Europe. Yet, one of the most challenging activities in such a context is the formation of the consortium, which requires the identification of adequate research collaborators. Traditional methods take this challenge by relying solely on social networks and, or the number of author citations, which proved to be limited in efficacy. This paper proposes an Agentic Graph Retrieval-Augmented Generation (RAG) method, that provides contextual and explainable recommendations, which are tailored to researchers' areas of expertise and project relevance, thus more effective than existing approaches. The proposed method combines Knowledge Graphs (KGs) and Large Language Models (LLMs) capabilities and has been developed following the Design Science research methodology. The new method has been evaluated by considering two of the highest-performant LLMs currently in the market: Claude Sonnet 3.5 and GPT-4o.

Keywords: Hybrid AI · Knowledge Graphs · Large Language Models · Retrieval Augmented Generation · Research Collaboration

1 Introduction

Research collaborations are vital for addressing complex, multidisciplinary challenges, advancing knowledge, and accelerating innovation. Traditional approaches to collaboration often rely on professional networking through conferences, workshops, and institutional partnerships [10]. These methods have proven effective in facilitating connections but are often constrained by geographic and logistical limitations. Digital platforms, including ResearchGate[1]

---

[1] https://www.researchgate.net.

and LinkedIn[2], have expanded the reach of collaborations, allowing researchers to network online, share results, and identify potential collaborators worldwide. However, these platforms focus primarily on social connectivity rather than intelligent matchmaking based on complementary expertise or shared goals. Recommender systems [11], widely used in commercial contexts such as e-commerce and streaming platforms, have shown significant potential for matching individuals with relevant objects or entities nowadays [7]. Although they traditionally include algorithms that make recommendations about the most relevant items for a particular user, such as Content-Based Filtering (CBF) and Collaborative Filtering (CF), the recent advancements in Deep Learning (DL) techniques based on neural networks have improved the recommender systems' performance. Further advancements of DL methods, such as LLMs, overcome the limitations of deep neural network in capturing users' preferences and diverse textual information [21]. Nevertheless, they continue to exhibit critical limitations in the explainability of results and this lack reduces their effectiveness in tasks requiring complex reasoning, such as research collaborator recommendations.

In recent years, hybrid Artifical Intelligence (AI) has emerged as a novel research field that combines approaches from Machine Learning and Knowledge Engineering [5,13,16]. Respectively, two emerging technologies are LLMs and KGs. These two have very recently been employed for developing intelligent and interpretable recommendation systems [21]. On the one hand, KGs enables the representation of structured information about entities and their relationships, providing a basis for reasoning and generating insights. On the other hand, LLMs have demonstrated remarkable abilities to both understand complex textual information and generate new (relevant) content.

When combined with RAG KGs, LLMs can overcome the limitations of DL models by integrating external knowledge sources, reducing hallucinations, and providing contextually enriched, explainable, and accurate recommendations [2].

This combination represents a promising way to make recommender systems more effective; therefore, in this work, we explored their applicability in recommending research collaborators.

The main research question of our study is as follows:

How can a KG and LLM-based approach enhance the process of suggesting collaborators for research projects?

To answer this research question we followed the Design Science Research (DSR) Methodology [6].

In the problem awareness phase, we analyzed the literature and real-world scenarios from which we derived design requirements. The suggested artifact combines Agentic with Graph RAG approaches, and leverages KGs and LLMs with the goal of generating explainable recommendations regarding potential collaborators in the domain of European projects.

The paper is structured as follows. In Sect. 2 related works are discussed and relevant requirements are listed, while in Sect. 3 we describe the dataset that

---

[2] https://www.linkedin.com.

emerged from the analysis of 5 EU research projects. In Sect. 4 the proposed system architecture and its implementation are discussed, while in Sect. 5 we describe the evaluation of the approach, which is done by running experiments over the prototype. Finally, Sect. 6 concludes the paper.

2   Literature Review

This section describes the state-of-the-art with respect to both the KGs and Recommender Systems in the context of project collaborators. Finally, a list of requirements is described, which influenced the design of the artifact.

2.1   Knowledge Graphs in Research Field

KGs have come up as a key technology in data management and AI, enabling sophisticated data integration, retrieval, and analysis. KGs are directed graph-based data structures representing real-world entities and their interrelations, providing a way to model complex domains and their underlying semantics. A KG consists of nodes (also called entities) and edges (also called relationships), forming a network of interconnected information. Well-known KGs and ontologies have significantly influenced the research field by providing structured representations of knowledge that facilitate data integration, retrieval, and analysis. One prominent example was the Microsoft Academic Graph (MAG), a mapping system of academic publications, authors, institutions and topics for analysing research trends and discovering collaborations [20]. After its discontinuation in 2021, OpenAlex emerged as an open-source successor, linking academic entities with rich metadata [14]. Semantic Scholar Academic Graph (S2AG) of the Allen Institute for AI is one of the largest research KGs, containing over 205 million publications and 121 million authors [19]. It integrates metadata from sources such as Crossref and PubMed, offering insights for Natural Language Processing (NLP), citation analysis, and research discovery. Wikidata, launched by the Wikimedia Foundation in 2012, is a collaboratively edited KG that serves as a repository of structured data in all fields [18]. By supporting Linked Open Data (LOD), Wikidata integrates with external datasets through globally recognised identifiers, improving knowledge connectivity. It is widely used in NLP, recommender systems, and AI-driven research. Open Research Knowledge Graph (ORKG) structures research contributions in a machine-readable format, facilitating systematic reviews and comparative studies. By aligning key concepts and methodologies, ORKG improves literature gap analysis, reproducibility, and self-reasoning [8]. The VIVO ontology forms the basis of the VIVO platform and models academic activities using semantic technologies such as Resource Description Framework (RDF) and Web Ontology Language (OWL) [1]. It defines relationships between researchers, publications, scholarship, and institutions while ensuring interoperability through external vocabularies such as Friend of a Friend (FOAF). FOAF facilitates the representation of researchers, social networks, and collaborations, promoting data sharing on the Semantic Web.

2.2   Recommender Systems in Research Field

Most of the existing works of recommender systems in the literature regarding the field of research are based on suggesting research papers. [17] proposed REFORE, a hybrid recommender system that helps researchers manage information overload by providing personalized paper recommendations. It integrates bibliometric measures (e.g., journal impact factors, author h-index) to assess quality and uses a CBF approach to match user preferences with paper metadata (keywords, abstracts, citations). Papers are represented as vectors with weighted keywords, dynamically building user profiles based on past publications and manual inputs. Additionally, they used CF to enhances recommendations by incorporating feedback from similar users. [9] proposed a research paper recommendation system that integrates citation and collaboration networks to enhance relevance. It addresses challenges like cold-start, data sparsity, and semantic ambiguity by constructing a multi-level citation network, where the focal paper serves as the central node. Citation relationships are analyzed up to six levels using bibliographic coupling and co-citation strengths to filter relevant papers. Centrality measures (betweenness, degree, closeness, eigenvector) rank papers by structural significance. [12] proposed a user-based CF research paper recommender to address information overload. The system analyzes user-paper interactions (e.g., ratings) and calculates cosine similarity between users to identify those with shared interests. Recommendations are generated by predicting ratings for papers based on similar users' preferences. A prediction rating mechanism refines suggestions, prioritizing highly rated papers. Additionally, a user-link formation step enhances the CF model by leveraging collective user behavior. [3] proposed ACR-ANE, a model for academic collaborator recommendations that integrates network topology and multi-type scholar attributes. Unlike existing methods, it incorporates non-local neighbors (identified via biased random walks and frequency filtering) to capture stronger academic ties. Six scholar attributes (e.g., research interests, H-index) are encoded with a deep auto-encoder, generating embeddings that preserve local and global network characteristics. The model constructs a multi-type relational network, enriching academic relationship representation. [22] explored the application of Graph Neural Networks (GNNs) to recommend research collaborators in the academic domain. The study focuses on leveraging dynamic and temporal aspects of research networks, addressing the challenge of identifying suitable collaborators in a rapidly evolving academic landscape. The authors utilize data from the MEDLINE database and implement two GNN-based models, GraphSAGE and Temporal Graph Networks (TGN), to capture both static and temporal dependencies among researchers.

Requirements from Relevant Literature. The following Literature Requirements (LRs) were selected from the relevant works in the literature. Several KGs exist in the research and scholarly fields, but no work uses them in the European research domain. The definition of an ontology and/or use of a KG in this domain is necessary in order to allow semantic representation of European projects (LR1). Among current research recommender systems, some exploit various filtering approaches including CBF. Generating content-based recommendation could be quite efficient (LR2), for example if based on a project description or abstract, recommend potential collaborators, who have collaborated on a project with that description similar to the one specified. Unfortunately, some DL-based recommender systems need data training to perform the assigned task. In some cases it may also be necessary to retrain the model. In these cases, generating recommendations without performing either training or other techniques such as fine-tuning helps to save computational power (LR3). Regarding the hop reasoning perspective, retrieving relevant information dynamically, using models such as GNNs, can require high computations on graphs, especially on large graphs (LR4).

3 Scenarios Analysis

This section describes the dataset used, and then introduces the relevant scenarios that were analysed to derive the application requirements.

3.1 Dataset and Scenarios

The Community Research and Development Information Service (CORDIS) dataset [15] was chosen as primary data source. CORDIS[3] serves as the European Commission's primary public repository for distributing information about EU-funded research projects. This dataset is a valid resource for analyzing research trends, understanding research project collaborations, and identifying potential research partners. The chosen dataset contains information about projects funded under two major European Union research initiatives: The Seventh Framework Programme (FP7) for Research and Technological Development , covering projects funded from 2007 to 2013; and the Horizon 2020 (H2020) Programme for Research and Innovation , covering projects funded from 2014 to 2020. The dataset consists of five distinct subsets. The projects subset includes details on participating organizations, legal basis information, topic classifications, project URLs, and categorization using the European Science Vocabulary (EuroSciVoc). The project deliverables subset contains metadata and links to project deliverables. The project publications subset provides metadata and links to publications. Similarly, the report summaries, which include periodic or final publishable summaries. Reference data, including information on programs, topics, topic keywords, funding schemes (types of action), organization types, and countries are also stored in the dataset.

Using data from CORDIS, the structures of five European research projects that are part of the H2020 programme were analysed. The selected projects are: "BIM-based holistic tools for Energy-driven Renovation of existing Residences", "Integrated and Replicable Solutions for Co-Creation in Sustainable Cities", "New integrated methodology and Tools for Retrofit design towards a next generation

---

[3] https://cordis.europa.eu.

of ENergy efficient and sustainable buildings and Districts", "Proactive synergy of inteGrated Efficient Technologies on buildings' Envelopes", and "Adaptive Multimodal Interfaces to Assist Disabled People in Daily Activities". As an output of this analysis a list of Application Requirements (APRs) has been derived. Each project was part of the Research and Innovation Action funding scheme and focused on **Building Information Modeling (BIM)** as the main topic. In the following we report a short list of the main APRs: the project description (APR1), objectives (APR2), field of science, programmes, topics, proposal call, funding scheme, and keywords (APR3). In addition, there are the most important details concerning the coordinating organisation (APR4) of the project, and all the organisations participating (APR5) in that project. Each organisation presents secondary information such as postal address, location (APR6), and main type of activity. The available information only concerns organisations. However, for the recommendation of collaborators it is important to also know which people from the relevant organisations are involved in the projects, therefore we considered it as an additional requirement (APR7).

4   Results

This section illustrates the architecture of the proposed system, describing the selected ontology and KG, and details the responsibilities of each component of the RAG approach. Finally, the technologies used to implement the system are shown.

4.1   Proposed Architecture

The proposed architecture integrates KGs and LLMs in a RAG pipeline, following and combining the GraphRAG and AgenticRAG paradigms together. This facilitates the recommendation of potential research collaborators without re-training the model (satisfied LR3). The architecture is built upon the EUropean Research Information Ontology (EURIO) KG, which provides a structured and semantically rich representation of (EU-funded) research projects (satisfied APR1, APR2), organizations (satisfied APR4, APR6), and participants (satisfied APR5, APR7). The EURIO ontology, developed by the Publications Office of the European Union[4], was found as a data model that conceptualizes, formally encodes, and makes available in an open, structured, and machine-readable format data about research projects funded by the EU's framework programmes for research and innovation (satisfied LR1). CORDIS is responsible for publishing the results of these projects, while EURIO provides a semantic model that enhances transparency, reusability, and accessibility. The EURIO ontology is built on top of well-known ontologies and vocabularies to ensure interoperability and semantic richness such as Dublin Core, Data Catalog Vocabulary, Data Integration for Grant Ontology, FRBR-aligned Bibliographic Ontology, Funding,

---

[4] https://op.europa.eu/en/.

Research Administration and Projects Ontology, FOAF, and Simple Knowledge Organization System. The EURIO Ontology also incorporates reference data, such as countries, funding schemes, types of action, the EuroSciVoc taxonomy, and the NUTS classification, to enhance the semantic representation of research information. It leverages the OWL 2 to formally define the semantics of domain-specific terms used to describe CORDIS entities (e.g., projects, organizations, etc.), their attributes (e.g., title, acronym, legal name, etc.), and their interrelations (e.g., the connection between a project and its participating organizations, etc.). The EURIO ontology defines multiple classes representing different concepts such as projects, organizations, funding schemes, grants, publications, and roles, along with associated data properties and object properties that define their relationships. The proposed system architecture is designed to generate recommendations regarding potential research collaborators for research projects. The user can enter their own research perspective as a prompt or, for example, provide a call for proposals that includes the project's description and objectives. As shown in Fig. 1, the architecture consists of three main components: the *Retrieval Component* is responsible for retrieving relevant information from the EURIO KG and the vector database, in which 25,000 embeddings of European project titles and abstracts are stored. An AgenticRAG approach is used in this component, in which there are three agents. These agents follow two agentic workflow patterns: the tool use pattern and the multi-agent collaboration pattern (satisfied LR4). The agent workflow is initiated by the master agent: the *project-participants-information agent*. This agent is responsible for returning information about projects, such as the (e.g. project abstract), and also for returning information about the participants involved in that project (e.g. person full name, organization details). To perform the retrieval of this information, the agent was specified to follow a template prompt, in which it is instructed to generate SPARQL Protocol and RDF Query Language (SPARQL) queries to query the EURIO KG from which to extract data. Depending on the task to be performed, the master agent will delegate that task to the agent responsible for that task, if necessary. The *potential collaborators agent* has the task of recommending research collaborators, given a project description as input. The *potential consortium organisations agent* has the task of creating several consortia formed by various organisations, which contribute to the consortium in a complementary way, i.e. there will be no consortia with organisations specialising in the same research area. These two agents use the "recommend collaborators" tool, and the "recommend consortium organisations" tool, respectively, to accomplish the tasks previously described, and they too are instructed with specific prompt templates to follow to achieve their goal. In addition, both use the "search web" tool (satisfied APR3), to enrich the information obtained, such as a researcher's areas of interest, which are not present within the EURIO KG. The *Augmentation Component*, in addition to combining the user query and prompt templates, with all the relevant information obtained from the similarity search (satisfied LR2), adds additional data that comes from the task executed by the agent workflow. Cosine similarity was used as metric for the semantic search to determine the similarity of embeddings. In this way, agents act autonomously and are capable of dynamic decision-making, leading to better results than a graphRAG. Finally, the *Generation Component* combines all previously retrieved and augmented information with the pre-trained knowledge of the LLM to generate contextually accurate and consistent responses.

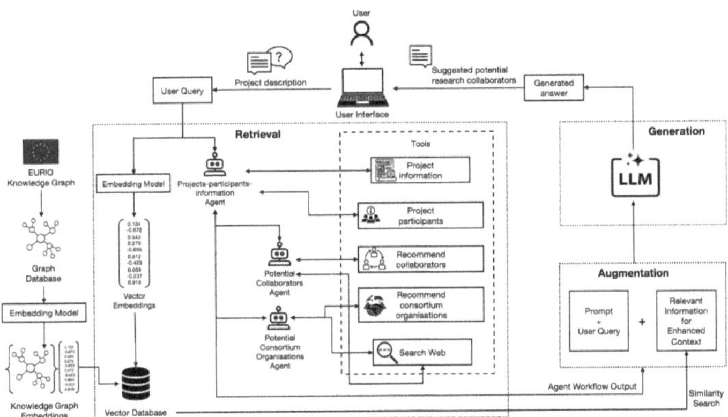

Fig. 1. The proposed Knowledge-Driven and Hybrid AI Architecture for Research Collaboration.

4.2   Technological Implementation

The proposed system is built entirely in Python, using Streamlit for both the back-end and front-end to simplify web app development and sharing. GraphDB by Ontotext was chosen as the graph database for its robust support for the RDF standard, enabling semantic data representation, efficient SPARQL querying, and easy integration with KGs for enhanced reasoning and retrieval. Additionally, Chroma serves as the vector database for storing KG embeddings due to its efficient similarity search, scalable storage, ensuring fast and accurate retrieval of relevant entities. We use the all-MiniLM-L6-v2 model for computing embeddings. This model is particularly well-suited for encoding short to medium-length text, making it ideal for our use case, where we store and retrieve project titles and abstracts from the EURIO dataset. By leveraging a lightweight transformer architecture, all-MiniLM-L6-v2 balances accuracy and computational efficiency, enabling fast and effective similarity search within our system. To implement our GraphRAG and AgenticRAG approach, we utilized two main frameworks: LlamaIndex was employed to build the agent workflow, coordinate agents, and integrate tools, while LangChain primarily facilitated the generation of SPARQL queries from user query inputs. For response generation, we utilized two state-of-the-art LLMs: GPT-4o, developed by OpenAI, and Claude 3.5 Sonnet, developed by Anthropic.

5   Experiments and Discussion

The effectiveness of the approach has been evaluated by testing the performance of the prototype in terms of how well the collaborators are recommended. For this, an evaluation dataset consisting of 10 user queries and 10 associated potential answers was built. For both types of recommendations, the user queries consist of the project description and objectives. Figure 2 shows an example of a query presented in our evaluation dataset (Fig. 2a), and the corresponding response (Fig. 2b) generated using GPT-4o in our system. (Fig. 2c) shows the response for a similar prompt but asking to find potential collaborators. Since the recommendations generated consist of one or more lists of consortia, the figure presents only part of this response. For a full inspection of the code, evaluation dataset and the results obtained, they can be found at the repository link[5]. This section describes the metrics used for the evaluation. Finally, we present a comparison of the performance of the candidate LLMs for the evaluation of our approach.

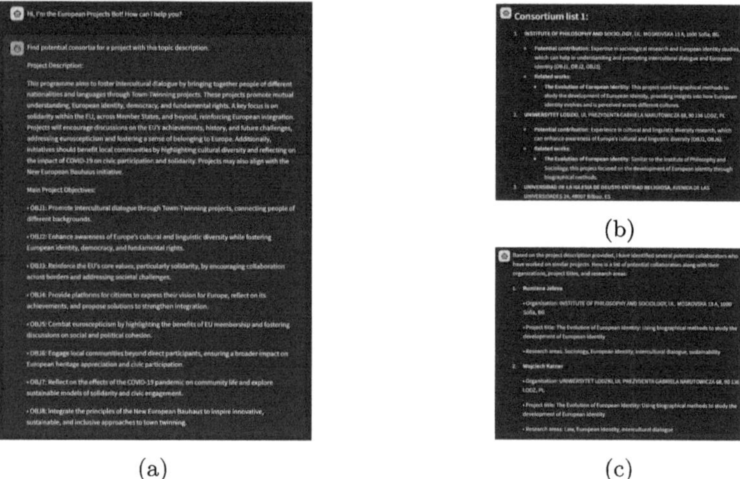

(a)

(b)

(c)

Fig. 2. Excerpts of the experiments. (a): The user need is to find organizations forming a consortium on intercultural dialogue. (b): The response recommends 4 organisations, their potential contributions, and related works, for the user query of Fig. 2a. (c): The response, related to a user query similar to Fig. 2a, recommends 2 research collaborators, their employment organisations, project titles similar to the one asked in the user query, and their research areas.

---

[5] Code and our experiments are available at https://github.com/Piermuz7/MasterThesisProject.git.

5.1   Evaluation Metrics

Evaluating RAG-based systems requires assessing both retrieval accuracy and LLM-generated responses. We focus on consortia recommendations, using the Retrieval-Augmented Generation Assessment (RAGAs) framework [4] to measure the relevance and consistency of suggested contributors. The evaluation metrics and results are presented below. *Faithfulness* assesses factual consistency between generated answers and retrieved context, scored between 0 and 1. *Answer Relevancy (AR)* measures alignment between the response and the input prompt, using cosine similarity. *Context Precision (CP)* evaluates how well top-ranked retrieved contexts match ground-truth data. *Context Recall (CR)* measures how comprehensively the retrieved content supports the answer. *Context Entity Recall (CER)* assesses whether key entities from the ground truth appear in retrieved contexts. *Answer Semantic Similarity (SS)* measures semantic closeness between generated and reference answers. *Answer Correctness (AC)* combines factual and semantic similarity to quantify overall accuracy.

5.2   LLMs Performance Comparison

The evaluation results provide a comparative analysis of GPT-4o 2024-05-13 and Claude 3.5 Sonnet 2024-10-22 on the Agentic Graph RAG approach, based on key retrieval and answer quality described in Sub-Sect. 5.1. Table 1 shows the results, which highlight differences in the LLM ability to retrieve relevant context and generate semantically accurate consortia recommendations. GPT-4o outperforms Claude 3.5 Sonnet in AR, AR, SS and AC, being more effective in generating relevant and accurate responses. Claude, while slightly better in faithfulness, struggles significantly in CP and CER, leading to less effective retrieval. Overall, GPT-4o provides more aligned, complete and contextually correct responses and recommendations, while Claude is more grounded but less effective in retrieving, structuring relevant information and thus recommending consortia. A better performance of GPT-4o also comes from the use of agents during experiments execution, where the *potential consortium organisations agent* was used correctly for all 10 queries. In contrast, Claude 3.5 Sonnet incorrectly called *potential collaborators agent*. As can be seen from the responses generated, Claude Sonnet's recommendations are much more concise than GPT's, in particular Sonnet has no relevant works associated with the recommended organisation and in several responses the potential contributions the organisation could make to the consortium are not even suggested. As a result of the Agentic Graph RAG approach, neither LLMs hallucinates.

Table 1. LLMs performance comparison in the used Agentic Graph RAG approach

Model	Faithfulness	AR	CP	CR	CER	SS	AC
GPT-4o 2024-05-13	0.314	0.93	0.076	0.266	0.298	0.716	0.469
Claude 3.5 Sonnet 2024-10-22	0.336	0.767	0.000	0.147	0.278	0.653	0.260

6   Conclusions and Future Work

This work introduced an Agentic Graph RAG method that provides contextual and explainable recommendations for research collaborators. The proposed method combines KGs and LLMs capabilities and has been developed following the Design Science research methodology. Experiments indicate that GPT-4o outperforms other LLMs in RAG-based recommendation metrics, demonstrating superior retrieval quality, contextual reasoning, and reduced hallucinations. Recommendations are tailored to researchers' areas of expertise and project relevance, thus making them more effective than existing approaches.

This work contributes to hybrid AI research approaches, in particular to the advancement of AI-assisted research networks, where the ultimate goal is to increase opportunities for collaboration and facilitate interdisciplinary research connections in a scalable and automated way. Our work also contributes significantly to society by providing an alternative approach to traditional collaboration practices, such as relying on personal contacts or informal networks, towards an inclusive and data-driven approach to research matchmaking. By leveraging explainable AI, the system makes access to potential collaborators more inclusive, ensuring transparency, and fairness, in consortia formation. This shift supports innovation across scientific domains and fosters more diverse and equitable research partnerships.

Potential future research work revolves around the automatic updating of the KGs (including information about Horizon Europe projects) to keep up with emerging research topics and thus keep the proposed approach relevant over time. In addition, the integration of academic KGs could be a useful resource to enrich the EURIO knowledge base and thus add context regarding the recommendation of papers and researchers.

Acknowledgments. This work has been funded by the European Union - NextGenerationEU under the Italian Ministry of University and Research (MUR) National Innovation Ecosystem grant ECS00000041 - VITALITY - CUP J13C22000430001.

References

1. Börner, K., Conlon, M., Corson-Rikert, J., Ding, Y.: Vivo a semantic approach to scholarly networking and discovery. Synth. Lectures Semant. Web: Theory Technol. **2**, 1–180 (2012)

2. Deldjoo, Y., et al.: A review of modern recommender systems using generative models (gen-recsys). In: Proceedings of the ACM SIGKDD International Conference on Knowledge Discovery and Data Mining, pp. 6448–6458. Association for Computing Machinery (2024)
3. Du, O., Li, Y.: Academic collaborator recommendation based on attributed network embedding. J. Data Inf. Sci. **7**, 37–56 (2022)
4. Es, S., James, J., Espinosa Anke, L., Schockaert, S.: RAGAs: automated evaluation of retrieval augmented generation. In: Proceedings of the 18th Conference of the European Chapter of the Association for Computational Linguistics: System Demonstrations, pp. 150–158. Association for Computational Linguistics (2024)
5. d'Avila Garcez, A., Lamb, L.C.: Neurosymbolic AI: the 3rd wave. Artif. Intell. Rev. **56**(11), 12387–12406 (2023)
6. Hevner, A., Chatterjee, S.: Design Science Research in Information Systems, pp. 9–22. Springer US, Boston, MA (2010). https://doi.org/10.1007/978-1-4419-5653-8_2
7. Hussien, F.T.A., Rahma, A.M.S., Wahab, H.B.A.: Recommendation systems for e-commerce systems an overview. In: Journal of Physics: Conference Series, vol. 1897. IOP Publishing Ltd (2021)
8. Jaradeh, M.Y., et al.: Open research knowledge graph: next generation infrastructure for semantic scholarly knowledge. In: Proceedings of the 10th International Conference on Knowledge Capture, pp. 243–246. Association for Computing Machinery, New York, NY, USA (2019)
9. Kanwal, T., Amjad, T.: Research paper recommendation system based on multiple features from citation network. Scientometrics (2024)
10. Katz, J., Martin, B.R.: What is research collaboration? Res. Policy **26**(1), 1–18 (1997)
11. Lü, L., Medo, M., Yeung, C.H., Zhang, Y.C., Zhang, Z.K., Zhou, T.: Recommender systems (2012)
12. Murali, M.V., Vishnu, T.G., Victor, N.: A collaborative filtering based recommender system for suggesting new trends in any domain of research. In: Proceedings of the 2019 5th International Conference on Advanced Computing & Communication Systems (ICACCS), pp. 550–553. IEEE (2019)
13. Prater, R., Laurenzi, E.: A hybrid intelligent approach for the support of higher education students in literature discovery. In: Proceedings of the AAAI 2022 Spring Symposium on Machine Learning and Knowledge Engineering for Hybrid Intelligence (AAAI-MAKE 2022), vol. 3121 (2022)
14. Priem, J., Piwowar, H., Orr, R.: Openalex: a fully-open index of scholarly works, authors, venues, institutions, and concepts (2022)
15. Publications Office of the European Union: Cordis reference data. Data set (2018). originally published in 2015
16. Rordorf, D., Käser, J., Crego, A., Laurenzi, E.: A hybrid intelligent approach combining machine learning and a knowledge graph to support academic journal publishers addressing the reviewer assignment problem (RAP). In: Proceedings of the AAAI 2023 Spring Symposium on Challenges Requiring the Combination of Machine Learning and Knowledge Engineering (AAAI-MAKE 2023), vol. 3433. CEUR-WS.org (2023)
17. Tejeda-Lorente, A., Porcel, C., Bernabé-Moreno, J., Herrera-Viedma, E.: Refore: a recommender system for researchers based on bibliometrics. Appl. Soft Comput. J. **30**, 778–791 (2015)
18. Vrandečić, D., Krötzsch, M.: Wikidata: a free collaborative knowledgebase. Commun. ACM **57**, 78–85 (2014)

19. Wade, A.D.: The semantic scholar academic graph (s2ag). In: Companion Proceedings of the Web Conference 2022, p. 739. WWW '22, Association for Computing Machinery, New York, NY, USA (2022)
20. Wang, K., Shen, Z., Huang, C., Wu, C.H., Dong, Y., Kanakia, A.: Microsoft academic graph: when experts are not enough. Quant. Sci. Stud. **1**, 396–413 (2020)
21. Zhao, Z., et al.: Recommender systems in the era of large language models (LLMs). IEEE Trans. Knowl. Data Eng. **36**(11), 6889–6907 (2024)
22. Zhu, J., Yaseen, A.: A recommender for research collaborators using graph neural networks. Front. Artif. Intell. **5** (2022)

Identification of Barriers that Lead to Problems in the Further Training of Employees

Natascha Sigle[1,2]($\boxtimes$) (iD) and Dieter Hertweck[1]

[1] Reutlingen University, Alteburgstraße 150, 72762 Reutlingen, Germany
{natascha.sigle,dieter.hertweck}@reutlingen-university.de
[2] University of Camerino, Via Madonna Delle Carceri 9, 62032 Camerino, MC, Italy

Abstract. The digital transformation presents companies with complex challenges, particularly in the area of employee training. This paper examines key barriers to the implementation of effective training concepts and analyzes practical solutions. Through a combination of in-depth literature research and expert interviews, key barriers are identified, including a lack of strategies for skills identification, inadequate documentation practices and a lack of management understanding of necessary qualifications. The results show that individualized training offers, internal knowledge exchange formats and the targeted use of managers in competence assessment are decisive for the success of further training. In addition, a concept matrix is presented that supports companies in the selection of suitable training models.

Keywords: Digital transformation · employee training · skills development · personnel development · strategic training management · training concepts

1 Introduction

1.1 Relevance

The convergence of economic and technological trends presents significant challenges for organizations. Companies are required to address demographic shifts and the evolving structure of their workforce [1], while simultaneously adapting to emerging technologies such as the Internet of Things (IoT), cyber-physical systems (CPS), artificial intelligence (AI), cloud computing, data analytics, blockchain, and additive manufacturing [1–4]. With the help of these technologies, it is possible, for example, to automate tasks with low added value through the use of robotic process automation applications or to create new manufacturing processes through the use of additive manufacturing processes. In order to be able to use the new technologies and opportunities listed profitably, a digital innovation and adaptation process is required that will permanently change the work and business processes in most organizations as well as the basic business model [5–7]. In this context, it should be noted that employees must constantly adapt to new technologies and changing conditions due to their increasingly intensive use [1, 8, 9].

F. Corradini et al. (Eds.): Society 5.0 2025, CCIS 2787, pp. 265–276, 2026.
https://doi.org/10.1007/978-3-032-15463-7_22

1.2 Problem Definition

Companies must not only anticipate technological developments, but also train their employees for these changes. There are significant obstacles: Identifying employees in need of further training is difficult due to the lack of standardized methods for assessing skills [10]. There is also a lack of clear alignment between company goals and training concepts, which impairs the effectiveness of training measures [11]. In addition, the willingness of the workforce to change is often not sufficiently taken into account, which causes adaptation processes to stall [12]. Financial restrictions, a lack of strategic approaches and an inadequate understanding of digital skills requirements on the part of management also make it difficult to implement sustainable training concepts [13]. These factors lead to a discrepancy between technological progress and qualification profiles, which can jeopardize the competitiveness of companies in the long term.

1.3 Objective of the Paper

The objective of this paper is to systematically identify and analyze the key barriers to employee training within the context of digital transformation. To achieve this, findings from a comprehensive literature review are combined with empirical insights gathered through company interviews. The study highlights the discrepancies between technological demands and existing employee competencies and critically evaluates existing training models using a concept matrix. Ultimately, the paper aims to develop strategic recommendations for addressing skills gaps and fostering sustainable workforce development.

2 Identification of Different Barriers

This chapter presents and compares the challenges found in the literature research and those identified in the exemplary interviews. The models found are then analyzed and differentiated using a concept matrix.

2.1 Literature Review

This paper uses the literature analysis according to Levy and Ellis (2006). In the first step of the research, the following databases for scientific articles were used: IEEE Xplore, JSTOR, ResearchGate, ACM Digital Library, Springer Link, ScienceDirect, Elsevier and EBSCOhost. The following search terms were used in the titles or abstracts: "Skill Development Challenges", "Skill Gap Model" and "Digitalization Business Model". The following inclusion criteria were defined: Publications had to be published in 2008 or later, be written in German or English and demonstrate a focus on digitalization and employee training. Publications that met these criteria were screened based on their title and abstract. A total of 51 publications were identified. Only one relevant publication was identified in the backward search, while two suitable literature sources were found in the forward search.

2.2 Obstacles to Further Training - from the Literature

The literature consistently emphasizes the importance of continuing vocational training as a key factor in managing digital transformation [1–3, 5, 6, 8, 9, 14–17]. However, there is limited focus on the systematic identification and development of the skills required for emerging roles and fields of work. While Hecklau et al. (2016) detail the general challenges companies face, and Pontes et al. (2021) present a model linking technological trends to new job profiles and associated training needs, the practical implementation of scalable training concepts remains largely unexplored. The barriers identified through the literature review are thematically grouped and summarized in Table 1.

Table 1. Obstacles in the literature (OL)

Abstraction	ID: Description
Suitability of the training for the employee's objectives	OL1: The training programs must be tailored to the employee's objectives and activities [19, 20]
Training courses that are tailored to individual needs	OL2: In order to achieve the greatest possible learning success, the training and further education opportunities offered must be individualized and geared to the needs of the individual. This applies not only to content aspects, but also to the level of difficulty or the didactic approach [19–22]
Identification of employees with a need for further training	OL3: Another problem for companies is identifying the employees who need further training [8, 9, 23, 24]
Evaluation of the ability to change	OL4: Another aspect is the evaluation of the individual employee's ability to change or the job profile [9]
Determining the future need for competencies and skills	OL5: Another obstacle is to identify qualifications with decreasing and qualifications with increasing demand [2, 3, 9, 23, 25]
Identifying the suitability of individuals	OL6: Companies are often confronted with the challenge of identifying highly qualified specialists for top positions who have the necessary skills [26]
Lack of understanding on the part of the management	OL7: One in four managers does not have a clear understanding of how digitalization will affect skills requirements [27]
Coordination of the training process	OL8: Companies must relate the training process to their corporate strategies, functions and processes. Only in this way is it possible to apply the concepts learned in practice and consolidate the skills gained [25, 28, 29]

2.3 Obstacles to Further Training - Practical Experience

In order to expand the state of knowledge in this field of research, gain a more comprehensive understanding of the situation and contribute to the "body of knowledge", information was collected through company interviews. These exemplary interviews are conducted on a small scale in this paper with the help of a guideline and the main statements are then grouped in * MERGEFORMAT Table 3. The questions formulated for this purpose are as follows:

1. Is there a need on the part of employers to train certain groups of employees, particularly with regard to the digital transformation?
2. Is there a defined strategy for implementing further training measures?
3. What specific challenges have arisen in the development and implementation of the concept?
4. What solutions are you pursuing to overcome the obstacles mentioned above? / What would help you to implement these solutions?

When selecting the interviewees, who are listed in Table 2, care was taken to ensure that people from different sectors were interviewed. This should help to obtain a picture of the existing obstacles that is as generalizable as possible, even with a small number of interviewees.

Table 2. List of interlocutors

ID	Industry	Size	Role	Professional experience
I1	Transport	Concern	Learning and Development Manager	15 Years
I2	Defense	Concern	Learning and Development Manager	30 Years
I3	IT system house	SME	HR Business Partner	26 Years

The main statements were identified and categorized in interviews I1 to I3:

Table 3. Obstacles in practice (OP)

Abstraction	ID: Description
Increase in employee efficiency	OP1: Employees must be able to make better use of the available resources, technologies and digital tools (I1, I2, I3)
External influences and requirements	OP2: Companies must keep pace with customer requirements, industry-specific developments, standards and technological changes (I1, I2, I3)
Inventory of competencies	OP3: Managers must assess individual skills and further training needs as part of the performance reviews (I1, I2, I3)

(continued)

Table 3. (*continued*)

Abstraction	ID: Description
Documentation of competencies	OP4: Employee profiles represent the current status of employees, but not a target status (I3). Competencies are documented in decentralized profiles, which makes it difficult to obtain a comprehensive overview of competencies (I1, I2)
Development paths	OP5: Development paths prepare employees for specialist or management tasks over several years by teaching them relevant skills (I1, I3)
Notification of requirements	OP6: The specialist departments currently report their skills requirements to the HR department on an ad hoc basis (I2)
Needs analysis	OP7: There are models for matching an employee's skills to an existing job, but none for defining future jobs or the skills required for them (I1)
Skills acquisition and exchange	OP8: In order to make use of existing skills and conserve the available training budget, knowledge is passed on through knowledge transfer sessions and internal training courses (I1, I2, I3)
Formats	OP9 Different training formats allow employees to choose their preferred learning format (I1, I2, I3)
Limitations - Budget	OP10: As training budgets are limited, it requires careful selection and timing of training to provide employees with the opportunity to develop relevant skills (I2, I3)
Limitations - minimum participants	OP11: Training courses offered have to be canceled because the minimum number of participants has not been reached, as employees do not find the time due to time pressure in ongoing projects (I2, I3)
Selection of training courses	OP12: The selection of training courses is coordinated between the Learning Hub partner and the specialist department (I2)
Leadership culture	OP13: The management works closely with the specialist departments and is involved in further training planning (I2, I3)

2.4 Comparative Analysis of Findings from Practice and Literature

After listing the obstacles identified in the literature in Table 1 and those identified in practice in Table 3, as well as strategies for overcoming them, these two tables are compared in text form below.

The interviews conducted confirm the need for continuous employee training as identified in the literature, primarily driven by the implementation of new technologies (OP1) and external requirements such as client-driven certification demands (OP2). A strong alignment between practice and literature is observed regarding the inventory of competencies (OP3, OP4) and needs analysis (OP6, OP7), as well as the challenges related to identifying employees requiring further training (OL3), predicting future competency demands (OL5), and assessing individual suitability (OL6).

In practice, the evaluation of employee competencies is carried out by direct supervisors during annual performance reviews and interim discussions (OP3, OP4, OP6, OP7). This decentralized approach effectively addresses the literature-identified need for systematic skills assessment. Although the evaluation of employees' change readiness (OL4) was not explicitly mentioned, it can be assumed that such considerations are inherently part of the managers' broader assessments.

The design of development paths (OP5) further supports the targeted selection of training programs by aligning employee goals (OL1) and individual learning needs (OL2) with organizational requirements. A variety of training formats (OP9), including distance learning, on-site courses, and online modules, enables personalized and flexible learning pathways.

Challenges such as budget constraints (OP10) and minimum participant requirements (OP11) were raised exclusively in practice and are not addressed in the reviewed literature. Nevertheless, they represent significant barriers to implementing training initiatives and are managed by prioritizing training offerings and optimizing the allocation of limited budgets (related to OL8).

Additionally, the practice of knowledge sharing sessions (OP8) complements formal training initiatives by promoting internal skill dissemination. The literature-reported issue of lack of management understanding (OL7) was not reflected in the interviews; on the contrary, managers were found to be actively involved in training planning and competency development processes (OP13).

In summary, while many obstacles identified in the literature are mirrored in practice, additional practice-specific challenges highlight the need for adaptable and context-sensitive training strategies.

2.5 Concept Matrix

In addition to the strategies and solutions developed in practice, models for overcoming various obstacles can also be found in the literature. In order to provide an overview of the models found and to find out whether there is a suitable model for the strategic further training of employees in the existing scientific literature that can be applied in particular in the context of the emergence of new activities and fields of work, the models found are differentiated in the following concept matrix (Table 4) according to Webster and Watson (2002) based on their object of consideration and the solution approach used.

Table 4. Concept matrix of models found in the literature

	Object of consideration						Solution approach	
	Maturity model	Needs analysis	Procedure model	E-learning optimization	Job Matching	Competence assessment	Analytics-based procedure	Organizational procedure
Acampora et al. (2008b)				X			X	
Acampora et al. (2008a)				X		X	X	
Berghaus (2016)	X							X
Bian et al. (2020)					X		X	
Çelik et al. (2013)					X		X	
Chen (2015)				X			X	
Cheng et al. (2018)				X			X	
Cordes and Weber (2021)			X					X
Dave et al. (2018)					X	X	X	
De Carolis et al. (2017)	X							X
Fiqri and Nurjanah (2017)				X		X	X	
Hogarth (2019)				X				X
Klötzer and Pflaum (2017)	X							X
McKenney and Handley (2020)					X	X	X	
Mok (2022)				X				X
Ng et al. (2018)			X					X
Ramamurthy et al. (2015)						X	X	
Remane et al. (2017)	X							X
Richter et al. (2007)					X		X	
Salas et al. (2012)		X						X
Schumacher et al. (2016)	X							X
Singh et al. (2017)					X		X	
Tonelli et al. (2016)	X							X
Umemoto et al. (2020)							X	
Vista (2020)						X	X	
Wei et al. (2015)					X		X	
Σ Occurrence	6	1	2	7	7	6	15	11

The methods classified under e-learning optimization, job matching and competence assessment belong to the methods with an analytics-based procedure. They use data-driven, algorithmic or model-based procedures to solve training issues. These methods focus on using technical means to enable precise, automated or scalable decisions. Maturity models, needs analysis and procedure models have an organizational approach aimed at structural, procedural or strategic measures within companies. These approaches are less technical, but more practical and easier to integrate into existing company processes. Six studies propose maturity models that enable companies to assess their digital readiness, such as the model by Berghaus [32], which utilizes employee surveys for benchmarking purposes. Only the publication Salas et al. (2012) addresses needs analysis, identifying future skill requirements without providing a methodology for company-specific assessments. In the category of process models two publications were found. In the first one by Cordes and Weber (2021) the authors highlight the crucial role that an organization's workforce plays in the success or failure of digital innovation. They emphasize the importance of a structured approach that supports organizations in training their employees in a targeted manner. The second publication in this category is the paper by [25], which pursues a similar objective and deals with the creation of a conceptual model for digitalization. Seven publications focus on e-learning optimization, often leveraging analytics-based methods to adapt content difficulty to individual user profiles, as demonstrated by Umemoto et al. (2020) and Acampora et al. (2008b). Additionally, seven studies explore job-matching approaches, aligning employee competencies with job requirements, such as the constraint programming-based method proposed by Richter et al. (2007). In the last category of skills assessment, there are six publications that use an analytical approach to assess the skills and qualifications of employees. Ramamurthy et al. (2015) rely on an algorithmic approach for this, while Vista (2020) pursues an approach using graph theory. In this respect, the development of an algorithmic and formulaic approach must be seen as far more complex because, as Gaula et al. (2022) point out, it must take a large number of parameters into account.

3   Results

The analysis of the literature identified three particularly relevant publications: The first, "Using the DSRM to Develop a Skills Gaps Analysis Model" by Cordes and Weber (2021), highlights the critical role of structured approaches to digital upskilling. To support organizations in this endeavor, the authors propose 15 design principles intended to provide both broad applicability and detailed practical guidance. They further emphasize the importance of personalized training recommendations and advocate for the development of systems capable of analyzing employee competencies and generating targeted development suggestions [14]. The second key publication, by Ng et al. (2018), addresses the challenges companies encounter during digital transformation, particularly those related to skill needs and organizational alignment (OL5, OL8). In response, the authors introduce a five-stage conceptual model that defines the core phases of digitalization and their interdependencies, calling for further refinement into a practical methodology for guiding digital reinvention. The third notable contribution comes from McKenney and Handley (2020), who focus on the identification and assessment of skills for specific positions. They present a combined skills gap analysis model that integrates components of existing approaches, enabling organizations to evaluate both position-specific requirements and the suitability of employees. Their model is assessed against five criteria designed to ensure comprehensive skills gap identification.

A key finding emerging from the comparative analysis is that, in practice, companies tend to address training needs on an ad-hoc basis rather than implementing systematic, long-term strategies. While the literature advocates standardized frameworks, such as maturity models, e-learning optimization, and job-matching approaches, the companies surveyed predominantly rely on decentralized processes, with managers independently identifying and addressing training needs. Several questions arise for future research. One promising avenue is the investigation of AI-supported systems for automating needs analysis and customising training programmes based on structured and unstructured company data. The contribution of standardised, centralised competence profiles to increasing organizational transparency would also be a subject for future investigation. In view of stagnating budgets in human resources development, research into costoptimised methods in continuing education planning could become more important in the future.

Disclosure of Interests.   The authors have no competing interests to declare that are relevant to the content of this article.

References

1. Chakrabarti, S., Caratozzolo, P., Norgaard, B., Sjoer, E.: Preparing engineers for lifelong learning in the era of industry 4.0. In: 2021 World Engineering Education Forum/Global Engineering Deans Council (WEEF/GEDC), pp. 518–523 (2021). https://doi.org/10.1109/WEEF/GEDC53299.2021.9657247
2. Pontes, J., et al.: Relationship between trends, job profiles, skills and training programs in the factory of the future. In: 2021 22nd IEEE International Conference on Industrial Technology (ICIT), pp. 1240–1245 (2021). https://doi.org/10.1109/ICIT46573.2021.9453584
3. Vista, A.: Data-driven identification of skills for the future: 21st-Century skills for the 21st-Century workforce. SAGE Open **April-June**, 1–10 (2020). https://doi.org/10.1109/ICIT46 573.2021.9453584
4. Weerasinghe, T., Vidanagamachchi, K., Nanayakkara, J.: Employee competencies development framework for Industry 4.0 adaptation in the healthcare sector. In: 4th International Research Symposium on Pure and Applied Sciences, Faculty of Science, University of Kelaniya, Sri Lanka (2020). Accessed 22 Dec. 2024. [Online]. Available: http://repository.kln.ac.lk/bitstream/handle/123456789/20656/155.pdf?sequence=1&isAllowed=y
5. Aagaard, A., Presser, M., Andersen, T.: Applying Iot as a leverage for business model innovation and digital transformation. In: 2019 Global IoT Summit (GIoTS), pp. 1–5 (2019). https://doi.org/10.1109/GIOTS.2019.8766397
6. Barann, B., Hermann, A., Cordes, A.-K., Chasin, F., Becker, J.: Supporting digital transformation in small and medium-sized enterprises: a procedure model involving publicly funded support units. HICSS (2019). https://doi.org/10.24251/HICSS.2019.598
7. Dudakov, G., Molchanov, N., Kostenarov, K.: The impact of digital transformation on building business models. In: Proceedings of the International Scientific Conference - Digital Transformation on Manufacturing, Infrastructure and Service, in DTMIS '20. Association

for Computing Machinery, New York, NY, USA (2021). https://doi.org/10.1145/3446434.3446489

8. Probst, L., Scharf, C.: The Lost Workforce in partnership with Upskilling for the Future (2019). Accessed 22 Dec. 2024. [Online]. Available: https://www.pwc.com/m1/en/world-government-summit/documents/wgs-lost-workforce.pdf

9. Singh, M., Ramamurthy, K.N., Vasudevan, S.: Propensity modeling for employee re-skilling. In: 2017 IEEE Global Conference on Signal and Information Processing (GlobalSIP), pp. 893–897 (2017). https://doi.org/10.1109/GlobalSIP.2017.8309089

10. Gurtner, A., Clerc, I., Scheidegger, L.: Digital human resource management. In: Schellinger, J., Tokarski, K.O., Kissling-Näf, I. (eds.) Digital Business: Analysen und Handlungsfelder in der Praxis, pp. 159–181. Springer Fachmedien Wiesbaden, Wiesbaden (2021). https://doi.org/10.1007/978-3-658-32323-3_8

11. Vladova, G., Heuts, A., Teichmann, M.: Dem Mitarbeiter zu Diensten. Weiterbildung und Qualifizierung als Personennahe Dienstleistung. HMD Praxis der Wirtschaftsinformatik **57**(4), 710–721 (2020). https://doi.org/10.1365/s40702-020-00626-7

12. Gast, O., Seifert, J., Werth, D.: Der Mensch im Fokus der digitalen transformation des Lernens: Erfolgreiche Aus- und Weiterbildung im Unternehmen. HMD Praxis der Wirtschaftsinformatik **58**(6), 1444–1455 (2021). https://doi.org/10.1365/s40702-021-00788-y

13. Schönbohm, A., Egle, U.: Controlling der digitalen transformation. In: Schallmo, D., Rusnjak, A., Anzengruber, J., Werani, T., Jünger, M. (eds.) Digitale Transformation von Geschäftsmodellen: Grundlagen, Instrumente und Best Practices, pp. 213–236. Springer Fachmedien Wiesbaden, Wiesbaden (2017). https://doi.org/10.1007/978-3-658-12388-8_8

14. Cordes, A.-K., Weber, J.: Design principles for digital upskilling in organizations. In: Ahlemann, F., Schütte, R., Stieglitz, S. (eds.) Innovation Through Information Systems, pp. 509–525. Springer International Publishing, Cham (2021)

15. Li, L.: Reskilling and upskilling the future-ready workforce for industry 4.0 and beyond. Inf. Syst. Front. **26**(5), 1697–1712 (2024). https://doi.org/10.1007/s10796-022-10308-y

16. Ratcheva, V., Leopold, T.A., Zahidi, S.: Jobs of Tomorrow: Mapping Opportunity in the New Economy. World Economic Forum, pp. 1–29 (2020). Accessed 22 Dec. 2024. [Online]. Available: https://www3.weforum.org/docs/WEF_Jobs_of_Tomorrow_2020.pdf

17. Salas, E., Tannenbaum, S.I., Kraiger, K., Smith-Jentsch, K.A.: The science of training and development in organizations: what matters in practice. Psychol. Sci. Public Interest **13**(2), 74–101 (2012). https://doi.org/10.1177/1529100612436661

18. Hecklau, F., Galeitzke, M., Bourgeois, S., Kohl, H.: Holistic approach for human resource management in industry 4.0. Procedia CIRP **54**, 1–6 (2016). https://doi.org/10.1016/j.procir.2016.05.102

19. Acampora, G., Gaeta, M., Loia, V., Ritrovato, P., Salerno, S.: Optimizing learning path selection through memetic algorithms. In: 2008 IEEE International Joint Conference on Neural Networks (IEEE World Congress on Computational Intelligence), pp. 3869–3875 (2008). https://doi.org/10.1109/IJCNN.2008.4634354

20. Bevis, K.: The challenges for sustainable skills development in the UK automotive supply sector. Manag. Res. Rev. **34**(1), 133–147 (2011). https://doi.org/10.1108/01409171111096513

21. Cheng, B., Zhang, Y., Shi, D.: Ontology-based personalized learning path recommendation for course learning. In: 2018 9th International Conference on Information Technology in Medicine and Education (ITME), pp. 531–535 (2018). https://doi.org/10.1109/ITME.2018.00123

22. du Boulay, B.: Jim Greer's and Mary Mark's reviews of evaluation methods for adaptive systems: a brief comment about new goals. Int. J. Artif. Intell. Educ. **31**(3), 622–635 (2020). https://doi.org/10.1007/s40593-020-00198-z

23. McKenney, M.J., Handley, H.A.: Using the DSRM to develop a skills gaps analysis model. IEEE Eng. Manag. Rev. **48**(4), 102–119 (2020). https://doi.org/10.1109/EMR.2020.3011704
24. Ramamurthy, K.N., Singh, M., Davis, M., Kevern, J.A., Klein, U., Peran, M.: Identifying employees for reskilling using an analytics-based approach. In: 2015 IEEE International Conference on Data Mining Workshop (ICDMW), pp. 345–354 (2015). https://doi.org/10.1109/ICDMW.2015.206
25. Ng, H.Y., Tan, P.S., Lim, Y.G.: Methodology for digitalization - a conceptual model. In: 2018 IEEE International Conference on Industrial Engineering and Engineering Management (IEEM), pp. 1269–1273 (2018). https://doi.org/10.1109/IEEM.2018.8607457
26. Richter, Y., Naveh, Y., Gresh, D.L., Connors, D.P.: Optimatch: applying constraint programming to workforce management of highly-skilled employees. In: 2007 IEEE International Conference on Service Operations and Logistics, and Informatics, pp. 1–6. IEEE (2007). https://doi.org/10.1109/SOLI.2007.4383953
27. Horlacher, A., Hess, T.: What does a chief digital officer do? Managerial tasks and roles of a new C-level position in the context of digital transformation. In: 2016 49th Hawaii International Conference on System Sciences (HICSS), pp. 5126–5135 (2016). https://doi.org/10.1109/HICSS.2016.634
28. Agrawal, S., De Smet, A.: How companies are reskilling to address skill gaps. McKinsey (2018). Accessed 29 Dec. 2024. [Online]. Available: https://www.mckinsey.com/capabilities/people-and-organizational-performance/our-insights/beyond-hiring-how-companies-are-reskilling-to-address-talent-gaps/
29. Ilyas, M., Hin, C., Adnan, Z.: Training aligned with business strategies: aiming at the 'strategic fit.' J. Sci. Res. Dev. **3**, 150–156 (2016)
30. Webster, J., Watson, R.T.: Analyzing the Past to Prepare for the Future: Writing a Literature Review. MIS Q. **26**(2), xiii–xxiii (2002)
31. Acampora, G., Gaeta, M., Loia, V.: An ontological approach for memetic optimization in personalised e-learning scenarios. In: 2008 Third International Conference on Convergence and Hybrid Information Technology, pp. 1204–1213 (2008). https://doi.org/10.1109/ICCIT.2008.405
32. Berghaus, S., Back, A.: Stages in digital business transformation: results of an empirical maturity study (2016)
33. Bian, S., et al.: Learning to match jobs with resumes from sparse interaction data using multi-view co-teaching network. In: CIKM '20. Association for Computing Machinery, pp. 65–74 (2020). https://doi.org/10.1145/3340531.3411929
34. Çelik, D., et al.: Towards an information extraction system based on ontology to match resumes and jobs. In: 2013 IEEE 37th Annual Computer Software and Applications Conference Workshops, pp. 333–338 (2013). https://doi.org/10.1109/COMPSACW.2013.60
35. Chen, S.: Skill management. In: Zeuch, M. (ed.) Dos and Don'ts in Human Resources Management: a Practical Guide, pp. 41–42. Springer Berlin, Heidelberg, Berlin, Heidelberg (2015). https://doi.org/10.1007/978-3-662-43553-3_13
36. Dave, V.S., Zhang, B., Al Hasan, M., AlJadda, K., Korayem, M.: A combined representation learning approach for better job and skill recommendation. In: CIKM '18. Association for Computing Machinery, pp. 1997–2005 (2018). https://doi.org/10.1145/3269206.3272023
37. De Carolis, A., Macchi, M., Negri, E., Terzi, S.: A maturity model for assessing the digital readiness of manufacturing companies. In: Lödding, H., Riedel, R., Thoben, K.-D., von Cieminski, G., Kiritsis, D. (eds.) Advances in Production Management Systems. The Path to Intelligent, Collaborative and Sustainable Manufacturing, pp. 13–20. Springer International Publishing, Cham (2017)
38. Fiqri, M., Nurjanah, D.: Graph-based domain model for adaptive learning path recommendation. In: 2017 IEEE Global Engineering Education Conference (EDUCON), pp. 375–380 (2017). https://doi.org/10.1109/EDUCON.2017.7942875

39. Hogarth, T.: Cedefop analytical framework for developing upskilling pathways for adults (2019) [Online]. Available: https://policycommons.net/artifacts/2078987/cedefop-analytical-framework-for-developing-upskilling-pathways-for-adults/2834285/
40. Klötzer, C., Pflaum, A.: Toward the Development of a Maturity Model for Digitalization within the Manufacturing Industry's Supply Chain (2017). https://doi.org/10.24251/HICSS.2017.509
41. Lily Mok: Use a Digital Talent Management Framework to Future-Proof the IT Workforce (2022). Accessed 12 Jan. 2025. [Online]. Available: https://www.gartner.com/smarterwithgartner/use-a-digital-talent-management-framework-to-future-proof-the-it-workforce
42. Remane, G., Hanelt, A., Wiesboeck, F., Kolbe, L.M.: Digital Maturity in Traditional industries-an Exploratory Analysis, p. 10. ECIS (2017)
43. Schumacher, A., Erol, S., Sihn, W.: A maturity model for assessing industry 4.0 readiness and maturity of manufacturing enterprises. Procedia CIRP **52**, 161–166 (2016). https://doi.org/10.1016/j.procir.2016.07.040
44. Tonelli, F., Demartini, M., Loleo, A., Testa, C.: A novel methodology for manufacturing firms value modeling and mapping to improve operational performance in the industry 4.0 era. Procedia CIRP **57**, 122–127 (2016). https://doi.org/10.1016/j.procir.2016.11.022
45. Umemoto, K., Milo, T., Kitsuregawa, M.: Toward recommendation for upskilling: modeling skill improvement and item difficulty in action sequences. In: 2020 IEEE 36th International Conference on Data Engineering (ICDE), 2020, pp. 169–180. https://doi.org/10.1109/ICDE48307.2020.00022
46. Wei, D., Varshney, K.R., Wagman, M.: Optigrow: people analytics for job transfers. In: 2015 IEEE International Congress on Big Data (BigData Congress), IEEE, 2015, pp. 535–542. https://doi.org/10.1109/BigDataCongress.2015.84
47. Gaula, M., Telukdarie, A., Munsamy, M.: 4IR skills development: a comparative analysis of the South African and global skills development systems. In: 2022 Portland International Conference on Management of Engineering and Technology (PICMET), 2022, pp. 1–6. https://doi.org/10.23919/PICMET53225.2022.9882657

Adaptability and Resilience in Cage Aquaculture: A Few-Shot Learning Approach to Question Answering

Ronald Tombe[1]([✉]) [iD], Vukosi Marivate[2,3] [iD], and Hanlie Smuts[3] [iD]

[1] Computing Sciences Department, Kisii University, Kisii 408-40200, Kenya
ronaldtombe@kisiiuniversity.ac.ke
[2] Department of Computer Science, University of Pretoria, Pretoria, South Africa
vukosi.marivate@cs.up.ac.za
[3] Department of Informatics, University of Pretoria, Pretoria 0083, South Africa
hanlie.smuts@up.ac.za

Abstract. Fish farming is a cornerstone of livelihoods across Sub-Saharan Africa, yet smallholder farmers often lack timely access to expert knowledge and decision-support systems. Cage aquaculture, a growing sector in sustainable food production, faces critical challenges such as water quality degradation, disease outbreaks, and greenhouse gas emissions. Traditional machine learning approaches, which rely on extensive datasets, struggle in data-scarce environments, limiting their effectiveness in supporting aquaculture resilience and adaptation. This study proposes an AI-driven Question-and-Answering (Q&A) algorithm that leverages Few-Shot Learning (FSL) to bridge the aquaculture knowledge gap. Unlike conventional fine-tuning methods that suffer performance declines with limited data, prompt-based fine-tuning techniques, such as FewshotQA and Null Prompting, enable models to generalize effectively from minimal examples. While these approaches have been explored in text classification, their application in domain-specific extractive Q&A for aquaculture remains underexplored.

Keywords: Meta-Learning · FewshotQA and Null Prompting · Transfer learning · Just Transition · Sustainability

1 Introduction

The global population growth necessitates increased food production, with fish playing a crucial role in providing high-quality protein and essential nutrients. However, overfishing and environmental degradation threaten fish availability, making cage aquaculture a promising alternative. Cage aquaculture, is a method of fish farming that involves rearing fish in mesh enclosures in natural water bodies [1]. Despite its potential, cage aquaculture in Africa faces challenges such as water quality degradation, fish kills due to low oxygen levels, and greenhouse gas

F. Corradini et al. (Eds.): Society 5.0 2025, CCIS 2787, pp. 277–288, 2026.
https://doi.org/10.1007/978-3-032-15463-7_23

emissions [2]. These challenges can potentially result to environmental variability, disease outbreaks, and resource management. Emerging technologies such as artificial intelligence (AI) and the Internet of Things (IoTs) offer potential innovative solutions to address these challenges and enhance the sustainability of cage aquaculture.

"Can machines think?" This fundamental question, posed by Alan Turing in his groundbreaking 1950 paper Computing Machinery and Intelligence [3], laid the foundation for modern artificial intelligence. Turing proposed that digital computers are designed to execute tasks traditionally performed by human minds, ultimately striving toward human-like intelligence. In recent years, rapid advancements in computing power (e.g., GPUs and distributed cloud platforms), access to vast datasets (e.g., large-scale environmental and operational datasets in aquaculture), and sophisticated AI models (e.g., transformer-based architectures like Large Language Models (LLMs) and Few-Shot Learning (FSL) techniques) have accelerated AI's capabilities across various domains. AI has surpassed human performance in tasks such as strategic gameplay, exemplified by AlphaGo [4] defeating world champions in Go, and image classification, where ResNet [5] outperforms humans on benchmark datasets.

Despite its advancements, current AI techniques struggle to generalize quickly from only a few examples. Many successful AI applications rely on training with large-scale datasets, whereas humans can rapidly adapt to new tasks by leveraging prior knowledge. For instance, a child who has learned addition can quickly grasp multiplication with minimal instruction (e.g., understanding that 2×3 is equivalent to $2 + 2 + 2$). Similarly, after seeing just a few photos of a stranger, a child can easily recognize the same person among many other images. Bridging this gap between AI and human learning remains a critical challenge. Machine learning, which focuses on developing systems that improve through experience [7], has introduced a novel paradigm known as Few-Shot Learning (FSL) [8] to address this issue. FSL enables AI models to learn from a few labelled examples by identifying transferable patterns. A notable application is character generation [9], where AI systems learn to parse and create new handwritten characters based on only a few samples. This process mimics human learning by decomposing characters into smaller, reusable components and reassembling them into new forms [10]. Beyond character recognition, FSL has significant implications for robotics [6], where machines are trained to replicate human actions with minimal data. Examples include one-shot imitation learning [11], multi-armed bandit algorithms for decision-making [12], visual navigation systems [13], and continuous control mechanisms [13]. These advancements pave the way for AI to operate more efficiently in data-scarce environments, making it particularly valuable for applications such as aquaculture management, where real-time adaptation and predictive insights are essential. FSL can also alleviate the challenge of collecting large-scale labelled datasets. While models like ResNet [5] surpass human performance on ImageNet, they require a substantial number of annotated images for each class, making data collection a labour-intensive process. By enabling learning from limited examples, FSL reduces the dependency on extensive datasets, making it particularly useful for data-intensive applications. Notable examples include image classification [17], image retrieval [18], object tracking [19] image captioning, visual question answering [21], and video event detection [22].

Traditional machine learning approaches often require large datasets to train models effectively, which can be a significant limitation in aquaculture due to the scarcity of labeled data. Few-shot learning (FSL) offers a promising solution by enabling models to generalize from a limited number of examples, making it particularly suitable for applications in cage aquaculture, where data is often scarce with a risk of overfitting. Overfitting occurs when a model learns to perform exceptionally well on the training data but fails to generalize to unseen data, a common issue in traditional machine learning models that rely on large datasets. FSL, by design, mitigates this problem through several innovative techniques, for instance, the Model-Agnostic Meta-Learning (MAML) [13] optimizes model parameters such that they can be fine-tuned with minimal data for new tasks, reducing the risk of overfitting to any single task. By learning a generalized initialization, MAML enables models to adapt quickly to new tasks with limited data, effectively balancing generalization and task-specific performance. FewshotQA and Null Prompting [14], is prompt-based fine-tuning technique in natural language processing (NLP), that enables models to generalize effectively from minimal examples by reformulating tasks as prompt-based queries. This reduces the need for extensive task-specific fine-tuning, thereby minimizing the risk of overfitting. Transfer learning [16] is a key strategy in FSL to combat overfitting through leveraging pretrained models on large, diverse datasets to new tasks with limited data. For example, pretrained models like BERT [15] in NLP or ResNet [5] in computer vision provide a strong foundation for few-shot tasks. These models are fine-tuned on small datasets, allowing them to adapt to new tasks without overfitting.

This paper proposes a FSL approach in cage aquaculture, focusing on its potential to enhance adaptability and resilience through improved question-answering systems. By leveraging prior knowledge and limited data, FSL can help aquaculture practitioners make informed decisions, optimize resource allocation, and mitigate risks associated with environmental and biological uncertainties.

2   Literature Review

2.1   Few-Shot Learning

Few-shot learning (FSL) is a specialized area within machine learning that focuses on achieving good learning performance with limited supervised information [23]. In traditional machine learning, a computer program improves its performance on a task T through experience E, measured by a performance metric P. For example, in image classification, a model improves its accuracy by training on a large dataset of labeled images. However, FSL deals with scenarios where the training set D_{train} contains only a few labeled examples, making it challenging to generalize effectively [25].

Formally, FSL is defined as a type of machine learning problem where the experience E consists of only a limited number of examples with supervised information for the target task T [23]. This definition distinguishes FSL from traditional machine learning, which typically requires large amounts of labeled data. FSL is particularly relevant in scenarios where acquiring large datasets is difficult, such as in drug discovery [24], where new molecules may have limited biological assay data due to toxicity or solubility issues. In the context of cage aquaculture, FSL can learn and generalize from a small number of examples, such as a few labeled images of fish diseases or a limited set of environmental data points. The goal is to develop models that can rapidly adapt to new tasks, such as identifying disease outbreaks or predicting water quality changes, with minimal data.

2.2   Similar Learning Approaches

FSL is closely related to several other machine learning paradigms, each with its own unique characteristics and challenges:

- **Weakly Supervised Learning** [26]. This involves learning from experience E that contains only weak supervision, such as incomplete or noisy labels. A subset of this is **semi-supervised learning** [27], where the model learns from a small number of labeled samples and a large number of unlabeled samples. Another subset is **active learning** [28], where the model selects the most informative unlabeled samples to query for labels. While weakly supervised learning often relies on unlabeled data, FSL leverages various forms of prior knowledge, such as pre-trained models or data from other domains.
- **Imbalanced Learning** [29]. This addresses learning from datasets where some classes are underrepresented. Unlike FSL, which focuses on learning from a few examples, imbalanced learning aims to handle skewed class distributions.
- **Transfer Learning** [30]. This involves transferring knowledge from a source domain with abundant data to a target domain with scarce data. Transfer learning is often used in FSL to leverage prior knowledge from related tasks or domains.
- **Meta-Learning** [31] Also known as "learning to learn," meta-learning improves performance on new tasks by extracting meta-knowledge from a set of related tasks. Meta-learning methods are particularly useful in FSL [32], as they can adapt quickly to new tasks with limited data by leveraging prior experience.

Each of these learning paradigms shares some similarities with FSL but differs in how they handle the lack of labeled data. FSL uniquely combines prior knowledge with a few labeled examples to achieve effective learning, making it a powerful approach for tasks where data is scarce as summarized in Table 1.

Table 1. Few-shot learning examples

Task T	Experience E		Performance P
	Supervised Information	Prior Knowledge	
Character Generation	A few examples of new characters		Pass rate of visual Turing test
Drug Toxicity Discovery	New molecule's limited assay		Classification accuracy
Image Classification	**A few labeled images**	Raw images or pre-trained models	Classification accuracy

3   Methods

3.1   A Few-Shot Learning Approach Formulation and Terminology

In the context of the learning task T, Few-Shot Learning (FSL) operates on a dataset, $D = \{D_{train}, D_{test}\}$, where: $D_{train} = \{(x_i, y_i)\}_{i=1}^{I}$ represents the training set, with I being a small number of labeled examples. $D_{test} = \{x_{test}\}$ represents the testing set used to evaluate the model's performance.

Let $p(x, y)$ denote the ground truth joint probability distribution of the input x and an output y, and let $\hat{h}$ represent the optimal hypothesis that maps x to y. The goal of FSL is to learn $\hat{h}$ by fitting the training data D_{train} and evaluating on D_{test}.

To approximate $\hat{h}$, the FSL model defines a hypothesis space H, which consists of hypotheses $(h.; \theta)$'s where θ represents the parameters of the hypothesis h. in FSL, a parametric model is typically used, as nonparametric models often require large datasets and therefore unsuitable for few-shot scenarios.

A FSL algorithm is an optimization strategy that searches the hypothesis space H to identify the parameters θ that defines the best hypothesis $h* \in H$ [23]. The performance of the FSL model is evaluated using a loss function $L(\hat{y}, y)$, which quantifies the discrepancy between the predicted output $\hat{y} = h(x; \theta)$ and the true output y.

3.2   Problem Formulation

In cage aquaculture, the ability to answer questions accurately with limited data for decision-making; for example:

- **Question.** "What is the optimal feeding schedule for fish in a specific water temperature range?"
- **Question.** "How can we detect early signs of disease in fish using limited historical data?"

To address these questions, we frame the problem as a FSL task:

1. *input(x)*. A question relate to aquaculture (e.g. water quality parameters, fish behavior).
2. *output(y)*. Answer to the question (e.g., feeding schedule, disease diagnosis)

3. $trainingdata(D_{train})$. A small set of labeled examples, such as historical data on feeding or disease outbreaks.

4. $testingdata(D_{test})$. unseen questions that the model must answer based on its learning from D_{train}

3.3   A Few-Shot Learning Framework for Question Answering

Algorithm 1 Few-Shot Learning for Aquaculture Question Answering

---

```
 1: Initialize Model:
 2: θ ← random_initialization()                      ▷ Initialize model parameters
 3:
 4: Preprocess Data:
 5: for (xᵢ, yᵢ) ∈ D_train do
 6:     xᵢ ← extract_features(xᵢ)                        ▷ Extract relevant features
 7:     xᵢ ← normalize(xᵢ)                                    ▷ Normalize features
 8: end for
 9:
10: Train Model:
11: for epoch = 1 to num_epochs do
12:     for (xᵢ, yᵢ) ∈ D_train do
13:         ŷᵢ ← h(xᵢ; θ)                                            ▷ Forward pass
14:         loss ← L(ŷᵢ, yᵢ)                                       ▷ Compute loss
15:         θ ← update_parameters(θ, loss)                       ▷ Backward pass
16:     end for
17: end for
18:
19: Evaluate Model:
20: for x_test ∈ D_test do
21:     y_test ← h(x_test; θ)                                    ▷ Predict answer
22:     predictions.append(y_test)
23: end for
24:
25: Fine-Tune Model:
26: θ ← train_model(D_train, θ)              ▷ Adjust hypothesis space or enrich data
27:
28: Deploy Model:
29: while True do
30:     x_test ← get_new_query()          ▷ Get new query from aquaculture system
31:     y_test ← h(x_test; θ)                                   ▷ Predict answer
32:     provide_answer(y_test)                           ▷ Provide answer to the user
33: end while
```

The FSL framework for question answering in aquaculture involves the following steps

1. Hypothesis Space (H)
   - The model defines a hypothesis space H, which consists of the possible mappings $h(.;\theta)$ from questions (x) to answers (y).
   - Each hypothesis h is parameterized by θ, which is learned from the small training dataset D_{train}.
2. Loss Function ($L(\hat{y}, y)$).
   - Performance of the model is evaluated using a loss function $L(\hat{y}, y)$ where: $\hat{y} = h(x; \theta)$ is the predicted answer, and y is the ground truth answer.
   - The loss function quantifies the discrepancy between the predicted and the actual answers, guiding the optimization process.
3. Optimization Strategy.
   - The FSL algorithm searches the hypothesis space H to find the optimal parameters θ that minimizes the loss function.
   - This process enables the model to generalize from a small number of examples and provide accurate answers to new questions.
4. A Few-shot learning framework is implemented by algorithm 1.

4   Algorithm Implementation Strategy

4.1   Dataset

The Aquaponics-Fish-Pond-Dataset-IoTPond10.cvs from Kaggle contains sensor data collected from a cage aquaculture environment, with each row representing a timestamped observation of various environmental and biological parameters. The columns in the dataset include created_at, which records the timestamp of the observation; entry_id, a unique identifier for each observation; TEMPER-ATURE, indicating the water temperature in degrees Celsius; TURBIDITY, a measure of water clarity; DISOLVED OXYGEN, representing the amount of oxygen dissolved in the water; pH, which measures the acidity or alkalinity of the water; AMMONIA, the concentration of ammonia in the water; NITRATE, the concentration of nitrate; Population, the number of fish in the pond; Length, the average length of the fish in centimeters; and Weight, the average weight of the fish in grams. These features provide a comprehensive view of the aquaculture environment and are used to monitor and predict fish health and growth.

The dataset consists of 620 rows (observations) and 11 columns (features). Some rows contain invalid values, such as –127 for TEMPERATURE or DIS-OLVED OXYGEN, which are replaced with NaN and subsequently dropped during preprocessing to ensure data quality. The Population column is used as the target variable in this example, but it can be replaced with other columns like Length or Weight depending on the specific task. The dataset captures a range of environmental and biological metrics, making it suitable for tasks such as predicting fish population, health, or growth based on water quality parameters.

4.2   Experimental Setup

The experimental setup for applying Few-Shot Learning (FSL) to the aquaculture dataset (IoTPond10.csv). First, the dataset is preprocessed to handle invalid values (e.g., replacing –127 with NaN and dropping missing rows) and normalize the features (e.g., temperature, dissolved oxygen, pH) using techniques like StandardScaler. The target variable, such as fish population, growth rate, or disease indicators, is selected based on the specific task. The dataset is then split into training and testing sets, with 80% of the data used for training and 20% for evaluation. A neural network model is designed with a few hidden layers and ReLU activation functions, tailored to the small dataset size. The model is trained using a small set of labeled examples (e.g., historical data with questions and answers) and evaluated on the test set to measure its performance using metrics like Mean Squared Error (MSE) or Mean Absolute Error (MAE). To simulate few-shot learning, the training data is further limited to a small subset (20 examples) to test the model's ability to generalize from minimal data. The experimental setup also includes validation steps to ensure the model does not overfit and can adapt to new, unseen questions. Finally, the model's predictions are compared against ground truth or domain knowledge to assess its accuracy and practicality for real-world aquaculture applications.

4.3   A Few Short-Learning Question and Answer Approach

Few-shot learning (FSL) questions and answers formulated for the dataset include:

1. **Feeding optimization,** *Question:* "What is the optimal feeding schedule for fish when the water temperature is $25\,°C$, dissolved oxygen is $6\,mg/L$, and pH is 7.0?"

   Answer: "Based on historical data, the optimal feeding schedule is twice daily at 8 AM and 4 PM when the water temperature is $25\,°C$, dissolved oxygen is $6\,mg/L$, and pH is 7.0."

2. **Disease Detection,** *Question:* "Are there signs of disease in the fish population when ammonia levels are $0.5\,mg/L$, nitrate levels are $20\,mg/L$, and turbidity is 50 NTU?"

   Answer: "Yes, there are signs of disease. High ammonia levels ($0.5\,mg/L$) and elevated turbidity (50 NTU) indicate poor water quality, which can lead to stress and disease in the fish population."

3. **Environmental Monitoring,** *Question:* "How will a $2\,°C$ increase in water temperature affect fish growth when dissolved oxygen is $5\,mg/L$ and pH is 6.5?"

Answer: "A 2 °C increase in water temperature may reduce fish growth by 10% due to lower dissolved oxygen levels (5 mg/L) and suboptimal pH (6.5), which can stress the fish."

4. **Population Prediction**, *Question:* "What is the expected fish population in the next month if the current temperature is 28 °C, dissolved oxygen is 7 mg/L, and ammonia levels are 0.2 mg/L?"

   Answer: "The expected fish population in the next month is 55, given the current temperature (28 °C), dissolved oxygen (7 mg/L), and low ammonia levels (0.2 mg/L), which are within optimal ranges."

5. **Water Quality Assessment**, *Question:* "Is the water quality suitable for fish survival when the pH is 8.0, ammonia is 0.1 mg/L, and nitrate is 10 mg/L?"

   Answer: "Yes, the water quality is suitable for fish survival. The pH (8.0) is within the acceptable range, and both ammonia (0.1 mg/L) and nitrate (10 mg/L) levels are below harmful thresholds."

6. **Impact of Nitrate on Fish Health**, *Question:* "How do nitrate levels above 30 mg/L affect fish health?"

   Answer: "Nitrate levels above 30 mg/L can lead to reduced growth, increased stress, and higher susceptibility to diseases in fish."

Example of Few-Shot Learning Setup

– **Training Examples**
   - *Input:* "What is the optimal feeding schedule when temperature is 25 °C, dissolved oxygen is 6 mg/L, and pH is 7.0?"
     Output: "Twice daily at 8 AM and 4 PM."
   - *Input:* "Are there signs of disease when ammonia is 0.5 mg/L, nitrate is 20 mg/L, and turbidity is 50 NTU?"
     Output: "Yes, signs of disease are present."
– **New Question:**
   - *Input:* "How will a 2 °C increase in temperature affect fish growth when dissolved oxygen is 5 mg/L and pH is 6.5?"
     Output: "Growth may reduce by 10% due to stress."

5   Discussion

Data scarcity is a key challenge in aquaculture, particularly for smallholder farmers in Sub-Saharan Africa, where timely access to expert knowledge and decision-support systems is often limited. Few-shot learning (FSL) holds transformative potential in addressing this issue, offering a solution tailored to data-scarce environments. Traditional machine learning approaches, which rely on extensive datasets, are often ineffective in such contexts, limiting their ability to support aquaculture resilience and adaptation. This study proposes an AI-driven Question-and-answer (Q&A) algorithm that leverages FSL to bridge the knowledge gap, providing a novel approach to overcoming the constraints of smallholder aquaculture.

One of the most significant advantages of FSL is its ability to adapt to small datasets, a critical feature in resource-constrained environments where collecting large amounts of labelled data is impractical. By enabling models to learn effectively from minimal examples, FSL provides actionable insights for tasks such as optimizing feeding schedules, monitoring water quality, and detecting disease outbreaks. These capabilities are essential for improving fish health and productivity, particularly in cage aquaculture, a growing sector in sustainable food production. Moreover, FSL supports cost-effective solutions by reducing the need for extensive data collection and labelling, making advanced decision-support tools accessible to small-scale farmers who lack the resources for traditional data-intensive approaches.

The ability of FSL to generalize to new scenarios further enhances its utility in dynamic aquaculture settings. For instance, models can predict the impact of environmental changes, such as temperature fluctuations or variations in dissolved oxygen levels, and provide recommendations for mitigating adverse effects. This adaptability is particularly valuable in addressing the unpredictability of aquaculture environments, where conditions can change rapidly. Techniques like prompt-based fine-tuning, including FewshotQA and Null Prompting, enable models to perform effectively even with limited data, overcoming the performance declines typically associated with conventional fine-tuning methods. While these approaches have been explored in text classification, their application in domain-specific extractive Q&A for aquaculture remains underexplored, presenting a promising avenue for future research.

6   Conclusion and Future Work

Few-shot learning (FSL) represents a transformative approach to addressing critical challenges in aquaculture, particularly in data-scarce environments such as smallholder farming systems in Sub-Saharan Africa. By enabling models to generalize effectively from minimal datasets, FSL provides actionable insights for key tasks, including feeding optimization, disease detection, water quality monitoring, and growth prediction. This capability is especially valuable in resource-constrained settings, where traditional data-intensive machine learning approaches are often impractical. Furthermore, FSL's adaptability to dynamic and unpredictable aquaculture environments, such as responding to temperature fluctuations or dissolved oxygen variations, underscores its potential to enhance resilience and productivity in the sector.

Future research should focus on several key areas to fully realize the potential of FSL in aquaculture. First, integrating FSL with Internet of Things (IoT) technologies could enable real-time monitoring and decision-making, further enhancing the precision and timeliness of insights provided to farmers. Second, leveraging transfer learning techniques could improve model performance by building on pre-trained models and domain-specific knowledge, reducing the need for extensive labelled data. Third, developing explainable AI (XAI) methods is crucial to building trust among users, particularly smallholder farmers, by making model outputs more interpretable and actionable. Additionally, exploring FSL's feasibility for cross-lingual question answering could improve the dissemination of expert knowledge across diverse linguistic and cultural contexts, further democratizing access to decision-support tools.

References

1. Taparhudee, W., Jongjaraunsuk, R., Nimitkul, S., Suwannasing, P., Mathurossuwan, W.: Optimizing convolutional neural networks, XGBoost, and hybrid CNN-XGBoost for precise red tilapia (Oreochromis niloticus Linn.) Weight estimation in river cage culture with aerial imagery. AgriEngineering **6**(2), 1235–1251 (2024)
2. Dauda, A.B., Ajadi, A., Tola-Fabunmi, A.S., Akinwole, A.O.: Waste production in aquaculture: sources, components and managements in different culture systems. Aquac. Fish. **4**(3), 81–88 (2019)
3. Akata, Z., Perronnin, F., Harchaoui, Z., Schmid, C.: Label-embedding for attribute-based classification. In: Proceedings of the IEEE Conference on Computer Vision and Pattern Recognition, pp. 819–826 (2013)
4. Silver, D., et al.: Mastering the game of Go with deep neural networks and tree search. Nature **529**(7587), 484–489 (2016)
5. He, K., Zhang, X., Ren, S., Sun, J.: Deep residual learning for image recognition. In: Proceedings of the IEEE Conference on Computer Vision and Pattern Recognition, pp. 770–778 (2016)
6. Craig, J.J.: Introduction to Robotics: Mechanics and Control, 3/E. Pearson Education, India (2009)
7. Mohri, M.: Foundations of machine learning (2018)
8. Fei-Fei, L., Fergus, R., Perona, P.: One-shot learning of object categories. IEEE Trans. Pattern Anal. Mach. Intell. **28**(4), 594–611 (2006)
9. Lake, B.M., Salakhutdinov, R., Tenenbaum, J.B.: Human-level concept learning through probabilistic program induction. Science **350**(6266), 1332–1338 (2015)
10. Lake, B.M., Ullman, T.D., Tenenbaum, J.B., Gershman, S.J.: Building machines that learn and think like people. Behav. Brain Sci. **40**, e253 (2017)
11. Wu, Y., Demiris, Y.: Towards one shot learning by imitation for humanoid robots. In: 2010 IEEE International Conference on Robotics and Automation, pp. 2889–2894. IEEE (2010)
12. Duan, Y., et al.: One-shot imitation learning. Adv. Neural Inf. Process. Syst. **30** (2017)
13. Finn, C., Abbeel, P., Levine, S.: Model-agnostic meta-learning for fast adaptation of deep networks. In: International Conference on Machine Learning, pp. 1126–1135. PMLR (2017)

14. Li, X., Yuan, S., Gu, X., Chen, Y., Shen, B.: Few-shot code translation via task-adapted prompt learning. J. Syst. Softw. **212**, 112002 (2024)
15. Garrido-Merchan, E.C., Gozalo-Brizuela, R., Gonzalez-Carvajal, S.: Comparing BERT against traditional machine learning models in text classification. J. Comput. Cogn. Eng. **2**(4), 352–356 (2023)
16. Liu, B.: Few-shot learning method based on data enhancement and transfer learning. Appl. Comput. Eng. **111**, 11–16 (2024)
17. Vinyals, O., Blundell, C., Lillicrap, T., Wierstra, D.: Matching networks for one shot learning. Adv. Neural Inf. Process. Syst. **29** (2016)
18. Triantafillou, E., Zemel, R., Urtasun, R.: Few-shot learning through an information retrieval lens. Adv. Neural Inf. Process. Syst. **30** (2017)
19. Bertinetto, L., Henriques, J.F., Valmadre, J., Torr, P., Vedaldi, A.: Learning feed-forward one-shot learners. Adv. Neural Inf. Process. Syst. **29** (2016)
20. Pfister, T., Charles, J., Zisserman, A.: Domain-adaptive discriminative one-shot learning of gestures. In: Fleet, D., Pajdla, T., Schiele, B., Tuytelaars, T. (eds.) ECCV 2014. LNCS, vol. 8694, pp. 814–829. Springer, Cham (2014). https://doi.org/10.1007/978-3-319-10599-4_52
21. Dong, X., Zhu, L., Zhang, D., Yang, Y., Wu, F.: Fast parameter adaptation for few-shot image captioning and visual question answering. In: Proceedings of the 26th ACM International Conference on Multimedia, pp. 54–62 (2018)
22. Yan, W., Yap, J., Mori, G.: Multi-task transfer methods to improve one-shot learning for multimedia event detection. In: BMVC, pp. 37–1 (2015)
23. Wang, Y., Yao, Q., Kwok, J.T., Ni, L.M.: Generalizing from a few examples: a survey on few-shot learning. ACM Comput. Surv. (csur) **53**(3), 1–34 (2020)
24. Altae-Tran, H., Ramsundar, B., Pappu, A.S., Pande, V.: Low data drug discovery with one-shot learning. ACS Cent. Sci. **3**(4), 283–293 (2017)
25. Zhang, H., Chen, S., Luo, L., Yang, J.: Few-shot learning with long-tailed labels. Pattern Recogn. **156**, 110806 (2024)
26. Zhou, Z.H.: A brief introduction to weakly supervised learning. Natl. Sci. Rev. **5**(1), 44–53 (2018)
27. Zhu, X.J.: Semi-supervised learning literature survey (2005)
28. Settles, B.: Active learning literature survey (2009)
29. He, H., Garcia, E.A.: Learning from imbalanced data. IEEE Trans. Knowl. Data Eng. **21**(9), 1263–1284 (2009)
30. Pan, S.J., Yang, Q.: A survey on transfer learning. IEEE Trans. Knowl. Data Eng. **22**(10), 1345–1359 (2009)
31. Hochreiter, S., Younger, A.S., Conwell, P.R.: Learning to learn using gradient descent. In: Dorffner, G., Bischof, H., Hornik, K. (eds.) ICANN 2001. LNCS, vol. 2130, pp. 87–94. Springer, Heidelberg (2001). https://doi.org/10.1007/3-540-44668-0_13
32. Co-Reyes, J.D., et al.: Meta-learning language-guided policy learning. In: International Conference on Learning Representations, vol. 3 (2019)
33. Vartak, M., Thiagarajan, A., Miranda, C., Bratman, J., Larochelle, H.: A meta-learning perspective on cold-start recommendations for items. Adv. Neural Inf. Process. Syst. **30** (2017)

The Effect of Self-Regulating Technology on Workplace Efficiency

Petrus Arnoldus van Zyl[(✉)] [iD] and Marie Hattingh [iD]

Department of Informatics, University of Pretoria, Pretoria, South Africa
vanzylarno@yahoo.com, marie.hattingh@up.ac.za

Abstract. The ubiquitous nature of technology in the age of Society 5.0, has necessitated the need for self-regulation technologies. Self-regulation technologies are applications or equipment that allow end users to govern and manage their own technology use. Research indicates that distractions in the workplace are one of the primary contributors to reduced productivity, lower task completion, and lower task success rates. Electronic devices commonly used in the workplace have increased employee distractions during daily work routines. This study analyzed how self-regulating technologies can promote workplace efficiency. The study employed a mono-method approach and compared the findings obtained from seventeen employees. Qualitative data were collected through semi-structured interviews. The results enabled an understanding whether self-regulating technologies can promote workplace efficiency. The study emphasized automated technology use and its influence on workplace efficiency. The research aims to provide an understanding of automated technology and how individuals in organizations can use the technologies available to them to ensure focus and attention on their job requirements. The study established that self-regulating technologies can help employees become more efficient and less stressed and distracted in their working environment while improving their work-life balance. Future research could expand the multitude of participants to include individuals from diverse working environments to obtain more information on the various types of self-regulating technologies being employed, whether the participants of the study deemed these technologies beneficial, and how easily these technologies can be incorporated into an average work routine.

1 Introduction

Society 5.0 is characterized by the symbiotic relationship between society and technology. It refers to a society that is sustainable and supports individuals by providing a safe and comfortable environment using technology [1]. Technological applications, software, and equipment have become essential commodities in everyday life. Whether it be as software through which we complete work assignments, applications used to aid learning experiences, or even technologies used for commuting from one place to another, technology is everywhere [2]. The responsible use of technology is essential due to the dependance people place on it and the extent to which it is integrated into our daily lives [3]. Responsible technology use is the process of managing, governing,

F. Corradini et al. (Eds.): Society 5.0 2025, CCIS 2787, pp. 289–300, 2026.
https://doi.org/10.1007/978-3-032-15463-7_24

and controlling technological use in a sound, safe, and ethical manner. How we think about technology and how we use technology is an ever-changing process where humans attempt to create, use, and innovate technological applications, software, or equipment; therefore, our derived utility from these technologies supports our flourishing as humans [4]. An important aspect that needs to be considered in Society 5.0.

For an individual to use technology responsibly, some level of self-regulation is required. Self-regulation can be defined as the ability to manage and control your behavior [5]. Self-regulation has been found to help improve the chances of goal attainment [6], consequently numerous technologies have been created to promote self-regulation.

Technology in the workplace should be used responsibly to ensure optimal workplace efficiency [7]. Workplace efficiency refers to the optimal utilization of time, effort, and resources to achieve a greater task turnaround and success rate. It involves various techniques used to streamline processes, minimize waste and in essence enhance an individual's overall effectiveness. An efficient workplace prioritizes organizational communication, and collaboration to ensure that tasks are completed timeously [8]. In the workplace, employees encounter technological distractions daily, such as unplanned conversations, and numerous distracting notifications from mobile devices and work equipment [9]. Furthermore, excessive use of social media is prevalent in the workplace and causes a significant distraction to employees [10].

Various approaches exist to restrict workplace distractions through self-regulating technologies [9, 11, 12]. However, the effectiveness of self-regulating technology in promoting workplace efficiency is still unclear. This research seeks to answer the following research question: *What impact does the daily use of self-regulating technology have on employee workplace efficiency?*

The rest of the paper is structured as follows: Sect. 2 provides background literature on self-regulation and workplace efficiency. Section 3 provides a brief description of the methodology followed in this study. Section 4 details the findings and analysis of findings which are discussed in Sect. 5. Section 6 concludes the paper with key implications and future research.

2   Literature Background

2.1   Self-Regulation

There are a set of key skills attributed to self-regulation, all of which relate to the development of control over one's attention, inhibitory control and working memory [13]. From this the intent behind self-regulation is to maintain, govern and control one's own behavior in any circumstance and centers around your own cognition. It involves self-management and self-awareness [14]. In the context of this study, self-regulation is a user's ability to govern and manage their technological interactions and is regarded as one of the critical factors of responsible technology use.

From a work environment, [15] established that self-regulation concerning work requirements and goal setting has become a crucial skill employees need to have in the modern work era.

2.2 Workplace Efficiency

In today's overly competitive and highly dynamic work environment, an efficient employee is a crucial resource for an organization's success. Workplace efficiency refers to the standard of quality an employee performs according to their job specifications and requirements and involves numerous metrics and measurement guidelines. It requires employee activities and performance standards [16].

The optimization of workplace efficiency directly contributes to a working environment with increased productivity, accompanied by better job satisfaction [17]. With the increased dependency on technology in the workplace, the importance of understanding what enables an employee to be efficient and how to foster an environment with increased efficiency is fundamental to an organization and that it should be incorporated into the corporate strategies of organizations [18].

2.3 Self-Regulation Technology (SRT)

SRTs encompass various tools and applications created to help individuals manage and improve their cognitive and emotional behavioral interactions with technology. These technologies are developed based on principles established in psychology, human computer interaction, and data sciences to promote healthier interactions with technologies in time management, goal acquisition, stress reduction, and technological addiction management. SRTs were created as a proactive response to the ever-changing technological landscape, with technology constantly expanding its grasp on everyday lives [19].

There are several ways technology can make users more self-aware of their technological interactions. One example would be machine learning to collect information about the end user's technological interaction, such as application usage and time spent (this is known as screen time). The second would allow the end user to customize the applications, notifications, call controls, and automatic replies through self-regulatory configuration [9].

SRTs in the form of focus applications are an example of technologies that help end users maintain their focus on tasks. Focus technologies are applications developed to minimize distractions and enforce an environment where the end users' goals are prioritized [20]. These applications are configurable per end users and strive to improve an individual's productivity.

3 Research Methodology

This interpretive study adopted a survey research strategy to collect data through semi-structured interviews from seventeen participants. The participants were recruited using a convenient snowball sampling strategy [21]. Participants were invited via Whatsapp for voluntary participation in the study. After informed consent was obtained from the participants, the following data was collected through semi-structured interviews on Google Meeting May – July 2023:

- Demographic data (age range, type of work, type of industry, office layout)

- Self-regulation technology current use (type of application, experience of use in workplace, influence of use on productivity, time management and work habits)
- Work environment distractions
- Workplace efficiency
- Self-regulation technology adoption barriers

All collected data were saved on an access restricted Google Drive. The collected data was analyzed using thematic analysis by using the six steps offered by [22].

4 Data Analysis and Findings

4.1 Demographic Data

The mean age for the participants was 33. 44% Software engineers, 19% Business Analysts, 19% General Manager, 6% UX/UI Engineer and 12% QA Engineer. Eight of the seventeen participants worked from home, six worked in an open plan office and three in a cubicle office environment. Three used Apple Focus mode, three did not use any SRT, two used Screen Timer, two used Forest App, one Google Tasks, three Samsung Focus mode. Two participants used three SRTs each: Confluence, Headspace and InsightTimer, and the other BlockSite, AdGuard and Screen Timer.

4.2 Main Findings and Discussion

The Notion of Self-Regulating Technology. The participants discussed the reasoning and notions behind using self-regulating technologies, whether the participants knew self-regulating technologies existed, what various technologies were available to them, what they were using, and their general perception of self-regulating technology. From these narratives, multiple sub-themes were identified, which provided insight into why participants opted to use self-regulating technology. These included participants needing to reduce distractions during the workday, to focus their attention on specific tasks with greater cognitive intent. Some agreed that using self-regulating technologies fosters an environment where positive habits are created. Table 1 illustrates the codes extracted from the quotations that describe the notion of self-regulation technology use by the participants.

The codes, or coding, as referred to in this research refers to the systematic process of organizing and categorizing textual or visual data to identify patterns, themes and relationships, within the information collected from the participants of the study. They represent generalized themes found from the data obtained.

The results obtained coincides with previous research undertaken into the notion of utilizing self-regulating technology. In [23] it was shown that higher education students used various strategies and reasoning behind adopting self-regulating technologies, and that lecturers should foster an environment where self-regulating technology adoption is promoted. The students using these applications indicated that there are many different factors which contributed to the adoption of these applications, including task management [23]. Furthermore, in [24] the utilization of meditation applications to help in stressful circumstances were investigated and it was noted that there was a range of

Table 1. The notion of self-regulating technology

Example quotations	Codes
"When I use my Mac or iPhone's work schedule (Focus Mode) while I'm busy with tickets or if I'm in meetings, I did notice that I can focus a bit more on my work" – Participant 1 "It does get rid of all the spam calls and messages I get through the day, and just by doing that, it definitely keeps me more focused on my work." – Participant 2 "I know some apps help you structure your work into focused intervals, and then a brief rest period, to try and boost your productivity." – Participant 6 "I use True Caller to get rid of the general annoyance of being bothered by phone calls at work, and it definitely helps alleviate the pain of unwanted spam. It's like putting a force field around distractions." – Participant 8 "They act as a helpful assistant to my self-discipline and reinforce positive habits, which I think ultimately leads to greater efficiency and accomplishment." – Participant 15 "By being limited on the amount of time I can spend on social media, it has helped me prioritize work and remain focused, as I am not focused on "staying on top of things" by checking every notification anymore." – Participant 12 "I can set my Focus Mode to allow only messages and calls from certain people or important contacts. It ensures I don't miss critical updates from my team or supervisors, which helps me stay informed…" – Participant 4 "It definitely helps me screen out what's important and what's not." -Participant 10 "It helps me get that time placement. Like today I'm doing this, this is my focus. And assist me in identifying the crucial goals of projects." – Participant 7"	Focus more Create habits Reduce distractions Stress relief Emotional regulation Improve time management skills Task prioritization Time limiting Prioritize communication Stay informed

positive results and benefits participants perceived in battling anxiety and stress. Some participants even created a 'more mindful' daily routine.

From this the notion of utilizing self-regulating technology lies in whether the technology can benefit the user, whether the technology can help accomplish goals set, and can the technology foster a healthier environment for the end user.

4.3 Emotional Influence of SRTs

A general topic introduced by the participants was the "level of annoyance" (Participant 3, Participant 8, Participant 9, Participant 10) they experienced during their workday with numerous distractions, and how self-regulating technology helped them manage these. They experienced "improved tolerance" (Participant 7) and "enhanced emotional regulation" (Participant 3). Some participants elaborated on how self-regulating technologies and the general gamification thereof helped them experience "a sense of self-completion" (Participant 5) on task performance while improving their job satisfaction.

Table 2 illustrates example quotations and derived codes from the data.

Table 2. The emotional influence of self-regulating technologies

Example quotations	Codes
"I've noticed that self-regulating technologies have had both positive and challenging impacts on my ability to recognize, understand, and manage emotions, both in myself and others. As someone who works in UX design, being empathetic and curious is part of my nature, and I'm usually good at picking up on people's emotions and state of mind. However, since the shift to remote work and increased reliance on technology, I've found it a bit more difficult to accurately gauge emotions." – Participant 6 "… These technologies grant great personal benefits that I didn't realize I was lacking." – Participant 12 "They act as a helpful assistant to my self-discipline and reinforce positive habits, which I think ultimately leads to greater efficiency and accomplishment." – Participant 15	Empathy toward others Sense of completion Reduced annoyance Self-awareness

Previous research undertaken supports the results found. [24] noted that individuals utilized self-regulating technologies to help respond to unwanted circumstances in a healthier manner and found that many benefits were perceived by participants with regards to their response to stressful environments.

Additionally, the research indicates that eight of the twelve employees worked from home. Working from home has become prevalent in the modern-work era [25, 26]. According to [26] this shift to remote work has significantly impacted employees, influencing various aspects of their personal and professional lives and with this shift many different advantages and disadvantages aspire.

Therefore, SRTs can be used as a medium to help respond to social situations in a healthier manner and ultimately helps support the improvement of one's own emotional intelligence and mental well-being.

The Concern of Distractions. A common subject for discussion in the narrative between the participants and the researcher was the participants' concern with distractions. Participants felt that with the increased usage of various communication platforms in their working environment, such as Microsoft Teams, Slack, WhatsApp, Discord, the increased communication channels went together with the distractions. From the list of participants, eleven remarked that they find it challenging to re-concentrate on work assignments after distractions occurred, indicating that the attentional resources required to re-concentrate on work requirements can be a draining resource; eleven of the participants indicated that they experience distractions regularly during the workday.

Table 3 illustrates example quotations and derived codes from the data.

Supporting this evidence, [27] investigated how the utilization of technology within an academic environment led to an increase of distractions observed and noted that

Table 3. The concerns of distractions

Example quotations	Codes
"It allows me to customize which notifications and apps I want to receive notifications and alerts from while I'm at work. By blocking unnecessary distractions, I can maintain my focus and make decisions without interruptions, and I feel this really boosts my productivity" – Participant 5 "… by using these apps, it creates an environment of uninterrupted work, you kind of cut yourself off from the world and can focus on one thing at a time. It really creates a calm space." – Participant 2 "… Just placing you in a scenario where you're not that easily distracted." – Participant 5	Reduce notifications Fear Of Missing Out

a measurement of self-regulation is required to help reduce the number of distractions perceived. Furthermore, [28] investigated how continuous notifications can be harmful to one's own mental well-being and stated that by utilizing batch notifications an individual feels less stressed and overwhelmed by the information provided.

From this it can be deduced that self-regulating technologies enable users to reduce the number of distractions they perceive throughout the workday, ultimately allowing them to focus on their job requirements with greater attention.

Commitment to Work. Participants discussed the increased commitment to work while using self-regulating technologies. A general assumption can be made based on the results that participants felt more committed to their work when they used self-regulating technologies. They felt that with the task tracking and time management features available to them in self-regulating technologies; they set visible goals and promoted their ambition to achieve them in a timelier fashion. Table 4 provides example quotations and codes from the participants.

Supporting the results obtained, previous research undertaken by [29] indicated that with the increased utilization of various communication tools available to employees they were more inclined to complete their job requirements in a timeous fashion, however accompanied with the continuous and always available communication, employee fatigue was more likely to occur.

From this the results obtained can be supported, with the utilization of self-regulating technologies employees can ensure that when they are required to focus on their job requirements their full attention and cognitive capacity can be spent on what is needed from them in the moment, allowing them to finish their tasks at a faster rate, and ensuring that deadlines are achieved.

Concerns of Using SRT. Participants were probed to discuss their concerns about using self-regulating technology. A general theme appeared that self-regulating technologies are not that appealing to use in the workplace constantly. Some concerns were raised about the data sharing and privacy policies of self-regulating technologies, and participants rarely felt comfortable sharing their working schedules and activities with third-party applications without clear and concise data usage policies. Participants were

Table 4. Commitment to work

Example quotations	Codes
"… it's like peanut butter and jelly… it helps me stay committed to my work." – Participant 1 "I appreciate self-regulating technologies that help me keep track of tasks, deadlines, and priorities." – Participant 6 "I can focus on what is needed from me with much greater attention." – Participant 8 "By utilizing these technologies, I can create structured routines and set clear priorities which keeps me on track of important deadlines." – Participant 14 "I'm able to get rid of 20% of my annoyances in the office…" – Participant 9 "I think they help me stay on top of my responsibilities and maintain a well-organized work routine." – Participant 14	Committed to work Narrows down requirements Greater attention

provided the opportunity to participate in an open discussion on the lacking features of self-regulating technologies, and a general concern was raised that the self-regulating technologies available had no appealing qualities or features, which made users want to use them specifically.

Table 5 illustrates the codes extracted from the quotations that describe how the participants remarked how self-regulating technologies have affected their commitment to work.

Table 5. Concerns of using SRT

Example quotations	Codes
"I am not the most organized person and in certain aspects I am not self-disciplined in capturing what I've done on a digital platform. Technology tools only help when you are committed to using them." – Participant 11 "I believe you might find that some of these technologies need regular adjustments to suit the working Joe's needs." – Participant 16 "I'm not a hundred percent comfortable with sharing my work routine with others. So, I think it's crucial for these apps to be completely transparent with their data collection procedures." – Participant 17 "… it'll need to be more addicting for me to use it constantly." – Participant 3 "Sometimes it does feel that when I use focus apps, I cut myself off from my team." – Participant 7	Commitment to usage Usefulness shortcoming Privacy concerns Addictive personalities

Technological adoption is a topic widely studied and contains various approaches and recommendations for application development and design to ensure continuous and positive technology adoption and utilization. [30] investigated user experience and technology acceptance with regards to iPad users and noted that application adoption is higher when individuals find the application useful.

Regarding self-regulating technologies and the research results, a consensus was reached among the research participants that there might be a low acceptance rate for implementing self-regulating technologies in organizations.

From this it should be noted that the adoption and usage of self-regulating technology is very dependent on the individual. To justify this, the participants were probed on whether they think that their personality traits have clashed with self-regulating technologies. Most participants agreed that self-regulating technologies does not conflict with their personality traits; however, one specified that:

"… Sometimes it does feel that when I use focus apps, I cut myself off from my team." – Participant 3

This relates to one of the common themes identified in the results, where users fear missing out. The fear of missing out (FOMO) is a feeling of anxiety or unease an individual experiences from the belief that they are missing something exciting or interesting happening somewhere else. This phenomenon is typically associated with social media and could lead to employees or individuals constantly checking their devices for updates on events that might be inappropriate in the situation [31]. This is coupled with most of the research participants indicating that they often use their personal devices for non-work-related activities during the workday, even though most believe that they are moderately capable and good at screening distractions in their working environment.

Furthermore, literature indicates that additional technostress is prevalent in the modern-day workplace due to social media usage at work [32]. The authors further noted that in the corporate world, social media addiction is rapidly increasing. Accompanying this self-regulation should be applied to help reduce the increased impact of social media addiction. Self-regulation effectively buffers the negative effects of social media overuse [32]. This can be supported by the research results obtained, where five of the seventeen participants noted specifically that they used self-regulating technologies to block out the addiction of social media usage at work.

"I actively use app blockers to resist the urge to check social media during work hours" – Participant 15

"…every time a notification came through you would find me, checking what happened, going to Instagram to get updates, Facebook, WhatsApp." – Participant 8

To conclude, by using self-regulating technologies, employees have a more significant arsenal available to them to help reduce the distractions perceived in their working environment, and by minimizing the distractions, employees can protect their own mental and cognitive capacity, allowing them to remain focused longer on tasks, and perform at a higher efficiency rate. Self-regulating technologies promote an efficient workforce.

5 Conclusion

The findings provide valuable insights into the intricacies of workplace efficiency and how self-regulating technologies can improve it. A key characteristic of creating a society 5.0 where a sustainable symbiosis exists between humans and technology.

In answering the research question, it can be concluded that the use of SRT in the workplace lead to:

- Improved efficiency: Thirteen of the participants agreed that self-regulating technology considerably influences their efficiency at work. Through the features self-regulating technology provides, such as goal tracking, time management, and application restrictions, these employees could complete their job requirements at a higher efficiency level and a greater success rate.
- Improved time management: Twelve research participants considered it necessary to raise those self-regulating technologies that enabled them to manage their time more effectively. Through self-regulating technology, allowing users to track their time spent on tasks and applications, it created an environment where the employees managed their time more effectively.
- Enhanced task focus: Thirteen of the participants agreed that, by using self-regulating technologies, they concentrated better on job requirements. This allowed them to reduce distractions during the day and keep their cognitive capabilities zoned on their job requirements.

The contribution of this research lies in that it provides an understanding of the multifaceted ways self-regulating technology affects workplace efficiency by exploring the various experiences perceived by participants who used such technologies during their workday. It uncovers the positive and negative effects of self-regulating technologies on workplace efficiency and emphasizes the importance of considering individual differences in employees' contexts.

This study reveals the effect of self-regulating technologies on employees' perception of their work environment and work-life balance. Participants reported that using self-regulating technologies helped them create a more positive working environment and improved their work-life balance.

From this research the following recommendations can be made to employees and organizations. Employees need to be made aware of the various types of self-regulating technologies they have at their disposal; organizations should not force the adoption of these technologies but rather create an environment where the usage of these technologies are supported. Technologies enable employees to create a personalized working experience where your attention and focus can maintain on your job requirements creating an environment where you can promote your overall efficiency. It can consequently be recommended that employees make use of self-regulating technologies, to find the applications which support their customized ways of working and adopt a new approach to distraction management.

Future research could expand the multitude of participants to include individuals from diverse working environments to obtain more information on the various types of self-regulating technologies being employed, whether the participants of the study deemed these technologies beneficial, and how easily these technologies can be incorporated into an average work routine.

References

1. Narvaez Rojas, C., Alomia Peñafiel, G.A., Loaiza Buitrago, D.F., Tavera Romero, C.A.: Society 5.0: a Japanese concept for a superintelligent society. Sustainability **13**, 6567 (2021). https://doi.org/10.3390/su13126567
2. Jacobs, J.V., et al.: Employee acceptance of wearable technology in the workplace. Appl. Ergon. **78**, 148–156 (2019)
3. Legault, G.A., Verchère, C., Patenaude, J.: Support for the development of technological innovations: promoting responsible social uses. Sci. Eng. Ethics **24**, 529–549 (2018)
4. Jirotka, M., Stahl, B.C.: The need for responsible technology. J. Responsible Technol. **1**, 100002 (2020)
5. Stosny, S: Self-Regulation | Psychology Today South Africa. https://www.psychologytoday.com/za/blog/anger-in-the-age-entitlement/201110/self-regulation. Accessed 26 Feb. 2025
6. Vancouver, J.B., Day, D.V.: Industrial and organisation research on self-regulation: from constructs to applications. Appl. Psychol. **54**, 155–185 (2005)
7. Bondanini, G., Giorgi, G., Ariza-Montes, A., Vega-Muñoz, A., Andreucci-Annunziata, P.: Technostress dark side of technology in the workplace: a scientometric analysis. Int. J. Environ. Res. Public Health **17**, 8013 (2020)
8. Pârjoleanu, R.: Work motivation efficiency in the workplace. Postmod. Open. **11**, 293–309 (2020)
9. Mark, G., Iqbal, S.T., Czerwinski, M., Johns, P.: Bored mondays and focused afternoons: the rhythm of attention and online activity in the workplace. In: Proceedings of the SIGCHI Conference on Human Factors in Computing Systems, pp. 3025–3034 (2014)
10. Song, Q., Wang, Y., Chen, Y., Benitez, J., Hu, J.: Impact of the usage of social media in the workplace on team and employee performance. Inf. Manag. **56**, 103160 (2019)
11. Zukriyani, F.A.M., Azizan, N.: Student academic planner system: a review. Malays. J. Sci. Health Technol. **9**, 63–73 (2023)
12. Orhan, M.A., Castellano, S., Khelladi, I., Marinelli, L., Monge, F.: Technology distraction at work. Impacts on self-regulation and work engagement. J. Bus. Res. **126**, 341–349 (2021)
13. Halfon, N., Forrest, C.B., Lerner, R.M., Faustman, E.M.: Handbook of life course health development (2018)
14. Bell, B.S., Kozlowski, S.W.: Adaptive guidance: Enhancing self-regulation, knowledge, and performance in technology-based training. Pers. Psychol. **55**, 267–306 (2002)
15. Lord, R.G., Diefendorff, J.M., Schmidt, A.M., Hall, R.J.: Self-regulation at work. Annu. Rev. Psychol. **61**, 543–568 (2010)
16. Jiang, J., Duffy, V.G.: Modern workplace ergonomics and productivity–a systematic literature review. In: HCI International 2021-Late Breaking Papers: HCI Applications in Health, Transport, and Industry: 23rd HCI International Conference, HCII 2021, Virtual Event, July 24–29, 2021 Proceedings 23, pp. 509–524. Springer (2021)
17. Kim, S., Christensen, A.L.: The dark and bright sides of personal use of technology at work: a job demands–resources model. Hum. Resour. Dev. Rev. **16**, 425–447 (2017)
18. Grant, A.M., Parker, S.K.: 7 redesigning work design theories: the rise of relational and proactive perspectives. Acad. Manag. Ann. **3**, 317–375 (2009)
19. Orben, A., Przybylski, A.K.: The association between adolescent well-being and digital technology use. Nat. Hum. Behav. **3**, 173–182 (2019)

20. Le, T., Senaratne, H., McQuaid, M., Tigwell, G.W.: Exploring a multifaceted framework to support the design of mobile apps for self-regulating anxiety. In: Extended Abstracts of the 2021 CHI Conference on Human Factors in Computing Systems, pp. 1–7 (2021)
21. Oates, B., Griffiths, M., McLean, R.: Researching Information Systems and Computing. SAGE, London (2022)
22. Braun, V., Clarke, V.: Using thematic analysis in psychology. Qual. Res. Psychol. **3**, 77–101 (2006). https://doi.org/10.1191/1478088706qp063oa
23. Yot-Domínguez, C., Marcelo, C.: University students' self-regulated learning using digital technologies. Int. J. Educ. Technol. High. Educ. **14**, 1–18 (2017)
24. Kellen, M., Saxena, D.: Calm my Headspace: Motivations and Barriers for Adoption and Usage of Meditation Apps during Times of Crisis. ICEB 2020 Proceedings (Hong Kong, SAR China) (2020)
25. Oakman, J., Kinsman, N., Stuckey, R., Graham, M., Weale, V.: A rapid review of mental and physical health effects of working at home: How do we optimise health? BMC Public Health **20**, 1–13 (2020)
26. Ipsen, C., Van Veldhoven, M., Kirchner, K., Hansen, J.P.: Six key advantages and disadvantages of working from home in Europe during COVID-19. Int. J. Environ. Res. Public Health **18**, 1826 (2021)
27. Dontre, A.J.: The influence of technology on academic distraction: a review. Hum. Behav. Emerg. Technol. **3**, 379–390 (2021)
28. Fitz, N., Kushlev, K., Jagannathan, R., Lewis, T., Paliwal, D., Ariely, D.: Batching smartphone notifications can improve well-being. Comput. Hum. Behav. **101**, 84–94 (2019)
29. Lee, S., Zhou, Z.E., Xie, J., Guo, H.: Work-related use of information and communication technologies after hours and employee fatigue: the exacerbating effect of affective commitment. J. Manag. Psychol. **36**, 477–490 (2021)
30. Hart, J., Sutcliffe, A.: Is it all about the apps or the device?: User experience and technology acceptance among iPad users. Int. J. Hum. Comput. Stud. **130**, 93–112 (2019)
31. Barry, C.T., Wong, M.Y.: Fear of missing out (FoMO): A generational phenomenon or an individual difference? J. Soc. Pers. Relat. **37**, 2952–2966 (2020)
32. Khan, N.A., Khan, A.N., Moin, M.F.: Self-regulation and social media addiction: a multi-wave data analysis in China. Technol. Soc. **64**, 101527 (2021)

Author Index

F. Corradini et al. (Eds.): Society 5.0 2025, CCIS 2787, pp. 301–302, 2026.
https://doi.org/10.1007/978-3-032-15463-7